THE PSYCHOLOGY
OF LEARNING AND MOTIVATION

Advances in Research and Theory

VOLUME 30

.

THE PSYCHOLOGY
OF LEARNING AND MOTIVATION

Advances in Research and Theory

EDITED BY DOUGLAS L. MEDIN

DEPARTMENT OF PSYCHOLOGY
NORTHWESTERN UNIVERSITY, EVANSTON, ILLINOIS

Volume 30

ACADEMIC PRESS, INC.
A Division of Harcourt Brace & Company
San Diego   New York   Boston   London   Sydney   Tokyo   Toronto

This book is printed on acid-free paper. ∞

Academic Press, Inc.
1250 Sixth Avenue, San Diego, California 92101-4311

United Kingdom Edition published by
Academic Press Limited
24–28 Oval Road, London NW1 7DX

International Standard Serial Number: 0079-7421

International Standard Book Number: 0-12-543330-1

PRINTED IN THE UNITED STATES OF AMERICA
93 94 95 96 97 98   BC   9 8 7 6 5 4 3 2 1

CONTENTS

SEPARATING CAUSAL LAWS FROM CASUAL FACTS: PRESSING THE LIMITS OF STATISTICAL RELEVANCE

Patricia W. Cheng

CATEGORIES, HIERARCHIES, AND INDUCTION

Elizabeth F. Shipley

CONTRIBUTORS

Numbers in parentheses indicate the pages on which the authors' contributions begin.

Felice Bedford, Department of Psychology and Program in Cognitive Science, University of Arizona, Tucson, Arizona 85721 (1)

Lyle E. Bourne, Jr., Department of Psychology, University of Colorado, Boulder, Colorado 80309 (135)

Bruce K. Britton, Department of Psychology, University of Georgia, Athens, Georgia 30602 (165)

Patricia W. Cheng, Department of Psychology, University of California, Los Angeles, California 90024 (215)

Deborah M. Clawson, Department of Psychology, University of Colorado, Boulder, Colorado 80309 (135)

Robert J. Crutcher, Department of Psychology, University of Illinois at Chicago, Chicago, Illinois 60680 (135)

K. Anders Ericsson,[1] Department of Psychology, University of Colorado, Boulder, Colorado 80309 (135)

Charles R. Fletcher, Department of Psychology, University of Minnesota, Minneapolis, Minnesota 55455 (165)

Rochel Gelman, Department of Psychology, University of California, Los Angeles, California 90024 (61)

[1] Present address: Department of Psychology, The Florida State University, Tallahassee, Florida 32306.

Alice F. Healy, Department of Psychology, University of Colorado, Boulder, Colorado 80309 (135)

Cheri L. King, Department of Psychology, University of Colorado, Boulder, Colorado 80309 (135)

Eileen Kintsch, Institute of Cognitive Science, University of Colorado, Boulder, Colorado 80309 (165)

Walter Kintsch, Institute of Cognitive Science, University of Colorado, Boulder, Colorado 80309 (165)

Suzanne M. Mannes, Department of Psychology, University of Delaware, Newark, Delaware 19716 (165)

William R. Marmie, Department of Psychology, University of Colorado, Boulder, Colorado 80309 (135)

Danielle S. McNamara, Institute of Cognitive Science, University of Colorado, Boulder, Colorado 80309 (135)

Mitchell J. Nathan, Learning Research and Development Center, University of Pittsburgh, Pittsburgh, Pennsylvania 15260 (165)

Suparna Rajaram,[2] Temple University School of Medicine, Philadelphia, Pennsylvania 19122 (97)

Timothy C. Rickard, Department of Psychology, University of Colorado, Boulder, Colorado 80309 (135)

Henry L. Roediger III, Department of Psychology, Rice University, Houston, Texas 77251 (97)

Vivian I. Schneider, Department of Psychology, University of Colorado, Boulder, Colorado 80309 (135)

Elizabeth F. Shipley, Department of Psychology, University of Pennsylvania, Philadelphia, Pennsylvania 19104 (265)

Mark A. Wheeler,[3] Temple University, School of Medicine, Philadelphia, Pennsylvania 19122 (97)

---

[2] Present address: Department of Psychology, State University of New York at Stony Brook, Stony Brook, New York 11794.

[3] Present address: Rotman Research Institute, Baycrest Centre, North York, Ontario, Canada M6A 2E1.

PERCEPTUAL LEARNING

Felice Bedford

I. Introduction

Most psychologists' familiarity with perceptual learning comes from the classic example of plasticity known as *prism adaptation*. That's the one instructors of all levels demonstrate to their students on a slow day. A volunteer straps on a pair of goggles, which has been fitted with a wedge prism, and tries to walk around the room. The task is not easy because the prism distorts vision so that objects are not where they appear to be. The prism displaces the visual image of the world to the side of the true location. There is something of a slapstick appeal, if nothing else, in watching the student bump into walls and knock things off desks or, when I was a student, miss the chalkboard erasers thrown for him to catch. Yet the comedy has its reward when the volunteer not only improves, but, if testing is done right, continues to have altered visual-motor behavior even when the goggles are removed. This usually comes as a surprise to the class, and to the perplexed volunteer as well.

   Despite its intuitive appeal, and a long history of experimentation, prism adaptation has remained something of an anomaly both from the standpoint of perception and from the standpoint of learning. It has earned the status of *plasticity,* the label reserved for things unclassified that seem to be both learning and not learning at the same time. Research interest waned by the 1970s, stayed low in the 1980s and, so far, in the 1990s. I would like to convince readers of this article that perceptual learning, of

1

which prism adaptation is a subset, should be a thriving enterprise. It is a perfect candidate for a specialized acquisition device, with its own rules, that could even serve as a model of study. While others have suggested the potential uniqueness of perceptual learning (e.g., Epstein, 1967; Gibson, 1969), they did so without the benefit of theoretical interest in modules and domain-specific acquisition systems developed largely in the last decade (e.g., Fodor, 1983; Keil, 1992; Rozin & Schull, 1988).

This article will illustrate the fruitfulness of the approach, largely with experiments from three paradigms used in my laboratory. The first consists of variations on the classic prism adaptation paradigm, designed to ask questions different from those typically addressed. The second looks at mappings with more modern advances of a computer monitor and a "mouse-like" pen and tablet, a paradigm that also adds a cognitive flavor. The third involves some new ideas about the phenomenon known as the McCollough effect (McCollough, 1965), which involves forming connections between properties of orientation and color. I begin first with some general considerations on learning.

II. Classification of Learning Processes

Perceptual learning phenomena would seem less anomalous if they were located within a broad classification of learning in general. Such categorization schemes, with or without perceptual learning, are too infrequent. One such categorization is briefly suggested here. At the top level, we begin most generally with *effects of experience*. The first division takes its inspiration from Paul Rozin and Jonathon Schull (1988), who in turn quote from ethologist K. Z. Lorenz (1981). To paraphrase, he asks us to contemplate why it is that learning always makes us better. If this philosophical comment causes hesitation, I suggest that is because it is so fundamental and integral to what is meant by learning as to go unnoticed. Like all things that are so obviously true, they get left out of definitions, theories, and classifications. An analogy may be the way three-dimensional space is taken for granted (Shepard, 1991). Shepard notes that people say things like "If only I had a larger office, I would have more room for my books"; but not "If only I had a four-dimensional office, I would have so many more degrees of freedom for arranging them!" (p. 3).

Figure 1 illustrates the division of *Experience* into "Experience that makes us better" and "Experience that makes us worse." The former category is what should be meant by learning. The latter category consists of experiences that leave us worse for wear, including the prototypic nonlearning effects such as fatigue and injury.

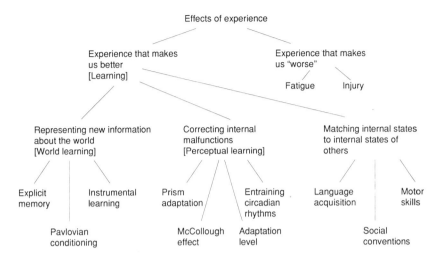

Fig. 1. Classification of different types of learning.

An illustration of how the division may capture intuition concerns the phenomenon known as *habituation*. A characterized scenario is about the family that lives by the train station, where noisy trains pass through once an hour. In reply to guests who ask how they can tolerate the trains, they remark, "What trains?" A more scientific example comes from animal behavior. An unexpected loud noise causes rats to startle; the response decreases with repetition of the noise, until the rat's behavior is uninterrupted by the noise. Not all scholars view habituation as a legitimate example of learning (see Rescorla & Holland, 1976, for discussion). The basic source of disagreement may be a matter of individual intuition about whether habituation makes us better equipped, or worse off, at dealing with the world than we were before the experience. Those who do not regard habituation as learning also tend to view the decreased responding as an unavoidable consequence of any physical system that is subjected to repeated use. On the other hand, those who think that habituation serves an adaptive function do regard the phenomenon as learning. The gist of many of these views is that it is sensible to ignore a repeating stimulus that is of little consequence, in order to free resources for other potentially more important events. The contrast suggests that the distinction in the learning classification does capture intuition about what should be regarded as learning, and as such may be useful.

Experiences that make us better can next be broken down into two major categories: processes that apprehend new information about the world and processes that correct internal malfunctions, or otherwise improve sensory systems. It is the former category that is most often regarded as *learning*. Well-known examples are the associative processes. For instance, Pavlovian conditioning may be "a primary means by which the organism represents the structure of its world" through learning relations among events (Rescorla, 1988, p. 152). A distinct process also in this category is *explicit memory*, where there is storage and conscious recollection of specific learning episodes or recently presented information.[1]

Yet the other category, while less familiar, should properly be regarded as learning in the broad sense defined above. Processes within both categories make us better equipped to deal with the world. The former, which we can call *world learning* or "external learning" does so directly, through the representation of environmental properties (e.g., Gallistel, 1990, Chap. 2). The latter, *perceptual learning* or "internal learning" does so indirectly, through improvements to the organism, which in turn make us better able subsequently to apprehend the world. The perceptual learning processes keep the sensory systems in good working order to allow subsequent world learning to occur.

Before turning to perceptual learning, I will mention that there is likely also a third category. The first category, *world learning,* involves matching one's own internal states to the world. The second category, *perceptual learning,* usually involves matching one's own internal states to one another. The third category involves matching one's own internal states to the internal states of others. One example in this category is language acquisition. Languages are not out in the world (e.g., Bloom, 1990; Chomsky, 1986), nor is their acquisition a matter of correcting malfunctions. Instead, what matters is that your language match some one else's language. Another example may be the acquisition of social conventions. The function of learning that Americans drive on the right side of the road is to avoid accidents with other Americans, who also drive on the right side of the road. More tentatively, but arguably, motor skills belong primarily in this category. Skiing is not something out in the world to be acquired, but is arbitrary; its acquisition is an attempt to acquire what someone else can do. Many of the motor abilities we need in order to interact with the world mature early (e.g., walking and running); motor skills may be a

---

[1] *Implicit memory* (Schacter, 1987; 1992) is intentionally omitted as a type of learning. The problem with the category is not that it is heterogeneous, but that it is held together by a concept that does not make it a meaningful category. The category is defined by processes in which conscious or intentional storage or recollection of information is *not* present. In a manner analogous to the way that "not the liver" or "not tables" would not be meaningful categories of body organs or furniture respectively, "not explicit memory" isn't a meaningful category of learning. Of course, the different phenomena from which the data are collected, most frequently certain "priming" effects, still need to placed within this categorization.

matter of putting together components in the correct order. (See Adams, 1987, for a review.) Similar arguments about skills not being in the world may extend to cognitive skills, like chess playing, and other skills such as music composition.[2]

III. Perceptual Learning: Beginning Anew

There are three primary questions to be asked of any potentially distinct acquisition system (Rescorla, 1988). "What are the circumstances which produce learning? What is the nature of that learning? How is the learning manifested in behavior?" (p. 151). To this can be added a fourth: What purpose does it serve? (e.g., Rozin & Schull, 1988). Deciding when we have a "natural-kind" category is a formidable task. A separate system should distinguish itself from other systems on at least some answers to the above questions. The first three are questions about process, dealing with input, internal states, and output, respectively. The last is a question of evolutionary function. I suggest that perceptual learning distinguishes itself from world learning on all four of these questions.

Beginning with the fourth question, the general function of perceptual learning is to improve sensory systems, which is particularly important if there is a malfunction. The processes responsible for perceptual learning do not represent new information from the environment external to the organism, the way world-learning processes do. Acquisition tasks with different goals have likely evolved different mechanisms to achieve them (Rozin & Schull, 1988). Consequently, answers to the other three questions may differ as well.

Continuing backward, learning will manifest itself by changes in what is actually seen, in the case of vision, or heard, felt and so forth in the other modalities. Perceptual learning can be observed if, as a result of experience, the same proximal stimulus leads to a new percept and continues to do so in the absence of new information.[3] In principle, perceptual learning

---

[2] It is interesting that many examples of "critical periods" for acquisition appear to fall into this third category. It is not clear whether this is coincidental, or whether it reflects something important about learning.

[3] The second part of the definition, "continues to do so in the absence of new information," may not be necessary. Many definitions of learning processes include some mention of stability or relative permanence, and I have succumbed to the same temptation. Definitions are often based on implicitly stated theories (Rescorla & Holland, 1976); the initial division into "experience that makes us better" and "experience that makes us worse" may also capture the intuition of longevity. Things that make us better are usually those that stay around for a while, whereas we hope that things that make us worse are temporary.

distinguishes itself from world learning, which can manifest itself as changes in knowledge, beliefs, and expectations, but which typically will not alter what is perceived. Of course, identifying when perception ends and knowledge begins presents both a theoretical and a methodological challenge. Some phenomena will likely be clear cases of perceptual change within any theory of perception; others will be more difficult.

For instance, if an object looks white under particular lighting conditions before experience, but afterward looks red under the identical physical conditions, then a change in what is seen has taken place. This example will be expanded later in the discussion of the McCollough effect. A phenomenon more in the "gray area" may be habituation. Under some views, the repeating stimulation becomes uninfluential because of a decrease in attention. Whether attention changes should be regarded as changes in perception depends on general theories of perception. A second clear example of a perceptual change occurs if an object is localized straight ahead of the nose before experience, but six inches to the left following experience. The change could occur in vision, so that the object looks as if it is in a different position,[4] or the change could be a different modality. For instance, if the same pattern of proprioceptive joint information produces a different conclusion as to where the arm is after experience, an object will be localized differently via touch. The example of perceived location change following experience will be expanded later in the discussion of adaptation to rearrangements of space.

At this point, however, we encounter a puzzle. The function of perceptual learning is to correct "malfunctions," and its occurrence can be observed by looking for a change in perception. But what could possibly be the circumstances that would cause such a change to occur?

IV. Paradox of Perceptual Learning

Most models of world learning assume that the output of sensory systems is correct, and begin the models from that point. New information about the world is conveyed via the sensory systems. If information about the world comes through the senses, why not always interpret a pattern of stimulation as reflecting the world? How could the mind ever know that the

---

[4] Such a change in perceived visual location is likely to result from a change in felt direction of gaze, where the same eye position signals (mostly efference information) are interpreted as a different eye position (e.g. Howard, 1982). This in turn affects the seen location of the target, which is dependent on both retinal position and eye position information.

proximal stimulus is due to an internal error, and that it is not simply reflecting another facet of the world?

Part of the answer is that not all knowledge of the world does come through the senses. Roger Shepard argues that enduring regularities in the world are likely to have been internalized by perceptual systems (Shepard, 1984, 1987, 1991, 1992). A few examples are the existence of three dimensions of space, the existence and nature of gravity, the 24-hr light/dark cycle, and the rigid motions of objects. We have evolved to know these things, presumably, because possession of this knowledge conveyed some advantage over having to acquire it during the lifetime of the individual through "trial and possibly fatal error" (Shepard, 1984, p. 432.) Elizabeth Spelke and colleagues (Spelke, 1990; Spelke, Breinlinger, Macomber, & Jacobson, 1992) have elucidated a number of principles, specifically about the behavior of objects, that young infants appear already to know with little or no input. Objects in our world are bounded, travel on continuous paths, do not mysteriously vanish, and so forth.

With knowledge about how the world works, new input encountered naturally or through experimental manipulations can now be in agreement with, neutral in relationship to, or inconsistent with the innate information. The majority of encounters are likely neutral with respect to these constraints, in which case new information is added to the preexisting knowledge base. If the new input is in perfect agreement with the internal knowledge, then there is no need for learning of any sort. If, however, the two sources of information are inconsistent, then there are two possible inferences: Either the constraint is abandoned as false, or the constraint is right and the fault is internal. There are likely a number of constraints never, or almost never, relinquished, such as the three-dimensionality of space. Information inconsistent with these constraints can provide the basis for perceptual learning to occur.

One constraint important for perceptual learning is that an object cannot occupy more than one place at one time (Bedford, 1993). Information discrepant with that a priori knowledge of the world will suggest an internal malfunction. If you localize a desired object a few inches to your right through vision, but simultaneously find the object physically to be somewhere else, then the information from the two modalities taken together has violated the constraint. These are precisely the conditions produced in a prism adaptation experiment, in which the wedge prism displaces the visual locations of objects from their locations as determined by the remaining modalities. The inconsistency will be encountered in nature as well because of physical growth in childhood (Held, 1965). As the shoulders get broader, for instance, the mind's sense of where the body is in space will be wrong. Consequently, that modality will produce a disagreement with vision over the location of objects. The disagreement may also be produced after periods in the dark when vision and proprioception drift with respect to each other possibly because all complex systems drift out of alignment without feedback (Howard, 1982). Two other possible sources of natural discrepancy are the visual distortions produced by different environments, such as lakes and rivers, and by injury (Howard, 1982).

It is typically accepted that the basis for adaptation occurs when there is a "discrepancy" between two cues that determine the same parameter and usually provide the same value (Wallach, 1968). Adaptation is the process by which the discrepancy is reduced or eliminated (e.g., Welch, 1978). The above analysis suggests why a mismatch is problematic. Were it not for the built-in constraint, the visual and motor inputs could be providing new information about the current world. For example, the mismatch could imply that the same object is in two places at once. Instead, the information suggests an internal malfunction. There will be an adjustment to one or both modalities such that the location constraint is upheld.

I turn now to more explicit discussion of adaptation to rearrangements of space. Much of the research described can be viewed as providing answers to the question "What is the content of learning?" for this type of perceptual learning.

V. Prism Adaptation: New Variants on a Classic Paradigm

Previous research on adaptation to rearrangements of one-dimensional space has been largely limited to the nearly uniform displacement produced by the prism. The relevant dimension of space is a set of positions from left to right in a horizontal plane. This physical dimension leads to at least two psychological dimensions: the positions as they are localized visually, and the same positions as they are localized with the hand, or proprioceptively (see Fig. 2). A uniform displacement of all visual positions with respect to motor positions is only one of an infinite number of mappings that can be arranged between the two continua. To describe just a few, there can be a discontinuous mapping where space is split down the middle and only regions to the left of straight ahead are pulled further to the left. There can be a many-to-one mapping, where, in the extreme, every single visual position would correspond to exactly the same location in motor space. This would imply that regardless of where you localized an object visually, you would always reach for exactly the same absolute location to obtain the object. Or we can impose an arbitrary mapping in which visual and motor locations chosen at random are paired! Figure 2

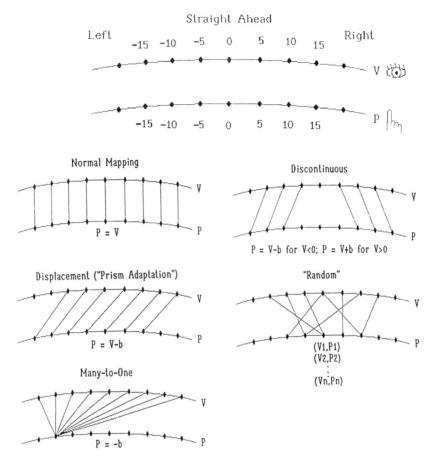

Fig. 2.   Some mappings between spatial dimensions. The connecting lines show which positions along the visual dimension (V) go with which positions along the proprioceptive dimension (P) for different mappings. In the equations beneath, "b" stands for a numerical constant.

shows a schematic of the visual and motor dimensions, the normal mapping, the displacement mapping, and the sample mappings.

To fully understand the rules of acquisition, we need to know not just how the system performs with simple lateral displacement but also what it will do for any conceivable mapping that could be imposed, no matter how bizarre or improbable. The research enterprise I have been conducting for the last few years is concerned with the question, What are the rules when two dimensions are to be connected (Bedford, 1989, 1992a, 1992b, 1993)? For instance, should a mapping between two entire dimensions be viewed as a collection of individual pairs of locations? One of the salient features of coordination is that an individual needs to know where to direct her hand not just for one location in space but for any location where an object may appear. If a mapping can be decomposed into a list of independent visual-motor pairs, then rules of acquisition may be similar to those of simple associative processes. Similarities between adaptation to rearrangements and simple associative learning have been noted (e.g., Epstein, 1976; Taub, 1968; Taylor, 1962); if they prove to be important, our theoretical task becomes simpler.

There are two complementary approaches for uncovering preexisting constraints. One is to provide ambiguous, or incomplete, information about a mapping by specifying the new arrangement for only very few regions of space. The logic of this manipulation is that there are an infinity of mappings that would be consistent with only a handful of visual–motor pairs. The particular interpretation imposed by the perceptual system will presumably reflect the internal rules. An analogy from the domain of natural language may come from the acquisition of word meaning, in which a novel label (e.g., *dog*) could map onto any one of an infinite number of concepts. The interpretation chosen by the child is believed to reflect internal biases, such as the "Whole Object assumption" (Markman, 1990). In the domain of spatial acquisition, we can determine which interpretation was favored by inspecting how behavior generalizes to locations different from those explicitly specified during training.

For instance, imagine you are in a dark room, with a single small target visible in the distance. Through the retinal position of that target, along with eye and head position information, you can recover where the target is located in body-centered coordinates—say straight ahead. Now imagine you reach for the target but discover that if you direct your hand straight ahead, the target is physically not there. Instead, your hand must be a few inches off straight ahead to find the target in motor space. The situation is repeated enough to rule out the possibility of a fluke. For that target, you begin to point to the side of straight ahead, but what should you do if a target appears in a different location?

Describing "one-pair training" in the above fashion is risky because it implies conscious awareness of the mismatch and conscious choice about how to generalize, neither of which need be present. In fact, I will argue later that other contexts, in which conscious intervention is more common, lead to radically different outcomes. This description serves to give a sense, however, of the problem facing the perceptual system if it receives minimal information.

The second approach starts from the other extreme by attempting to provide unambiguous, or complete, information about the nature of a mapping. This is done by experimentally specifying visual–motor pairs for many points in space, thereby dramatically reducing the set of mappings logically consistent with training. Rather than inspecting generalization, here we look to see how well the novel arrangement was accommodated. Presumably mappings easily accommodated are "natural" in some sense, whereas those that create difficulty go against the internal structure. In addition, the structure may also be revealed by studying the errors that result when a mapping is poorly acquired.

The first strategy is optimal for revealing the hidden biases brought to the task, whereas the second may be more useful for identifying the absolute constraints on learning. Note that the general questions of rules and constraints are different from the research question most frequently asked of prism adaptation: Which system changes? The change in pointing observed following exposure to rearrangements could be due to a change in vision, such that you point in a different location because you see the object in a different location. Or it could be due to a change in body proprioception, so that you point to a different location because your hand feels that it is in a different location. (See Harris, 1965). The study of which type of experience with the prism leads to which outcome has been extensive, and research on this issue continues (e.g., Redding & Wallace, 1988a, 1988b). For instance, moving your hand from side to side while watching through a prism produces a change in the felt position of the hand, whereas seeing the hand only at the end of pointing motion adds a visual change as well. The different possible sites of adaptation to rearrangements and the experiences that lead to them will not be reviewed here; thorough reviews can be found in the works of Harris (1965), Howard (1982), Redding & Wallace (1992), and Welch (1978, 1986).

Before discussing the outcome of manipulations with a few novel pairs (strategy of ambiguous information) and of more complicated mappings defined over all of space (strategy of unambiguous information), I will first briefly describe the methodology. This section has two purposes: to explain the general paradigm and to make clear how the location constraint is violated experimentally.

A. METHODOLOGY

As in many prism adaptation experiments and other studies designed to test for effects of experience, the procedure consists of three mains phases: an initial testing phase (known as *pretest* in the prism literature), a training phase (*exposure*), and a final testing phase (*posttest*). The observer sits at the center of a semicircular array of lights, which are located every few degrees (Fig. 3). Lights are illuminated one at a time, and a

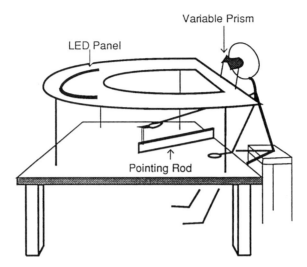

Fig. 3.   Apparatus for prism adaptation experiments. From "Constraints on Learning New Mappings between Perceptual Dimensions" by F. L. Bedford, 1989, *Journal of Experimental Psychology: Human Perception and Performance, 15.* Copyright © 1989 by the American Psychological Association. Reprinted by permission.

subject is asked to point to the light. The room is dark, and pointing must occur without the benefit of visual guidance. The purpose of this phase is to provide a measure of how accurately subjects point before receiving any training.

The training phase is especially designed to allow the two strategies to be implemented. The subject wears a single light on the finger, and, as before, a light in space is illuminated in the darkened room. The subject is told that if she points accurately to the light in space, the light on her finger (*finger LED*) will light up. Varying arm position by a fraction of a degree on either side turns the finger LED off again. The subject's task is to light the finger LED and keep it lit as much as possible during each trial.

If vision were undistorted, the task would be especially simple. Even without visual guidance, it is easy to direct the arm to a target in space, an action that would cause the finger LED to turn on. But the subject looks through a prism, making the target appear to the side. Therefore, the subject initially points to the side of the target's true location, failing to illuminate the finger LED. She is encouraged to explore, and usually with one or two attempts finds the correct position, which causes the finger LED to light up. (See Fig. 4, top two panels; the third panel is discussed later in the article.) The subject is misinformed that it is "disorienting being

PERCEPTUAL LEARNING

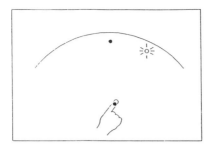

Initial Attempt

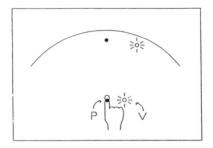

Successful Attempt

COGNITIVE LEARNING

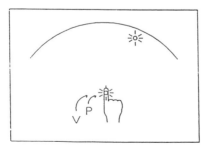

Successful Attempt

Fig. 4.   Pointing with the finger LED. Top two panels show an initial and a successful attempt, both made while looking through a prism (Perceptual Learning). The bottom panel shows a successful attempt using a different "Cognitive Learning" paradigm. V, visual position of the finger; P, felt (proprioceptive) position of the finger. From "Perceptual and Cognitive Spatial Learning" by F. L. Bedford, in press, *Journal of Experimental Psychology: Human Perception and Performance*. Copyright © by the American Psychological Association. Adapted by permission.

in the dark," a small deception that she readily believes to be the source of her difficulty. Further practice is usually required to keep the finger LED on steadily, a difficulty that keeps the subject's attention on the task. When the finger LED is successfully illuminated, the subject is localizing the light on her finger through proprioception in one location, but sees the light (also through the prism) in a different location. This situation creates the apparent violation of the constraint that an object can be in only one place at one time, because the finger is detected in two different locations.

The paradigm essentially isolates individual "points" in space because the room is completely dark and visual feedback is provided for only a very small region of the finger. A successful illumination of the finger LED provides information about only one visual–proprioceptive pairing. Environmental input can therefore be limited to only one, or a few, locations, enabling the research strategy of ambiguous information to be easily implemented. This arrangement differs from the typical training procedure used in adaptation experiments in which the mapping is specified over a large continuous range of locations, for example, watching one's hand while pointing to targets in full-room illumination. In addition, mappings other than uniform displacements could be created by using a variable prism under computer control. The prism enabled lateral shifts of anywhere from 13° to the left to 13° to the right. Choosing different shifts for different locations permitted complicated mappings to be created.

Following training, testing occurs again. The change in pointing from before the experience to after the experience serves as the measure of acquisition.

B. AMBIGUOUS INFORMATION

What happens when the input is limited to only one or two points? I find that following repeated training trials at only one location, behavior generalizes in a rigid fashion (Bedford, 1989). That is, however far you pointed off from the trained location, you point that amount off for all positions, even those a fair distance away. This appears to be true regardless of where the trained location occurs, although central training produces larger overall shifts. Figure 5 shows the change in pointing for two training conditions, one when the single location was straight ahead, and the other where it was not. The x axis shows the position of the test target, from left (−) of straight ahead (0) to the right (+). The y axis shows the change in pointing from pretest to posttest. If the experience had no effect, there would be a change of 0, and the data would lie along the 0-degree horizontal line. Input at one location proved sufficient to affect both that location and other locations.

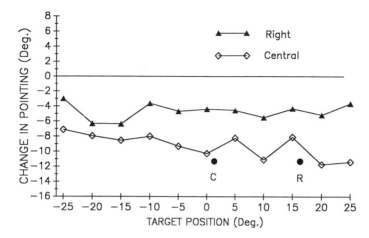

Fig. 5. Training with one pair located either straight ahead (C) or to the right (R). Location of training pair shown by filled circle. From "Constraints on Learning New Mappings between Perceptual Dimensions" by F. L. Bedford, 1989, *Journal of Experimental Psychology: Human Perception and Performance, 15*. Copyright © 1989 by the American Psychological Association. Adapted by permission.

What if training is inconsistent with a rigid shift for all of space? Consider the additional information provided by a second target in a new location. The second pair can be chosen so as to be consistent with a rigid shift, or to violate that solution. If touch is offset from vision by exactly the same amount for both locations, (e.g., 10° to the right) then interpolation to intervening locations is rigid. The result is not unexpected, given that only a single pair is needed to produce a uniform shift. If the offsets are in opposite directions (e.g., when the target is to the left, point further to the left, but when it's to the right, point further to the right), then behavior can be described as a rescaling of space. One dimension gets uniformly stretched with respect to the other. The intervening locations are filled in accordingly, even though the mapping was never encountered at those locations (Fig. 6).

The consequences of one- and two-pair input argue for two main conclusions. First, a mapping between visual space and motor space cannot be thought of as a collection of individual pairs of locations. If it were, the pairs would be largely independent and we would expect the system to generalize differently. We would be more likely to obtain the familiar generalization gradient surrounding each trained pair. Each trained location would provide minimal information about others, and the impact would decline rapidly with increasing distance from the trained location.

Felice Bedford

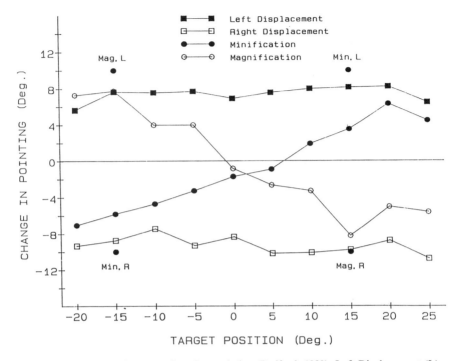

Fig. 6.   Training with two pairs—interpolation (Bedford, 1989). Left Displacement (L): Both visual positions shifted to the left. Right Displacement (R): Both visual positions shifted to the right. Minification (Min): Left visual position shifted to right; right visual position shifted to left. Magnification (Mag): Left visual position shifted to left; right visual position shifted to right. From "Constraints on Learning New Mappings between Perceptual Dimensions" by F. L. Bedford, 1989, *Journal of Experimental Psychology: Human Perception and Performance, 15*. Copyright © 1989 by the American Psychological Association. Reprinted by permission.

In the intuitive description given earlier for one-pair training, this would be the equivalent of adopting a strategy, perhaps wisely, of not generalizing the learned response to locations far removed from the conditions of training. Another way to think of the failure to get independence is that training two pairs simultaneously would not always be predictable from training each pair by itself and combining them additively.

Instead, training seems to influence the entire dimension. Note that information at only a single location was needed to drive the change for all of space. Mechanisms for which only minimal input is needed from the environment for acquisition are usually indicative of highly constrained, rule-governed, specialized learning organs.

Second, the "constraint" revealed by these manipulations can be described as *linear*. Of the infinite number of possible mappings consistent with the limited input, linear mappings were chosen. The generalized pattern always conformed either to a rigid shift (intercept parameter) or to a uniform rescaling (slope parameter). Note that within linearity, intercept changes seem to be preferred. Scale changes occurred only with information inconsistent with a change in a single intercept parameter.

C. EXTRAPOLATION

We were struck by an unexpected feature of the data. Although interpolation between trained positions conformed to a sloping line, when an intercept shift was not possible, the same was not obviously true for positions that did not fall within the two end points of training. Rather than extrapolating along the fitted line, pointing seemed to level off, perhaps even to drop back (refer to Fig. 6). Figure 7 shows the outcome of some manipulations tried in order to further explore the issue.

1. Absolute Size

Is the result simply a performance limitation? Perhaps the maximum permissible shift in pointing is something like 9°. If so, requiring anything greater than that amount, as might be required by extrapolation, would not be seen in behavior. This possibility proved insufficient. A two-pair training situation was designed such that the extrapolation, if it occurred, would fall within the 9 or so degrees known to be permissible based on prior experiments. Figure 7A shows the training pairs and the data. In addition, the dotted line shows the "interpolation line," calculated from the data of the three test locations that are within the two training end points. Here too, extrapolation along the same line that is interpolated does not occur, suggesting that this is a general phenomenon.

2. Centrality

We investigated the conditions under which extrapolation may be more likely to occur. Thus far, extrapolation would require generalizing from two points straddling a central region (e.g., 7° to the left of straight ahead and 7° to the right) to a non-central region (e.g., 7° to 25°). Yet many systems are known to be linear only over a central range. Perhaps this knowledge has been internalized in some sense, so that a linear function in the middle of a spatial continuum would not be generalized to a non-central region in the absence of solid proof. It may be easier to go in the other direction.

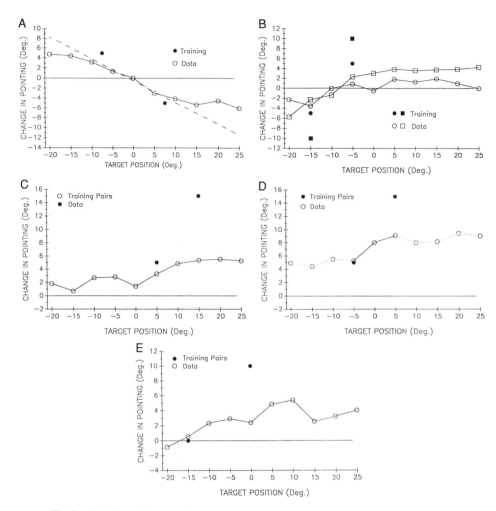

Fig. 7. Training with two pairs—extrapolation. Dashed line in panel A shows interpolation line fit to the three test locations between the two training positions. A: From "Constraints on Learning New Mappings between Perceptual Dimensions" by F. L. Bedford,
1989, *Journal of Experimental Psychology: Human Perception and Performance, 15.* Copyright © 1989 by the American Psychological Association. Adapted by permission. E: From
"Perceptual and Cognitive Spatial Learning" by F. L. Bedford, in press, *Journal of Experimental Psychology: Human Perception and Performance.* Copyright © by the American
Psychological Association. Reprinted by permission.

The two training pairs were "moved" to the side, such that both visual
locations were to the left of straight ahead. Figure 7B shows the pattern of
generalization. The primary outcome is that extrapolation along the interpolated line does not occur to central regions either. This result occurred

for two different sets of training pairs, one with 5° offsets and the other with 10° offsets.

3. Relative Size

Intuitively, the most difficult requirement of extrapolation may be having to infer a change that is *larger* than any experienced during training. If the two trained locations required pointing shifts of 5 degrees (one leftward, and one rightward), it may be incautious to assume that some locations must require pointing shifts of 6° or 8°, or even more. One difficulty is that there is no natural stopping point: At what value would the extrapolation end? What if the two input pairs required a different best-fit line, which, if extrapolated, would produce changes in pointing that were only smaller than those encountered in training?

Instead of moving the two pairs to the side, they were slid upward. That is, instead of the two offsets between visual and proprioceptive positions going in opposite directions, the offsets of the pairs were in the same direction but were of different sizes. In one of the manipulations, the two visual locations were on the same side of straight ahead, to assess the combination of this factor along with "centrality" (Fig. 7C). In another, they were on opposite sides of straight ahead. The data are most striking in Fig. 7D, where extrapolation to the right would require a larger response and to the left a smaller response. There appears to be little difference: Extrapolation in a downward direction does not occur either.

4. Normal Experience

Finally, a condition was chosen that seemed certain to produce a different pattern of generalization. If you receive training at two pairs, so that the offsets are in opposite directions, or so that the offsets are in the same direction but have different amounts, it is arguably difficult to know how to go beyond the specific training instances. However, suppose one of the two pairs had no offset at all. For instance, when a target is localized straight ahead, you must reach slightly to the right, but you also observe that when it appears somewhere else (e.g., 15° to the left), you just reach directly at the target, just as you always do. How do you extrapolate?

It seems that the most conservative strategy is to assume that, unless there is information to the contrary, the straight-ahead position is simply the "odd man out." Whereas the other manipulations were conditions chosen as most likely to produce linear extrapolation along the fitted line, this manipulation was chosen in order to have the opposite influence, that is, to produce more standard generalization decrements.

This did not occur (Fig. 7E); if anything, there was more extrapolation here than in any of the other conditions!

Overall, the pattern of data suggests that a sloping line fit between two points is not extended to locations outside that range, even under conditions in which it seems sensible and/or easy to do so. Nor does pointing drop back toward zero, even when that decision would be conservative. Under a variety of different conditions, the data may best be described as "leveling off," so that however much the system shifted at an end point, that same shift is continued for all locations beyond. For some of the conditions, there appears to be a little extrapolation along a line with a shallower slope than that of the interpolated line. Part of this effect may be due to consequences of presenting visual stimuli all to one side of straight ahead, or of presenting the two training pairs very close together. Whether some minimal extrapolation remains has not yet been determined. Extrapolation experiments are difficult to do. They are more likely than interpolation experiments to produce a few subjects with wildly aberrant means and variability. At present, the data appear to reflect a tendency for the system to extrapolate with caution.

D. UNAMBIGUOUS INFORMATION

I turn now to a few manipulations using the opposite strategy. To present "complete" mappings, typically approximately nine distinct locations were chosen. The experiments reported do not reflect a systematic exploration, but rather loosely follow one particular line of thought.

1. Isolation

The type of generalization following degraded input suggests a preference for modifying all the locations along a spatial continuum, rather than only one. As discussed, ncither the presentation of a single shifted location nor the special case in which a second location was consistent with the normal mapping led to the modification of only one small region of space. However, these results do not prove that a dimension *can't* be broken into small independent regions. If breaking a dimension into small independent pieces is less preferred than are linear functions, that ability could easily be hidden under circumstances in which the decision is left up to the system. To determine whether one location could be singled out, a mapping was created for which just about any interpretation other than "only one region has changed" would be a failure to learn correctly.

When a target appeared straight ahead, its physical location was actually to the right, but when it appeared anywhere else, coordination could proceed normally. Figure 8 (top) shows the outcome following training

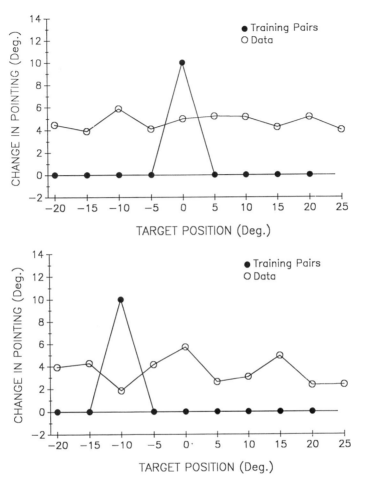

Fig. 8. Training with many pairs to isolate one region. Atypical location either straight ahead (top panel) or to the left (bottom panel). Top: From "Perceptual and Cognitive Spatial Learning" by F. L. Bedford, in press, *Journal of Experimental Psychology: Human Perception and Performance*. Copyright © by the American Psychological Association. Reprinted by permission.

with the one location shifted, and the remaining locations unchanged. The system was, in fact, unable to accommodate this intuitively simple transformation. If a mapping was really a collection of independent pairs, this particular transformation would be easily learned. However, it appears unlikely that the dimension can ever be divided, even under conditions in which it is highly adaptive to do so.

That which subjects impose on this mapping converges with what they interpolate following degraded input. Though the mapping was not learned correctly, pointing did change. There was a roughly uniform shift for all locations, by an amount roughly in between the 10° offset and zero. This is precisely the best-fit linear function under the circumstances (50% of the training occurred at the straight ahead position, and 50% was equally distributed among the remaining locations). Unfortunately, the fit is not always perfect. Figure 8 (bottom) shows what happens following similar training, except where the odd-man-out target is off to the side rather than at straight ahead. Whereas the best-fit linear function would be a sloping line, the change was instead a rigid shift. This may be another manifestation of the greater preference for intercept over slope changes, as seen with one- and two-pair training. Clearly this issue needs further investigation.

Why wasn't the intuitively simple isolation mapping acquired? One possibility is that only linear functions can be used to realign the two spaces. A second possibility is that the mapping was particularly difficult because it violated topological properties, as well as linear ones. Shepard (1989) while referring to neural representations and models, suggests that a rearrangement of space that disrupts topology is not likely to be learned because that would ". . . completely defeat the local connectivities of the topographically organized system" (p. 128). Figure 9A shows how locations in visual space get mapped into locations in motor space for the mapping where only the straight-ahead position was changed. Note that the property of being a one-to-one mapping has been destroyed, as has the initial order of points, both of which are topological properties.

2. Topology

Are topological properties relevant for realigning dimensions? Two mappings were devised that used identical visual locations and identical offsets, except that one of them violated topology and the other did not. For one group, all visual locations to the left of zero required pointing further to the left by 10° and all locations to the right required pointing further to the right by 10°. The straight-ahead position remained normal, that is, a 0° offset. For the other group, the directions were reversed so that all visual locations to the left of 0 required pointing further to right and locations to the right required pointing further to the left. As in the other group, straight ahead was unchanged. Figure 9B shows the distortion of space produced by these mappings; it can be seen that the uncrossed group is a one-to-one mapping with original order preserved and that the second, crossed, group is not. For instance, in the crossed group, if you wanted to obtain physically a stimulus that appeared either straight ahead, 10° to the left, or 10° to

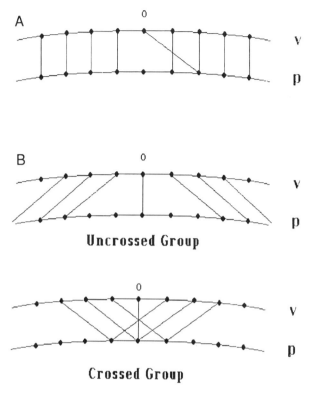

Fig. 9.   Mapping required in the isolation (A) and topological (B) experiments. v, Positions along the visual dimension; p, positions along the proprioceptive dimension.

the right, you would do so by reaching straight ahead for all three locations. In the uncrossed group, the distinctness of these three locations remains.

The data are presented in Fig. 10, which shows how pointing changes as a function of target position in the two groups; the figure also shows a comparison of the size of slope changes. The changes in slope are different in the two groups, with the uncrossed mapping (.28) producing more than double the amount of change than does the crossed mapping (.11). (Both slopes are significantly different from 0, and from each other.) Slopes were compared because, interestingly, only linear components reached significance when the changes in pointing were tested for polynomial components up to Degree 9. The mappings would be more accurately captured by a cubic, which would reflect two "bends" in the data. The data for at least the uncrossed group look as if they were heading in that direction.

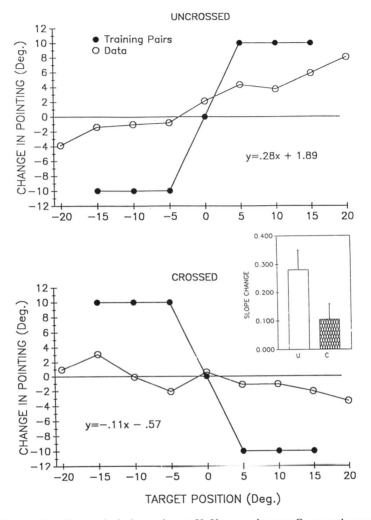

Fig. 10.   Data for topological experiment. U, Uncrossed group; C, crossed group.

Whether more training with the uncrossed mapping would produce more
accurate results remains to be determined. It is possible that the preferred
linear function is present in intermediate stages and then gets refined
accordingly. Because statistically there is evidence only for a linear fit,
whether transformations that are nonlinear but that preserve topological
properties can be accommodated is not yet known. However, either way,

there clearly is a sensitivity to topological properties, as demonstrated by greater change to mappings that are one to one and that preserve order.

Does the fact that there was some change in the crossed group suggest that even gross distortions of space can be accommodated? The answer is no. Figure 11 shows the mappings actually acquired, in which it can be seen that for the crossed group as well as the uncrossed group visual–motor behavior never became many-to-one, nor did it switch order. There appears to be a sensitivity to topological properties, so that mappings that do not violate topology are more easily dealt with. In addition, there is so far no evidence that violations of topology are ever acquired. Whether some topological properties are more influential than others is currently under investigation.

3. Discontinuity

A different strategy for dealing with the uncrossed mapping would be one in which the system split up the space, so that the left half of space were

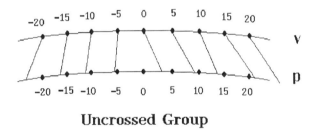

Uncrossed Group

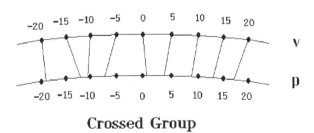

Crossed Group

Fig. 11.   Mappings acquired in the topological experiment. v, Positions along the visual dimensions; p, positions along the proprioceptive dimension.

pulled further left, and the right half further right. This would be a nonto-
pological transformation because destroying the continuity of points, like
destroying distinctness and order, destroys the topology. However, the
system is good at rigid shifts, and in addition, more than one adaptive state
can be present at the same time when they are contingent on different cues
(e.g., Hay & Pick, 1966; Kohler, 1964; Taylor, 1962; Welch, 1971; see
Welch, 1978, pp. 96–99 for a review.) It might be possible to code the
uncrossed mapping as two intercept parameters, each relevant for a different half of space. This solution may have been discouraged by the visual–
proprioceptive pair for which the straight-ahead position remained normal
(0,0).

Consequently, the mappings were repeated, except with the (0,0) pair
omitted. Statistically, the results were little different from the prior experiment. A linear, but not cubic, component was present for the uncrossed
and for the crossed group. Like the other study, the uncrossed group
showed greater change than the crossed group (slopes = .24 and −.14,
respectively) reflecting again the sensitivity to topological properties. Although it is difficult to rule out definitely that separate intercept parameters
were fit to the two halves of space, the data do not overwhelmingly support
this solution. It may well be that some type of external cue is needed upon
which different adaptive states must be contingent, and that space is not
easily split otherwise.

E. A DISSOCIATION

What makes this learning perceptual? As discussed earlier, location
mismatches between vision and touch for the same object suggest an
internal malfunction because internal knowledge about objects has been
violated. The inputs that make up the visual-motor mappings are used
along with preexisting structure to correct the internal malfunction as best
as possible. The research program described suggests some rules governing the acquisition of the new internal states. We can now ask whether the
rules are different from learning processes that function to apprehend new
information about the world. Another way to phrase the question is
whether there is a dissociation between perceptual and world learning on
the issue of "the content of what is learned" in addition to the issue of the
circumstances that produce learning.

For two of the permutations explored and described above, we directly
compared the outcome to a "cognitive" learning task with the same formal
properties (Bedford, in press). Would people be able to learn the mapping
where only one region had been changed, when not under the control of

the perceptual learning system? In addition, how would they choose to generalize to novel locations following two-pair training?

We needed a task that presented the same mappings but that removed the internal inconsistency between sensory systems. Instead of the prism, the visual–motor offsets were produced through computer software. For instance, a target light located straight ahead would require the arm to be 10 degrees to the right to illuminate the finger LED. Contrast this with the perceptual learning procedure, which also requires that a target appearing straight ahead be pointed to 10° to the right. In that procedure, when the subject is successful, the "hand" looks as if it's also straight ahead, and looks as if it's pointing to the target. This situation occurs because the target's actual position is at 10°, and both it and the hand are seen through the prism. In the cognitive procedure, the hand looks simply where it actually is, at 10°, and it looks as if it is pointing to the side of the target. Because there is no prism, there is no discrepancy between where the finger feels it is and where it appears to be. (Compare the second and third panels of Fig. 3.) Yet, the visual–motor pairings can be made to match any permutation created with the perceptual learning procedure. For the cognitive paradigm, subjects were told from the beginning that this was a learning task. A subject was told that she had to try to figure out and to remember where to put her arm for each different light, and that she would be tested on it afterward.

Without the need for internal correction, and without the ensuing motivation for perceptual learning, the consequences of the particular mappings were quite different. People were able to learn the mapping when one region was shifted and eight regions required accurate pointing (Fig. 12, top), consistent with intuition that this should be an easy rule to acquire. Even more notable was the different pattern of generalization when one region was shifted and one region required accurate pointing. This "discrimination" experiment produced a generalization gradient of the sort more familiar to learning researchers, in which a newly acquired response is used less and less as a function of distance from the explicitly trained stimuli (Fig. 12, bottom).

In these tasks, some type of "cognitive" abilities were used to acquire new information about the environment and to go beyond the exact training stimuli. These processes appear to allow spatial continua to be broken into individual pieces. Models assuming that associations between individual stimuli are the correct units of acquisition may be applicable under these circumstances. This is in contrast to the perceptual learning system, which seems constrained to operate on the dimension as a whole.

One clarification may be useful. In prism adaptation and its variants, the subject's behavior, *as viewed by an outside observer,* is to point to the side

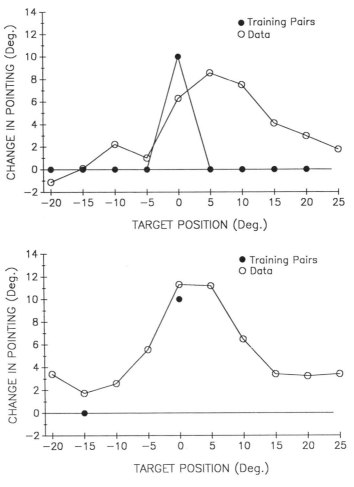

Fig. 12.   Data from cognitive learning paradigm. Top panel shows many-pair training. Bottom panel shows two-pair training. From "Perceptual and Cognitive Spatial Learning" by F. L. Bedford, in press, *Journal of Experimental Psychology: Human Perception and Performance*. Copyright © by the American Psychological Association. Reprinted by permission.

of a target's true location. This behavior appears identical to what a subject would do in the cognitive learning task discussed above. However, in perceptual learning there is never a representation that objects are to be found in different places with the visual system and with the motor system. The constraint that an object can be in only one place is upheld. Instead, there is a change within one or both systems, so that the two sensory systems again coincide. A subject looks as if she points to the side because her hand's position is mislocalized as further to the side or because the target appears to the side. As far as the perceptual system is concerned, she is pointing directly at the visual location. This is in contrast to the cognitive learning context, in which presumably there is a representation to point to the side of the targets seen position.

Another potential difference between the two types of learning concerns the role of conscious awareness. Subjects need not be aware of any discrepancy in order to adapt to rearrangements of space (see Welch, 1978), whereas the cognitive task that we used forced subjects to be aware that there was something new to be acquired. How awareness influences perceptual learning is currently under investigation.

F. SUMMARY OF RULES

How can we characterize the rules by which the perceptual system accommodates new mappings? Using the strategies of ambiguous and unambiguous information, we have thus far uncovered the following biases:

1. Acquiring a mapping is not a collection of individual visual–motor associations, but instead involves connecting entire dimensions.
2. There is a preference for linear functions to relate the two continua.
3. Within linearity, there is a preference for intercept changes over slope changes.
4. Extrapolation of a fitted function occurs cautiously, if at all.
5. There is a sensitivity to topological properties of space.
6. There is no evidence that space can be broken into "left half" and "right half."

Linearity clearly plays an important role. We are pursuing the possibility that rigid shifts and uniform stretches and squashes are precisely the internal changs that would be needed to correct for growth of the body in childhood, or the drift between sensory systems in adulthood.

VI. Hierarchy of Transformation Geometry

While linearity is important, it may not be sufficient. For instance, it does not account for the sensitivity to topological properties, nor can it by itself explain the preference for intercept over slope changes. One possible, admittedly speculative, integration of the findings comes from transformation geometry. In brief, the view is that a mapping should be considered more difficult than another if more geometric properties are altered by the mapping.

The transformation approach to geometry originated with mathematician Felix Klein who showed that different geometries could be ordered on the basis of the number of properties remaining unchanged as a result of a group of transformations (e.g., 1893/1957). The familiar Euclidian geometry concerns all those properties left intact by transformations that move a form in its entirety. A square that has been slid over changes nothing about the "squareness," but alters only its location. All the properties that remain intact—angle, parallelism, size, distance between two points, and so forth—are properties of Euclidian geometry (laboriously studied in high school). Those altered—absolute location—are not in the study of that geometry. Thus, a square, and a square 3 in. away, are equivalent forms in Euclidian geometry. But there are other, more radical, transformations that can be applied that lead to other geometries. For instance, consider pulling on one side of a square to turn it into a rectangle. Such a transformation alters more than location—for example, it alters size and distance between points. Only those properties that remain intact are part of this geometry, for example, parallelism and the property of being a straight line. Whereas in Euclidian geometry a square and a rectangle are distinct individual forms, in affine geometry they are equivalent. Klein laid out a series of transformations, each more radical than the last, and showed how each was the basis of a different-sized geometry. Although his concern with the transformations was the resulting geometry, it is the transformations themselves that most concern us here.

We can imagine visual space as a form, and different mappings as transformations on the form, which turn it into motor space. The more geometric properties altered by the transformation, the more complex the mapping. In the two-dimensional hierarchy, as devised by Klein, there are five distinct levels. They are shown in Fig. 13. What follows is an informal description of the different levels of transformations. Good formal discussions can be found in Modenov and Parkhomenko (1965). The simplest possible transformation picks up the visual space in its entirety and puts it elsewhere, altering only the absolute location. For instance, a square could be rotated or displaced to another location. This as described above as the group of transformations underlying Euclidian geometry. The next, slightly more complex, "similarity" transformations allow uniform expansions and contractions to both dimensions equally. That is, they alter the property of size as well as location, but all the remaining shape properties are unaltered. A square could be transformed into a larger square, or a rectangle into a larger rectangle with unchanged width-to-height ratio, and so forth. Next are the Affine transformations, also mentioned above. Here

Properties
Altered

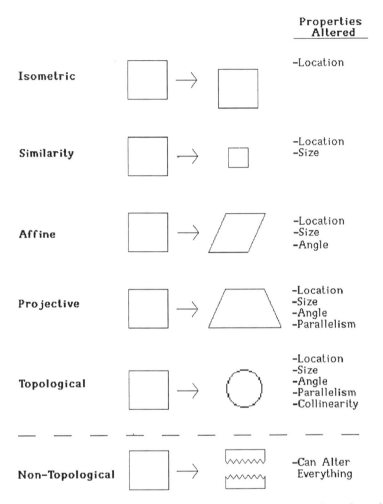

Isometric	-Location
Similarity	-Location -Size
Affine	-Location -Size -Angle
Projective	-Location -Size -Angle -Parallelism
Topological	-Location -Size -Angle -Parallelism -Collinearity
Non-Topological	-Can Alter Everything

Fig. 13.   Sample transformations within Klein's (1893/1957) hierarchy of transformations for two-dimensional space.

uniform expansions and contractions can be applied separately to two orthogonal dimensions. These transformations can turn squares into rectangles, or into rhombuses. Typically, they alter the property of angle, while leaving other shape properties intact, such as collinearity (straightness), parallelism, and order. Affine transformations are the most general type of linear changes. The fourth group are projective transformations, which alter the parallelism of sides as well. Squares, for instance, can turn into trapezoids. Finally, we have topological transformations. These are the most radical because all transformations of the original form are allowed, provided that distinct points are not glued together (1-to-1) and that continuous points are not split (continuity). These transformations have the power to turn squares into circles, preserving little of what we think of as form, except aspects such as the property of being a closed curve.

For one-dimensional space only, the second, third, and fourth levels collapse to a single level, which we will refer to as "affine." Clearly, a proper test of this view must come from visual–motor mappings in two dimensions of space. This consideration in part motivated the paradigm to be discussed next. Yet from the data that we do have in one dimension of space, the outcome appears consistent with the different levels. The isometric level corresponds to rigid shifts, which we found to be the most highly preferred. Affine transformations were next preferred, which in one-dimensional space correspond to slope changes. These were easily accommodated when the input was inconsistent with a rigid shift. Uniform stretching was, in turn, easier than any topological transformation, reflected by the tendency to fit straight lines to nonlinear mappings. Next, we saw that mappings preserving topological properties produced more change than those that did not. Finally, there was no evidence that non-topological properties can be acquired.

Why pursue this hierarchy? First, if nothing else, it is useful to have a taxonomy of some sort to guide research. There are an infinite number of possible mappings, and clearly no research program could try them all. The existence of a manageable number of distinct classes of mappings allows systematic exploration.

Somewhat more strongly, it should be noted that these different levels are not arbitrary classifications. The different levels are different *groups,* in a mathematical sense. For instance, if one transformation produces a particular mapping, in order to be a group there must also be a transformation that restores the original (presence of an inverse). Although going through the requirements to be a group is beyond the scope of the chapter, the major point is that the concept of a group is mathematics' way of carving nature at its joints. It may be the mind's way as well.

While the different levels must each be a group, that still leaves an infinite number of ways of parsing mappings. Why this one? One based on geometry seems a better candidate than do other schemes, such as polynomials of increasing order. Geometry is the study of form. To the extent that space can be considered to have form, formal properties of geometry are relevant to space and therefore potentially to the perception of space.

There are, however, an infinite number of geometries and corresponding transformations in addition to those described above. Mathematical schemes are "restricted by no other rule than that of avoiding contradictions" (Cassirer, 1944, p. 4). What makes Klein's levels special? While the geometries described are not all Euclidian, they are all within the Euclidian framework. That is, they all share certain fundamental axioms, none of which violate the way our world works (Euclidian with the most axioms, and topology, the least). The correct reflection of our world is not true of other goemetries, for example, that of Reimann. Cheng and Gallistel (1984) argue that although an organism may not represent all properties of the world, it would be crazy to have evolved a rule that gets things systematically wrong. Thus, while mathematics is not restricted by the way the world works, reality greatly limits which schemes are likely relevant for psychological problems.

One final issue on which I will comment concerns the direction of preferences (assuming that the levels are in some sense internalized). For instance, why assume that all of space is a rigid shift (isometric) unless given information to the contrary? Why not assume some other level? A useful analogy here may be the subset principle (Berwick, 1985) in language acquisition. If you have two languages, one of which is the subset of another, children assume the smaller language first and switch to the larger grammar only when given information inconsistent with the smaller one. The logic behind the principle is that it is easier to switch from the smaller to the larger universe than it would be to do the opposite, given the kinds of inputs for language. Children typcially get samples of correct language (*positive evidence*), but don't hear samples of ungrammatical utterances (*negative evidence*). To switch from the subset to the superset, you need only hear a grammatical sentence inconsistent with the subset. But there is no obvious way to get from the superset to the subset, because nothing tells you that you are wrong.

In the current domain, each level of transformations is a subset of all the ones above it. For example, all affine transformations are also topological transformations, but not all topological transformations are affine. While the subset rule is usually thought of as specific to the specialized language-acquisition module, the two domains face similar problems that may have led to similar solutions. As in language acquisition, the goal is to acquire something infinite. Because space has an infinite number of points, no look-up table will suffice (see also Hay, 1974). Thus, as with language acquisition, what is acquired is a generative system, rather than specific instances. In addition, as with language acquisition, environmental input is impoverished, especially for our cases where only one or two locations are specified. Although specific issues of positive and negative evidence may not be relevant to spatial mappings, the subset rule may still be sensible. It may always be more efficient under these conditions to infer the smaller infinity so as never to have to unlearn something inferred incorrectly.

VII. Computer Mappings

The second paradigm to be described permits novel visual–motor mappings to be produced in two-dimensional space. Visual positions are presented on a standard computer monitor. Motor positions are produced using a pen attached to a tablet, which is lying flat on a table. The pen and tablet work similarly to a computer mouse: The position of the pen on the tablet is represented on the screen by a visual character. Moving the pen causes the visual character to move appropriately on the screen in real time with no noticeable delay. Figure 14 shows a rough layout of tablet and monitor. Novel mappings can be imposed via software that alters how the tablet locations are mapped onto the screen. For instance, a mirror reflection would cause the cursor to move to the left when you moved your hand to the right. Helen Cunningham (1984) was the first to document this paradigm as useful for the study of visual–motor mappings.

The first question we asked was whether two dimensions of space are independent of one another. When detecting and accommodating new visual–motor relations, do orthogonal dimensions get processed separately from one another? If they do, then it should be possible to learn about one dimension (e.g., x), without regard to what is done to the other (e.g., y). Consider two mappings, both of which create exactly the same transformation of x but with differing manipulations to y. Both mappings shrink motor space in the horizontal direction to half its former size. For instance, moving the pen left to right by 2 in. on the tablet causes the cursor to move 4 in. left to right on the screen. One of the mappings also shrinks y

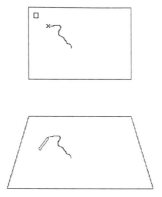

Fig. 14.   Sketch of computer monitor (top) and tablet surface (bottom) used to produce computer mappings. Pen on tablet represented on monitor with an ''x.''

by the same amount as x, whereas the other mapping leaves y unchanged from normal.

The mappings can be characterized by very simple linear equations. The normal relation between visual position and the tablet position before transformation is: $T_x = V_x + 0$ for x, and $T_y = V_y + 0$ for y. The relation under Mappings 1 and 2 is as follows:

Mapping 1

$$T_x = 0.5V_x + 0 \quad \text{(Minify both } x \text{ and } y)$$
$$T_y = 0.5V_y + 0$$

Mapping 2

$$T_x = 0.5V_x + 0 \quad \text{(Minify only } x)$$
$$T_y = 1.0V_y + 0$$

If the orthogonal dimensions of space are independent of one another, then the novel x relation should be learned equally effectively in both groups because it is the same in both groups. If they are dependent, then learning about x will depend on what is done to y as well. If so, then there are two main possibilities. Shrinking just x (Mapping 2) may be easier than shrinking both x and y (Mapping 1) because on average, positions move less under that transformation. The system may be trying to minimize the amount of change. Alternatively, the system may be trying to minimize the number of geometric properties altered. This rule would make the opposite prediction, that is, Mapping 1 is easier than Mapping 2. Referring back to the hierarchy of transformations, shrinking both x and y by the same amount is less radical a transformation than shrinking only x. The former mapping (similarity) alters only the size, but the latter mapping (affine) alters shape properties as well. Mapping 1 turns a square into a small square, and Mapping 2 turns a square into a rectangle.

Thus, we can determine whether the two dimensions of space are independent, and if they are not, get some idea of how they are linked. We assigned subjects to one or the other mapping. As in the prism adaptation paradigm, normal visual–motor performance was first determined. In this paradigm, a small square target appeared on the computer monitor on each trial. Subjects moved the pen without feedback so that the cursor produced by the pen (an "X") was invisible. Subjects were told to move the pen to the position on the tablet that *would* make the X fit in the square, if it were visible, and were tested on different positions. Practice with the novel transformation was subsequently provided by making the X cursor visible. With the distorted mapping in place, on each trial subjects tried to move the X into the small square target. There were nine different positions that together would make up a large square: three on the top row, three in the middle, and three on the bottom. Subjects practiced for a total of 9 min (135 trials), and were tested again without feedback.

The outcome was surprising and did not match any of the specific predictions. When the mapping minified both x and y, both x and y did shrink. That is, subjects did use a smaller range of the tablet for both x and y directions than they did before practice. When the mapping minified only x, x did shrink—and by an amount comparable to the other mapping. However, the y direction also became smaller, even though it should not have! The data are shown in Fig. 15 in which it can be seen that basically a square turned into a smaller square for both groups, even though for one it should have been turned into a particular rectangle. Although the results were unexpected, they do support the view that preserving geometric properties may be important. Shape was preserved, even when it meant imposing a transformation that was not correct. It is apparently easier to rescale both x and y equally, then just to minify x. The slope parameters describing the data are as follows:

Mapping 1 (Minify both x and y)

Pretransformation	Posttransformation
$T_x = 1.13V_x$	$T_x = 0.80V_x$
$T_y = 1.07V_y$	$T_y = 0.75V_y$

Mapping 2 (Minify only x)

Pretransformation	Posttransformation
$T_x = 1.17V_x$	$T_x = 0.83V_x$
$T_y = 1.12V_y$	$T_y = 0.85V_y$

But did y really shrink because of x, or would it have happened anyway? Note that before any transformation, a larger area of the tablet was used than should have been (pretransformation slopes start out greater than 1.0). Perhaps the range would shrink anyway following any kind of practice with the equipment. Figure 16 (top) shows that this is not the case. When an equal amount of practice is given with the normal mapping instead of a novel mapping, the y range of the tablet (as well as the x range) does not shrink. In fact, initially the range expands even more. This may occur because the tablet is larger than the computer screen and there may

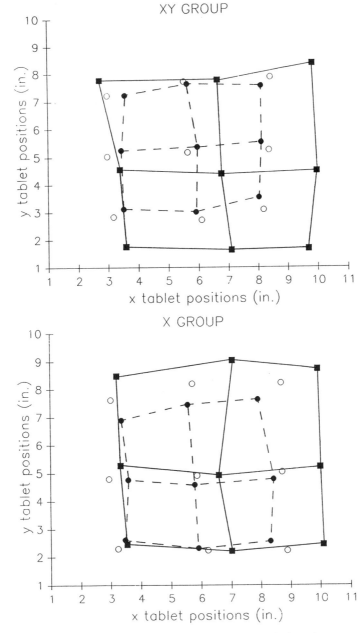

Fig. 15. Tablet positions before and after training for the "independence experiment." Connected squares show positions before training, unconnected (unfilled) circles after 6 min. of training, and connected (filled) circles after 9 min. Lower left corner of tablet is located at (0,0). "*XY* group" is the mapping that shrinks both *x* and *y*; "*X* group" is the mapping that shrinks only *x*.

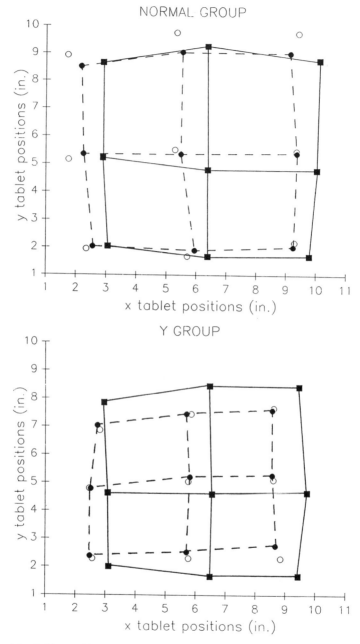

Fig. 16.   Tablet positions before and after training for the "independence experiment."
Connected squares show positions before training, unconnected (unfilled) circles after 6 min.
of training, and connected (filled) circles after 9 min. Lower left corner of tablet is located at
(0,0). "Normal Group" is the mapping in which neither x nor y is changed; "Y group" is the
mapping that shrinks y.

be a natural tendency to map the whole tablet to the whole screen. A tendency to use a larger tablet range than the normal mapping dictates can account for the pretransformation values as well.

But there is at least one puzzle. To complete the fourth permutation, we ran another group where y was shrunk, but not x. Figure 16 (bottom) shows that y does not pull x with it as obviously as x influences y. The asymmetrical influence may be due to the asymmetry imposed by the paradigm. The x dimension maps straightforwardly from the tablet to the screen, but the y dimension does not. Moving the hand from left to right on the tablet causes the cursor to move from left to right on the screen. Moving the hand in a forward direction (close to far) on the tablet, which lies flat on the table, causes the cursor to move from the bottom to the top of the screen. There is evidence from research on interpreting "you are here" and other maps of the environment, that people naturally assume *forward* corresponds to *up* (Levine, 1982). Yet perhaps subjects are not completely certain of that correspondence and may not know how to align those two distinct spatial dimensions. In this paradigm, the y dimension may consequently be more labile than x in the sense that it takes guidance from the more certain dimension, especially given novel transformations. One of the many intriguing questions that remain to be investigated is whether x and y will be dependent or independent, and whether they will be symmetrical or asymmetrical, when the y mapping from tablet to screen is made more straightforward.

Having determined that at least under some conditions x and y are dependent, and that shape-preserving transformations seem preferred, we still wanted to test whether the hierarchy of transformation geometry is a useful way to categorize mappings. The following experiment should be viewed as exploratory, with both more data analyses and experiments needed. Five different mappings corresponding to the five different levels of the hierarchy were given to the same subjects on different days and in different orders. The particular mappings chosen are as follows. The isometric mapping shifted motor space down with respect to visual space by 1.5 in. That is, the position of the pen on the tablet is lower than where it appears on the screen, for all positions. The similarity mapping uniformly shrunk both x and y to half their normal range, as in the last experiment. The affine transformation sheared space by essentially "pulling" x axes diagonally so that the y position on the tablet depends on the x position on the screen. For instance, to get a path on the screen to be perfectly horizontal from left to right requires moving the pen diagonally from lower left to upper right. A square region of the screen is turned into a sheared square on the tablet. The projective transformation turned a square region into a trapezoid. And finally, the topological transformation we chose mapped straight lines of space to curved lines and turned a square into a small circle. The transformations all moved the upper left target down by exactly the same amount (1.5 in.). The left column of Fig. 17 shows how the transformations should alter behavior to the nine test targets if learning were perfect; the right side of Fig. 17 shows what actually was learned for each transformation.

Overall, the results are promising. The more geometric properties altered by the transformation, the harder the mapping was to acquire. The first three levels can be compared relatively directly by fitting linear equations, because all three are linear mappings in two dimensions. Figure 18 (top) shows the change in the parameter(s) that should have changed, as a percentage of optimal amount of change for that transformation. The Y displacement mapping was learned 100% (change in y intercept); next was the minification mapping at an average for both parameters of 70% (change in x slope, change in y slope), followed by shear at 26% (change in y as a function of x).

To compare all the groups, the positions for perfect acquisition for each mapping were determined, followed by a calculation of how far the pen position was from the optimal position for each target (average square root of x^2 and y^2). The average distance from the optimal positions following training are shown in Fig. 18 (bottom). The Y displacement group is closest to the destination, followed by circle, minification, shear, and trapezoid. The circle group appears better accommodated than was predicted from the hierarchy; however, this result comes from accommodating the minification part of the transformation, rather than from altering the shape. There is little evidence that the straight lines of the square became curved lines of a circle.

Although promising, the data are not conclusive. The distance measure is problematic because it does not take into account the shape of the mappings, and could be misleading. There are different possible interpretations of the outcome of the experiment. For instance, the data could support a view that transformations of scale are easy, and everything else difficult. The geometric hierarchy as well as other possibilities are being explored.

Is this perceptual learning? It is difficult to determine whether the constraint that an object cannot be in two places at once, or any other constraint, has been violated in the pen and tablet paradigm. Without information that there is an internal error, the motivation for perceptual learning would be absent. If we consider again the prism adaptation paradigm, the error is suggested by feeling an object (the hand) in one place but seeing the object (the hand) in a different place. Welch (1972; 1978; 1986, p. 10; Welch & Warren, 1980) points out that the object localized by the two modalities must be judged as the *exact same object*. Otherwise, there is no discrepancy between the modalities. If you feel your hand straight ahead of your body, but assume that the visual image you see a few inches away is someone else's hand, then there is no motivation for adaptation. The information wouldn't be in violation of any constraint, because different objects can be in different places (see also Bedford, 1992a).

Returning to the digitizing tablet, are there sufficient cues present to assume that the information obtained visually and the information obtained through the hand refer to the same object? The motor information is the feel of the hand's (and pen's) position and motion on the tablet, yet the visual information isn't of a hand, or part of a hand, or the pen. It's the character "X", an abstract representation. This is also to a large extent true of our prism adaptation paradigm, where only a small, round LED on the hand was visible. However, in the digitizing tablet paradigm, the hand/pen and its visual representation are also located very far from one another, which could decrease the same object assumption. The paradigm imposes three spatial transformations of its own, even if the normal mapping is used: The tablet is lower down than the screen (a y displacement), it's closer to the observer (a z displacement), and it's flat on a table, whereas the screen is upright (rotation around an x axis). Large lateral displacements in prism adaptation produce less percentage adaptation, which could be due in part to some object assumption breaking down. If you look at your hand through a prism that displaces the image $10°$, your hand temporarily feels as if it's located where you see it (visual capture). If you look at your hand through a $30°$ prism, visual capture breaks down and your hand looks and feels as if it's in two different positions.

Yet there could be other factors that compensate for the large differences in spatial position produced by the digitizing table paradigm. Held and Durlach (1989) suggest that motion plays a major role in object identity. The visual- and motor-motion information are highly correlated, with the movements occurring at the same time and with the same velocities and accelerations. The bottom line is that exact circumstances under which two distinct samples will be judged, by the perceptual system, to refer to the same object are not precisely known.

Another approach would be to see whether the change in aiming for the target is due to a genuine perceptual change, in which either the hand feels as if it's in a different position on the tablet, or the target on the screen looks as if it's in a different position. We asked subjects after each experiment to describe any transformation that they were aware of, although not in those words. Some of the subjects report intentionally using a strategy to get the "X" in the square—such as moving their hands a smaller amount on the tablet in the minification of the x and y conditions—and

YDISPLACEMENT TARGETS

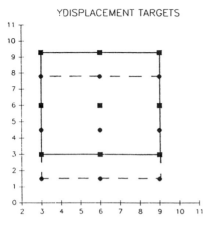

YDISPLACEMENT

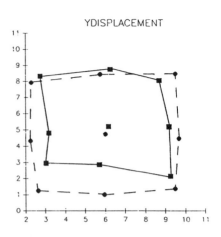

MINIFICATION TARGETS

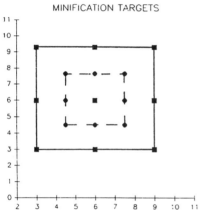

MINIFICATION

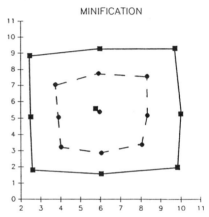

SHEAR TARGETS

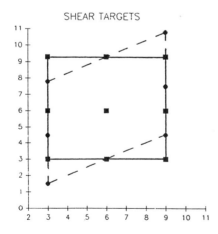

SHEAR

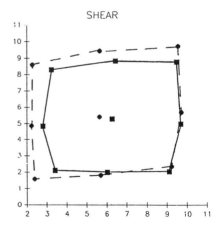

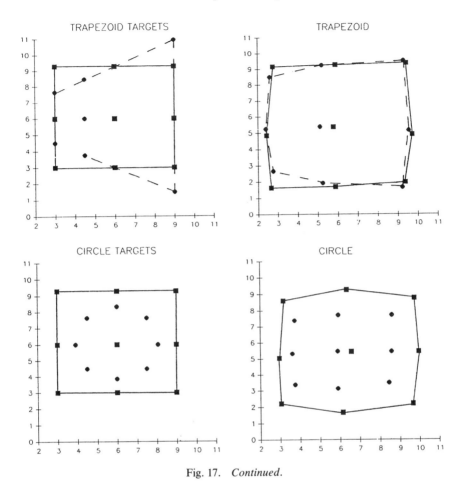

Fig. 17. *Continued.*

using that strategy for testing as well. Interestingly, so far the data for those subjects appear indistinguishable from the others. Yet the presence or absence of conscious awareness does not necessarily map neatly onto cognitive and perceptual learning anyway. Direct tests of perceptual changes, such as transfer to entirely visual tasks or entirely motor tasks, are being investigated.

Note that in any event, the paradigm remains of interest. The ease with which people use computer mice and learn video games may suggest that

Fig. 17. Geometry experiment. Left column shows the transformation of space required of subjects for the nine test targets. Right column shows the outcome. Data shown before training (connected squares) and after 6 min of training (connected circles). The circle data are not connected.

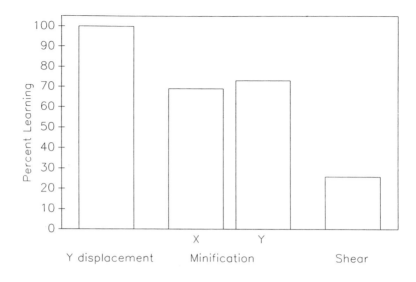

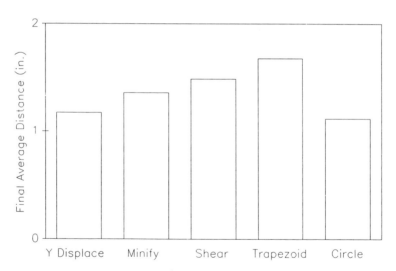

Fig. 18. Geometry experiment. Top panel shows the percentage change in the relevant
parameter(s) for the three linear transformations. Bottom panel shows the average distance
from the optimal positions following training for all five transformations. (See p. 40.)

the rules of perceptual–motor coordination and its maintenance are accessible for purposes other than to correct sensory systems. Tasks with
similar characteristics—such as needing mappings between entire dimensions, and referring to space—may be "parasitic" on perceptual learning

proper, even when an internal error has not, strictly speaking, been detected. This view may be similar to the view of "accessibility" of adaptive specializations (Rozin, 1976), in which mechanisms evolved for one purpose can be exploited for other purposes. Although these ideas may weaken the modular story of perceptual learning to some extent, they may nonetheless prove true.

Adaptation to the rearrangements of space and to learning new mappings between spatial dimensions appear to differ in significant ways from apprehending new information about the world. Is adaptation unique, or do other processes differ from world learning also? I turn now to a different phenomenon, which has recently been gaining in interest.

VIII. The McCollough Effect

An example of plasticity entirely within the visual system is a phenomenon known as the McCollough effect or the orientation-contingent color aftereffect, discovered in 1965 by Celeste McCollough. A vertical grid consisting of alternating black and magenta bars is shown for a few seconds, followed by a grid of horizontal bars colored black and green (see Fig. 19). The two patterns are alternated repeatedly for several minutes. This experience leads to the perception of colors that are contingent on the orientation of a stimulus. The white portion of black and white vertical bars look slightly green, and white horizontal bars look pink.

The explanation for this phenomenon has proved elusive, candidates ranging all the way from fatigue within simple neural detectors to a Pavlovian conditioning interpretation (e.g., Dodwell & Humphrey, 1990; Harris, 1980; McCollough, 1965; Murch, 1976; Seigel & Allan, 1992). I suggest first that the phenomenon is properly thought of as an instance of *learning* as described in the first section. It is a change from experience that evolved to make us better. Precisely what function it serves will be elaborated

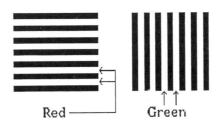

Fig. 19.   Stimuli for a McCollough effect experiment.

later. Second, within the category of learning, it belongs within the division of internal perceptual learning, rather than that of apprehending new information about the world. This point can be illustrated by an experiment conducted recently in my laboratory, showing that the mechanism responsible for the contingent aftereffect cannot make use of properties in the world. In the standard McCollough effect, tilting one's head to the side by 90° causes the illusory colors seen on the test patterns to reverse (Ellis, 1976; McCollough, 1965). For example, if vertical lines appear pink and horizontal lines green, then tilting the head makes vertical lines appear green and the horizontal lines pink. Yet when you tilt your head, objectively vertical lines continue to be perceived as vertical even though the retinal orientation becomes horizontal. That is, the illusory colors appear yoked to the retinal orientation, rather than to the perceived or objective orientation of a stimulus.

Karen Reinke and I (Bedford & Reinke, 1992) pursued this finding by asking whether color *could* be made contingent on the objective or perceived orientation. When inducing the standard McCollough effect, color is paired both with retinal and with objective/perceived orientation. Logically, acquiring either dependence will correctly reflect the contingencies of the environment. It is possible that when both contingencies are made available, the retinal properties overshadow the regularity involving the real orientation. Under these artificial circumstances, learning about the world may be prevented. In the real world, it can be argued, the continual motion of an observer may prevent any longterm retinal correlation. That is, it could be that the purpose of the mechanism reflected by the McCollough effect is to apprehend new features of the environment—that vertical lines and red color go together in some sense. We asked, if subjects received only pairings between color and objective orientation, would they learn the connection?

To answer this question, we dissociated retinal from perceived coordinates during training by having each subject view the stimuli with her head tilted 90° for half of the trials. Consider a red grating, which is objectively vertical, alternating with a green grating, objectively horizontal. If viewed when upright, red is paired with both actual vertical and with retinal vertical, and green with both actual and retinal horizontal. If those same stimuli are next viewed with the head tilted, red remains paired with actual vertical and green with actual horizontal, but the retinal relation has reversed. Red is now paired with retinal horizontal, and green with retinal vertical. Equal numbers of trials when the head is upright and when it is tilted produce a zero retinal contingency where both retinal horizontal and vertical lines will each be red half the time and green the other half. The colors remain perfectly correlated with the actual orientation of the stimuli (red-vertical/green-horizontal). We found that very little was learned in this condition compared both to a standard condition in which both contingencies are present, and to a condition that left only the retinal contingency. It appears to be extremely difficult to get the illusory color under the control of the actual orientation of a stimulus.

We use this finding as a plausibility argument to suggest that some classes of explanation for the McCollough effect will not be very useful. Any account for which the goal is to apprehend new information about the world would be ill served by a process that is insensitive to that information. We suggest instead a theory that is based heavily on perceptual learning as distinct from other forms of learning.

The theory has two assumptions, the first a condition necessary to produce learning and the second a claim about the content of what is learned (Bedford, 1992a). The assumptions are first summarized and then followed by a more detailed explanation.

1. Objects should not change their color when the head (or object) is tilted. If they appear to do so, then an internal correction is necessary the manifestation of which we call the McCollough effect.
2. The McCollough effect involves a mapping between entire dimensions of orientation and color rather than learning two specific red-vertical and green-horizontal associations.

According to the first assumption, when an experimental induction procedure pairs a vertical grating with red, and a horizontal grating with green, it is actually providing the visual system with the information that as the retinal orientation of an object—the grating—changes, so does its color. This is problematic because when the orientation of an object on the retina changes, whether due to head tilt or object tilt, color should not. Objects do not change their color when the head (or object) is tilted. If they appear to do so, an internal correction is necessary, the manifestation of which we call the McCollough effect. There will be an internal correction for the perceived color differences, so that different orientations of the same object will no longer have different colors. Red vertical lines and green horizontal lines should eventually appear as exactly the same color if learning is perfect. If tested on white lines, vertical will appear green and horizontal will look red.

Unless there is some information to inform the visual system that it is malfunctioning, perceptual learning will not occur. I suggest that we have a constraint that an object does not change its "color" over time, analogous to the constraint that an object cannot be in two places at the same time. If information contained in the proximal stimulus does not contradict the constraint, then internal changes are not necessary and will not occur.

Consequently the co-occurrence of colors and orientations is problematic, from the viewpoint of the visual system, only if the different colors refer to the *same* object in different orientations. Different objects can have different colors. This assumption makes strong predictions about when contingent aftereffects will and will not occur, an issue that has been the subject of continuing debate (e.g., Dodwell & Humphrey, 1990; Harris, 1980; Seigel, Allan & Eissenberg, 1992; Skowbo, 1984).

The extent to which an induction procedure is successful will depend on the extent to which the perceptual system is convinced that the same object is involved. In the standard phenomenon, red and green are paired with vertical and horizontal gratings, which leads to illusory colors contingent on orientation. Also successful have been red and green paired with a single vertical and single horizontal bar, a triangle pointing up and a triangle pointing down, (vertical) wide stripes and (vertical) narrow stripes, two concentric circle patterns of different spatial frequencies, two different directions of motion, two different velocities, two disks of different lightnesses, and two different lightnesses of a surrounding frame (Breitmeyer & Cooper, 1972; Harris, 1980; Hepler, 1968; Lovegrove & Over, 1972; Mayhew & Anstis, 1972; Siegel, Allan & Eissenberg, 1992; see Stromeyer, 1978, for a review). All these stimuli lead to color contingent on the appropriate feature.

In the present interpretation, these successes are sensible because in all cases the two members of the pair can be interpreted as referring to a single object. Two concentric-circle patterns of different spatial frequencies can refer to the exact same concentric-circle pattern seen at different distances, because spatial frequency changes as a function of distance. A vertical bar and a horizontal bar can refer to the exact same bar viewed either with the head upright, or with the head tilted by 90°. A light-gray disk and a dark-gray disk can be the same disk under different overall levels of illumination. Gratings moving up and moving down on the retina can result from the exact same grating viewed with different up and down head motions. Different velocities can result from different speeds of head motion. Once the "same-object" constraint is met, then one of the required conditions for a discrepancy is met. When the retinal image of a single object tilts, its color should not; when the distance between an object and an observer changes, the object's color should not; when the distance from an object changes, the object's velocity should not, and so on.

Stimuli that do not succeed are those not readily interpretable as different states of the same object. Concentric circles of one color alternated with radiating lines of another did not produce a color effect. Pairing one direction of motion with small disks, and the other with small triangles also did not produce a contingent aftereffect, nor did alternating a green cross and a red square (Fidell, 1968, reported in Skowbo, Timney, Gentry & Morant, 1975; Foreit & Ambler, 1978; Mayhew & Anstis, 1972). There is a bias toward reporting successes, but a number of researchers have concluded that arbitrarily chosen stimuli tend not to work (e.g., Dodwell & Humphrey, 1990; Skowbo, 1984). As White and Riggs (1974) note, no one has ever reported color contingent on different makes of automobiles. From the viewpoint of the visual system, none of these results are problematic. For instance, the square and cross were ineffective because the retinal image of a cross and the retinal image of a square cannot refer to the same object—assuming objects maintain rigidity. Pairing a red square and a green cross requires no action, because different objects can be different colors. The same argument holds for pairing small triangles and small circles. There is no normal transformation that turns triangles into circles. That is, retinal images of triangles and circles always refer to different objects. No internal malfunction will be detected, or corrected, and no illusory colors manifested.

The above is a simplified version for sake of clarity, dividing conditions into simply whether they will work or won't work. It is likely that the distinction is one of more or less effectiveness, rather than of all or none. For instance, it is probably more accurate to say that the retinal image of a circle and of a triangle is *less likely* to refer to the same object than a small circle and a large circle. Non-natural transformations are apparently sometimes acceptable for object identity (see Shepard, 1984, pg. 430). This probably explains why a (red) square and a (green) cross are ineffective when using the same procedure that is sufficient for oriented lines and color (Foreit & Ambler, 1978), but why the aftereffect can be detected when using a test procedure designed for measuring very small effects (Siegel, Allan & Eissenberg, 1992). As noted earlier in the section on computer mappings, the circumstances under which two distinct instances are judged by the perceptual system to refer to the same object are not precisely known. It should be possible to use the criteria of object identity uncovered in other areas, such as apparent motion (e.g., Chen, 1985; Warren, W. H., 1977), certain types of priming (see Kahneman, Treisman & Gibbs, 1992), and unity in infants (Spelke, 1990) to predict how effective stimuli will be in the McCollough effect.

Stimuli can fail to suggest a malfunction in ways other than by referring to different objects. The two stimuli can refer to the same object, but not undergo a change in color. For example, the alternation of a vertical grid colored green and a horizontal grid also colored the same color green does not induce any contingent aftereffect (Humphrey, Dodwell & Emerson, 1985). In the current interpretation this result is sensible because different retinal orientation of the same object did not change color. There is no discrepancy here, just a green object.

Other learning-based accounts have had difficulty explaining and predicting which stimuli can and cannot induce contingent aftereffects. The most well developed traditional learning account maintains that the McCollough effect is an instance of Pavlovian conditioning (e.g., Allan & Siegel, 1986; Murch, 1976; Siegel & Allan, 1992; Westbrook & Harrison, 1984). A naive instantiation of this view predicts that any arbitrarily chosen stimuli can be associated, an account clearly falsified by the data. A more sophisticated view argues that based on phenomena of selective association in animal learning (e.g., taste aversions), not all stimuli have to be equally associable (see, e.g., Harris, 1980). This would allow for failures as well as successes. However, it does not allow one to specify *which* stimuli will work, unlike the present interpretation (see Bedford, 1992 for additional problems).

Once the circumstances that induce perceptual learning are present, something gets learned. The question becomes, What is the content of that learning? The second assumption is that part of what is acquired is a mapping between the dimensions of orientation and of opponent red/green color (cf., Hurvich & Jameson, 1957). This suggestion is in contrast to associative models, which assume that what is learned is the specific red-vertical and/or green-horizontal pairs presented during induction. Models based on independent connections between individual stimuli make different predictions from those based on connecting entire dimensions, including whether one can distinguish the trained stimuli from the untrained stimuli in performance and whether individually trained pairs would combine additively to produce all possible combinations of trained pairs (see Bedford, in press; Koh & Meyer, 1990). I focus here on one particular difference, the information necessary for a correlation, because there is relevant data from the McCollough effect and because the interpretation of the data has been controversial.

The successful correlation of two individual stimuli, such as red and vertical, requires integrating information about the presence and absence of one of those stimuli with the presence and absence of the other. Figure 20 shows the four possible combinations along with different outcomes. For instance, if S_1 and S_2 co-occur often, and S_1 does not occur without S_2, nor S_2 without S_1, then the correlation between S_1 and S_2 is high—S_1 and S_2 appear and disappear together. If S_1 and S_2 co-occur often, but S_1 also occurs often without S_2, and S_2 without S_1, then the correlation is low—S_1 and S_2 are independent and the co-occurrences were coincidental. Thus, a mechanism correlating two individual stimuli would have as input the information in those cells.

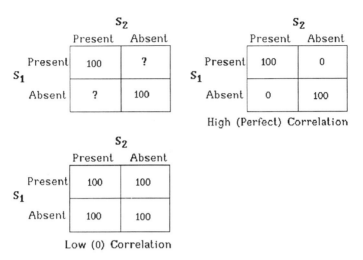

Fig. 20.   High and low correlation between two stimuli (S_1 and S_2) with number of pairings between S_1 and S_2 held constant (100).

If instead a mechanism correlates the values along two entire dimensions, it is not obtaining information showing that the dimensions appear and disappear together, but rather that *if* the two stimulus dimensions co-occur, then the values of one dimension may (high correlation) or may not (low correlation) be systematically related to the values along another (in a linear fashion for simple linear regression). The relevant information does not come from the four cells described above, but from all pairs of values from the two dimensions. For instance, the correlation of height and weight takes as its input pairs of height-weight values. If the weight of a 6-ft person was unknown, it would not affect the correlation, whereas if the weight of a 6-ft person was 90 it would[5].

Now we can consider the controversial finding from the McCollough effect. If trials of a red homogeneous patch are interspersed among red-vertical and green-horizontal induction trials, they do not reduce the magnitude of the contingent aftereffect that results (Skowbo & Forster, 1983). This is problematic for a single stimulus account because, as described above, this manipulation decreases the correlation between the two stimuli. However, the finding is well accommodated within a dimension account. The presence of red without vertical is simply a missing data point,

---

[5] The correlation of two individual stimuli can be viewed as a simplified subset of correlation proper, where the "dimension" for an individual stimulus consists only of two values—presence and absence.

analogous to entering height without weight into a correlator. It also accounts for why interspersing, instead, achromatic vertical lines (i.e., vertical lines without red) does reduce learning. This is not a missing data point because achromatic vertical lines do pair orientation with color; *vertical, white* will be entered into the correlation.

The dimension approach suggests manipulations that largely have not been conducted. For instance, mappings between dimensions shift the focus from simply whether you get a connection, to the type of connection. Must orientation and red/green color always be related linearly? If we pair vertical lines with green, and horizontal lines with a less saturated green rather than red, will the illusory colors seen be related linearly to orientation? How about the presentation of multiple orientation–red/green color pairs rather than only two pairs? Will linear functions always be fit even if the relation presented is nonlinear? Are some mappings more preferred and more easily learned than others? It is easy to see why research has been limited to only two pairs. Because only two points are needed to determine a line, two pairs are sufficient to recalibrate the entire dimension. Under these circumstances, it can appear as if one or two specific associations are the core phenomenon, rather than reflecting a degraded version of the actual phenomenon of mappings between entire dimensions. Note that with rich internal constraints on this learning system, even a single pair can be sufficient to drive a change throughout the dimension, as in prism adaptation (see Bedford, 1992a).

In addition to dimensions, another answer to the question of the content of learning should involve which system changes, an often ignored aspect of the McCollough effect. Why does color become contingent on orientation and not vice versa? In fact, that relation can also be learned (Held & Shattuck, 1971) but the factors that lead to one or the other have not been systematically explored. The perceptual learning view approaches this question by asking which system is malfunctioning. If an error is detected, correct resolution requires first inferring the source of the error. Does the color dimension need recalibration because it is erroneously varying with changes in retinal orientation (head tilt)? Or is it the orientation dimension that needs recalibrating, because it is erroneously varying with changes in relative luminance? A related problem that must be solved is whether color is erroneously varying with orientation (if that direction is inferred), or with some other dimension. Research that can be viewed as related involves effects labeled *blocking,* in which past experience can bias decisions about the source of the error (e.g., Brand, Holding, & Jones, 1987; Sloane, Ost, Etheridge, & Henderlite, 1989; Westbrook, & Harrison, 1984; Siegel & Allan, 1985). Framing the problem this way should also enable selective control over which system changes by trying to bias one or the other interpretation.

Having elaborated briefly on the two assumptions, I will discuss a few related general questions to keep in mind. Why does it make evolutionary sense to have these internal corrections? We need to know how such a mechanism could have arrived there in the first place, and why it would be adaptive in an evolutionary sense of the word to have such a mechanism. Clearly at an abstract level, it is advantageous to have optimally functioning sensory systems, without which fatal errors are more likely to result. But we need more specific hypotheses for the specific internal corrections. In the case of the McCollough effect, why have a mechanism prepared to correct for observed color changes of an object seen in different orientations, if an object does not change its selective reflectance of wavelength?

I suggest that the function is an extension of maintaining perceptual constancy. *Constancy* refers to perception of the property of an object remaining constant despite continually varying input. For instance, size constancy refers to the perception of the size of an object remaining constant, despite changes in retinal size with distance. Color constancy refers to the perception of the color of an object remaining constant despite changes in relative luminance that result from different lighting conditions. The point in both instances is that the size and "color" of an object in the world typically do not change. Consequently, it is advantageous to perceive them as non-changing, so as to represent the world accurately. It would defeat the purpose of constancy, if sometimes the color on an object erroneously appeared to change with head tilt. It may therefore be useful to ensure that when you tilt your head, not only shouldn't perceived orientation change ("primary constancy"), but neither should perceived size or color or motion, and so forth ("secondary constancy"). But why prepare for that possibility if it can never happen? Is nature paranoid enough to prepare for experimenter intervention?

The missing piece of the puzzle may be provided by Held (1980), who points out that there are natural situations in which the color can indeed appear to change when viewed from different orientations. There is a common optic defect in which the optical axis of the lens is not aligned with the fixation axis. As the "ocular prism" moves with the eye, color fringes at edges will appear that are contingent on the orientation of the stimulus with respect to the observer. Thus, there appears to be a naturally occurring situation that would create the otherwise impossible covariation between orientation and color. Consequently, it is sensible that a corrective mechanism already exists to handle the natural discrepancy, which can also be tapped by experimenters who artificially induce a similar discrepancy. We refer to these mechanisms as maintaining *secondary constancy*, to distinguish them from classic perceptual constancy, which we can call *primary constancy*. Due to the importance of keeping perception constant and veridical while besieged with bodily movements and changes in lighting conditions, the evolution of corrective mechanisms would be adaptive to the organism.

What happens if the motivation for perceptual learning is absent? The present view does not claim that nothing will be learned in some situations where stimuli co-occur. For instance, if a triangle is repeatedly red and a circle repeatedly green, an organism would be foolish not to take notice of the pervasive contingency. However, what will be learned will be about the external world and not about internal perceptual systems. Such learning could manifest itself as changes in thoughts, expectations, beliefs, or behaviors, but there is no need to alter what is seen because there is no internal malfunction.

IX. Conclusion

The general direction of this chapter has been to argue that *perceptual learning* is a distinct type of learning, with its own inputs, internal states, outputs, and function. In addition, the issue of how this category is related to other changes that result from experience was briefly discussed in the beginning.

Considering the issue of internal states, or content of learning, one important idea involves dimensions. Perceptual learning processes may be constrained to operate on entire dimensions, rather than on individual stimuli along those dimensions. Adaptation to rearrangements of space involves rules about entire dimensions rather than rules simply about individual associations between discrete locations of space. In addition, I suggested that study of the McCollough effect might benefit from viewing what is learned as a connection between entire dimensions of orientation and opponent color, rather than as the formation of specific associations such as *vertical* and *magenta*. The emphasis on dimensions for perceptual learning may distinguish itself from world learning, which does not have the same limitations.

It is sensible that world learning not be restricted to dimensions. Objects that are perceptually similar do not necessarily have the same consequences; consider, for instance, cats and mountain lions. The world acts on individual objects and events, and the learning mechanisms should reflect this. Consequently, mechanisms that apprehend new information about the world should be equipped to handle individual stimuli as independent. On the other hand, perceptual learning may be subject to different pressures. These processes keep sensory systems functioning optimally, and sensory systems may instead be built upon entire stimulus continua. Some fundamental dimensions both at the psychological and physiological levels appear to be spatial frequency, spatial location, orientation, and distance (e.g., Graham, 1992). Entire systems get recalibrated when learning is needed.

Other perceptual learning phenomena may involve dimensions as well. One example is the "criterion shift rule" (Warren, R. M., 1985) or "adaptation level" (Helson, 1964), not to be confused with adaptation to rearrangements of space. This set of effects involves shifting the interpretation of an entire stimulus dimension as a result of experience with a few instances along the dimension. For instance, a temperature of 65°F feels cool in Tucson, Arizona, because of the usually higher temperatures, but feels warm in Montana because of the usually lower temperatures. A given physical weight will feel heavier or lighter as a function of the weight of objects experienced previously. These effects differ from adaptation to spatial rearrangements discussed in this chapter. The criterion shift rule does not refer to detection of new relations between pairs of dimensions, but instead to the reception of information from a single dimension. Yet, like all perceptual learning phenomena, its purpose is to keep perceptual systems functioning optimally (Warren, R. M., 1985). In addition, it appears to operate on dimensions.

Another phenomenon that may involve dimensions is the maintenance of an accurate internal clock, known as the *entrainment of circadian rhythms*. The process is not usually regarded as perceptual learning. However, entrainment may be better thought of as perceptual learning than as the representation of information from the world. Our internal sense of the time of day is kept correct by input from daylight from the environment. The function of the environmental information is not to create the underlying representation of time—that already exists. Instead, it is used to check whether the clock is accurate, similar to other perceptual learning systems that make use of environmental input to check accuracy. For the present discussion, one critical aspect is that entrainment appears to operate on dimensions also. Limited input from the environment at one time of day is sufficient to reset the clock for the remaining hours of a 24-hr day.

The view of dimensions as important to perceptual learning suggests that whenever a phenomenon appears to be perceptual learning, we should investigate whether the underlying mechanism acts on dimensions, and in addition, that whenever a mechanism appears to operate on dimensions, we should investigate whether it is really an instance of perceptual learning. Whether all perceptual learning phenomena involve dimensions, or whether that property identifies one particular subclass of perceptual learning, is a potentially important question that remains to be answered.

Considering the issue of input, or circumstances that produce learning, perceptual learning first requires the inference that internal sensory systems are functioning suboptimally. This condition is not required for world learning. One way the inference can occur is if new information obtained via vision, audition, and so forth is discrepant with internal assumptions about real-world objects. The assumption challenged in a prism-adaptation experiment is that an object occupies only one place at one time, and for a McCollough effect experiment that an object stays the same color over time. Both of these laboratory phenomena tap into mechanisms needed in the real world for accurate spatial localization and color constancy, respectively.

In addition, verifying that a constraint has been seemingly violated may involve a decision about object identity. In prism adaptation, what you are seeing and what you are touching may or may not refer to the same object. In the McCollough effect, the two samples obtained at different times (e.g., vertical grid and horizontal grid) may or may not refer to the same object. For both phenomena, if the two samples are judged to refer to the same object, then a problem will be detected, and if not, then there is no evidence of internal malfunctions. Different objects can be in different places and can have different colors. The decision about when two distinct samples refer to the same object, whether they are from two different modalities at the same time, or at two different times from the same modality, is critical both for perception and perceptual learning. The study of perceptual learning will benefit from a good understanding of how this decision is made.

If we consider the issues of output, and of function, perceptual learning is manifested by actual changes in how the world is perceived under identical physical stimulation. Perceptions are modified, which preserves internal constraints about objects and restores the systems to what is believed to be good working order. Perceptual learning processes keep perception accurate to allow world learning to occur.

The field of cognition has started to recognize that learning processes must play a central role. It is hoped that the rigorous study of perceptual learning will contribute to this momentum.

ACKNOWLEDGMENTS

Thanks to the participants of my fall 1992 graduate seminar on "Plasticity and Cognition" for helpful discussions, especially colleagues Paul Bloom and William Ittelson. Thanks also to Doug Medin for helpful editorial comments, and to Elizabeth Niswander for dozens of hours of figure preparation. This work was supported by a grant from the National Science Foundation (BNS-8909825).

References

Adams, J. A. (1987). Historical review and appraisal of research on the learning, retention, and transfer of human motor skills. *Psychological Bulletin, 101*, 41–74.

Allan, L. G., & Siegel, S. (1986). McCollough effects as conditioned responses: Reply to Skowbo. *Psychological Bulletin, 100*, 388–393.

Bedford, F. L. (1989). Constraints on learning new mappings between perceptual dimensions. *Journal of Experimental Psychology: Human Perception and Performance, 15*, 232–248.

Bedford, F. L. (1992a). *Constraints on perceptual learning: Objects and dimensions.* Submitted for publication. Manuscript available from author.

Bedford, F. L. (1992b). *Coordinating spatial maps: Rules of extrapolation.* Submitted for publication.

Bedford, F. L. (1993). Perceptual and cognitive spatial learning. *Journal of Experimental Psychology: Human Perception and Performance.*

Bedford, F. L., & Reinke, K. S. (in press). The McCollough effect: Dissociating retinal from spatial coordinates. *Perception and Psychophysics.*

Berwick, R. (1985). *The acquisition of syntactic knowledge.* Cambridge, MA: MIT Press.

Bloom, P. (1990). [Review of *Cognition and representation*] *Mind & Language, 5*, 166–173.

Brand, J. L., Holding, D. H., & Jones, P. D. (1987). Conditioning and blocking of the McCollough effect. *Perception and Psychophysics, 41*, 313–317.

Breitmeyer, B. G., & Cooper, L. A. (1972). Frequency specific color adaptation in the human visual system. *Perception and Psychophysics, 11*, 95–96.

Cassirer, E. (1944). The concept of group and the theory of perception. *Philosophy and Phenomenological Research, 5*, 1–36.

Chen, L. (1985). Topological structure in the perception of apparent motion. *Perception, 14*, 197–208.

Cheng, K., & Gallistel, C. R. (1984). Testing the geometric power of an animal's spatial representation. In H. Roitblat, T. G. Bever & H. Terrace (Eds.), *Animal cognition* (pp. 409–423). Hillsdale, NJ: Lawrence Erlbaum.

Chomsky, N. (1986). *Knowledge of language: Nature, origin, and use.* New York: Prager.

Cunningham, H. A. (1984). An Apple microcomputer-based laboratory for the study of visual–motor behavior. *Behavior Research Methods, Instruments, and Computers, 17*, 484–488.

Dodwell, P. C. & Humphrey, G. K. (1990). A functional theory of the McCollough effect. *Psychological Review, 97*, 78–89.

Ellis, S. R. (1976). Orientation constancy of the McCollough effect. *Perception and Psychophysics, 19*, 183–192.

Epstein, W. (1967). *Varieties of perceptual learning.* New York: McGraw-Hill.

Epstein, W. (1976). Recalibration by pairing: A process of perceptual learning. *Perception, 3*, 59–72.

Fodor, J. A. (1983). *Modularity of mind.* Cambridge, MA: MIT Press.

Foreit, K. G., & Ambler, B. A. (1978). Induction of the McCollough effect I: Figural variables. *Perception and Psychophysics, 24*, 295–230.

Gallistel, C. R. (1990). *The organization of learning.* Cambridge, MA: MIT Press.

Gibson, E. J. (1969). *Principles of perceptual learning and development.* New York: Appleton-Century-Crofts.

Graham, N. (1992). Breaking the visual stimulus into parts. *Current Directions, 1*, 55–61.

Harris, C. S. (1965). Perceptual adaptation to inverted, reversed, and displaced vision. *Psychological Review, 72*, 419–444.

Harris, C. S. (1980). Insight or out of sight? Two examples of perceptual plasticity in the human adult. In C. S. Harris (Ed.), *Visual coding and adaptability* (pp. 95–149). Hillsdale, NJ: Lawrence Erlbaum.

Hay, J. C. (1974). Motor-transformation learning. *Perception, 3,* 487–496.

Hay, J. C., & Pick, H. L., Jr. (1966). Gaze-contingent prism adaptation: Optical and motor factors. *Journal of Experimental Psychology, 72,* 640–648.

Held, R. (1965). Plasticity in sensory–motor systems. *Scientific American, 213,* 84–94.

Held, R. (1980). The rediscovery of adaptability in the visual system: Effects of intrinsic and extrinsic chromatic dispersion. In C. S. Harris (Ed.), *Visual coding and adaptability* (pp. 69–94). Hillsdale, NJ: Lawrence Erlbaum.

Held, R. & Durlach, N. (1991). Telepresence, time delay, and adaptation. In S. R. Ellis (Ed.), *Pictorial communication in virtual and real environments* (pp. 232–246). London: Taylor and Francis

Held, R. & Shattuck, S. R. (1971). Color and edge-sensitive channels in the human visual system: Tuning for orientation. *Science, 174,* 314–316.

Helson, H. (1964). *Adaptation-level theory: An experimental and systematic approach to behavior.* New York: Harper & Row.

Hepler, N. (1968). A motion-contingent aftereffect. *Science, 162,* 376–377.

Howard, I. P. (1982). *Human visual orientation.* Chichester, New York: John Wiley & Sons.

Humphrey, G. K., Dodwell, P. C., & Emerson, V. F. (1985). The roles of pattern orthogonality and color contrast in the generalization of pattern-contingent color aftereffects. *Perception and Psychophysics, 38,* 343–353.

Hurvich, L. M., & Jameson, D. (1957). An opponent-process theory of color vision. *Psychological Review, 64,* 384–404.

Kahneman, D., Treisman, A., & Gibbs, B. J. (1992). The reviewing of object files: Object-specific integration of information. *Cognitive Psychology,* 175–219.

Keil, F. C. (1992). The origins of an autonomous biology. *The Minnesota Symposium on Child Psychology, 25.* Hillsdale, NJ: Lawrence Erlbaum.

Klein, F. (1957). *Vorlesungen uber hohere geometrie* [Lectures on higher geometry] (3rd ed.). New York: Chelsea. (Original work published 1893)

Koh, K., & Meyer, D. E. (1989). Induction of continuous stimulus-response relations. In G. Olsen & E. Smith (Eds.), *Proceedings of the Eleventh Annual Conference of the Cognitive Science Society* (pp. 333–340). Hillsdale, NJ: Erlbaum.

Kohler, I. (1964). The formation and transformation of the perceptual world. *Psychological Issues, 3*(4), 1–173.

Levine, M. (1982). You-are-here maps: Psychological considerations. *Environment and Behavior, 14,* 221–237.

Lorenz, K. Z. (1981). *The foundations of ethology.* New York: Springer-Verlag.

Lovegrove, W. J., & Over, R. (1972). Color adaptation of spatial frequency detectors in the human visual system. *Science, 176,* 541–543.

Markman, E. M. (1990). Constraints children place on word meanings. *Cognitive Science, 14,* 57–77.

Mayhew, J. E. W., & Anstis, S. M. (1972). Movement aftereffects contingent on color, intensity, and pattern. *Perception and Psychophysics, 12,* 77–85.

McCollough, C. (1965). Color adaptation of edge detectors in the human visual system. *Science, 149,* 1115–1116.

Modenov, & Parkhomenko (1965). *Geometric transformations* (Vols. 1 & 2). New York: Academic Press.

Murch, G. M. (1976). Classical conditioning of the McCollough effect: Temporal parameters. *Vision Research, 16,* 615–619.

Redding, G. M., & Wallace, B. (1988a). Adaptive mechanisms in perceptual–motor co-ordination: Components of prism adaptation. *Journal of Motor Behavior, 20*, 242–254.

Redding, G. M., & Wallace, B. (1988b). Components of prism adaptation in terminal and concurrent exposure: Organization of the eye–hand coordination loop. *Perception and Psychophysics, 44*, 59–68.

Rescorla, R. A. (1988). Pavlovian conditioning: It's not what you think it is. *American Psychologist, 43*, 151–160.

Rescorla, R. A., & Holland, P. C. (1976). Some behavioral approaches to the study of learning. In M. R. Rozenzweig and E. L. Bennett (Eds.), *Neural mechanisms of learning and memory*. Cambridge, MA: MIT Press.

Rozin, P. (1976). The evolution of intelligence and access to the cognitive unconscious. In J. A. Sprague & A. N. Epstein (Eds.), *Progress in psychobiology and physiological psychology: Vol. 6* (pp. 245–280). New York: Academic Press.

Rozin, P., & Schull, J. (1988). The adaptive-evolutionary point of view in experimental psychology. In R. C. Atkinson, R. J. Herrnstein, G. Lindzey, & R. D. Luce (Eds.), *Handbook of experimental psychology* (pp. 503–546). New York: Wiley-Interscience.

Schacter, D. L. (1987). Implicit memory: History and current status. *Journal of Experimental Psychology, Learning, Memory and Cognition, 13*, 501–518.

Schacter, D. L. (1992). Understanding implicit memory: A cognitive neuroscience approach. *American Psychologist, 47*, 559–569.

Shepard, R. N. (1984). Ecological constraints on internal representation: Resonant kinematics of perceiving, imagining, thinking, and dreaming. *Psychological Review, 91*, 417–447.

Shepard, R. N. (1987). Evolution of a mesh between principles of the mind and regularities of the world. In J. Dupre (Ed.), *The latest on the best: Essays on evolution and optimality*. Cambridge, MA: MIT Press.

Shepard, R. N. (1989). Initial representation of universal regularities: A challenge for connectionism. In L. Nadel, P. Culicover, L. A. Cooper, & R. M. Harnish (Eds.), *Neural connections, mental computations*. Cambridge, MA: MIT Press/Bradford Books.

Shepard, R. N. (1991). *Can natural selection yield universal principles of mind?* Paper presented at AAAS, Washington, DC, Feb. 1991.

Shepard, R. N. (1992). The three-dimensionality of color: An evolutionary accommodation to an enduring property of the world. In J. Burkow, L. Cosmides, & J. Tooby (Eds.), *The adapted mind: Evolutionary psychology and the generation of culture* (pp. 495–536). New York: Oxford University Press.

Siegel, S., & Allan, L. G. (1985). Overshadowing and blocking of the orientation-contingent color aftereffects: Evidence for a conditioning mechanism. *Learning and Motivation, 16*, 125–138.

Siegel, S., & Allan, L. G. (1987). Contingency and the McCollough effect. *Perception & Psychophysics, 42*, 281–285.

Siegel, S., & Allan, L. G. (1992). Pairings in learning and perception: Pavlovian conditioning and contingent aftereffects. In D. Medin (Ed.), *Psychology of learning and motivation, 28*, 127–155.

Siegel, S., Allan, L. G., & Eissenberg, T. (1992). The associative basis of contingent color aftereffect. *Journal of Experimental Psychology: General, 121*, 79–94.

Skowbo, D. (1984). Are McCollough effects conditioned responses? *Psychological Bulletin, 46*, 215–226.

Skowbo, D., & Forster, T. (1983). Further evidence against a classical conditioning model of McCollough effects. *Perception and Psychophysics, 34*, 552–554.

Skowbo, D., Timney, B. N., Gentry, T. A., & Morant, R. B. (1975). McCollough effects: Experimental findings and theoretical accounts. *Psychological Bulletin, 82,* 497–510.

Sloane, M. E., Ost, J. W. P., Etheridge, D. B., & Henderlite, S. E. (1989). Overprediction and blocking in the McCollough aftereffect. *Perception and Psychophysics, 45,* 110–120.

Spelke, E. S. (1990). Principles of object perception. *Cognitive Science, 14,* 29–56.

Spelke, E. S., Breinlinger, K., Macomber, J., & Jacobson, K. (1992). Origins of knowledge. *Psychological Review, 99,* 605–632.

Stromeyer, C. F. (1978). Form–color aftereffects in human vision. In R. Held, H. Leibowitz & H. L. Teuber (Eds.), *Handbook of sensory physiology, Vol. 8. Perception* (pp. 97–142). New York: Springer-Verlag.

Taub, E. (1968). Prism compensation as a learning phenomenon: A phylogenetic perspective. In R. Held, E. Taub, & S. J. Freedman (Eds.), *Neuropsychology of spatially oriented behavior* (pp. 77–106). Chicago, IL: Dorsey Press.

Taylor, J. G. (1962). *The behavioral basis of perception.* New Haven, CT: Yale University Press.

Wallach, H. (1968). Adaptation based on cue discrepancy. R. Held, E. Taub, & S. J. Freeman (Eds.), In *Neuropsychology of spatially oriented behavior* (pp. 235–259). Illinois: Dorsey Press.

Warren, R. M. (1985). Criterion shift rule. *Psychological Review, 92,* 574–584.

Warren, W. H. (1977). Visual information for object identity in apparent movement. *Perception and Psychophysics, 25,* 205–208.

Welch, R. B. (1971). Discriminative conditioning of prism adaptation. *Perception and Psychophysics, 10,* 90–92.

Welch, R. B. (1972). The effect of experienced limb identity upon adaptation to simulated displacement of the visual field. *Perception and Psychophysics, 12,* 453–456.

Welch, R. B. (1978). *Perceptual modification.* New York: Academic Press.

Welch, R. B. (1986). Adaptation of space perception. In K. R. Boff, L. Kaufman, & J. P. Thomas (Eds.), *Handbook of perception and human performance* (Vol. 1) (pp. 24–45). New York: Wiley-Interscience.

Welch, R. B., & Warren, D. H. (1980). Immediate perceptual response to intersensory discrepancy. *Psychological Bulletin, 88,* 638–667.

Westbrook, R. F., & Harrison, W. (1984). Associative blocking of the McCollough effect. *Quarterly Journal of Experimental Psychology, 36A,* 309–318.

White, K. D., and Riggs, L. A. (1974). Angle-contingent color aftereffects. *Vision Research, 14,* 1147–1154.

A RATIONAL-CONSTRUCTIVIST ACCOUNT OF EARLY LEARNING ABOUT NUMBERS AND OBJECTS

Rochel Gelman

I. Introduction

This article features my rational-constructivist account of cognitive development. The rationalist side of the theory captures the assumption that our young bring a skeletal outline of domain-specific knowledge to their task of learning the initial concepts they will share with others. The constructivist side of the theory captures the assumption that, from the start, our young actively join in their own cognitive development. Even as beginning learners, skeletal principles motivate them to seek out and assimilate inputs that nurture the development of these structures. To develop these assumptions I consider work on two topics: (1) conceptions of objects during infancy and (2) numerical concepts in infants and beginning language users. Special attention is given to the need to consider whether differences in performance levels across tasks are due to limits on the conceptual competence under investigation or to limits on the procedural and interpretative competences needed for successful performance.

There is no a priori reason to assume that the rational and the constructivist positions are inconsistent or contradictory. I join Marler in his challenge of those who still "think of learning and instinct as being virtually antithetical . . . [that] behavior is one or the other, but not both" (p. 37, 1991). In the history of science, key terms shifted their meaning when

61

understanding of the phenomena to which they refer changed. For example, developments in physics, mathematics, and biology led to changes in the meaning of *movement, zero,* and *alive* (see Carey, 1985; Kitcher, 1982; Kuhn, 1970; Mayer, 1982; and Wiser, 1987). Likewise, recent advances in neuroscience, animal learning, and ethology are producing shifts in the meaning of phrases or terms like *biological underpinnings* and *innate*. The more we understand about the acquisition of complex actions, the more we appreciate that they depend on organisms' opportunities to interact with and assimilate relevant environments. To say that genetic history contributes to the development of some classes of behavior is not to say that these will appear full-blown at a given point in time. Without opportunities to engage with and learn about the kinds of environments that nurture the potential given by the genetic history, development either will be abnormal or will fail to occur. Normal development is intricately tied to opportunities to interact with and process relevant environments. The story of how the young male white-crowned sparrow comes to learn his species-specific adult song provides an elegant example of these points.

The male white-crowned sparrow is born with a template specifying basic features of his adult song. However, he must hear examples of the correct conspecific song during a critical period early in development. If he is reared in an environment that does not include examples of his adult dialect, he is able to learn a nonpreferred song. Therefore, the learning process that supports acquisition of the conspecific song can yield unexpected or inappropriate outcomes, given sufficient atypical experience. Nevertheless, "errors" seldom occur because learning typically takes place in a supporting ecology.

Similarly, the opportunity to interact with the environment supports another key step in song development. The initial song, which is first produced well after the above critical period, is far from the adult song. Production of the adult crystallized song is preceded by a lengthy trial-and-error period. Although the bird does not have to hear any further inputs from other birds during this period, it appears that he does have to hear himself produce what are called *subsongs* and *plastic songs*. It seems as if the remembered song provides birds with a standard against which to compare their output, much as memories of recordings or performances can aid music students as they practice.

Such examples help to illustrate how the meaning of terms and phrases like *learn, innate,* and *biological contributions* are changing. Indeed, Marler (1991) now writes of "the instinct to learn" and refuses to pit terms like *practice, trial-and-error, variability,* and *learn* against ones like *constraint, innate, biological, genetic,* and so on. Parallel shifts in meaning can be found in writings about animal learning (Gallistel, 1990; Rozin &

Schull, 1988) and cognitive development (e.g., Carey & Gelman, 1991; Karmiloff-Smith, 1992; Keil, 1981). These developments serve as the backdrop for my rational–constructivist account of knowledge acquisition. I have been especially concerned with the specification of the nature of relevant inputs and the laws of learning that apply for such an account.

II. Different Accounts of Initial Concepts

A. ASSOCIATION THEORIES OF LEARNING

There have been important developments in associative accounts of learning, especially regarding the need for the conditioned stimulus (CS) to predict the unconditioned stimulus (UCS) (Rescorla & Wagner, 1972). Still, the empiricists' assumptions about the acquisition of knowledge remain as core assumptions in modern associationist accounts of concept development and learning. These assumptions are that all knowledge can be traced to our ability to process sensory inputs and to form associations between these sensations (S-S connections) and/or to our responses to these sensations (S-R connections). In the case of the infant, what is given is the ability to receive punctate sensations of light, or sound, or pressure, and so forth, and to form associations between these according to the laws of association (frequency and proximity). Sensations and responses that occur close together (in time or space) and repeatedly are more likely to be associated than those that are infrequent and far apart. As associations between sensations and responses are impressed on the infant's blank mental slate, these too become associated with incoming data or each other and lay the groundwork for knowledge of the world at a sensory and motor level. These further associations in turn support knowledge acquisition at the perceptual level. Experiences at the perceptual level provide the opportunity for cross-modal associative learning and thus for the eventual induction of abstract concepts that cut across concepts about particular perceptual information.

B. DEVELOPMENTAL THEORIES OF LEARNING

Developmental textbooks often pit learning theoretic (read as "associationist") accounts against developmental ones. In this context, the idea is that development involves more than "mere" learning. Cognitive development proceeds through stages, and the way learners interpret inputs of a given kind is influenced by the stage they have achieved. For example, during the first two years of life, Piaget's sensorimotor infants can build schemes relating actions to what they see, hear, touch, and so on; however, they will not be able to represent a set of objects in terms of class inclusion until they reach concrete operations at about 6 to 9 years of age.

Paired with the assumption of stages is the related assumption that learners actively interpret inputs with reference to their available knowledge and mental structures. In the Piagetian framework, the construction of the "correct" interpretation of the transformations performed on quantities must await the child's advance to concrete operational thought. The younger child's belief that the amount of water in a glass changes as it is poured into another, different-shaped glass, reflects reliance on perceptual information (Piaget, 1952).

As we shall see, there are important differing foundational assumptions of the associationist and developmental accounts of infant-knowledge acquisition. Still, the two classes of characterizations of an infant's initial world are more similar than not. For example, Piaget limits an infant's initial knowledge to a level that is controlled reflexively. The active practice of these reflexes leads to their adaptation into sensorimotor schemes. The active use of the consequent scheme leads to the development of intercoordinated schemes of action. The more such intercoordinations, the more likely that the infant builds a world of three-dimensional objects in a three-dimensional space.

In the associationist account, infants gradually build up a notion of an individual object by associating the primitive sensations generated by different objects. Somehow, by forming associative clusters for many different objects, young learners eventually produce the concept of an object as something that exclusively occupies a volume of space at a particular time and that has properties such as color, shape, weight, and so on.

To be sure, associations are not Piaget's fundamental building blocks of cognition; sensorimotor schemes are. Nevertheless, his infant must have repeated interactions with objects in order to achieve more coordinated memories among those sensorimotor schemes that are used with a given object. These action-based representations help move the infant from a state of out-of-sight, out-of-mind to states that lead to a concept of an object. Only then does the infant finally know that an object persists over time and in space, whether or not it is covered and/or moved through invisible displacements.

Some of Piaget's foundational assumptions about the nature of the data required to drive development apply to the developmental theories advanced by Bruner, Vygotsky, and Werner. In each case, learners are assumed to approach objects on the basis of simple motoric, sensory, or perceptual features. Given suitable opportunities to develop further knowledge of these features, the child is able to induce more abstract concepts. Initial "concepts," whose core consists of sensorimotor associations or perceptual rules of organization, are variously labeled as graphic collections, preconcepts, complexes, pseudo-concepts, and chain concepts.

In sum, whether the account of the origins of knowledge is rooted in an associationist view or one of the classical theories of cognitive development, the assumption is that first-order sense data, for example, sensations of colored light, sound, pressure, and so forth, serve as the foundation upon which knowledge is developed. Principles that organize the buildup of representations of concepts, as a function of experience and the opportunity to form associative networks or sensorimotor schemes, are induced.

C. MORE ON THE RATIONAL-CONSTRUCTIVIST ACCOUNT

A key assumption that I make is that cognitive development is channeled by innate, domain-specific principles—even in infants. Another is that infants build models of the world in accord with these first principles. What follows expands on these notions. As we shall see, this view has implications regarding which data are relevant for concept acquisition. In order to show why this is so, it helps to have a way to identify a domain.

1. Defining a Domain of Knowledge

I define a domain of knowledge in much the same way that formalists do, by appeal to the notion of a set of interrelated principles. A given set of principles, the rules of their application, and the entities to which they apply together constitute a domain. Because different structures are defined by different sets of principles, we can say that a body of knowledge constitutes a domain of knowledge to the extent that we can show that a set of interrelated principles organize the entities and related knowledge as well as the rules of operation on these. Note that there is nothing in this definition that requires that domain-specific knowledge be built on an innate foundation. Whether a domain is acquired or not is an orthogonal issue.

Counting is a part of a number-specific domain, because the representatives of numerosity (what I call "numerons") generated by counting are operated on by mechanisms informed by, or obedient to, arithmetic principles. For counting to provide the input for arithmetic reasoning, the principles governing counting must complement the principles governing arithmetic reasoning. For example, the counting principles must be such that sets assigned the same numeron are in fact numerically equal and the set assigned a greater numeron is more numerous than a set assigned a lesser numeron. Similarly, the analysis of the causation of movements is based on a domain-specific set of principles. This is the case because there are principles that govern reasoning about the causes of motion and perceptual mechanisms that are informed by complementary principles, those that recognize different categories of causation for the movements of biological objects as a whole as opposed to the movements of inanimate objects as a whole (Gelman, 1990).

In contrast, general processes, like discrimination, or general-purpose processing mechanisms, like short-term memory, do not constitute domains any more than the process of applying rewrite rules, which is common to all formal systems, constitutes a domain of mathematics. Nor does a script structure constitute a domain. Scripts are analogous to the heuristic prescriptions for solving problems in mathematics, which should not be confused with the mathematical domains themselves (algebra, calculus, theory of functions, etc.).

In sum, when we suspect that something is a conceptual domain, we can test whether this is so by seeing whether it is possible to characterize it in terms of a coherent set of operating principles and their related entities. I must emphasize an important aspect about the definition of a knowledge domain that I favor. This is that it is neutral about whether it starts as an innate skeletal set of principles or whether it is learned from scratch. For a related reason there is no necessary link between the idea that knowledge is domain specific and when the knowledge within the domain is acquired. Given my definition of a domain, expert chess players possess domain-specific knowledge of chess. Yet, surely they were not endowed with innate knowledge of the structure that organizes the domain, the entities, and the permissible moves. Similarly, my attribution of some domain specific knowledge to infants does not block me from using domain-general learning principles, that is, ones that apply across domains as part of my account of cognitive development.

2. On Granting Innate Knowledge of a Domain

What does it mean to say that some domains of knowledge are innately given? When I postulate that early cognitive development is directed by domain-specific principles, I find it helpful to use the metaphor of a skeleton. Were there no skeletons to dictate the shape and contents of the bodies of pertinent knowledge, then the acquired representations would not cohere. Just as different skeletons are assembled according to different principles, so too are different coherent bodies of knowledge. Skeletons need not be evident on the surface of a body. Similarly the underlying axiom-like principles that enable the acquisition of coherent knowledge need never be accessible.

The aptness of the skeleton metaphor is less than perfect. It carries the implication that all principles are in place before their respective bodies of knowledge are acquired. This is unlikely. In fact, it is possible that only some subset of principles of a domain serve as part of the initial skeleton. Further, initial principles might even be replaced or expanded over the course of learning, especially if the learner acquires new or extremely enriched theories (Carey, 1985), or has the capacity for mapping language onto principles that are not at first statable or even symbolically represented (Karmiloff-Smith, 1986).

3.   Adding the Constructivist Side of the Theory

We assume that all learners actively apply their available structures, no matter how young they are. If we allow that infants use skeletal structures, we account for their tendencies to attend selectively and to respond in structurally coherent ways to their environment. The knowledge that infants acquire when they actively apply their nascent skeletal structures to the world feeds the development of these structures. This occurs because the principles function both to define the constraints on the class of relevant inputs and to store, in a coherent fashion, experiences with these inputs. As relevant inputs are assimilated to these principles, they feed the coherent development of knowledge within their respective domains.

The principles that define a domain of conceptual development need not be represented within the system in a symbolic or linguistic form. Rather they can be, and most likely are, first represented within the structure of the information-processing mechanisms that assimilate experience and direct action (cf. Karmiloff-Smith, 1992). Marr (1982) presents many cases where the algorithms by which the visual system processes visual input implicitly incorporate various principles about the structure of the world. Gallistel, in 1990 (see also Cheng & Gallistel, 1984), argued that the principles of Euclidean geometry are implicit in the mechanisms by which the rat constructs and uses a map of its environment. Knudsen's (1983) work on the development of the tectal circuitry for representing the angular positions of distal stimuli apprehended by different sensory modalities in the barn owl provides a clear example of how a principle can be implicit in a developmental mechanism. Implicit in the mechanism that controls the development of tectal circuitry of the owl is the principle that the spatial matrix for experience is unitary and transcends sensory modality. An object cannot have one location in the space apprehended through the visual modality and a different location in the space apprehended through the auditory modality. Thus, when the mapping of visual locations is experimentally put out of register with the mapping of auditory locations, the maturing circuitry reorganizes so as to bring the mappings back into register.

Because skeletal principles give the young constructivist mind a way to attend to and selectively process data, they similarly contribute to the nurturing and development of the concepts that limn the domain in question. No matter how skeletal these first principles may be, they still can organize the search for, and assimilation of inputs that can feed the development of the concepts of the domain. Actively assimilated inputs help flesh out the skeletal structure. The more structured knowledge there is, the more it is possible for the learner to find domain-relevant inputs to attend to and actively assimilate to the existing structure. The positive feedback set up underlies the continual buildup of the knowledge structure within the domain. For a related discussion of structure mapping in vision see Bedford (this volume).

In sum, first principles help focus attention on inputs that are relevant for the acquisition of concepts in their domain. It matters not that these first principles are implicit, preverbal and sketchy in form. What matters is that they are structured. Their active application leads infants and young children to find and store experience in domain-relevant ways.

The above has implications for what counts as primary data within a rational-constructivist account of concept acquisition. Since the relevant primary data are defined in terms of abstract principles, they must be relational. Simple sensations no longer are the basic data for concept acquisition. If infants come to the world with both skeletal knowledge and a tendency to apply it, we should expect them to attend selectively to domain-relevant inputs that are appropriately structured. If, for example, infants are endowed with principles that focus their attention on things in the world, they might attend to a three-dimensional thing before attending to its color. Similarly, infants might take a set of things as an opportunity to apply implicit nonverbal counting principles before they attend to whether the things are the same color or shape. These possibilities, of course, reverse the assumptions that associationist theories make about what is initially salient and pertinent to both perceptual and cognitive development. Such "possibilities" are in fact more than possible outcomes. They are well-established results. The pertinent studies took advantage of infants' tendencies to explore their environments with whatever responses they have in their limited repertoire of behaviors. Infants look, listen, and even suck more when presented with a stimulus of interest. The rates or strength of these responses decline as the novel becomes familiar.

Infants resume responding when they detect a change in the input. Thus, the tendency to dishabituate can index an infant's ability to differentiate between different input conditions. This all supports the assumption of a constructivist infant mind—one that is data seeking and data integrating. The fact that these tendencies often are applied to structurally complex data motivates a theory that pairs constructivism with rationalism to generate an infant mind that assimilates data in accord with abstract principles.

Piaget and others using his procedures have repeatedly found that 4- to 8-month olds will reach for and even grasp a toy only as long as they can see it. They stop reaching or looking as soon as the toy disappears behind a barrier. Their failure to continue to be interested in objects once they are covered led Piaget to conclude that young infants lack a representation of an object. They behave as if governed by an "out of sight, out of mind" epistemology. The long-standing assumption that young infants do not represent objects has been challenged by two series of studies, one from Baillargeon's lab and one from Spelke's. These investigators offer evidence that infants come to the world prepared to behave as if there are three-dimensional objects that occupy space and do not move through each other. The contrast between Piaget's conclusions, on the one hand, and Baillargeon's and Spelke's, on the other hand, provides an especially compelling case example of how much displays of competence can vary across tasks.

In Baillargeon, Spelke, and Wasserman (1985), 6- to 8-month-old infants were first shown a screen as it rotated toward and away from them, through an 180° arc. When their interest in the moving screen declined, that is, when the infants habituated, they were shown a new display. This consisted of an object that was held stationary in an upright position to the left side of the screen. Once an infant looked at the object, the experimenter moved it behind the screen. This set the stage for the post-habituation phase of the experiment. Once again the screen rotated toward and away from the infant. Given the physics of the situation, the screen should have stopped at about the 120° position of its rotation. When it continued through a 180° arc (thanks to the use of trick mirrors or trap-doors), it contributed to the adult perception of an impossible event. It looked as if the (unseen) block behind the screen were repeatedly crushed and uncrushed as the screen rotated forward and backward through a 180° arc. The event is impossible for adults because for them—save in the world of spirits and ghosts—one solid object cannot pass through another one. If, as Piaget suggests, infants this young believe that objects disappear once they are no longer in view, then the 180° rotation event should not bother them. Indeed, they should continue to be bored by the screen that passes through a full 180° arc. Instead, they should treat as more novel the event in which the screen rotates through only a 110° arc. However, they did not. The infants in the experiment in fact looked more at the impossible event. Therefore, they must have reinterpreted the 180° arc event. Otherwise they could not have "seen" a different event, one in which a screen seemed to go through (or crush) the (hidden) object.

Baillargeon (1986) also has shown that 6- to 8-month-old infants are surprised when a train that moves behind a barrier follows a trajectory that passes right through a rigid object. Unseen events serve to achieve what looks like an impossible outcome. Spelke (1991) provides similar evidence with still younger infants. She first ran 3- to 4-month-old infants in a three-step habituation event. To start each habituation trial, a ball was held up in the air over a screen. It was then dropped behind the screen. Finally, the screen was removed to reveal the ball resting on the surface of a table. This event sequence was repeated until infants habituated, that is, until they looked less than half as long during a trial as they once did. During the post-habituation phase, the event sequence was the same for its first two steps; in the final, third step, infants viewed the object resting either on top of or under a novel shelf that had been placed surreptitiously into the display. For the latter case, the ball ended up in a familiar position, on top of the table. However, to get there, it would have had to pass through the shelf that sat between the point and the table. Therefore, although both of the post-habituation events were novel, only the latter (on-the-table) one was impossible. Once again, infants looked longer at the impossible events. In a control set of conditions, infants saw the exact same final displays in the post-habituation phase, but the balls were not dropped. Therefore, neither outcome was impossible. Now infants preferred to look at the ball that was resting in a novel place, that is, on the shelf, as opposed to on the floor (and under the shelf). This pattern of results suggests that even some 3- to 4-month-olds care about impossible events, a possibility that gains credence given that Baillargeon (1987) finds that a reliable number of a sample of $3\frac{1}{2}$- to $4\frac{1}{2}$-month-olds respond to the rotating screen conditions as did the older infants in Baillargeon et al. (1985).

Spelke has appealed to findings like the above to conclude that, from the start, infants behave as if the world has three-dimensional things "out there," things that occupy space and maintain both their coherence and boundaries as they move. Principles of object perception can support this outcome. Additional conceptual principles are needed to account for infants' reactions to the presentation of impossible physical events. The principles of perception that can lead infants to find three-dimensional things are as follows: (1) Two surfaces will be perceived as part of the same object if they touch each other; and (2) two surfaces that move together at the same time and speed along parallel paths in three-dimensional space—even if their connection is concealed—will be perceived as the surface of the same object. The ability to react correctly (with surprise or renewed attention) to the seeming ability of objects to pass through each other suggests that infants also have implicit conceptual principles about objects, including that they are solid.

The foregoing perceptual principles are neutral as to whether infants can or cannot perceive color, shape, and size. They are neutral because the principles do not need to use such information to support the ability to find three-dimensional things. Therefore, these primary sense data are not foundational in the Spelke account of how infants perceive three-dimensional objects. It is not that Spelke denies infants the ability to use sensations like these. Rather, her view is that sensory abilities work in the service of the perceptual principles. Once objects are located, infants then learn about their attributes, what goes with what, and so on. Infants could even count these things, whether or not they have learned about their characteristic attributes, because counting principles are indifferent to the attributes of objects.

My suggestion that infants, or anyone, might count objects even if they know nothing or very little about these things is inconsistent with the associationist, stage theoretic and logicist account of number. In all of the latter accounts, number concepts are treated as higher and later-learned abstractions. It is therefore not surprising that those who favor these theories of number concepts are the same individuals who offer non-numerical accounts of infants' ability to respond to the numerical information in displays.

There are many demonstrations that infants attend to the numerical information in displays (Cooper, 1984; Sophian & Adams, 1987; Starkey, 1992; Starkey Spelke, & Gelman, 1983, 1990; Strauss, 1984; Wynn, 1992a). For example, Starkey et al. (1990) show that infants prefer to look at a slide that contains the same number of heterogeneous household items (two or three) that they hear in a sequence of drum beats (two or three). Infants of 12 months or younger also keep track of the effects of surreptitious additions and subtractions (Starkey, 1992; Wynn, 1992a), which means that they can order the set sizes they encounter (see also, Baillargeon, Miller, & Constantino, 1992; Sophian & Adams, 1987; Strauss & Curtis, 1984).

Additionally, infants respond to numerosity when the items in a set each move on separate paths during a trial (van Loosbroek & Smitsman, 1990), that is, when any pattern is obscured. They also match the number of heterogeneous items they see with the number of drum beats they hear, whether or not time is constant or varied across the drum-beat events (Starkey, Spelke, & Gelman, 1990). Whatever the account of these findings, it must deal with infants' ability to respond amodally to numerical information. The next section focuses on possible explanations, including my rational–constructivist explanation. Like Spelke and Baillargeon, I do *not* claim full-blown knowledge, either of numbers or of objects and their properties. All of us are concerned with what is learned, as well as with explanations of the difference between our findings and those of others, especially Piaget's. We are particularly interested in developing a learning theory that explains systematic across-task and within-tack variability in performances that depend on the same conceptual competence (Gelman, 1991; Gelman, Massey, & McManus, 1991).

III. On Variability

Some authors argue that findings like those reviewed above are obtained under too limited a set of conditions and therefore do not justify the attribution of principled knowledge about objects and numerosity. For example, Fischer and Biddle (1991) take the fact that 4- to 8-month-old infants fail even the simple Piagetian covering tasks as compelling reason to reject Baillargeon's and Spelke's attributions of conceptual competence for objects to such very young infants. To be sure, systematic within- and across-condition variability in the extent to which performance conforms to abstract principles is consistent with traditional learning and developmental theories. For both classes of theories, unprincipled "habits" are acquired prior to the induction of principles. However, contrary to widespread assumption, rational accounts of cognitive development do not predict errorless performance from the start. It therefore behooves us to consider more carefully the way systematic cross-task variability is treated in different accounts of concept development.

Gelman and Greeno (1989) point out that there are a number of systematic sources of variability that can mask conceptual competence, including limited procedural and interpretative competence. Because Gallistel and Gelman's (1992) competence model of preverbal counting makes use of mechanisms whose outputs are inherently variable, it is also necessary to find ways to relate details of variability at this level to choices of models.

In their 1989 paper Gelman and Greeno expand on their initial proposal (Greeno, Riley & Gelman, 1984) that competent plans of action require the successful integration of *conceptual, procedural* (planning), and *interpretative* (utilization) competence. A competent plan of action must honor the constraints of conceptual competence. For example, for a plan of counting to be competent, it must incorporate the constraints of the one-for-one counting principle. The plan must not embrace component acts of double-tagging, item-skipping, or tag repeating. Additionally, the plan has to be responsive to constraints on the interpretations of the task setting, instructions, domain-related terms, conversational rules, and so forth. The limited development or misapplication of setting relevant conversational rules can lead to faulty plans of action in a given setting and therefore to variability in success levels across studies or tasks. This possibility is illustrated in Gelman, Meck and Merkin's (1986) use of the doesn't-matter counting task that asked children to count a row of items in a novel way.

The doesn't-matter task begins when the experimenter points to an object that is not at an end of a row of items and asks the child to make that object "the one" and to count all of the objects. To accomplish this, a child has to skip back and forth over the items while counting, switch the designated item with one that is at an end, or count as if the row of items were in a circle. Interestingly, very young children who were given a chance to count a row of items before they started the doesn't-matter task did more poorly than children who had no pretest counting experience. Inspection of their error patterns on the experimental task revealed that the latter group tried to find a way to meet the constraints of the new task while counting from one end of the array to another. It is as if they took their regular counting experience as an instruction to continue to count in the conventional way.

The Gelman and Meck (1986) follow-up to Briars and Siegler (1984) supports this interpretation. If young children are asked to say whether a puppet's count is correct or not, they can fall into the trap of saying that novel but error-free trials of the kind generated in the doesn't-matter task are "wrong." This will happen more often than not if care is not taken to communicate that they should not mix up trials that violate conventions with those that violate principles. We did this by sharing with children the distinction between silly-but-OK ways to count, the regular way to count, and not-OK ways to count. Even if children interpret a setting correctly and know how to count, limits on procedural competence can cause errors (Smith, Greeno, & Vitolo, 1985). For example, to honor the constraints of the one-for-one count principles, one must have a way to keep separate tagged and to-be-tagged items. Limits on one's ability to generate plans with suitable sorting procedures can increase the tendency for one to loose track during a count. Likewise, children must learn to pace the rate at which they point to items in a display before pointing can help them to honor constraints against double-counting or skipping items (see below).

The Gallistel and Gelman (1992) model of nonverbal counting illustrates how there also can be systematic variability that follows from some aspects of the operation of the machinery in whose structure the implicit principles of the conceptual competence resides. In our model the preverbal counting mechanism generates mental magnitudes to represent numerosities; there is trial-to-trial variability in the magnitudes generated to represent one and the same set size; and this variability obeys Weber's law, that is, the standard deviation of the distribution increases in proportion to its mean. Given an additional systematic source of variability, increasing tendencies to loose track of what has been counted and what remains to be counted as set size increases, it is likely that the spread on the distributions as set size increases is even wider than predicted from the Weber law. This is important in understanding a potent within-task source of systematic variability in children's numerical performance, the effect of the set size.

A. ACCOUNTING FOR VARIABILITY IN THE ASSESSMENT OF
   NUMERICAL COMPETENCE

1. Set Size Effects

It is well established that variations in set size have a systematic effect on the tendency of infants and young children to respond correctly to the numerical information in a display. Infants' ability to use numerical information apparently is limited to set sizes of three to four. This fact has encouraged many to conclude that infants use perceptual mechanisms in lieu of mechanisms that embody implicit numerical principles. The favored perceptual mechanism is *subitizing,* an example of a process that is assumed to allow subjects to make discriminations between set sizes without any implicit or explicit understanding of numerical principles (e.g., Cooper, 1984; Cooper, Campbell, & Blevins, 1983; Fischer, 1991/92; Sophian, 1991/92; von Glaserfeld, 1982).

The preferences for a subitizing account of how infants respond to variations produced by different set sizes are tied to studies of adults' time for stating the number of dots in an array. Over the entire range of numerosities, the greater the numerosity, the longer the reaction time, but the first few increments in reaction time per additional dot in the display are smaller. (See Gallistel & Gelman, 1992; Mandler & Shebo, 1982, for reviews.) Because the slope of the reaction times functions in the small-number range ($N < 5$) is shallower than in the large-number range, it is commonly assumed that different processes underlie the responses to the small and large sets, subitizing and counting respectively. If one yokes infants' failures on larger sets to the assumption that a counting mechanism is needed for larger set sizes, it follows that infants are limited to the use of a subitizing process. This would allow infants to succeed with very small sets but make it impossible for them to succeed on larger sets. On the subitizing model, the ability to discriminate threeness from twoness is akin to the ability to discriminate "treeness" from "cowness"; unlike counting processes, this ability does not depend in any way on numerical principles.

There is no model for the kind of perceptual classification ability that is taken for granted by those who attribute infants' use of small-set information to subitizing. Still, we can ask whether this kind of account is consistent with the findings on numerical estimation in infants, children, and adults. The answer is, probably not. Whatever the classification process, classifications need not honor ordering principles. First, there is no reason for cowness to be mastered before treeness, or for the time needed to process "cow" to be systematically longer than the time needed to process "tree," and so on. Second, the perceptual hypothesis offers no account of why reaction times and error rates increase as a function of set size for both children (Chi & Klahr, 1975) and adults (Mandler & Shebo, 1982), no matter how small and how much they are practiced. Further, the postulated perceptual mechanism is peculiar in that it has to be indifferent to all sensory characteristics of the input. However, in order to recognize a cow, one must encounter cow-like stimuli, ones that look like cows, have cow parts, sound like cows, move like cows, and so on. To some extent the size, color, posture, and so on can vary, but overall shape or kinds and arrangements of parts cannot. In contrast, whatever the subitizing mechanism, it has to handle the fact that there are no restrictions on the degree to which inputs can vary in terms of size, color, orientation, and so forth. For geometric reasons there are some limits on the shapes that can be represented with a small number of distinct items, but nevertheless there is always more than one way to arrange sets of at least two items. Likewise, there are many common arrangements that can be imposed on larger sets.

If subitizing is a general perceptual process, then why should judgments of numerosity, even for small sets, serve as inputs for numerical reasoning processes? What is there about the perception of cowness or treeness that would lead one to ponder the effect of adding or subtracting items or to wonder whether one display has more (or fewer) items in it? Yet, we know that infants 12 months old and younger order different set sizes (Cooper, 1984; Starkey, 1992; Wynn, 1992a) and take into account surreptitious changes in the number in an expected set (Sophian & Adams, 1987; Starkey, 1992; Wynn, 1992a).

Whether the field should continue to favor an apprehension-like mechanism to account for the non- or pre-verbal numerical abilities of infants must await the development of a detailed model of this kind. Only then can it be determined whether it can handle the empirical and formal constraints covered here. For now, we prefer the Gallistel and Gelman (1991, 1992) nonverbal-counting model of performance in the subitizing range because it can handle the data from infant studies as well as the characteristics of

Rochel Gelman

the range of adult findings in the literature. It also is consistent with the Meck and Church (1983) model of the known abilities of animals to keep track of largish sets, in some cases as large as 50. An example of this ability in rats is shown in Fig. 1.

Platt and Johnson (1971) required rats to press a lever N times to arm a feeder that operated silently across blocks of trials as the N varied from 4 to 24. The N presses on the lever had to occur before the rat poked its head into the feeding alcove. If a rat failed to press the requisite number of times before he poked his head into the alcove, the counter was reset to zero. There are a number of features of the Platt and Johnson results that merit attention. First, the median number of presses corresponds to the required value of N. Second, note that the variance of the distribution for each N increases as does N. That is, the greater the numerosity to be represented, the more likely it was that the animals confused it with adjacent or nearly adjacent values of N. Third, there is even some overlap in the distributions around the mean for the smaller values. The Meck and Church (1983) nonverbal counting process, a process that the authors intended to have honor the Gelman and Gallistel (1978) counting principles, generates representations of numerosities as well as the characteristics of the Platt and Johnson data. Therefore, the data in Fig. 1 suggest an explanation for the failure of infants to discriminate between sets greater than three and four items.

If infants use a preverbal counting process like Meck and Church's, the fact that their discrimination is consistent for two versus three items but variable for three versus four items is as expected, given the Weber variance of the proposed nonverbal counting mechanisms. The increasing variance in the magnitudes that represent a given numerosity makes confusion of adjacent numerosities increasingly likely as set size increases. Put

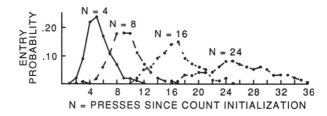

Fig. 1. Redrawing of the Platt and Johnson (1971) evidence that rats represent numerosities as large as 24—the probability of the rat breaking off to enter the food-delivery area as a function of n, the number of presses made since the initialization of the response counter, for various values of N, the required number of presses before the rat should enter the feeder. (The redrawing is from Fig. 1 of Gallistel & Gelman, 1992; with permission of the authors and publishers.)

differently, the animal experiments in effect measure the tendency to confuse one N with another as a function of the numerical distance between the Ns. Infants' numerical discrimination is scored as either correct or not. But this will not allow one to differentiate between errors that are due to increases in the inherent variability or an inability to use a preverbal counting process. It is therefore necessary to find ways to obtain from infants estimates of variability as a function of set size.

The Meck and Church (1983) mechanism for generating magnitudes to represent numerosities is a counting mechanism, not a pattern-perception mechanism; hence item kind is irrelevant, the representatives of numerosity are inherently ordered in accord with the set sizes and the representations of numerosity that can be related to the effects of addition and subtraction. The hypothesis that infants extract representations of numerosity by means of a preverbal magnitude-generating counting process dispenses with the need to postulate the rich abstraction and classification abilities that Piaget and others have taken to be the sine qua non of numerical concepts. First-order sense data are no longer primary. The primary elements are the objects qua discrete objects. The counting mechanism takes no account of their sensory attributes. Nor is there a requirement that a linguistic tag be used.

In the preverbal counting mechanism, mental magnitudes are used in place of count words. The process that generates these magnitudes is like the verbal counting process only in that it, too, honors the principles that define counting processes: the one-one assignment of numerons to the objects in the set, the stable ordering in the assignment of successive numerons, and the use of the final numeron assigned to represent the numerosity of the set. Given that variability is expected to increase as function of set size, both because of the nature of the magnitude-generating process and because of increasing information-processing demands of counting, the existing infant data cannot be used to reject the idea that infants use a preverbal counting process. Indeed, the data that are available are consistent with the Gallistel and Gelman (1991, 1992) model of infants' nonverbal counting competence.

2. Variable Performance across Tasks

I hold that nonverbal counting principles help beginning language learners to identify that set of speech units that can serve their learning of verbal count principles. There is some support for this proposal (Gelman, 1990; Shatz & Backscheider, 1991). Nevertheless, when 2- and young 3-year-olds are asked "how-many" questions, they do not do well. They either count without giving the cardinal answer, state the N without apparent counting, or even state some other N (Fuson, 1988; Wynn, 1990). Fuson takes this as reason to favor a model that has children acquiring separate component skills or rules before they achieve principled understanding of counting. Wynn uses these kinds of data to reject our proposals that nonverbal counting principles direct learning and that beginning language-users have implicit understanding of the verbal cardinal principle. She favors the hypothesis that verbal counting principles are induced as a function of counting-word experience with small sets. She defends her view by showing that comparably young children also have difficulty with two further verbal counting tasks, one that asks them to produce X items ("Could you give Big Bird two [three . . .] dinosaurs to play with?" p. 171) and one that asks them to match one of two sets to a numeral stated by the experimenter. My efforts to understand these reports and the consequent challenges to my theory led to the development of alternative ways to look at young children's verbal counting. They also took us back to some of our magic-task studies.

There is a cross-task contrast between the results for very young children from how-many, give-X, and other tasks and those from the "magic" task that I have used to uncover early understanding of addition and substraction as number-relevant operations. In work in progress, we have been exploring the factors that are responsible for the systematic effects of these tasks. We have also worked to develop new counting tasks that seem especially well suited for use with very young children. Below I summarize the findings from a new analysis that Gelman and Meck (1991) did with the protocols from a magic study that included $2\frac{1}{2}$-year-olds. These data, in conjunction with those from a new number task, help illuminate the subtle roles of interpretative and procedural competence as factors in determining between-task variability in very young children.

a. The Magic Task Reconsidered   Gelman & Meck (1991/92) reported a new analysis of the Bullock and Gelman (1977) "magic" experiment that was designed to determine whether $2\frac{1}{2}$- to 5-year-old children could reason with and about numerical relations. The method embeds a magic show in a two-phase game. In the first phase, the experimenter hides a plate with one item under one can, and another plate with two items under a second can. Without mentioning the numerical values, the experimenter points to either the one-plate or the two-plate (the fewer and more conditions, respectively) and proclaims it "the winner." The displays are then covered with cans and shuffled. Children first guess which can might be hiding the winner, then look under the can they pick, and finally tell us whether they were correct. The trials of Phase 1 serve to establish expectancies for the displays. Phase 2 starts when the experimenter surreptitiously adds two items to each display. Children now have to decide which of the uncovered new values (three or four) is a "winner." Those who were initially rewarded for finding the one-plate now have to designate three the winner; those who were first rewarded for finding two now have to choose the four-plate to be scored as correct.

Bullock and Gelman reported that although 3- , 4- , and 5-year-olds succeeded in Phase 2 of the magic experiment, the youngest children did not, that is, the 2½-year-olds did not choose reliably on the basis of a common numerical relationship between Phase 1 and Phase 2. Bullock and Gelman's second experiment, dubbed the *control condition* by Gelman and Meck (1991/92) in their report of their new analyses of Phase-2 protocols, tested the possibility that the youngest children in what Meck and Gelman called the *regular condition* did not interpret the task as intended, that is, that they did not think to transfer the knowledge they acquired in Phase 1 when they encountered novel values in Phase 2. Two variants of the follow-up experiment provided hints to do this. In one, the initial displays were left in place with their covers on so as to suggest that there was something about these that was relevant to the way children should answer in Phase 2. In the other condition, the initial displays were left in an uncovered place in order to determine whether children's failures during the second phase occurred because they could not remember enough about the initial displays. Then, in Phase 2 of the control condition, the experimenter introduced a new game "like the one just played" and put two new covered displays on the table. A reliable number of 2½-year-olds now chose relationally in Phase 2, that is, correctly selected the four-item (*more*) or three-item (less) display. Bullock and Gelman concluded that limits on the youngest children's ability to think to transfer learning across conditions were responsible for their poor performances in the regular condition. Because it is unlikely that such limits are domain-specific, they should be considered whenever one interprets how very young children do on transfer tasks. In any case, since the hints to transfer worked for Bullock and Gelman, it was possible for us to return to the Phase-2 protocols to determine whether they contained evidence that these young children applied the how-to-count principles.

After children first answered the Phase 2 winner questions for the altered display(s), Bullock and Gelman continued with an interview to determine whether they knew how many items were present during both Phases 1 and 2, how many were added or removed, and so on. Because these questions were asked for different values that were either physically present or to-be-remembered, this is a setting in which children might interpret correctly how-many questions. Indeed, because children had reason to compare different set sizes (those in front of them as well as those from the first phase), they also had reason to count more than once. Such efforts generated the data for the Gelman and Meck (1991/92) conclusion that these children did use verbal counting principles, despite the fact that the sets represented very small N's.

The details that influenced Wynn's conclusions led us to focus on whether children's use of number in Bullock and Gelman reflected an ability to count *and* to offer the cardinal value for set sizes of three or smaller. Wynn acknowledges that young children will count small sets when asked to do so; her claim is that they cannot relate these counts to a verbal cardinal principle. Behaviorally, this translates into a prediction that they will not count and offer the cardinal value of even small sets when asked about cardinal number. Therefore, in one of our analyses of the transcripts, we only scored subjects as having given both a cardinal and a counting response if they either (1) did so spontaneously, or (2) offered two kinds of answers to the same question ("How many?" or "Can you count . . . ?"). Pairs of trials in which children used the cardinal value on their own but counted only after we asked a question were not scored for this analysis. Nevertheless, more than 60% of the children gave evidence of using the cardinal count principle under these conditions, a percentage that is reliably greater than expected on the basis of Wynn's data.

In sum, the reanalysis of the Bullock and Gelman experiments provides some evidence that $2\frac{1}{2}$-year-olds can apply their implicit understanding of counting principles—at least given the conditions like those that hold in the magic experiment. What is it about the magic task that brings out this competence? My answer is that there was a reason for the children to count and relate the result to the cardinal values they actually saw as opposed to those they had expected, for they encountered unexpected changes in set size. How-many questions do not share these conversational conditions. Because we are not supposed to repeat what is known, the child who shares knowledge of the verbal counting principle with an interviewer might assume that it is sufficient to provide either the cardinal value or the count. When a speaker counts aloud, there is no need to repeat the last count to signal its status as the cardinal value of the set; the auditor can hear the last count word. It would be a violation of conversation rules to signal something so obvious to an adult listener. Conversely, the statement of the cardinal numerosity may be taken to imply that there was a count. We checked our intuitive beliefs about the force of these conversational rules in this context by running adults in a how-many study. When we asked undergraduates a how-many question about 18 blocks, all of them counted but only one bothered to repeat the last count word said. Repeats of the question elicited puzzlement, some recounting, and so forth, the kinds of responses that index the fact that we violated the conversational rule *don't ask about what is given*—in this case the numerosity implied by the count. The implication is clear: To repeat the how-many question is to run the risk of confusing subjects as well as confounding assessments of interpretative and conceptual competence.

The reader might object that what is so for adults may not be so for beginning language users. It is therefore necessary to find ways to obtain better evidence that very young children can and do use verbal counting principles—even on small set sizes. A new study with $2\frac{1}{2}$- and young 3-year-olds accomplishes this. It also allows us to tease apart the contributions of interpretative, procedural and conceptual competence.

b.   The What's on This Card? Study   We spent a great deal of time watching and comparing beginning talkers' reactions to a variety of number-relevant conditions, as opposed to non-numerical ones. (This study was done in collaboration with Betty Meck and Lisa Kaufman.) We were repeatedly impressed with how much their attention wandered when we tried to keep them focused on how-many questions or other instructions that started out asking about numbers. In contrast, if we asked them to label objects or kinds of displays, they were more likely to stay on task. This contrast led us to a new number task that takes advantage of these very young children's interest in labels. In this new task, the experimenter starts by showing a child a card with one sticker on it, for example, a bee, and asks, "What's on this card?" Children invariably say "a bee," at which point the adult responds, "That's right, *one* bee." Then she shows the child a card with two bees on it and asks, "What's on this card?" Invariably the eight children in our pilot study next used a cardinal number in their answer and said, "Two bees." Given additional trials with more items of the same kind, the children started to count to answer that they were looking at an *N*-bee card. As the experimenter continued to introduce cards with yet more bees, some children adopted yet another answering style. Now they counted and gave the cardinal value of the display but dropped any reference to the item type. When we finally shifted to cards with a new kind of item, some children once again gave both the kind and cardinal value that went with their count. This answering pattern fits well with conversational rules (Siegal, 1991) and suggests that children even this young know to leave unstated information that is old and already given (Clark & Brennan, 1991). Although there is no reason to keep labeling an object that has already been talked about by both conversational partners, one should provide the label when the subject is queried about a new item.

We have gone on to a more extensive study with the what's-on-this-card task. The latter followed a pretest session that assessed how well children in three different age groups could count and answer how-many questions for set sizes from 2 to 10. The groups' median ages were 2 years, 7 months (range = 2 years, 6 months–2 years, 10 months); 3 years, 2 months (range = 2 years, 11 months–3 years, 2 months); and 3 years, 4 months (range = 3 years, 3 months–3 years, 5 months), respectively. Below these the groupings are referred to as the 2½-year-old, youngest 3-year-old, and oldest 3-year-old groups.

To start the counting pretest, we placed two or three figures on a table and asked how many "people" were on the table. Since there were to be repeated trials, variants of the question (e.g., "How many are on the table now?"; "How many are there?") were allowed. The question "How many?" prompted both counting and cardinality responses. If necessary, the experimenter assisted the subject by either pointing to the items while the child provided the labels or by suggesting that the child begin the count sequence with "one." Then the experimenter again asked, "How many?" Additional trials (anywhere from two to seven trials per set size) were allowed in order to maximize the chance of the subjects counting a given set.

The what's-on-this-card session(s) followed on another day. Our design of this task called for the children to respond to what's-on-this-card trials for N's of at least 2 through 5 and, as many as possible for those planned for set sizes six and seven. Materials for each set size were homogeneous collections of seven kinds of stickers (cats, frogs, candy canes, apples, bees, hearts, shoes) glued onto cards in either in one or two rows. The order of item type and set size within the subset of cards with the same items varied save for two exceptions: Every child started with the one-item and two-item cards for each new item kind. If counting difficulties were not evident during pretest trials, the child usually was presented all values (one–seven) of a given kind of sticker. In any case, we planned to test all children on all cards with values of two through five and told experimenters to persist with the study at least this far. If a child seemed to tire or wanted to stop, the interview was to continue on yet a third day. As in the counting assessment phase, although the interviewer could point for children during the counting phase, she could not help on a cardinal trial and the pointing help could be offered only after the child tried the trial on his or her own.

Different initial responses to the what-kind question led to different subsequent inquiries. For example, some children responded to, "What kind of card is that?" by simply stating the number of items without counting. In this case, the child was asked one or more probe questions, for example, "How do you know that's_____?"; "Can you check to make sure?"; "Can you show me?", and so on. Similarly, children who counted but did not repeat the cardinal value (e.g., "one, two, three bees," as opposed to "one, two, three; three bees") were asked, "So, what is on the card? How many X's is that? or How many?" and so on.

Children were strikingly more likely to apply all of the one-one, stable and verbal cardinal count principles on the what's-on-this-card task than they were on the pretest where we asked how-many questions. (See Table I.) Comparisons of a child's best trial during the pretest as opposed to the same child's best trial during the experimental session favored the what's-on-this-card task. So did a comparison of the number of correct trials per set size (Sign test, $p < .001$). As in our counting assessment pretest, the what's-on-this-card task brought out very young children's ability to apply the verbal one-one, stable order and cardinal count principles. For example Subject 2 (2 years, 7 months) answered with "Three bees; . . . 1, 2, 3 bees," and Subject 13 (3 years, 0 months) answered "1, 2, 3, 4, 5 . . . 5." For the pretest and experimental sessions, to be credited with knowledge of how to apply the verbal one-one, stable, and cardinal count principles, children had to (1) count and state the cardinal value correctly on at least half of their trials for a given set size; or (2) achieve a count of $N \pm 1$ and to pair it with the last tag of their $N \pm 1$ count. Additionally, if, on their first trials with set sizes of two and three, children simply stated the cardinal value, we required evidence that they were not simply "labeling" the set size before we credited them the cardinal principle. Such evidence could involve successful counts that were combined with correct statements of the cardinal value for larger set size or a show of N fingers at the same time that a cardinal value was provided on the smallest set sizes. Experimenter-assisted counts (that is, ones on which the experimenter pointed) were scored as having honored the one-one and stable order principles if children correctly used the requisite N conventional tags (or ones from their own idiosyncratic list). To receive credit also for use of the cardinal principle, children had to tell us the cardinal number (either N or $N \pm 1$ if a count was of this form) *on their own*.

A second scoring of children's success levels followed the same rules as those above with one exception. Now assisted trials were excluded from the summary counts used to determine whether a child met the at-least-50%-correct criterion. An even more stringent rule was adopted for a third scoring of the data. If, for a given N, there were any assisted trials, that child was scored as having failed to apply the count principles on that set size. Figure 2 shows the results of the most lenient analysis as a function of age and set size. The results from the two alternative ways of scoring success levels are shown in the bar graphs in Fig. 3. These results are presented with bars for the more lenient analyses shown in Fig. 2.

Figure 2 summarizes performance levels when correct assisted trials were counted in the at-least-50%-correct criterion for crediting a child with

Rochel Gelman

TABLE I

A Comparison of Children's Ability to Use One-One,
Stable, and Cardinal Count Principles Trials on How-
Many? and the What's-on-This-Card? Counting Tasks[a]

Age group and set size	Counting task			
	How many[b]		What's on this card	
	Assisted	Unassisted	Assisted	Unassisted
2½ yr				
2	30	20	90	90
3	30	20	70	70
4	10	10	70	40
5	30	20	70	30
6	10	0	30	10
7 or more[c]	10	10	30	10
Youngest 3's (2;11–3;2)				
2	90	90	100	100
3	80	80	100	90
4	60	40	100	80
5	60	50	90	90
6	30	30	80	80
7 or more	50	60	80	80
Youngish 3's (3;3–3;5)				
2	80	80	100	80
3	80	80	80	80
4	70	70	80	80
5	70	70	80	80
6	60	50	90	80
7 or more	60	50	80	60

[a] Summaries are based on best trials.

[b] During the how-many counting pretest, subjects were asked how many "people" there were on the table. Because there were to be repeated trials, variants of the question, e.g., "How many are on the table now?"; "How many are there?" were allowed. Set sizes could range from 2 to 10. If necessary, the experimenter assisted the subject by either pointing to the items while the child provided the labels or suggesting that the child begin the count sequence with "one." Then the experimenter again asked "how many?" Additional trials (anywhere from two to seven trials per set size) were allowed in order to maximize the chance of subjects counting a given set.

[c] Children received credit in this case if they used all three principles correctly on at least one of their trials with a set size of seven or more.

all three verbal how-to-count principles. As compared to the findings for the how-many task in the literature (e.g., Wynn, 1990) and our pretest, the what's-on-this-card task yielded clearer evidence that very young children can use verbal counting principles. Save for our "oldish" 3-year-old

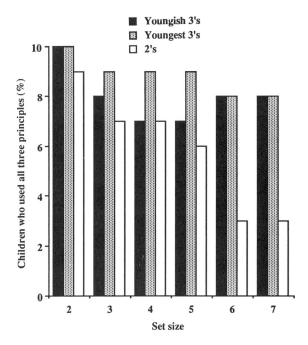

Fig. 2.   The percentage of children in each age group in the what's-on-this-card task who used all three verbal how-to-count principles on different set sizes.

group, the children are below the average age for which we should see such results according to other investigators (e.g., Fuson, 1988: Wynn, 1990). Even when tested on set sizes of five, six out of ten 2-year-olds gave us some evidence of knowing how and when to use verbal instantiations of the counting principles in these ranges. And both of the other age groups provided even more substantial evidence to this effect.

If we apply more stringent criteria, we reduce the set size range for which we might attribute this competence. Figure 3 reveals a notable Age Group × Set Size × Scoring Criterion interaction. The younger the children, the more the effect of the scoring criteria. This is due to the fact that it was primarily the youngest children who improved when the experimenter pointed to the items being counted, especially as set sizes increased. Should this dependence on an adult helping them be counted against them? I think not. First, a considerable majority of the two youngest groups passed the most stringent criterion on set sizes of two and three, that is, when they were least likely to have an adult point for them. Even this extent of the ability to both count and apply the related cardinal value

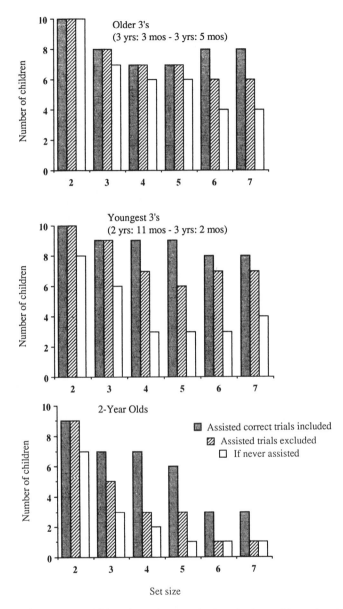

Fig. 3. Evidence that children in each group in the what's-on-this-card task used all three verbal how-to-count principles on different set sizes as a function of scoring criteria.

exceeds expectations, given results from standard tasks. Therefore, such evidence alone is consistent with an attribution of conceptual competence.

Second, Gelman and Greeno (1989) have noted that, unlike the ability to repeat the last tag of a count, pointing behaviors are not uniquely linked with the counting principles. They become counting linked because they help one honor counting principles, much as they help one sort items. For this reason, we propose that the data fit well with our idea that young children's conceptual competence can be masked by limits on their procedural competence. We never offered children clues regarding the cardinal value of the set, and even the youngest children performed well without assistance on small sets. Because they are shaky counters when left on their own with larger set sizes, the odds are that they have not had much experience in this range. This makes it unlikely that they were simply mimicking others, especially when adults may not offer such models (Gelman, Massey & McManus, 1991). Conversational rules inhibit their pointing out the obvious, as we showed in our how-many study with adults (Gelman & Meck, 1991/92).

When we watched the videotapes from this new experiment, it seemed that an adult's pointing worked in part because it kept the youngest children more task-oriented. Thus younger children's better performance on assisted trials also could have been related to matters that bear on interpretative competence. Because it is unlikely that the youngest children would have had occasion to learn to perform such tasks on their own (Siegal, 1991), the assisted trials could have served to create a setting of the social kind young children expect when they are to show others what they know (Rogoff, 1990; Siegal, 1991; Vygotsky, 1978). Analyses of the success children had with different kinds of questions provide evidence for our belief that very young children are sensitive to these kinds of interpretative matters.

As indicated above, we were prepared to ask children to justify their answer with different kinds of probe questions. These included "How do you know?"; "Can you show me why (it's 4)?"; "Show me"; "Can you (let's) check." Because beginning language learners are far from fluent with mental verbs (Shatz, Wellman & Silber, 1983), but very good with verbal requests for action (Shatz, 1978), the fact that we varied these formats gave us a direct assessment of the extent to which interpretative competence played a role in children's ability to reveal understanding of the counting principles and the relation between the verbal one-one and stable principles, on the one hand, and the cardinal verbal principle, on the other hand. As shown in Table II, the pattern of answering is consistent with the proposal that interpretative competence interacts with young children's conceptual competence for counting. All age groups of children

TABLE II

Effect of Question Type on Children's Ability to Answer

	Kind of question					
	Show			How know		
Age group	Mean no. questions asked[a]	Number answer (%)	Irrelevant or no answer (%)	Mean no. questions asked[a]	Number answer (%)	Irrelevant or no answer (%)
2½	6 (10)	78	22	3 (7)	50	50
Youngest 3's	5 (10)	88	12	3.3 (9)	33	66
Youngish 3's	3.3 (6)	95	5	3 (10)	44	54

[a] Number in parentheses is the N of the 10 subjects/age group who contributed to the mean number of times this question was asked.

were better able to deal with show as opposed to know-how questions. In fact, the rate at which the children answered questions like "How do you know that it is five?" is far from impressive—no matter what their age group. Since this is a commonly asked question in how-many studies, here is yet another source of interpretative competence that confounds assessments of young children's understanding of verbal count principles.

Overall then the evidence from the what's-on-this-card study helps develop our ideas about the need to consider the sources of variable performance when reaching conclusions about a given kind of competence. The role of interpretative competence is surely of significance when subjects are beginning language users. Since there is good reason to say that they will apply conversation rules variably, especially ones that suit experimental settings, this alone can confound the assessment of conceptual competence. Similarly, the young have problems coordinating actions. This too can influence how competent a performance they will render. Rather than insisting on the use of tasks that require such skills, we should make every effort to control these problems or to get around them. For it is certain that the younger the child, the less her ability to output the requisite plans of action. From this point of view, complaints about studies of early competence that minimize action requirements (e.g., Fischer & Biddell, 1991) should be redirected to finding out whether the young recognize the relevance of suitable actions, even if they themselves have limited or no ability to execute them. Our pointing during a counting trial can be viewed this way, as can studies on preschool children's abilities to choose between correct but novel and incorrect counting sequences that are generated by a puppet (Gelman & Meck, 1986). The conditions of the latter task resemble language use studies that ask individuals to discriminate between grammatical and ungrammatical utterances. To do so requires implicit understanding of the rules that characterize the class of acceptable utterances in one's language. Similarly, a child cannot not succeed at discriminating "errorful" from unusual, but acceptable, count trials without implicit principled knowledge of counting. Parallel data pertaining to the question of whether young infants possess an object can be used to buttress the idea that limits on the ability to generate and execute action plans can mask one's conceptual competence in a domain.

B.   VARIABILITY ACROSS ASSESSMENTS OF INFANTS' CONCEPT
   OF AN OBJECT

If the planning system needed to generate a competent plan of action is limited or not even developed, then the risk is high that a child will fail no matter how much she knows about the content domain at hand. Piaget's tests of the infant's understanding of the object concept all require the deployment of a competent plan of action. Yet, there is every reason to presume that infants' abilities to generate coordinated actions go through a protracted developmental course. Might it be that the conclusions Piaget reached about the development of infants' understanding of object permanence are better thought of as developments in infants' ability to assemble suitable plans and related action sequences? Fortunately, there are studies that bear on this question and the interpretation of the A-not-B error that infants make when they watch as an object is first hidden at one place (A) and then visibly moved to another hiding place (B). There is a point in development when an infant who can retrieve an object that is hidden at position A fails to retrieve the same object that they have just seen being displaced and hidden in position B. Within Piagetian theory, their tendency to look for the object at the first hiding place (A), as opposed to the second one (B), is taken as evidence that they do not understand that objects remain intact as they are visibly displaced through space. There is another account of the A-not-B error pattern.

To start, we know that the information-processing demands of the task vary as a function of development. Diamond (1985) finds clear effects of varying how long an experimenter waits to move the object from Position A to Position B, as well as of when the infant is allowed to reach for the hidden object. If the delay between the end of the hiding phase and the beginning of the retrieval phase is less than 2 sec, $7\frac{1}{2}$-to-8-month-old infants do not make the A-not-B error; instead they do look for the object in its second hiding place. If the interval exceeds this time, they make the typical error of returning to the original hiding well. By 9 months of age, infants can tolerate delays up to 5 s, and by 12 months up to 10 s. Bjork and Cummins (1984) used a five-well hiding arrangement to show that infants who erred had a clear tendency to choose an item that was near the first hiding place.

But it is not just the limits on memory that hinder the immature infant's ability to reach for the correct item. Diamond (1991) details a number of variables that limit the 5- to 7-month-old infant's ability to assemble and/or produce a competent plan of action. For example, younger infants have trouble inhibiting reflexes that are elicited if they accidentally touch the side of an object that happens to be near the one they have to get. Additionally, they have trouble meeting the requirement of putting two separate acts together. Baillargeon, Graber and Black (1990) also make it clear that there are action-specific limits, that is, limits that are not tied to knowledge about object permanence, that can mask the infant's knowledge of objects. These authors show that $5\frac{1}{2}$-month-old infants know the difference between actions that can and cannot support the retrieval of an object that is hidden behind a screen. In one experiment infants watched an object being retrieved under a possible and impossible action condition. To set the stage for the relevant part of the experiment, it was first necessary to have infants watch one of two kinds of hiding events. The first one involved the hand of the experimenter placing a toy teddy bear on a table, the subsequent movement of a screen in front the bear, and then a hand reaching behind the screen and pulling out the teddy bear, a perfectly possible event. In the second one, a toy teddy bear was placed on a table with a see-through cup over it, and then a screen was moved to occlude the display. Then, while the screen was in place, the infant again watched as someone's hand reached behind the screen and pulled out the teddy bear, an impossible outcome. Infants responded appropriately to these two different events. In subsequent conditions they also were able to indicate appreciation of the fact that a more complex action sequence was required for retrieval of the teddy bear in the second condition, the one in which the cup would have to be removed before the bear.

I share with Baillargeon and Diamond the view that at least part of the difference between outcomes in studies that use habituation of looking as opposed to reaching responses to evaluate whether infants believe in object permanence, has to be attributed to general limits on the ability to produce suitable action sequences. Diamond's demonstration of comparable action problems in delayed-matching-to-sample and novel-object-reaching tasks adds weight to the conclusion that there is much to learn about the development of action planning, and therefore procedural competence, during the first few years of life. Together such studies also serve to answer those who want to dismiss findings by Baillargeon and Spelke on the grounds that they come from only one task, the habituation of looking paradigms. Even if this were true, it is not a fair criticism, because infants in habituation and visual-preference studies have been tested under a wide range of stimulus conditions, including ones in which balls fall to the floor, trains go down tracks, blocks and toys are hidden, objects are felt but not seen, and so forth. The studies that now show infants able to discriminate between relevant and irrelevant retrieval acts and to pass the Piagetian task if they are tested under the right conditions help corroborate the conclusions that were based on habituation methods. Additionally, they give me further reason to argue that part of what develops is an ability to relate conceptual competence to procedural competence.

My position leads me to conclude that there is a sense in which Piaget was right to focus on the role of action in thought. However, I differ on how to interpret the development of more and more coordinated actions. For Piaget, thought and action are almost one and the same. For me they are different. Infants start life with immature and limited abilities even to perform, let alone put together, those acts into a competent plan that can satisfy conceptual competence. It is wise therefore to use assessment techniques that minimize demands on the procedural side if the question of interest is what conceptual competencies infants might have. It is better still to attempt to find more than one such method, or at least to vary the test materials across experiments. As these variations increase, so does one's confidence in the attribution of the competence in question. It is because there are many different studies of very young infants' ability to treat objects as permanent that we are now able to show that there are systematic sources of variability in Piaget's task that are not due to the extensive kinds of conceptual limits that Piaget would want us to place on infants.

IV. Conclusions

In case it is not clear by now, my position is not that our young come to the world with full conceptual competence in a domain. The choice of a skeleton as metaphor is meant to make this obvious. My claim is that this learning is much aided by the presence of structures of mind, no matter how limited these might be, because whenever it is possible for an individual to use his or her own organizations to interpret and store new inputs,

learning is facilitated. Conversely, learning is much harder when one has
no ideas as to how to interpret or organize novel inputs.

First principles can aid learning whenever the inputs do or can share the
structure of the domain. If the structure of the inputs cannot be mapped
onto some mental structure, no matter how limited the structure might be,
then learning is likely to be at risk, because one is confronted with the
conceptual analogue of having to get to the middle of a lake without a row
boat. There is nothing akin to a skeletal structure to support correct
interpretations of inputs and/or a coherent storage of them. Somehow we
have to build up a structure at the same time that we accrue bits of
knowledge that can feed the development of the structure that is being
assembled. Elsewhere I take on the question of how schoolchildren start to
succeed at this extremely difficult task. My focus in Gelman (1991) is on an
account of how they get beyond the belief that numbers are just those
things we get when we count things. To understand that fractions are
numbers, one has to understand that a fraction is one cardinal number
divided by another. However, the counting principles cannot support this
notion. In the absence of a relevant mental structure, the task then becomes one of finding mental steppingstones. One source for the development of such "stones" is the repository that results from the mapping of a
bit of a system that is already understood to a bit of a conceptual system
that we might come to know. I intentionally say "might come to know"
because it is clear that learning about new domains or new ways to con-
strue knowledge within a domain is far from easy. Children might readily
agree that they can count 1, $1\frac{1}{2}$, 2, $2\frac{1}{2}$ . . . but insist that there are no
numbers between 0 and 1 (Gelman, 1991). To accept the latter is to give up
the idea that numbers always involve counting things. Put differently, it is
not easy to build conceptual competence in the absence of an existing
knowledge base or at least a skeletal set of principles.

In sum, performances reveal understandings that are the result of a
collaboration between several different competencies. There is conceptual
competence, which is the ability to generate a relevant representation and
to apply appropriate principles of reasoning to that representation. An
example of this kind of competence is the ability to generate a representation of an object and to apply the principle that two different objects may
not both occupy the same part of space (the principle that makes the full
backward rotation of the screen impossible). Another example is the
ability to generate representations of numerosity and to recognize the
ordering of these representations and the effects of adding and subtracting
them. By experimenting with different tasks, it has been possible to obtain
strong evidence that these conceptual competencies are present in infancy. As we vary the tasks within a conceptual domain, we bring into play

various interpretive and planning competencies. Our understanding of the underlying conceptual competencies has enabled us to begin to tease out the contribution made by these other competencies to the lack of success or to the failure that we observe across tasks that are supposed to tap the same conceptual competencies. Our understanding of the characteristics of the preverbal counting process has also allowed us to model the child's inability to make reliable discriminations between adjacent numerosities outside the range of three or four items. All of these results strengthen the case for a constructivist–rationalist model of eary cognitive development. The domain-specific principles that underlie conceptual competence are present at a very early age. They guide the active assimilation of the relevant aspects of experience. These aspects are not the first-order sense data or elementary action patterns that have been assumed to be the foundation of cognitive development. Rather, they are the aspects that satisfy the structural constraints imposed by the domain-specific principles that guide development. Were there no first principles, our young would have as much difficulty acquiring their first understandings as do individuals who come to master understandings that cannot build off first principles or existing knowledge schemata.

ACKNOWLEDGMENT

The reported research and preparation of this chapter were funded by NSF grants BNS 89-16220 and DBS-9209741 to the author.

REFERENCES

Baillargeon, R. (1986). Representing the existence and the location of hidden objects: Object permanence in 6- and 8-month-old infants. *Cognition, 23,* 21–41.

Baillargeon, R. (1987). Object permanence in 3.5- and 4.5-month-old infants. *Developmental Psychology, 23,* 655–664.

Baillargeon, R., Graber, M., Devos, & Black, J. (1990). Why do young infants fail to search for hidden objects? *Cognition, 36,* 255–284.

Baillargeon, R., Miller, K. F., & Constantino, J. (1992). *Ten-month-old infants' intuitions about addition.* Unpublished manuscript. University of Illinois, Champaign-Urbana.

Baillargeon, R. S., Spelke, E. S., & Wasserman, S. (1985). Object permanence in the five-month-old infant. *Cognition, 20,* 191–208.

Bjork, E. L., & Cummins, E. M. (1984). Infant search errors: Stage of concept development or stage of memory development. *Memory & Cognition, 12,* 1–19.

Briars, D., & Siegler, R. S. (1984). A featural analysis of preschoolers' counting knowledge. *Developmental Psychology, 20,* 607–618.

Bullock, M., & Gelman, R. (1977). Numerical reasoning in young children: The ordering principle. *Child Development, 48,* 427–434.

Carey, S. (1985). *Conceptual change in childhood.* Cambridge, MA: MIT Press/Bradford Books.

Carey, S., & Gelman, R. (Eds.), (1991). *The epigenesis of mind: Essays on biology and cognition.* Hillsdale, NJ: Lawrence Erlbaum.

Cheng, K., & Gallistel, C. R. (1984). Testing the geometric power of an animal's spatial representation. In H. L. Roitblatt, T. G. Bever, & H. S. Terrace (Eds.), *Animal cognition* (pp. 409–423). Hillsdale, NJ: Lawrence Erlbaum.

Chi, M. T. H., & Klahr, D. (1975). Span and rate of apprehension in children and adults. *Journal of Experimental Child Psychology, 19,* 434–439.

Clark, H., & Brennan, M. (1991). Grounding in communication. In L. Resnick, J. Levine, & S. Teasley (Eds.), *Perspectives on socially shared cognition* (pp. 127–149). Washington, D.C.: American Psychological Association.

Cooper, R. G., Jr. (1984). Early number development: Discovering number space with addition and subtraction. In C. Sophian (Ed.), *The origins of cognitive skills* (pp. 157–192). Hillsdale, NJ: Lawrence Erlbaum.

Cooper, R. G., Jr., Campbell, R. L., & Blevins, B. (1983). Numerical representations from infancy to middle childhood: What develops? In D. Rogers & J. A. Sloboda (Eds.), *The acquisition of symbolic skills* (pp. 523–533). New York: Plenum.

Diamond, A. (1985). The development of the ability to use recall to guide action, as indicated by infants' performance on the $\overline{AB}$. *Child Development, 56,* 868–883.

Diamond, A. (1991). Neuropsychological insights into the meaning of object concept development. In S. Carey & R. Gelman (Eds.), *The epigenesis of mind: Essays on biology and cognition* (pp. 67–110). Hillsdale, NJ: Lawrence Erlbaum.

Fischer, J-P. (1991/2). Subitizing: the discontinuity after three. In J. Bideaud, C. Meljac, J-P. Fischer, (Eds.), *Pathways to number: Children's developing numerical abilities* (pp. 191–208). Hillsdale, NJ: Lawrence Erlbaum. (French edition was published in 1991 by Presses Universitaires de Lille.)

Fischer, K. W. & Biddle, T. (1991). Constraining nativist inferences about cognitive capacities. In S. Carey & R. Gelman (Eds.), *The epigenesis of mind: Essays on biology and cognition* (pp. 199–235). Hillsdale, NJ: Lawrence Erlbaum.

Fuson, K. C. (1988). *Children's counting and concepts of number.* New York: Springer-Verlag.

Gallistel, C. R. (1990). *The organization of learning.* Cambridge, MA: MIT Press/Bradford Books.

Gallistel, C. R., & Gelman, R. (1991). The preverbal counting process. In W. E. Kessen, A. Ortony, & F. I. M. Craik (Eds.), *Thoughts, memories and emotions: Essays in honor of George Mandler* (pp. 65–81). Hillsdale, NJ: Lawrence Erlbaum.

Gallistel, C. R., & Gelman, R. (1992). Preverbal and verbal counting and computation. *Cognition, 44,* 43–74.

Gelman, R. (1990). First principles organize attention to and learning about relevant data: Number and the animate-inanimate distinction as examples. *Cognitive Science, 14,* 79–106.

Gelman, R. (1991). Epigenetic foundations of knowledge structures: Initial and transcendent constructions. In S. Carey & R. Gelman (Eds.), *The epigenesis of mind: Essays on biology and cognition* (pp. 293–322). Hillsdale, NJ: Erlbaum Associates.

Gelman, R., & Gallistel, C. R. (1978). *The child's understanding of number.* Cambridge, MA: Harvard University Press.

Gelman, R., & Greeno, J. G. (1989). On the nature of competence: Principles for understanding in a domain. In L. B. Resnick (Ed.), *Knowing and learning: Issues for a cognitive science of instruction* (pp. 125–186). Hillsdale, NJ: Lawrence Erlbaum.

Gelman, R., Massey, C., & McManus, M. (1991). Characterizing supporting environments for cognitive development: Lessons from children in a museum. In J. M. Levine, L. B. Resnick, & S. D. Teasley (Eds.), *Perspectives on socially shared cognition* (pp. 226–256). Washington, DC: American Psychological Association.

Gelman, R., & Meck, E. (1986). The notion of principle: The case of counting. In J. Hiebert (Ed.), *The relationship between procedural and conceptual competence* (pp. 29–57). Hillsdale, NJ: Lawrence Erlbaum.

Gelman, R., & Meck, E. (1991/92). Early principles aid initial but not later concepts of number. In J. Bideaud, C. Meljac, J-P. Fischer (Eds.), *Pathways to number: Children's developing numerical abilities* (pp. 171–190; addendum, pp. 385–86). Hillsdale, NJ: Lawrence Erlbaum. (French edition was published in 1991 by Presses Universitaires de Lille.)

Gelman, R., Meck, E., & Merkin, S. (1986). Young children's numerical competence. *Cognitive Development, 1,* 1–29.

Greeno, J. G., Riley, M. S., & Gelman, R. (1984). Conceptual competence and children's counting. *Cognitive Psychology, 16,* 94–134.

Karmiloff-Smith, A. (1986). From meta-processes to conscious access: Evidence from children's metalinguistic and repair data. *Cognition, 23,* 95–147.

Karmiloff-Smith, A. (1992). *Beyond modularity: A developmental perspective on cognitive science.* Cambridge, MA: MIT Press/Bradford Books.

Keil, F. C. (1981). Constraints on knowledge and cognitive development. *Psychological Review, 88,* 197–227.

Kitcher, P. (1982). *The nature of mathematical knowledge.* New York: Oxford University Press.

Knudsen, E. (1983). Early auditory experience aligns the auditory map of space in the optic tectum of the barn owl. *Science, 222,* 939–942.

Kuhn, T. S. (1970). *The structure of scientific revolutions* (2nd ed.), Chicago, IL: University of Chicago Press.

Mandler, G., & Shebo, B. J. (1982). Subitizing: An analysis of its component processes. *Journal of Experimental Psychology: General, 11,* 1–22.

Marler, P. (1991). The instinct to learn. In S. Carey, & R. Gelman (Eds.), *The epigenesis of mind: Essays on biology and mind.* (pp. 37–66). Hillsdale, NJ: Lawrence Erlbaum.

Marr, D. (1982). *Vision.* San Francisco: Freeman.

Mayer, E. (1982). *The growth of biological thought: Diversity, evolution, and inheritance.* Cambridge, Mass.: Belknap/Harvard University Press.

Meck, W. H., & Church, R. M. (1983). A mode control model of counting and timing processes. *Journal of Experimental Psychology: Animal Behavior Processes, 11,* 591–597.

Moore, D., Benenson, J., Reznick, S., Peerson, M., Kagan, J. (1987). Effects of auditory numerical information on infants' looking behavior. *Developmental Psychology, 23,* 665–670.

Piaget, J. (1952). *The child's conception of number.* London, England: Routledge & Kegan Paul.

Platt, J. R., & Johnson, D. M. (1971). Localization of position within a homogeneous behavior chain: Effects of error contingencies. *Learning and Motivation, 2,* 386–414.

Rescorla, R. A., & Wagner, A. R. (1972). A theory of Pavlovian conditioning: Variations in the effectiveness of reinforcement and nonreinforcement. In A. H. Black, & W. F. Prokasy (Eds.), *Classical Conditioning II* (pp. 64–99). New York: Appleton-Century-Crofts.

Rogoff, B. (1990). *Apprenticeships in thinking: Cognitive development in social context*. Oxford, England: Oxford University Press.

Rozin, P. & Schull, J. (1988). The adaptive-evolutionary point of view in experimental psychology. In R. C. Atkinson, R. J. Herrnstein, G. Lindzey, & D. R. Luce (Eds.), *Steven's handbook of experimental psychology*. New York: W. J. Wiley.

Shatz, M. (1978). On the development of communicative understandings: An early strategy for interpreting and responding to message. *Cognitive Psychology, 10*, 271–308.

Shatz, M. & Backscheider, A. (1991, November). Acquiring the normative concepts of color and number. Presented at the annual meeting of the Psychonomic Society, Seattle, WA.

Shatz, M., Wellman, H., & Silber, S. (1983). The acquisition of mental verbs: A systematic investigation of the first reference to mental state. *Cognitive Psychology, 14*, 301–21.

Siegal, M. (1989). A clash of conversational worlds: Interpreting cognitive development through communication. In J. M. & R. Levine (Eds.), *Socially shared cognition* (pp. 1–27). Washington, DC: American Psychological Association.

Siegal, M. (1991). *Knowing children: Experiments in conversation and cognition*. Hillsdale, NJ: Lawrence Erlbaum.

Smith, D. A., Greeno, J. G., & Vitolo, T. V. (1989). A model of competence for counting. *Cognitive Science, 13*, 183–211.

Sophian, C. (1991/1992). Learning about numbers: Lessons for mathematics education from preschool number development. In J. Bideaud, C. Meljac, J-P. Fischer (Eds.), *Pathways to number: Children's developing numerical abilities* (pp. 19–40). Hillsdale, NJ: Lawrence Erlbaum. (French edition was published in 1991 by Presses Universitaires de Lille.)

Sophian, C., & Adams, N. (1987). Infants' understanding of numerical transformations. *British Journal of Developmental Psychology, 5*, 257–264.

Spelke, E. S. (1991). *Physical knowledge in infancy: Reflections on Piaget's theory*. In S. Carey, & R. Gelman (Ed.), *The epigenesis of mind* (pp. 133–169). Hillsdale, NJ: Lawrence Erlbaum.

Starkey, P. (1992). The early development of numerical reasoning. *Cognition, 43*, 93–126.

Starkey, P., Spelke, E. S., & Gelman, R. (1983). Detection of intermodal correspondences by human infants. *Science, 222*, 179–181.

Starkey, P., Spelke, E. S., & Gelman, R. (1990). Numerican abstraction by human infants. *Cognition, 36*, 97–127.

Strauss, M. S., & Curtis, L. E. (1984). Development of numerical concepts in infancy. In C. Sophian (Ed.), *Origins of cognitive skills* (pp. 131–155). Hillsdale, NJ: Lawrence Erlbaum.

Von Glaserfeld, E. (1982). Subitizing: The role of figural patterns in the development of numerical concepts. *Archives de Psychologie, 50*, 191–218.

van Loosbroek, E., & Smitsman, A. W. (1990). Visual perception of numerosity in infancy. *Developmental Psychology, 26*, 916–922.

Vygotsky, L. S. (1978). *Mind in society: The development of higher psychological processes*. Cambridge, MA: Harvard University Press.

Wiser, M. (1987). The differentiation of heat and temperature: History of science and novice-expert shift. In S. Strauss (Eds.), *Ontogeny, phylogeny, and historical development* pp. 28–48. Norwood, NJ: Ablex.

Wynn, K. (1990). Children's understanding of counting. *Cognition, 36*, 155–193.

Wynn, K. (1992a). Addition and subtraction by human infants. *Nature, 358*, 749–750.

Wynn, K. (1992b). Children's acquisition of the number words and the counting system. *Cognitive Psychology, 24*, 220–251.

REMEMBERING, KNOWING, AND
RECONSTRUCTING THE PAST

Henry L. Roediger III
Mark A. Wheeler
Suparna Rajaram

I. Introduction

A central issue in the psychology of learning and memory is how memories change over time. This issue was first addressed experimentally by Ebbinghaus (1885/1964, Chap. 7) and has been pursued assiduously ever since. A related issue, raised only briefly by Ebbinghaus, is our state of awareness concerning our memories. For some memories, even distant ones, we feel a sense of reexperiencing the events during their recollection. In remembering other past events, we feel less engaged: We know the event occurred, but the act of recollection does not carry with it the strong feeling of reliving it. In other cases we may know that events happened to us, but we cannot remember their occurrence at all. In still other cases, experiences may have considerable impact on our behavior, but we cannot recollect them at all (see Jacoby, Kelley, & Dywan, 1989, for examples). These two topics—the course of retention over time and the phenomenological experience of the rememberer—represent two focuses of the present chapter. The third is an issue that did not much exercise Ebbinghaus, but which has interested researchers ever since: How accurate are our memories for distant events?

THE PSYCHOLOGY OF LEARNING
AND MOTIVATION, VOL. 30   97

When Ebbinghaus conducted his pioneering experiments on the temporal course of retention, he learned lists to the criterion of two perfect recitations and then, at some later point in time, relearned the lists. Retention was measured by savings in relearning. Ebbinghaus advocated this method for studying retention because it obviated the need to consider states of conscious awareness; people might still show savings for the events even if they were unaware that the events had ever occurred. All readers are familiar with the beautiful logarithmic forgetting function that Ebbinghaus discovered when he plotted savings against time. Virtually all studies confirm the general shape of the function in a variety of situations, with the main point of dispute being whether the function flattens out for general knowledge obtained years previously (e.g., Bahrick, H. P., Bahrick, P. O., & Wittlinger, 1975) or instead continues to decline very slowly even over long intervals (e.g., Squire, 1989).

We bother to recount the familiar tale of Ebbinghaus's research here because we want to remind readers of a methodological detail that was introduced by Ebbinghaus and that has been carried forward in almost all later research concerned with forgetting. To wit, when Ebbinghaus learned lists and tested himself on them later, he always tested different lists at the varying retention intervals. Thus, a list was studied and tested only once. Today we would say that Ebbinghaus used a within-subject, between-lists design. Most researchers following in his footsteps have made a similar choice; indeed, the overwhelming preference of researchers has been to use between-subjects designs in which different groups of subjects learn the same material but are then tested at different points in time from the learning episode. The reason that researchers have chosen between-subjects (or at least between-lists) designs probably has to do with their beliefs concerning effects of repeatedly testing the same material, as would occur in a within-subjects, within-lists design in which the same subjects learn and are repeatedly tested on the same material. In this latter design, the first test given may carry over and affect the later tests in unknown ways. Therefore, researchers have sensibly avoided the repeated-testing design as involving interpretive difficulties in tracing the course of forgetting.

Although the dominant mode of investigating forgetting has been the between-subjects or between-lists design, the repeated-testing design has not been entirely overlooked. Typically, subjects study lists of words or pictures and are tested repeatedly, without feedback or intervening study opportunities. Indeed, many celebrated investigations in cognitive psychology have used this arrangement, including those of Ballard (1913), Brown (1923), Bartlett (1932), Estes (1960), Tulving (1967) and Erdelyi and Becker (1974), to take some cases in their chronological order of occurrence. The first part of this chapter will seek to unravel some puzzles and paradoxes raised by such experiments in which subjects' memories are tested repeatedly for the same events.

We can think of several good reasons to examine performance in repeated testing paradigms, even though they have been avoided by most psychologists interested in learning and memory. First, the alleged contaminating influence of a test is of interest in its own right. Having subjects successfully recall material on a first test powerfully enhances performance on later tests (e.g., Hogan & Kintsch, 1971; Thompson, Wenger, & Bartling, 1978). A test of memory is not a neutral event to gauge subjects' knowledge, but affects that knowledge when it is displayed on later tests (e.g., Brown, 1923; Spitzer, 1939; Tulving, 1967). This testing effect, as it is sometimes called, may have wide educational impliciations (Glover, 1989) and therefore seems worthy of study. On the other hand, a second important consideration is that sometimes a test may have the opposite effect on the later test, causing interference and forgetting of the original material (e.g., Hastie, Landsman, & Loftus, 1978). We shall report experiments in this chapter revealing this effect and will then attempt to answer the critical question of when a test will facilitate or interfere with later recall. A third reason to study how memories change when they are repeatedly tested is the external validity of such a situation. People repeatedly recollect the important events of their lives either to relate them to others or to reflect on them privately. Therefore, if systematic changes in the content of memories occur as a function of such repeated recollections, the proper way to discover them is through experiments with repeated tests. Between-subjects or between-lists designs will not answer the important questions in this case.

As the astute reader will by now have surmised, this chapter is largely about the operation of retrieval processes as revealed through repeated testing of subjects on the same material. In the next section of the article we describe a puzzle that arose from prior work using this paradigm—why some experiments have shown improvements from repeated testing whereas others showed the opposite—and report experiments that solve the puzzle. We also show a powerful positive effect of taking one test on performance on a similar test a week later. In the next section of the chapter we consider the question of when an earlier test can have a deleterious effect on a later test and report experiments documenting this effect. These experiments show that a test conducted under the appropriate circumstances can create interference and harm performance on a later test. The effect seems similar to the misinformation effect in eyewitness testimony investigated by Loftus (1979, 1991). After this section, we consider the phenomenological experience of recollection by investigating two types of awareness referred to as *remembering* and *knowing* by Tulving (1985) and Gardiner (1988). In both cases people are aware that they are making reports about their past experiences, but in the former the recollection is accompanied by a feeling of traveling back in time, in some sense, to reexperience the events as they are recollected. In the latter case, that of knowing, people are confident of their recollections of events as being in their past, but the retrieval is not accompanied by the rich experience of remembering the original event. The experiments reported here add to those of Gardiner and his colleagues (summarized by Gardiner & Java (1993) in showing that these two bases of recollection are separable and can be dissociated by experimental variables. We conclude the chapter by suggesting directions for future research.

II.   Disparate Effects of Repeated Testing

Psychologists have used repeated testing paradigms for many different purposes; therefore, several different traditions of this research have become established, often with little cross-referencing. In this section we describe research from early in this century in which investigators tested memory repeatedly and reached diametrically opposed conclusions about its operation. Curiously, to our knowledge no one noticed the paradox posed by this early research until two of the current authors raised it in 1992 (Wheeler & Roediger, 1992).

In some of the most well known research in cognitive psychology, Bartlett (1932) reported his famous experiments in which he had English college students read an American Indian story, "The War of the Ghosts," and then recall it several times. Typically, the first recall attempt occurred 15 min or so after initial study, and later tests might occur days, weeks, or months later. On later tests Bartlett found dramatic distortions in recall of the story, with many omissions, alterations of meaning, and occasional additions. Bartlett emphasized the constructive nature of memory and argued that his subjects likely used the schema of a fairy tale, a common form to these students, in encoding and reconstructing the story. Supernatural elements were deemphasized, and the story was often made more consistent and rational. Therefore, from his repeated-reproduction technique, Bartlett (1932) concluded that memories often become more error prone over repeated tests.

It is worth noting that Bartlett (1932) produced no aggregate data in support of his conclusions, but rather presented sample protocols and anecdotes to bolster his conclusions. Interestingly, we can cite only one attempted replication of Bartlett's (1932) pioneering research—one published by Gauld and Stephenson (1967) and discussed below—that tried to confirm his claims using the repeated-reproduction technique. "The War of the Ghosts" has been used in a great deal of later research, but this work rarely involved repeated testing and was usually conducted for purposes other than examining the reconstructive nature of memory.[1] By the same token, much research has been conducted on the reconstructive nature of memory, but rarely has this interesting work involved repeated testing; it is more customary to assess memory via a single recognition test for information that might have been inferred but not actually stated in a prose passage (e.g., Johnson, Bransford, & Solomon, 1973) or via misinformation given in a narrative after subjects have witnessed some event (e.g., Loftus, 1979, 1991).

   Curiously, Bartlett (1932) did not mention that his repeated testing research conflicted with other research dating back at least 20 years, also conducted in England. Ballard (1913) gave schoolchildren passages of poetry to memorize and then tested them repeatedly for intervals of up to one week later. Ballard found that children would often recall lines of poetry on later tests that they could not recall on earlier tests, a phenomenon he termed *reminiscence*. The basic observations of recall on a later test of material that had been missed on earlier tests were confirmed in later research (e.g., Brown, 1923) conducted well before Bartlett (1932) published his book, so it is curious that he did not at least cite it. However, the basic findings of Ballard and Brown were directly contrary to Bartlett's observations and conclusions; rather than dramatic forgetting and distortion of memory, Ballard and Brown had reported actual improvements over time in subjects' abilities to recollect their experiences. In fairness, Bartlett's celebrated book was intended to report his new experiments, which apparently began in 1913 (Bartlett, 1932, p. v). However, he might have added to the social factors that influence historical memory the tendency to disregard published evidence at odds with one's conception.

   The observations of Ballard (1913) and Brown (1923) indicating positive effects of repeated testing on overall recall were examined for some years before being abandoned, for a time, as an object of serious study. Buxton (1943) reviewed the literature and concluded that reminiscence was an ephemeral phenomenon that failed to occur about as often as it appeared. However, Payne (1987) argued that Buxton (1943) reached his conclusion because the phenomenon of reminiscence had been redefined over the

[1] Many of Bartlett's (1932) experiments used a serial reproduction technique in which one subject read "The War of the Ghosts" and recalled it later, and then a second subject read the first subject's protocol and later recalled it, and so on. This technique has been used in later research (e.g., Paul, 1959), and Bartlett's observations were generally confirmed.

years. Ballard's (1913) original definition of the term was of material that could not be recalled on a first test that was recovered on a second (or later) test. Whenever total recall improves between two tests, reminiscence must have occurred; therefore, Ballard sometimes used overall improvement between tests as an index of the occurrence of reminiscence. This now seems a mistake, because it led later researchers such as Buxton (1943) to redefine reminiscence as overall improvement in recall between tests. However, it is perfectly possible to have reminiscence (defined as "intertest recovery") without having overall improvement between tests, because forgetting between tests can offset the reminiscence or recovery. Therefore, when Buxton (1943) concluded that the phenomenon was unreliable, he referred to an overall improvement between tests, not to reminiscence defined as intertest recovery, which was widely obtained. Nonetheless, his review is generally credited with diminishing research in this area for several decades.

Research on the topic of improvements in recall across repeated tests was resuscitated by Erdelyi and Becker (1974). They presented subjects with pictures or concrete words and had subjects recall them on three successive tests, each lasting 7 min. They also used a new procedure, forced recall, in which subjects basically engaged in a free-recall test but were forced to produce a preset number of responses that was greater than the number of items subjects could recall. This procedure was used to overcome the argument that gains observed on later recall tests should be attributed to relaxed recall criteria on these tests. (We examine the effects of forced recall on memory in a later section). Erdelyi and Becker reported overall improvements across tests in recall of pictures but not of words. They labelled this improvement *hypermnesia* (the opposite of amnesia, or forgetting).[2]

It is worth noting that virtually all experiments employing free or forced recall have reported strong reminiscence in recall of both pictures and words (e.g., Erdelyi, Finkelstein, Herrell, Miller & Thomas, 1976), although in the case of words the improvement between tests is offset by intertest forgetting in many experiments. (However, some researchers have reported reliable hypermnesia for words; e.g., Payne & Roediger, 1987). There is by now a large literature on hypermnesia (see Erdelyi, 1984; Payne, 1987; and Roediger & Challis, 1989 for reviews). The point

[2] Today the term *reminiscence* is used to refer to recall of events on a later test that were not recalled on an earlier test; reminiscence is intertest recovery, which agrees with Ballard's (1913) original definition of the term. However, reminiscence can be offset by intertest forgetting. Hypermnesia refers to overall gains in recall between two tests, that is, when reminiscence reliably outweighs intertest forgetting. Thus one can obtain reminiscence without hypermnesia, but the reverse case is impossible.

we want to establish here, however, is simply that the phenomena of reminscence and hypermnesia are real and often replicated. In one interesting experiment, Scrivner and Safer (1988) showed subjects a videotape of a burglary and then gave them repeated tests in recalling critical details of the event. Recall improved steadily across four repeated tests. The generality of the phenomenon of hypermnesia leads us back to the initial question as to why two different traditions of research, both employing repeated testing, can arrive at such disparate conclusions regarding retrieval processes in memory.

Wheeler and Roediger (1992) examined past research and isolated two likely factors as potential causes of the different findings and conclusions: the type of material used and the length of the interval between tests. Bartlett (1932) used prose passages in most of his memory experiments, such as "The War of the Ghosts." On the other hand, much of the research showing improvements between tests used lists of words, pictures, or similar materials. (Payne, 1987, reviewed 172 such experiments documenting the phenomenon, all using lists.) Another potential factor is the intertest interval; Bartlett (1932) used rather lengthy intervals between tests, often days and sometimes months, whereas researchers studying hypermnesia usually interpose only five minutes or less between tests.

It is not obvious from prior research which of these factors should be more important, or whether both are critical. For example, Ballard (1913) obtained hypermnesia for passages of poetry, which might be considered connected discourse like prose. Similarly, Roediger, Payne, Gillespie and Lean (1982) obtained hypermnesia in recall of categories (presidents, birds, sports), which are also in well-structured sets. On the other hand, some researchers have obtained hypermnesia across long intervals. In the experiment by Scrivner and Safer (1988) described above, hypermnesia was obtained between tests over a 48-hr interval. Similarly, Erdelyi and Kleinbard (1978) obtained hypermnesia for a list of pictures over a week by testing subjects three times a day with a forced-recall procedure.

Wheeler and Roediger (1992) examined both retention interval and type of material as the possible factors underlying prior discrepant results in several experiments. They had subjects study 60 pictures under one of two conditions before taking forced-recall tests on the pictures. In one case, subjects heard a story and the names of the 60 pictured objects occurred in the story. They were told to learn both the story and the names of the pictures. Other subjects saw the same 60 pictures presented in the same order, but they heard the names of the pictures as they were being presented. These two conditions were meant to simulate, to some degree, the difference between Bartlett's materials (schematic processing of prose) in the pictures + story condition, on the one hand, and the list-learning conditions of the typical hypermnesia experiment in pictures + names conditions, on the other. Wheeler and Roediger's procedure arranges this comparison with the target material held constant between conditions, so one need not make a comparison between prose recall on the one hand and recall of some completely different material presented in lists, on the other.

The other main variable in the Wheeler and Roediger (1992) experiment was the schedule of testing subjects received after seeing the 60 pictures in one of the two conditions. All subjects received a brief questionnaire asking them about various features of the experiment, such as estimating the number of pictures presented. One third of the subjects were dismissed at this point and told to return a week later. (The questionnaire was created to give subjects in this condition a plausible rationale for having participated.) Another third of the subjects received one test for the pictures; they were given sheets numbered 1–60 and were told to recall the names of as many of the 60 pictures they had previously studied as possible, but that they should guess to fill up the 60 spaces. Seven minutes were permitted for recall. The final third of the subjects were treated the same way, except that they were given three 7-min forced-recall tests, with 1-min breaks between tests. Finally, all subjects returned a week later and then received three consecutive forced-recall tests for the 60 pictures that had been studied the previous week.

In summary, subjects studied either pictures in a list or in the context of a story, then took zero, one, or three forced-recall tests on the pictures, and then returned the next week and took three more tests. We anticipated that subjects taking the three immediate tests would show hypermnesia (improved recall over tests), at-least in the condition where they studied pictures and their names (replicating Erdelyi & Becker, 1974, among many others). However, we expected that forgetting (not improvement) would occur between tests with a week lag between them, and that this forgetting might be more pronounced in the pictures + story condition with its schema-driven processing.

The basic results are shown in Table I. The six groups of subjects are labelled on the left, with the first number indicating the number of tests taken on the day subjects studied the pictures (0, 1, or 3) and the second number indicating the three tests taken a week later (always 3). Recall of pictures was greater in the pictures + story conditions than in the pictures + names conditions; collapsing across all other conditions, the difference was about four items. However, the type of material is irrelevant to the main point here, so let us focus on the picture + story recall in the bottom of Table I to answer four questions of interest. First, did recall improve in the three immediate tests? The answer is clearly *yes:* Recall

TABLE I

NUMBER OF PICTURES RECALLED AS A FUNCTION OF PRESENTATION
CONTEXT AND TESTING SCHEDULE[a]

Context and group	Immediate tests				Delayed tests			
	1	2	3	$T_3 - T_1$	1	2	3	$T_3 - T_1$
Pictures plus names								
3–3	26.6	27.2	28.4	1.8[b]	25.2	26.3	26.0	0.8
1–3	25.7	—	—	—	20.2	21.7	23.0	2.8[b]
0–3	—	—	—	—	16.7	17.5	17.5	0.8
Pictures plus story								
3–3	32.7	35.0	36.4	3.8[b]	31.8	33.0	33.4	1.6[b]
1–3	31.8	—	—	—	23.3	25.0	25.6	2.3[b]
0–3	—	—	—	—	17.4	17.2	18.4	1.0

[a] Data are from Wheeler and Roediger (1992) and are reprinted by permission of the Cambridge University Press.
[b] These conditions demonstrated reliable hypermnesia across the three tests.

improved by 3.8 items across the tests, and the hypermnesia was even greater in the pictures + story condition than in the more typical pictures + names condition. Clearly, hypermnesia can be obtained in recall following a story (albeit of pictures embedded in the story).

The second question of interest is whether forgetting occurred between tests when a week rather than few minutes elapsed between them. Again, the answer is *yes*. In Group 3–3 in the pictures + story condition, recall dropped from 36.4 items recalled to 31.8 over the week; in Group 1–3, the drop was from 31.8 to 23.3. Successive tests with a week between tests produce forgetting, not hypermnesia. These results show that it is likely the delay between tests and not the type of material that produced the disparate outcomes in Ballard's (1913) and Bartlett's (1932) experiments.

The results in Table I can also be used to address two other issues that are of some interest. Can hypermnesia be obtained after a week retention interval if short intervals occur between successive tests after the week's delay? The answer given from the six conditions in the right side of Table I seems to be *yes*. In all six cases subjects recalled more on the third test than on the first test and an analysis of variance on only the delayed test data produced a significant effect for the number of tests, $F(2, 114) = 14.35$, $MS_e = 5.03$, $p < .001$. However, the effect is not particularly robust because it was significant on only three of the six conditions in individual ANOVAs. Nonetheless, in all likelihood, hypermnesia can be reliably obtained after a week's delay.

The final point to draw from Table I is the power of a test in aiding later recall. Subjects who took three immediate tests recalled more pictures a week later than did subjects who took only one test, but these subjects in turn recalled the pictures much better than did subjects who had no tests after studying the pictures initially. These results are portrayed graphically in Fig. 1, where performance on the three delayed tests has been averaged and plotted as a function of the number of immediate tests. The three groups of subjects in either the pictures + names and pictures + story condition were treated identically up to the point of the first test and then when they returned a week later. The only difference between conditions that could affect performance on the later tests was the number of tests taken during the initial session. Nonetheless, as Fig. 1 shows, delayed recall increased monotonically with the number of prior tests and the enhancing effect of testing affected delayed recall much more powerfully in the pictures + story than in the pictures + names condition. We have no ready interpretation of this last outcome, but our point here is mainly to document the powerful effect that taking a test has on later retention.

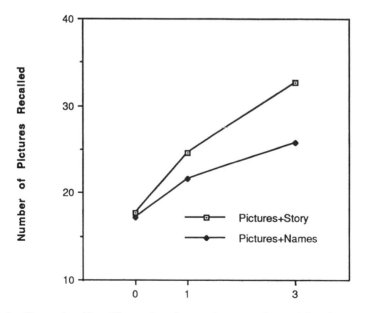

Fig. 1.   The testing effect. The number of tests taken soon after studying pictures greatly affected recall one week later.

Many others have made this point, too (e.g., Glover, 1989; Izawa, 1971; Spitzer, 1939; Thompson et al., 1978).

To return to the main point of the experiment, Wheeler and Roediger (1992) argued that their experiment resolved the puzzle posed by prior inconsistent studies of Ballard (1913) and Bartlett (1932). The answer is rather straightforward: If there are short intervals between tests, then one usually finds hypermnesia over repeated testing. If the intervals are long (a week, in our experiment), then one obtains forgetting between tests. Of course, this latter point must be true in the limiting case—say, with 5 years between tests—but also occurs with intervals as short as a week.

We conclude that type of material played little role in the earlier discrepancies between outcomes, because we found no interaction with other variables between pictures presented in a list (the pictures + names condition) and those presented in a story context (the pictures + story condition). However, this conclusion can be challenged, because in a sense we used the same materials—a series of 60 pictures—in both conditions. Wheeler and Roediger (1992) conducted two further experiments to see whether the basic findings could be obtained with prose materials. Can hypermnesia be obtained with short intervals between tests and forgetting be obtained when the interval is lengthened to one week?

The two experiments were similar, except for the types of materials and the fact that one was conducted as a classroom demonstration and the other was conducted under more controlled laboratory conditions. Nonetheless, the outcomes were very much alike. In the classroom experiment, students in a cognitive psychology course at Rice University read "The War of the Ghosts" twice at a comfortable rate and then spent 5 min recalling U.S. presidents. They were then given 8.5 min to recall the story as well as possible; following this free-recall attempt, they recalled U.S. states for 5 min and then recalled the story again for 8.5 more minutes. One week later students were given a surprise test and asked to recall the story again. The laboratory experiment was conducted under generally similar conditions with an excerpt from a John Updike short story, "The Kid's Whistling," serving as the target material.

The results of the two experiments are shown here in Table II. For both types of materials, subjects showed modest but statistically significant improvements between the first two tests. Following others (e.g., Mandler & Johnson, 1977), we scored the results in terms of the number of idea units (significant phrases or ideas in the passage) that were recalled. The improvement between the two initial tests looks modest, but each idea unit is composed of seven to eight words, on average, so the improvement would look greater if scored in this manner (which, however, is difficult with prose materials). In both cases the improvement was quite consistent

TABLE II

NUMBER OF IDEA UNITS RECALLED IN TWO EXPERIMENTS, USING DIFFERENT PROSE PASSAGES[a]

Material	Test 1	Test 2	Delayed test
"The War of the Ghosts"[b]	21.4	22.9	19.0
"The Kid's Whistling"[c]	12.1	13.2	10.7

[a] Data are from Wheeler and Roediger (1992) and are reprinted by permission of the Cambridge University Press.
[b] 42 idea units.
[c] 41 idea units.

across subjects (see Wheeler & Roediger, 1992 for details). Furthermore, in both experiments recall decreased between the second test and the third one a week later. However, in neither case did subjects display gross confusion and inaccuracy on the delayed test, which might have been expected from Bartlett's (1932) results. We return to this point later.

We conclude from the experiments described thus far that, for recently learned material, recall improves between tests when short intervals separate them but that forgetting occurs when the interval is increased to one week. Bahrick and Hall (1993) have argued that this conclusion may hold only for episodic memory situations, because when subjects are repeatedly tested on relatively permanent knowledge (e.g., of public events or famous faces), they show improvements over long delays between tests. Bahrick and Hall (1991) reported improvements over one month, as did Hermann, Buschke, and Gall (1987). In a rather different paradigm, Squire, Haist, and Shimamura (1989) reported significant improvements with one year between tests. These reports indicate that hypermnesia may be obtained with long intervals between tests, but Roediger and Wheeler (1993) noted that one possible interpretation of these gains in knowledge between tests is that subjects may be exposed to the relevant material from magazines, newspapers, television, or books during this time. (In some cases, such as research by Squire et al. [1989], the test procedure exposed subjects to the correct answers.) It is inherently difficult to test general knowledge with widely spaced intervals and not to have intervening study opportunities for the material. Indeed, the first test may sensitize subjects to relevant information and lead them to pay more attention if they are exposed to it later (but see Bahrick & Hall, 1991). Nonetheless, the results described by Bahrick and Hall (1993) are interesting and deserve further study.

To conclude this section, we think we have resolved the paradox posed by the disparate results from repeated testing in episodic memory by showing that the interval between tests is the critical variable. For recently learned material such as pictures or prose passages, repeated testing with short intervals between tests produces improvement in overall recall (hypermnesia). (If Bartlett, 1932, had used short intervals between tests he might have reached very different conclusions about the reconstructive nature of memory.) When the interval between tests is extended to one week, then recall declines. However, even with this longer interval, most of the forgetting occurred as omissions of material; there were few errors and confabulations introduced, and most of these were minor. This was true in the classroom experiment with "The War of the Ghosts" and with the other types of material, too. Does this evidence indicate that remembering is not as reconstructive as Bartlett (1932), among many others, would have us believe? We turn to this issue in the next section.

III. Interference and Reconstruction

Bartlett (1932) concluded from his research that remembering was highly constructive, because his subjects' recollections of "The War of the Ghosts" were so distorted during delayed tests. The distortions were not caused by misleading suggestions planted in other material, but were created by the subjects themselves in their previous recall attempts, or so the story goes. As previously noted, Bartlett's (1932) experiments have never been successfully replicated, to our knowledge. This seems a curious state of affairs for some of the most widely cited observations in cognitive psychology, especially because the original observations themselves were almost anecdotal. In light of more recent evidence we might wonder indeed whether the findings of reconstructed recall *can* be replicated.

In an interesting series of experiments, Gauld and Stephenson (1967) explored the possibility that Bartlett's (1932) instructions to his subjects may have led them to construct rather than to remember. Bartlett never says exactly what instructional set he encouraged in his subjects and indeed seemed to be deliberately vague in his instructions: "I thought it best, for the purposes of these experiments, to try to influence the subjects' procedure as little as possible" (1932, p. 78). Gauld and Stephenson (1967) note that if subjects took their task as retelling a story rather than as remembering it, Bartlett's results showing invention and construction would be expected. As they say:

Most people who retell a story are unlikely to care very much whether the story they retell is the same, detail by detail, as the story they originally heard. In other words, they are most unlikely to take pains that what they come out with is always what they remember rather than what they guess at or even consciously invent. Now if the changes and inventions in reproductions of stories . . . are to serve as the foundation for a theory of remembering, [then it should be established that the subjects] were indeed seriously trying to remember, and were not more or less consciously guessing or romancing in order to fill in gaps in their memories." (Gauld & Stepenson, 1967, p. 40)

Gauld and Stephenson (1967) conducted three experiments that led to the conclusion that Bartlett (1932) must have used rather loose instructions, ones encouraging subjects to tell a good story rather than to remember conscientiously. When subjects recalled "The War of the Ghosts" under instructions to remember the story as well as possible, there were relatively few errors, just as Wheeler and Roediger (1992) reported 25 years later. In addition, subjects were generally good at recognizing their own errors when asked to judge them. If Bartlett's (1932) instructions did emphasize that his subjects should tell a good story rather than try to accurately recall the story, "reconstructive memories" would be expected; if subjects are told to construct a story, they will. However, they may well not confuse this process with remembering if they were asked to make such a judgment. We report some observations below that bear on this issue.

In the modern era, the study of reconstructive memory has employed different techniques from Bartlett's (1932) method of repeated reproduction. Perhaps the most widely used is the so-called misinformation paradigm pioneered by Elizabeth Loftus and now widely studied (e.g., Loftus & Palmer, 1974; Loftus, 1979; Loftus, 1991). This paradigm capitalizes on a form of retroactive interference of the sort obtained in the A–B, A–D paradigm, in which subjects are taught two different responses to the same stimulus situation. Not surprisingly, people become confused about how to respond in Situation A if they have learned conflicting responses. If subjects are told to produce the response that they originally learned (B), but instead they produce D by mistake, they have wrongly reconstructed the original event because of the retroactive interference created by the interpolated learning.

In the standard form of the misinformation paradigm introduced by Loftus, subjects witness a series of events in which some critical items are embedded. For example, they may see a wrench. Later, subjects in an experimental condition read a narrative in which the suggestion is made that the tool in the original slide sequence was a hammer. Control subjects read the same passage except that the misinformation about a hammer appearing is not included (a neutral word such as *tool* is used). Later subjects are given a test in which they are asked to recognize which item appeared in the original slide sequence, *wrench* or *hammer*. Subjects in the experimental (misinformation) condition erroneously pick *hammer* much more often than control subjects, demonstrating the misinformation effect (or retroactive interference). Loftus (1979) interprets the results as indicating that subjects' memories are altered by the misinformation so that, at test, they believe that their recoded version of the memory is the actual event they saw. This interpretation is akin to the notion that the original information is unlearned and then replaced by the new information, one of the two factors in classic interference theory (Melton & Irwin, 1940).

McCloskey and Zaragoza (1985) have argued that Loftus' standard paradigm is not the appropriate one to determine whether subjects' memories of the original event (the appearance of the wrench, in the above example) has been altered. They suggested that a modified recognition test, in which subjects are given a choice between the original item (*wrench*) and a new exemplar from the same general category (say, *screwdriver*), is a more appropriate test of whether the misinformation reduced accessibility to the original target item. In a series of experiments McCloskey and Zaragoza (1985) found that subjects in the experimental (misinformation) and control conditions performed about equally well on the modified recognition test (see, too, Zaragoza & Koshmider, 1989; Zaragoza, McCloskey & Jamis, 1987). They interpreted this outcome as indicating that the misinformation produced no alteration in the representation of the original event. The standard effect, they argued, was due to response competition when subjects were given two plausible competing responses that were both familiar. Of course, response competition is the second major factor in classic two-factor interference theory, the one that later caused so much debate on how to eliminate it from measures of retention (e.g., Barnes & Underwood, 1959).

In more recent experiments Loftus (1991) and others (e.g., Ceci, Ross & Toglia, 1987) have found the misinformation effect even on the modified recognition test, but its magnitude has been quite small relative to the outcomes on the standard recognition test employed by Loftus and others. Typically, subjects are only 5–6% worse on the modified test in the experimental condition than in the control condition, when the effect is obtained at all. In some sense, failing to find the misinformation effect on recognition tests is not too surprising, because in an earlier era researchers also had trouble finding retroactive interference in the standard A–B, A–D paradigm on recognition tests (e.g., Postman & Stark, 1969). Curiously, there are relatively few reports in which recall tests are used in the misinformation paradigm, although both prior research in the interference tradition and considerations of external validity would seem to argue that such tests should be preferred. The preference on the latter grounds is that witnesses to crimes are frequently asked to recall the information, in response either to open-ended questions with general contextual cues ("Tell me what happened to you") akin to free recall, or to specific questions, as in cued recall procedures. Comfortingly, some experiments that have used recall procedures do tend to show misinformation effect (e.g., Lindsay, 1990).

The next experiments we report here can be thought of as a new way of studying reconstructive memory that contains features of both Bartlett's (1932) and Loftus' (1979) procedures, using recall tests. Bartlett's subjects in some sense provide their own misinformation because (he argued) on later recall attempts they were recalling their own prior recollections into which errors had been introduced. Loftus gained experimental control over the misinformation by planting the conflicting information in a narrative read after the original events were seen. However, misleading information from someone else may not pose as potent a source of interference as that generated by oneself. We have developed a technique in which we ensure that subjects are exposed to misleading information about recently experienced events and that they produce this information themselves. We can then examine whether this misinformation harms memory for the original events on later tests. The experiments in which we employed this technique were originally devised for a different purpose, so first we provide the relevant background.

Roediger and Payne (1985) were interested in the question of why some researchers routinely found hypermnesia for words (e.g., Roediger & Thorpe, 1978; Roediger et al., 1982) and others did not (e.g., Erdelyi & Becker, 1974; Erdelyi & Kleinbard, 1978), even with comparably short intervals between tests. One difference between experiments conducted in the different laboratories was that Erdelyi and his colleagues used forced-recall procedures whereas Roediger and his colleagues used free recall, with a warning against guessing. (Because intrusion rates did not increase over tests, they assumed that increased guessing was not a problem.) Roediger and Payne (1985) performed the straightforward experiment to find out whether the differences in the recall test led to the discrepant findings. Subjects studied a list of 70 words and then received three tests under one of three instructional conditions. Free-recall subjects were asked to recall the material as well as possible and were warned against guessing; forced-recall subjects were told to recall as many items as possible and were told that, before the test period was over, they needed to fill at least 50 spaces on their response sheets, guessing when necessary. A third group of subjects were given what Bousfield and Rosner (1970) called "uninhibited" recall instructions: They were told to recall the information as well as possible, but to hold nothing back and to produce every response that occurred to them. (Recall was not to be inhibited by withholding responses for any reason. The instruction is essentially one to free associate during recall.)

Roediger and Payne's (1985) basic results are given in Table III. Briefly, the type of instruction had no effect on the amount of hypermnesia obtained, and reliable improvements were obtained in all three conditions. Thus they did not solve the puzzle that had been the reason for the experiment—to explain why some researchers found hypermnesia for words and others did not. However, they noted that the results posed a more interesting puzzle for students of learning and memory: why huge variations in recall criteria had no effect on the amount recalled. An assumption ingrained in our theories of remembering is that guessing should produce benefits in performance, even if such benefits would not reflect true remembering but rather chance hits due to guessing (e.g., Klatzky & Erdelyi, 1985). However, Roediger and Payne's (1985) results do not show this: Response criteria were manipulated by almost a factor of 10 (2.5 intrusions in free recall and 23.8 in forced recall), and yet the number of items correctly produced did not vary (recall was actually 0.4 items worse for forced-recall subjects, though this slight difference was not significant). Apparently the assumption—implicit in most theories but explicit in certain versions of generate/recognize theories (e.g., Kintsch, 1970)—that subjects recall so little under free-recall conditions because they adopt a strict criterion for responding and therefore do not produce some correct responses that they generate, is wrong. If subjects are encouraged to produce every item they think of (the uninhibited-recall

TABLE III

Mean Recall, Intrusions, and Hypermnesia for Three Types of Test[a]

Type of recall test	Test			Hypermnesia $T_3 - T_1$	Mean recall[b]	Mean intrusions
	1	2	3			
Free	25.1	26.6	28.2	3.1	26.6	2.5
Uninhibited	24.3	26.4	28.4	4.1	26.4	9.6
Forced	25.1	26.0	27.4	2.3	26.2	23.8
Mean	24.8	26.3	28.0	3.2	26.4	

[a] Data are from Roediger and Payne (1985) and are reprinted from *Memory & Cognition, 13*, pp. 1–7, by permission of the Psychonomic Society, Inc.

[b] Means are averaged across the three tests.

condition) or are even forced to write reponses that are guesses (the forced-recall condition), they produce no more correct targets than under free-recall conditions.

Of course, there must be limits to the conclusion that guessing does not affect recall. Imagine that subjects are presented with the names of six of the months of the year tachistoscopically, so that they cannot be perceived very well. One group of subjects now engages in forced recall (being instructed to respond with 12 month names), whereas the other group is tested by free recall, with the customary warning against guessing. It would hardly be a surprise that the forced-recall group "recalled" correctly more presented months than the free-recall group. (Of course, the greater number of hits would be offset by more intrusions, too, so memory for the six presented months might be equal in the two conditions if an appropriate correction for guessing were applied to the data). In short, if subjects are given a constrained or guessable set of material, guessing is likely to help correct responding, but at the expense of many more errors, so that some correction must be used to try to estimate accurate recall.

Roediger and Payne (1985) used lists of more or less random words that would be difficult to guess and showed that instructions to guess did not benefit raw recall hit rates, even without worrying about corrections for guessing. Erdelyi, Finks, and Feigen-Pfau (1989) compared free and forced recall for a set of pictures and found that forced-recall subjects showed a small benefit relative to free-recall subjects, but at the expense of more intrusions. However, picture lists tend to be categorized lists (some animals, some plants, some toys, etc.) and so may be more guessable, a result that, in fact, Erdelyi et al. (1989) showed. Although overall responding was greater for the forced-recall condition than for the free-recall condition, if performance were somehow corrected for guessing, then the difference might evaporate, as pointed out by Roediger, Srinivas and Waddill (1989).

This concern with recall criteria led us to the current experiments, although now they seem more interesting from the perspective of the reconstructive approach to memory, as a new way of studying the interfering effects of misinformation supplied by the subjects themselves. In the forced-recall procedure subjects are told to try to recall as many target items as possible, but to guess to fill up the preset number of required responses before the recall period is over. We have found that subjects do not like to comply with the request for forced recall, because they know they are engaged in sheer guessing toward the end of the recall period. However, our interest in forced recall for present purposes is how this procedure will affect subjects' memories when they are tested later. If subjects study a set of material and then engage in either forced recall or free recall, we know that (1) the two groups will produce about the same number of target items, and (2) the forced-recall group will produce many more intrusions than the free-recall group. The question of present interest is what will happen when these two groups are asked to judge the accuracy of their responses. Will forced-recall subjects falsely recognize some of their confabulated responses as having occurred in the list? Will this tendency increase over repeated tests? That is, will subjects who took a forced-recall test initially later show poor retention for the original list because they supplied their own misinformation in the form of the intrusions generated on the first test? Subjects' own erroneous responses, their confabulations in attempting to recall the material, may provide a potent source of interference relative to the free-recall conditions where intrusions are rare. If so, then the phenomenon might be a workable addition to our techniques for studying reconstructive aspects of remembering, blending a strength of Bartlett's (1932) approach of having subjects be misled by their own prior recalls while still gaining some control over the nature of the misleading information, as in Loftus (e.g., 1979, 1991).

We describe here one experiment, in a series to be reported in full elsewhere (Roediger, Challis & Wheeler, in preparation), that used this paradigm. Subjects in this experiment studied 60 pictures in the context of a story, as in the Wheeler and Roediger (1992) experiment described above (although these pictures and the story were different). This story was 805 words long and revolved about a central character, "Sam the Alligator." The story had a plot but was somewhat eclectic, with an unpredictable theme, to miminize guessing from a stereotyped script (such as a visit to the zoo). Subjects were told that they would hear a story and would see pictures representing objects in the story. Their task was to remember as many of these objects as possible for a later test. A slide representing each picture was presented while the name of the object was mentioned in the story. During some of the time, when no critical objects were being mentioned in the story, the screen was blank. The presentation of the story and pictures lasted about 6 min.

After the presentation, half the subjects were dismissed from the experiment with instructions to report back the following week. The other half of the subjects took a test, either a free-recall test with a warning against guessing, or a forced-recall test. The instructions for this latter test said that subjects should try to recall as many items (names of the pictures) as possible, but that they should produce 60 responses before the 7-min recall period ended. They were told that they could produce more than 60 responses or guesses if they wanted to. A week later all subjects returned to the laboratory; half now took a free-recall test and half a forced-recall test. Subjects who had taken an immediate test received the same type of test a week later. Therefore, the experiment employed four between-subjects test conditions: One group received a free-recall test both immediately after study and after a week delay; the second group received forced-recall tests at both times; and two other groups received only delayed tests, either free recall or forced recall. The contrast between the groups taking two tests and those taking a single delayed test permits examination of the effects of the immediate test on a delayed test.

A final important detail of the procedure is that subjects were required, after taking each test, to go back and to rate each item they had produced on a 1–6 scale in terms of their confidence that it had appeared in the original list of pictures. Ratings of 4, 5, or 6 represented increasing levels of confidence that the items had appeared in the original set of pictures; ratings of 3, 2, or 1 represented increasing confidence that the item was new and had not appeared in the list. Therefore, a response of 1 indicated that subjects were certain that the response was new, and a rating of 6 indicated that subjects were certain the item was from the original set of pictures they had seen.

Consider first the immediate-recall results under free- and forced-recall conditions, shown in Table IV. The number of target items correctly produced is about the same in the two conditions, 35.9 and 35.6 produced, despite the large difference in the number of intrusions (0.9 and 25.9). These results replicate those of Roediger and Payne (1985) in showing that a huge variation in recall criterion has no effect on the number of responses correctly produced. However, these results go beyond those, because subjects were asked to rate each produced word on a 6-point confidence scale as to whether they believed it was from the list. Ratings of 4, 5, or 6 indicated that subjects judged the produced item as from the list. As can be seen from Table IV, subjects in the free-recall condition judged that virtu-

TABLE IV

NUMBER OF TARGET ITEMS PRODUCED AND RECOGNIZED, AND THE NUMBER OF INTRUSIONS AND THOSE FALSELY RECOGNIZED, IN THE IMMEDIATE TEST CONDITIONS[a]

Type of recall test	Targets produced	Targets "recognized"[b]	Intrusions produced	Intrusions "recognized"[b]
Free	35.9	35.6	0.9	0.8
Forced	35.6	32.8	25.9	5.0

[a] Data are from Roediger, Challis, and Wheeler (in preparation).
[b] Subjects gave a rating of 4, 5, or 6 on the recognition test.

ally all their produced items were from the list (the items received ratings of 4 or higher). However, this was not the case for subjects who engaged in forced recall. They produced 2.8 items that they failed to recognize as studied; apparently, they thought that these were guesses they had generated in complying with the experimenter's request to produce a large number of responses. In addition, they falsely recognized 5.0 of the 25.9 erroneous responses as having actually occurred in the list. Thus, unlike free recall, the forced-recall procedure leads subjects into two types of errors: recognition failure of recallable words and erroneous recognition as old of items that were not studied but that were generated on the tests.[3] The requirement for subjects to confabulate a large set of responses creates confusion or a reality-monitoring problem (Johnson & Raye, 1981) on the test. In complying with the forced-recall instruction, subjects generate their own misinformation (or set of interfering responses). If these responses create interference as to which items occurred in the set of studied pictures on the immediate test, just after the responses have been produced, the interference is likely to be even more potent after a delay.

The results in Table V, showing performance on the delayed test, indicate this to be the case for at least one type of error. First, note that on the delayed free-recall tests there is no strong evidence of the two sorts of confusion just defined, although some errors are apparent. Items free recalled by subjects (whether target items or the few intrusions) are generally judged to be from the list. This pattern occurs both for subjects who received an initial test a week earlier and for those who did not. However, data from both of the forced-recall test conditions show evidence of great confusion; both types of errors seen in forced recall on the immediate test appear on the delayed test. For example, subjects in both the forced-recall conditions produced about five more items actually from the target list than they recognized, producing 30.9 and 22.4 and recognizing 25.9 and 17.3, respectively. Thus they showed heightened recognition failure of recallable words relative to the free-recall test conditions. Similarly, forced-recall subjects frequently falsely recognized their generated responses that were not from the set of pictures as actual list members. Subjects who had a prior test falsely recognized 7.6, or 20%, of their incorrect responses as "old"; those who had not had a prior test averaged 12.1, or 28% of the generated (incorrect) responses as this sort of error.

---

[3] We are obviously assuming that it is appropriate to analyze absolute numbers of errors in the two conditions. A different set of conclusions would emerge if proportions were calculated.

TABLE V

NUMBER OF TARGET ITEMS PRODUCED AND RECOGNIZED, AND
THE NUMBER OF INTRUSIONS AND THOSE FALSELY
RECOGNIZED IN THE DELAYED TEST CONDITIONS[a]

Type of recall test	Targets produced	Targets "recognized"[b]	Intrusions produced	Intrusions "recognized"[b]
Free				
Prior test	29.6	29.5	2.1	1.9
No prior test	15.4	14.3	3.6	2.5
Forced				
Prior test	30.9	25.9	38.6	7.6
No prior test	22.4	17.3	43.9	12.1

[a] Data are from Roediger, Challis, and Wheeler (in preparation).
[b] Subjects gave a rating of 4, 5, or 6 on the recognition test.

We find these figures interesting on two counts. First, the absolute number of these false recognitions seems quite high. Subjects were required to produce these interfering responses, yet tended to judge over 20% as "memories" of external happenings. To reiterate, having subjects generate their own responses constitutes a potent source of interference. Second, we find it interesting that the interference on the delayed test was no greater for subjects who were tested a week earlier than for those who took a single test after a week. A plausible scenario is that subjects who engaged in forced recall on the first test would be especially prone to interference a week later, and to confuse the studied pictures with their own responses generated soon after. The fact that both groups' performances on the delayed test were so similar suggests that processes operating during forced recall create the false recognitions, rather than that they carry over from a prior test. One other feature of the data in Table V is worth noting, even though it does not play a role in our present discussion: In both free and forced recall, the positive effect of taking a prior test was observed on delayed-recall performance, in terms of both the total number of correct responses produced and their correct recognition. Thus we see the power of taking a test on later retention yet again, as in much earlier work (Spitzer, 1939; Thompson et al., 1978; Wheeler & Roediger, 1992).

The main point to be gleaned from the experiment just described is that subjects' own responses provide a potent source of interference. The forced recall procedure requires subjects to confabulate; later they confuse their confabulations with items presented in the target set. One type of error is generating items that were actually in the target set, but failing to recognize them. Production of these items may constitute a type of priming akin to that observed in implicit memory studies where subjects are asked to free associate to a cue (e.g., Srinivas & Roediger, 1990); the failure to recognize such generated responses as members of the target set qualifies as an instance of the recognition failure of recallable (or at least producible) words (e.g., Watkins & Tulving, 1975). The second sort of error is the one more commonly expected in studies of reconstructive memory: Subjects generate and then recognize as old (or remember as their own experiences) events that never happened in the target set but that were instead produced as confabulations. If numerous forced recalls were given, this tendency might be expected to increase, as generated items became more familiar over time.[4] This procedure of repeated recall accompanied by con-fabulation, which is induced by the forced-recall technique, should prove useful in future studies of reconstructive memory. As previously remarked, it seems to blend the best aspects of Bartlett's repeated-reproduction procedure (of having subjects generate their own interfering responses) with Loftus's control over the interfering events, at least to some degree.

One might complain that the experiment described here is artificial in several ways, and indeed it is. People rarely engage in forced recall in the sense of being required to generate material they believe to be erroneous. However, we think that the experiment just described (the basic findings of which have been replicated; see Roediger et al., in preparation) actually captures the nature of reconstructive memory quite well. When people see a complex event such as a crime and then try to recall it later, they probably respond to tacit demands from others to go beyond the information that they can accurately retrieve and to tell a plausible story, just as our subjects are asked to respond with plausible candidates for the pictures in the set. Once people respond with plausible guesses, they may later recall their guesses as actual occurrences. These self-generated guesses may provide a more potent source of misinformation or interference than would information planted in a narrative, as in the standard misinforma-toin paradigm. If Gauld and Stephenson's (1967) analysis of Bartlett's (1932) experiments is correct and Bartlett's subjects were instructed to create plausible renderings (rather than accurate memories) of "The War of the Ghosts," then his claims of massive reconstruction and erroneous recall are more plausible. Indeed, we would predict that after creating

---

[4] Of course, as noted, there was no greater tendency for false recognitions for forced-recall subjects on a second test than on a first test in this experiment. We suspect that the tendency to falsely recognize generated events will increase when they are generated many times, although this is an empirical question. Note that the difference in Table V is in the opposite direction from that predicted.

plausible stories related to the general theme, subjects would be unable, even if they tried, to accurately recall the story. Just as in our experiments with forced recall, subjects would have trouble sorting out fact from fiction after repeated retellings of plausible stories related to the target story. That such repeated callings to mind of invented "facts" can establish the inventions as memories might be illustrated in Jean Piaget's famous anecdote of his vivid memory of being narrowly saved from a kidnapping when he was a young child, which later turned out to be a fabrication of his nurse at the time. He credited the false memory to the family's repeated recollections of the event during his childhood, which he then projected into the past as an actual memory. Having subjects repeatedly tell themselves such erroneous information seems a natural way to study the reconstructive aspects of remembering. We plan to use this method in future investigations of this topic.

We end this section with a few methodological points. First, to reiterate the most obvious, we believe that the method of having subjects confabulate plausible candidates for recall on a test and then examining whether these creations are falsely recognized, and whether they will appear in later reconstructions of events, to be a good method to study the reconstructive aspects of remembering. The emphasis on recall helps broaden the arsenal of techniques used to study reconstructive aspects of memory. Various recognition procedures have been standard in the literature, but it has always been notoriously difficult to observe retroactive interference with certain recognition procedures (McCloskey & Zaragoza, 1985; Postman & Stark, 1969; Loftus, 1991).

A second implication of these results is somewhat less obvious yet just as clear: the forced recall procedure introduced by Erdelyi and Becker (1974) is flawed in regard to accurately estimating what is remembered. This is especially true on a delayed test, as the data in Table V show, but the same confusions observed there occur in lesser degree even on an immediate test (see Table IV). Forced recall was introduced as a praiseworthy way to control possible response-criterion effects by requiring subjects to produce the same number of responses across tests. The procedure does this, but the production of a correct response does not indicate that it is a product of conscious recollection. Responding is not remembering. On implicit memory tests even amnesic patients may respond with a recently studied item, but they do not remember the experience of having studied the item before (e.g., Graf, Squire, & Mandler, 1984). Jacoby (in press) points out that responding even on ostensibly explicit-memory tests, those involving conscious recollection, may involve correct response production through some automatic process (*priming,* in the jargon of implicit-memory researchers; see Roediger, 1990;

Schacter, 1987), and not through conscious recollection. Apparently, forced recall produces considerable responding of this sort relative to free recall, as the data in Tables IV and V reveal. Items are often produced that are not recognized as being from the list.

The objections to using forced recall are similar to those raised against using hypnosis to aid memory retrieval (e.g., Smith, 1983). Witnesses who are hypnotized and who then attempt to retrieve events often confabulate during their recall attempts, and then, when testifying later, may confuse the events created under hypnosis with real events. Like hypnosis, forced recall forces people to confabulate. Several reports have shown that highly hypnotizable subjects are likely to become increasingly confident that their errors represent true memories across repeated recall tests (Nogrady, McConkey, & Perry, 1985; Whitehouse, Dinges, E. C. Orne, & M. T. Orne, 1988). The experiment just reported shows that it is not necessary to have highly hypnotizable subjects or to use hypnosis to produce false recognitions of confabulated responses: The forced-recall procedure creates a similar effect. Poole and White (1991) reported similar results with repeated questioning. When asked about an event of which they had been given little information, subjects sometimes speculated about the correct answer. On a later test, their answers to the question became more certain.

The practical implication is that we should reexamine prior studies that use forced recall so that we can determine whether effects observed are based on remembering or on response production that combines both remembering and more automatic production of responses. Many basic findings obtained with forced recall, such as hypermnesia, seem quite secure, because they have been obtained in free-recall procedures during which subjects are more purely engaged in conscious recollection (at least judging by the recognition responses in Tables IV and V). However, forced recall experiments such as those of Wheeler and Roediger (1992) described above may deserve further scrutiny, but we suspect that the main conclusions are secure. If anything, correcting response production in forced recall for items actually remembered (recognized) would likely reveal greater forgetting over the week retention interval than that shown now in Table I, whereas the hypermnesia with short intervals between tests would remain intact (see the data in Table III from Roediger & Payne, 1985).

In the forced-recall procedure subjects produce responses that may be in the target set but that may not actually be remembered, and they may remember items that they produce as being from the target set when in fact they are not. In the Roediger et al. (in preparation) experiments, we used the procedure of having subjects give recognition-confidence ratings for their produced responses to ascertain their status as either products of conscious recollection or products of some more automatic process. However, subjects are capable of providing more detailed judgments than confidence ratings. In the next section we describe experiments in which subjects try to apportion their correct responses in memory tests on more qualitative bases.

IV.   Remembering and Knowing Past Events

In 1970 Tulving and Madigan remarked that theories and models of memory had neglected to incorporate "one of the truly unique characteristics of human memory: its knowledge of its own knowledge" (p. 477). The situation in the intervening 23 years has evidenced a remarkable change in this state of affairs, with the advance in the study of metamemory (see Nelson's, 1992, excellent collection of readings in this area). Investigators have pursued the study of the feeling of knowing (e.g., Nelson, 1984; Schacter, 1983), reality monitoring (Johnson & Raye, 1981), and the overconfidence of judgments (e.g., Fischhoff, 1975). In each case researchers make use of subjects' abilities (or, sometimes, inabilities) to evaluate the status of their own knowledge.

Tulving (1985) proposed that people may be able to differentiate their past experience in two ways, or that there are two ways of accessing knowledge about the personal past. When we say we remember past events, we usually mean that we can actually recollect their occurrence—we can remember vivid details, we can (in some sense) reexperience the events as we remember them. However, Tulving noted that our memories for past events can also be more impersonal: We can know, with certainty, that something happened to us but not be able to recall the event in the sense just described. Tulving (1985) reported a demonstration experiment that showed that subjects could reliably make "Remember" and "Know" judgments about their experiences; further, the more powerful the retrieval cues given during a test, the greater the preponderance of Know judgments relative to Remember judgments do subjects provide. More recently, Gardiner and his colleagues (1988; Gardiner & Java, 1990, 1993) have used the Remember/Know paradigm to separate different bases of responding in recognition memory.

Several researchers have proposed that recognition may have two separate bases for positive responses. Mandler (1979, 1980) proposed a distinction between integration of an experience as a perceptual unit (intra-item integration) and elaboration on the unit by relating it to other knowledge. These different encoding processes give rise to two bases for recognition:

familiarity-based responding (based on intraitem integration) and retrieval (based on elaborative processing). Jacoby (1983a, b; Jacoby & Dallas, 1981) proposed a similar distinction between responding on the basis of perceptual fluency (similar to familiarity in Mandler's proposal) or by conscious recollection (see Jacoby, 1991). Further, Jacoby (1983b) proposed that the fluency-based responding should be affected by data-driven variables, or those that affect basic perceptual processing (such as modality of presentation), whereas manipulation of meaning (or conceptual manipulations) affect conscious recollection. There is considerable evidence in agreement with recognition memory having two bases, although there is contrary evidence in the literature, too (Watkins & Gibson, 1988).

The distinction between experiences that are remembered and those that are known to have occurred but are not remembered maps naturally onto this distiction between two bases of responding in recognition. Briefly, Remember judgments should reflect elaborative or conceptual processing, whereas Know judgments would indicate responding on the basis of familiarity or perceptual fluency. Evidence provided by Gardiner (1988) and Gardiner and Java (1990) generally agrees with this proposal, although one problem will be noted below. The general paradigm they have used involves presenting subjects with words under various study conditions known to affect recognition memory and then giving subjects a recognition-memory test in which, for each item deemed "old" or previously studied, subjects are required to judge whether they remember the occurrence of the word in the list or rather know that it was there on some other basis. Subjects are told to judge an item as remembered if they can recollect its actual presentation in the list (e.g., they can recollect some feature of the context, or their own reaction). If they are sure it was in the list, but cannot remember its actual occurrence, then they are to provide a Know response. Although this distinction seems difficult, with proper instructions subjects provide sensible and reliable judgments. In most of Gardiner's experiments, variables that strongly affect recognition are shown to have their basis in Remember responses. That is, when the overall recognition responses are decomposed into the two components, the independent variable is shown to affect the Remember responses but to leave Know responses unaffected. This result is in accord with the idea that recognition largely reflects conscious recollection, but it also can be partly driven by perceptual fluency or familiarity that is reflected in Know responses.

One worry that emerges from the pattern of results described above is that Know responses are rather insensitive; perhaps subjects use this category only when they have low confidence that an event occurred. Gardiner and Java (1993) have argued that Remember and Know judgments are not to be equated with high- and low-confidence recognition judgments, respectively. The most compelling sort of evidence to document the claim that these judgments reflect distinct means of knowing the personal past is to show that a variable has opposite effects on the two judgments (rather than affecting one but not the other). Gardiner and Java (1990) accomplished this in one experiment by having subjects study words and nonwords and then receive a recognition memory test on old and new words and nonwords. Not surprisingly, words were recognized better than nonwords overall. However, when responding was decomposed into its components, words received more Remember responses than did nonwords, but nonwords received more Know responses than did words.

The experiments we report here are a selection from those that Rajaram (1990, 1993) reported as part of her PhD thesis. The general goal of the dissertation was to examine further factors that might affect Remember and Know judgments differently; the more specific goal was to investigate Gardiner's (1988) claim that Remember judgments are more affected by conceptual factors and that Know judgments are more driven by perceptual factors. Rajaram (1993) reasoned that factors affecting perceptual (or data-driven) implicit-memory tests should also affect Know responses. One such variable that greatly affects verbal implicit-memory tests such as word-fragment completion and word-stem completion is the symbolic form in which items are studied (i.e., items are given as words or pictures). When subjects study mixed lists of words and pictures, pictures are better recalled (e.g., Paivio, Rogers & Smythe, 1968) and better recognized (Madigan, 1983) than are words, even when the mode of responding is verbal (i.e., with subjects recalling words—the names of the pictures—or recognizing the picture names). This picture-superiority effect is generally credited to conceptual factors, either dual coding of pictures (e.g., Paivio, 1986) or greater analysis of pictures' meaning (Nelson, 1979). On the other hand, words produce much more priming than do pictures on verbal implicit-memory tests such as word-fragment completion, word-stem completion, and perceptual identification (e.g., Weldon & Roediger, 1987; Rajaram & Roediger, in press).

Given these considerations, Rajaram (1993) reasoned that the symbolic format variable might produce opposite effects on Remember and Know judgments. Specifically, overall recognition should be greater for pictures than for words (replicating Madigan, 1983, and others), but when recognition responses were decomposed into Remember and Know components, opposite effects would appear. Specifically, Remember judgments should be greater for pictures than for words, but Know judgments (driven by perceptual fluency) should be greater for words than for pictures.

Subjects studied 60 items in the first phase of Rajaram's (1993) Experiment 2, half as words and half as pictures, at the rate of 5 sec per item. After studying the list, subjects solved unrelated word fragments for 15 min prior to the test. During the testing phase subjects were given 120 words, half studied (30 as pictures, 30 as words) and half not studied. (Items were counterbalanced across studied and nonstudied conditions and, within studied conditions, across presentation as pictures or words.) The test words were given in a booklet, and subjects were instructed to decide if each item had been studied in the prior list as either a word or a picture, placing a "Y" for *yes* or an "N" for *no* next to each item. Further, if subjects placed a Y next to the item, signaling its recognition, they were further instructed to write an "R" for Remember or a "K" for Know next to the other response. The instructions for this response were modeled closely after those of Gardiner (1988). Instructions are critical in making subjects understand the distinction and those used in the experiments described here are presented in an appendix of Rajaram (1993). In brief, subjects were told to judge the recognized item as Remembered when they could recall the actual experience of its presentation. On the other hand, Know responses should be made:

> when you recognize that the word was in the study list but you cannot consciously recollect anything about its actual occurrence, or what happened or what was experienced at the time of its occurrence. In other words, write "K" (for "know") when you are certain of recognizing the words but these words fail to evoke any conscious recollection from the study list. (p. 102)

Rajaram's (1993, Experiment 2) results are presented in Table VI, where it can be seen that a picture-superiority effect occurred in recognition: The hit rate for pictures was .90 and for words was .69, with a .09 false alarm rate.[5] However, when the overall hit rate was decomposed into Remember and Know responses, then opposing patterns occurred. Remember responses in recognizing pictures greatly exceeded those in recognizing words, .81 to .51, consistent with the idea that the picture-superiority effect is conceptual in nature and therefore shows up in Remember responses. On the other hand, Know responses were greater following recognition of words (.18) than of pictures (.09), consistent with the notion that Know responses are driven by the same sort of perceptual operations that produce priming on perceptual implicit-memory tests. Interestingly,

---

[5] Subjects were actually recognizing words, so the match in physical features between study and test tokens was greater when subjects studied words than when they studied pictures. Despite this, pictures were recognized better than words, as reported by many others (e.g., Madigan, 1983).

TABLE VI

PROPORTIONS OF HITS AND FALSE
ALARMS FOR REMEMBER AND KNOW
JUDGMENTS FROM RAJARAM'S
EXPERIMENT 2[a]

	Target items		
	Pictures	Words	Lures
Recognition "Yes"	.90	.69	.09
Remember	.81	.51	.01
Know	.09	.18	.08

[a] Data are from Rajaram (1993), Experiment 2, and are reprinted from *Memory & Cognition, 21*, pp. 89–102, by permission of the Psychonomic Society.

false alarms in recognition were almost entirely Know responses; the subjects felt that the item was familiar, but could not remember its occurrence in the list because it had not occurred. Rajaram's data shown in Table VI strongly implicate Remember and Know judgments as independent components of recognition that are affected by different factors, in agreement with Gardiner's (1988) hypothesis.

The research reviewed thus far has revealed two patterns of dissociation between Remember and Know responses. Variables either affect Remember judgments and not Know judgments, or variables have opposite effects on the two types of responses, as in the data of Table VI. If the two bases of responding are independent, then it should be possible to find the remaining type of interaction: A variable that would affect Know responses but not Remember responses. Rajaram (1993) sought to find this sort of dissociation in a further experiment (Experiment 3). The trick was to increase the perceptual fluency of the target word without affecting the ability to recollect it consciously.

Rajaram (1993) used the masked repetition paradigm (Forster, 1985) in order to enhance perceptual fluency of the target. In this paradigm, a target item is preceded by its own masked presentation, so during a test trial subjects receive a forward mask (a series of ampersands), a very brief exposure to the target, and then the target is presented until the response is made. Subjects are unable to see the first presentation of the target, but this presentation is presumed to enhance the perceptual fluency of the target when it is presented clearly. Several previous experiments have shown that when a target is immediately preceded by its own masked presentation in the course of a recognition memory experiment, subjects produce more hits, relative to the case in which an unrelated word is the masked prime (Forster, 1985; Jacoby & Whitehouse, 1989; Rajaram & Neely, 1992). Jacoby and Whitehouse (1989) also reported that masked repetition increased the false-alarm rate, which would be expected if the prime increased perceptual fluency and this fluency made recognition more likely. Rajaram (1993) reasoned that masked repetitions should therefore affect Know responses (believed to be driven by perceptual operations) and not Remember responses.

In Rajaram's (1993) Experiment 3, subjects studied words in a list and then took a recognition test in which studied and nonstudied words were intermingled. Subjects were instructed to write Y or N to signal their recogniton of items as old or new and, in the case of items receiving a Y, to respond with Remember and Know judgments. Half the items were tested in the masked-repetition condition where the target was briefly preceded by its own copy; half were tested with an unrelated masked item preceding the target. The results are shown in Table VII. Masked repetition of targets increased both the hit rate for targets and the false-alarm rate for lures, by 7% and 5%, respectively. When Rajaram decomposed subjects' overall responding into Remember and Know components, the masked repetition variable enhanced the Know responses for both targets and lures and did not affect Remember responses. Thus, she had found the type of interaction missing from the literature: a variable that affected Know responses and not Remember responses. Further, the effect of masked repetition was predicted to affect only Know responding on the basis of Gardiner's (1988) hypothesis that perceptual operations affect such responses. In another experiment, Rajaram (1993, Experiment 4) showed that masked-repetition

TABLE VII

PROPORTIONS OF HITS AND FALSE ALARMS FOR REMEMBER AND KNOW JUDGMENTS FROM RAJARAM'S EXPERIMENT 3[a]

	Targets		Lures	
	Masked repetition	Unrelated primes	Masked repetition	Unrelated primes
Recognition "Yes"	.67	.60	.23	.18
Remember	.43	.42	.05	.05
Know	.24	.18	.18	.13

[a] Data are from Rajaram (1993), Experiment 3, and are reprinted from *Memory & Cognition, 21,* pp. 89–102, by permission of the Psychonomic Society.

priming did not have the same effect on confidence judgments as on Remember and Know judgments, further supporting the idea that Know responses are not simply low-confidence recognition responses.

The evidence we have just reviewed strongly supports the idea that Know responses are driven by the same factors that are responsible for perceptual priming. However, at least one source of evidence contradicts this idea. Rajaram (1993, Experiment 1) manipulated the modality of presentation of words (auditory or visual) and then later gave subjects a recognition test in which they were required to make Remember and Know judgments for items judged "old" in recognition. Modality of presentation consistently produces large differences in priming on perceptual implicit-memory tests (e.g., Blaxton, 1989; Rajaram & Roediger, in press), so the expectation is that modality should similarly affect recognition responses and that the difference should be localized in the Know component rather than the Remember component. However, Rajaram's (1993) results failed to verify this prediction because she found that modality had no effect on overall recognition and did not differentially affect either Remember or Know judgments. Gardiner and Java (1993) reported the same null finding. At this writing it is unclear how to reconcile the null results of modality with the contrasting results from manipulations of symbolic form (picture or word) and other variables. The preponderance of the evidence supports the idea that Know responses are driven by the same perceptual factors that produce priming on perceptual implicit-memory tests, but the clear failure of manipulations of modality to produce the expected results indicates that the story must be more complicated than the rather straightforward account provided here. In addition, the general failure of modality to affect recognition responses seems problematic for theories such as Mandler's (1980) or Jacoby's (1983a, b), which argue that perceptual factors increase fluency of responding and hence familiarity.

Remembering and Knowing are the mental states produced by two independent means of accessing the past. Knowing seems to tap some more automatic feature of memory, perhaps akin to priming on implicit-memory tests. If this is so, then perhaps Know responses can be driven by conceptual factors as well as perceptual factors, because conceptual implicit-memory tests show robust priming in memory-impaired patients as well as in normal subjects (e.g., Graf, Squire, & Mandler, 1984; Rappold & Hashtroudi, 1991; Srinivas & Roediger, 1990). Indeed, Blaxton (in press) has used the Remember/Know technique to study the mnemonic abilities of memory-impaired patients. However, as useful as the Remember/Know technique is, bear in mind that its use omits the possibility that responding may occur that is affected by past experience but in which responses may not be recognized. In the forced recall conditions of the Roediger et al. (in preparation) experiment described earlier, subjects often produced responses that had appeared in the target list (and therefore were unlikely to have been produced at random) and yet failed to recognize the responses as list members. If responses are not recognized as old, then of course the Remember/Know technique cannot be applied.

V. Conclusions

This article has been concerned with the processes of remembering, knowing and reconstructing past events. Memory refers to all these processes, and others, but we can separate different bases and mental states in our knowledge of the past. Remembering, as used here, refers to the recollection of past events when details of these events can be retrieved; the events can be mentally reexperienced (Tulving, 1985; Gardiner, 1988). Subjects claim to have such "remembering" experiences more frequently after deep as opposed to shallow levels of processing of material, after generating rather than reading words, and following the study of pictures rather than words (Gardiner & Java, 1993; Rajaram, 1993).

Subjects can know that events happened in their past without being able to remember them. We can know that we returned to our home for a Christmas vacation a decade ago without remembering the trip. In the lab, Know responses occur more often for words than for pictures and nonwords relative to words (Rajaram, 1993; Gardiner & Java, 1990). Knowing the past, in this sense, represents an interesting challenge for theory. We know something about an episode in our lives, but the knowledge seems impersonal, like the knowledge of any fact from semantic memory, because we cannot recollect the detailed occurrences that would provide the basis for true remembering. Our knowledge of the trip home is like our knowledge that William McKinley was President of the United States; both memories refer to true occurrences, but neither carries the features—the remembrance of details, the warm feeling of reexperiencing the event—that are the signature of remembering.

Reconstruction of the events of our lives involves our weaving together episodes and facts that we remember and those that we know into a plausible story of our past. In the process we may add details that did not actually occur. We described the new method of studying reconstructive memory by having subjects engage in forced recall during a memory test. In forced recall, subjects try to remember the events as well as possible, but then must also confabulate responses. The interest centers on subjects' tendencies to recognize their confabulated responses as actual memories. We used confidence ratings to estimate their subjective experience of remembering, but it would be interesting to ask subjects on a delayed forced-recall test to provide Remember and Know responses for the information they claim to recognize as having occurred (when in fact it did not). Would subjects claim to know that the events occurred in the target set but not to be able to remember them, as they do to false alarms in recognition tests? Or would subjects exhibit a propensity to say that they actually remember the occurrence of events which, in fact, they had only produced themselves? This latter category of response would be the clearest indication of reconstructive memory: Subjects claim to remember the experiencing of an event when in fact they produced it themselves on an earlier test. The methods described here—the forced-recall technique, making Remember and Know judgments—permit a new attack on the problem of reconstructive remembering, one that is just beginning.

ACKNOWLEDGMENTS

Some of the research reported here was supported by Grants 91-0253 and F49620-92-J-0437 from the Air Force Office of Scientific Research. The authors are grateful to Brad Challis, Beth Loftus, Doug Medin, and Mary Sue Weldon for commentary on an earlier version of the article and to Ulric Neisser for helpful correspondence.

REFERENCES

Bahrick, H. P., Bahrick, P. O., & Wittlinger, R. P. (1975). Fifty years of memory for names and faces: A cross-sectional approach. *Journal of Experimental Psychology: General, 104,* 54–75.

Bahrick, H. P., & Hall, L. K. (1991). Preventive and corrective maintenance of access to knowledge. *Applied Cognitive Psychology, 5,* 1–18.

Bahrick, H. P., & Hall, L. K. (1993). Long intervals between tests can yield hypermnesia: Comments on Wheeler and Roediger. *Psychological Science, 4,* 206–207.

Ballard, P. B. (1913). Oblivescence and reminiscence. *British Journal of Psychology Monograph Supplements, 1,* 1–82.

Barnes, J. M., & Underwood, B. J. (1959). "Fate" of first-list associations in transfer theory. *Journal of Experimental Psychology, 58,* 97–105.

Bartlett, F. C. (1932). *Remembering: A study in experimental and social psychology.* Cambridge, England: Cambridge University Press.

Blaxton, T. A. (1989). Investigating dissociations among memory measures: Support for the transfer-appropriate processing framework. *Journal of Experimental Psychology: Learning, Memory, and Cognition, 15,* 657–668.

Blaxton, T. A. (in press). The role of the temporal lobes in recognizing nonverbal materials: Remembering versus knowing. *Neuropsychologia.*

Bousfield, W. A., & Rosner, S. R. (1970). Free vs. uninhibited recall. *Psychonomic Science, 20,* 75–76.

Brown, W. (1923). To what extent is memory measured by a single recall trial? *Journal of Experimental Psychology, 6,* 377–382.

Buxton, C. E. (1943). The status of research in reminiscence. *Psychological Bulletin, 40,* 313–340.

Ceci, S. J., Ross, D. F., & Toglia, M. P. (1987). Suggestibility of children's memory: Psychological implications. *Journal of Experimental Psychology: General, 116,* 38–49.

Ebbinghaus, H. (1964). *Memory: A contribution to experimental psychology.* (H. A. Ruger & C. E. Bussenius, Trans.) New York: Dover. (Original work published 1885)

Erdelyi, M. H. (1984). The recovery of unconscious (inaccessible) memories: Laboratory studies of hypermnesia. In G. H. Bower (Ed.), *The psychology of learning and motivation: Advances in research and theory* (Vol. 18, pp. 95–127). New York: Academic Press.

Erdelyi, M. H., & Becker, J. (1974). Hypermnesia for pictures: Incremental memory for pictures but not for words in multiple recall trials. *Cognitive Psychology, 6,* 159–171.

Erdelyi, M. H., Finkelstein, S., Herrell, N., Miller, B., & Thomas, J. (1976). Coding modality vs. input modality in hypermnesia: Is a rose a rose a rose? *Cognition, 4,* 311–319.

Erdelyi, M. H., Finks, J., & Feigin-Pfau, M. B. (1989). The effects of response bias on recall performance, with some observations on processing bias. *Journal of Experimental Psychology: General, 118,* 245–254.

Erdelyi, M. H., & Kleinbard, J. (1978). Has Ebbinghaus decayed with time? The growth of recall over days. *Journal of Experimental Psychology: Human Learning and Memory, 4,* 275–289.

Estes, W. K. (1960). Learning theory and the new "mental chemistry." *Psychological Review, 67,* 207–233.

Fischhoff, B. (1975). Hindsight ≠ foresight: The effect of outcome knowledge on judgment under uncertainty. *Journal of Experimental Psychology: Human Perception and Performance, 1,* 288–299.

Forster, K. I. (1985). Lexical acquisition and the modular lexicon. *Language and Cognitive Processes, 2,* 87–108.

Gardiner, J. M. (1988). Functional aspects of recollective experience. *Memory & Cognition, 16,* 309–313.

Gardiner, J. M., & Java, R. I. (1990). Recollective experience in word and nonword recognition. *Memory & Cognition, 18,* 23–30.

Gardiner, J. M., & Java, R. (1993). Recognizing and remembering. In A. Collins, S. Gathercole, & P. Morris (Eds.), *Theories of memory* (pp. 168–188). Hillsdale, NJ: Erlbaum.

Gauld, A., & Stephenson, G. M. (1967). Some experiments related to Bartlett's theory of remembering. *British Journal of Psychology, 58,* 39–49.

Glover, J. A. (1989). The testing phenomenon: Not gone but nearly forgotten. *Journal of Educational Psychology, 81,* 392–399.

Graf, P., Squire, L. R., & Mandler, G. (1984). The information that amnesic patients do not forget. *Journal of Experimental Psychology: Learning, Memory, and Cognition, 10,* 164–178.

Hastie, R., Landsman, R., & Loftus, E. F. (1978). Eyewitness testimony: The dangers of guessing. *Jurimetrics Journal, 19,* 1–8.

Hermann, D. J., Buschke, H., & Gall, M. B. (1987). Improving retrieval. *Applied Cognitive Psychology, 1,* 27–33.

Hogan, R. M., & Kintsch, W. (1971). Differential effects of study and test trials on long-term retention and recall. *Journal of Verbal Learning and Verbal Behavior, 10,* 562–567.

Izawa, C. (1971). The test trial potentiating model. *Journal of Mathematical Psychology, 8,* 200–224.

Jacoby, L. L. (1983a). Perceptual enhancement: Persistent effects of an experience. *Journal of Experimental Psychology: Learning, Memory, and Cognition, 9,* 21–38.

Jacoby, L. L. (1983b). Remembering the data: Analyzing interactive processing in reading. *Journal of Verbal Learning and Verbal Behavior, 22,* 485–508.

Jacoby, L. L. (1991). A process dissociation framework: Separating automatic and intentional uses of memory. *Journal of Memory and Language, 30,* 513–541.

Jacoby, L. L. (in press). Measuring recollection: Strategic vs. automatic influences of associative context. In C. Umilta & M. Moscovitch (Eds.), *Attention and Performance.* Vol. 15. Cambridge, MA: Bradford.

Jacoby, L. L., & Dallas, M. (1981). On the relationship between autobiographical memory and perceptual learning. *Journal of Experimental Psychology: General, 110,* 306–340.

Jacoby, L. L., Kelley, C. M., & Dywan, J. (1989). Memory attributions. In H. L. Roediger & F. I. M. Craik (Eds.), *Varieties of memory and consciousness: Essays in honour of Endel Tulving* (pp. 391–422). Hillsdale, NJ: Erlbaum.

Jacoby, L. L., & Whitehouse, K. (1989). An illusion of memory: False recognition influenced by conscious perception. *Journal of Experimental Psychology: General, 118,* 126–135.

Johnson, M. K., Bransford, J. D., & Solomon, S. K. (1973). Memory for tacit implications of sentences. *Journal of Experimental Psychology, 98,* 203–205.

Johnson, M. K., & Raye, C. L. (1981). Reality monitoring. *Psychological Review, 88,* 67–85.

Kintsch, W. (1970). *Learning, memory, and conceptual processes.* New York: Wiley.

Klatzky, R. L., & Erdelyi, M. H. (1985). The response criterion problem in tests of hypnosis and memory. *International Journal of Clinical and Experimental Hypnosis, 33,* 246–257.

Lindsay, D. S. (1990). Misleading suggestions can impair eyewitnesses' ability to remember event details. *Journal of Experimental Psychology: Learning, Memory, and Cognition, 16,* 1077–1083.

Loftus, E. F. (1979). *Eyewitness Testimony.* Cambridge, MA: Harvard University Press.

Loftus, E. F. (1991). Made in memory: Distortions in recollection after misleading information. In G. H. Bower (Ed.), *The psychology of learning and motivation.* (Vol. 27, pp. 187–215). New York: Academic Press.

Loftus, E. F., & Palmer, J. C. (1974). Reconstruction of automobile destruction: An example of the interaction between language and memory. *Journal of Verbal Learning and Verbal Behavior, 13,* 585–589.

Madigan, S. (1983). Picture memory. In J. C. Yuille (Ed.), *Imagery, memory, and cognition: Essays in honour of Allan Paivio* (pp. 65–89). Hillsdale, NJ: Erlbaum.

Mandler, G. (1979). Organization and repetition: Organization principles with special reference to rote learning. In L. Nilsson (Ed.), *Perspectives on memory research* (pp. 293–327). Hillsdale, NJ: Erlbaum.

Mandler, G. (1980). Recognizing: The judgment of previous occurrence. *Psychological Review, 87,* 252–271.

Mandler, J. M., & Johnson, N. S. (1977). Remembrance of things parsed: Story structure and recall. *Cognitive Psychology, 9,* 111–151.

McCloskey, M., & Zaragoza, M. (1985). Misleading postevent information and memory for events: Arguments and evidence against memory impairment hypotheses. *Journal of Experimental Psychology: General, 114,* 1–16.

Melton, A. W., & Irwin, J. M. (1940). The influence of degree of interpolated learning in retroactive inhibition and the overt transfer of specific responses. *American Journal of Psychology, 53,* 173–203.

Nelson, D. L. (1979). Remembering pictures and words: Appearance, significance, and name. In L. S. Cermak & F. I. M. Craik (Eds.), *Levels of processing in human memory* (pp. 45–76). Hillsdale, NJ: Erlbaum.

Nelson, T. O. (1984). A comparison of current measures of the accuracy of feeling-of-knowing predictions. *Psychological Bulletin, 95,* 109–133.

Nelson, T. O. (Ed.). (1992). *Metacognition: Core readings.* Needham Heights, MA: Allyn and Bacon.

Nogrady, H., McConkey, K. M., & Perry, C. (1985). Enhancing visual memory: Trying hypnosis, trying imagination, and trying again. *Journal of Abnormal Psychology, 94,* 195–204.

Paivio, A. (1986). *Mental representations: A dual coding approach.* New York: Oxford University Press.

Paivio, A., Rogers, T. B., & Smythe, P. C. (1968). Why are pictures easier to recall than words? *Psychonomic Science, 11,* 137–138.

Paul, I. H. (1959). Studies in remembering: The reproduction of connected and extended verbal material. *Psychological Issues, 1* (Monograph 2).

Payne, D. G. (1987). Hypermnesia and reminiscence in recall: A historical and empirical review. *Psychological Bulletin, 101,* 5–27.

Payne, D. G., & Roediger, H. L. (1987). Hypermnesia occurs in recall but not recognition. *American Journal of Psychology, 100,* 145–156.

Poole, D. A., & White, L. T. (1991). Effect of question repetition on the eyewitness testimony of children and adults. *Developmental Psychology, 27,* 975–986.

Postman, L., & Stark, K. (1969). The role of response availability in transfer and interference. *Journal of Experimental Psychology, 79,* 168–177.

Rajaram, S. (1990). *Components of recollective experience: Remembering and knowing.* Unpublished doctoral dissertation, Rice University, Houston.

Rajaram, S. (1993). Remembering and knowing: Two means of access to the personal past. *Memory & Cognition, 21,* 89–102.

Rajaram, S., & Neely, J. H. (1992). Dissociative masked repetition priming and word frequency effects in lexical decision and episodic recognition tasks. *Journal of Memory and Language, 31,* 152–182.

Rajaram, S., & Roediger, H. L. (in press). Direct comparison of four implicit memory tests. *Journal of Experimental Psychology: Learning, Memory, and Cognition.*

Rappold, V., & Hashtroudi, S. (1991). Does organization improve priming? *Journal of Experimental Psychology: Learning, Memory, and Cognition, 17,* 103–114.

Roediger, H. L. (1990). Implicit memory: Retention without remembering. *American Psychologist, 45,* 1043–1056.

Roediger, H. L., & Challis, B. H. (1989). Hypermnesia: Improvements in recall with repeated testing. In C. Izawa (Ed.), *Current Issues in Cognitive Processes: The Tulane Floweree Symposium on Cognition* (pp. 175–199) Hillsdale, NJ: Erlbaum.

Roediger, H. L., Challis, B. H., & Wheeler, M. A. (in preparation). Effects of confabulation on later recall.

Roediger, H. L., & Payne, D. G. (1985). Recall criterion does not affect recall level or hypermnesia: A puzzle for generate/recognize theories. *Memory & Cognition, 13,* 1–7.

Roediger, H. L., Payne, D. G., Gillespie, G. L., & Lean, D. S. (1982). Hypermnesia as determined by level of recall. *Journal of Verbal Learning and Verbal Behavior, 21,* 635–655.

Roediger, H. L., Srinivas, K., & Waddill, P. (1989). How much does guessing influence recall? Comment on Erdelyi, Finks, and Feigin-Pfau. *Journal of Experimental Psychology: General, 118,* 255–257.

Roediger, H. L., & Thorpe, L. A. (1978). The role of recall time in producing hypermnesia. *Memory & Cognition, 6,* 296–305.

Roediger, H. L., & Wheeler, M. A. (1993). Hypermnesia in episodic and semantic memory: Response to Bahrick and Hall. *Psychological Science, 4*, 207–208.

Schacter, D. L. (1983). Feeling-of-knowing in episodic memory. *Journal of Experimental Psychology: Learning, Memory, and Cognition, 9*, 39–54.

Schacter, D. L. (1987). Implicit memory: History and current status. *Journal of Experimental Psychology: Learning, Memory, and Cognition, 13*, 501–518.

Scrivner, E., & Safer, M. A. (1988). Eyewitnesses show hypermnesia for details about a violent event. *Journal of Applied Psychology, 73*, 371–377.

Smith, M. C. (1983). Hypnotic memory enhancement of witnesses: Does it work? *Psychological Bulletin, 94*, 387–407.

Spitzer, H. F. (1939). Studies in retention. *Journal of Educational Psychology, 30*, 641–656.

Squire, L. R. (1989). On the course of forgetting in very long-term memory. *Journal of Experimental Psychology: Learning, Memory, and Cognition, 15*, 241–245.

Squire, L. R., Haist, F., & Shimamura, A. P. (1989). The neurology of memory: Quantitative assessment of retrograde amnesia in two groups of amnesic patients. *The Journal of Neuroscience, 9*, 828–839.

Srinivas, K., & Roediger, H. L. (1990). Testing the nature of two implicit tests: Dissociations between conceptually-driven and data-driven processes. *Journal of Memory and Language, 28*, 389–412.

Thompson, C. P., Wenger, S. K., & Bartling, C. A. (1978). How recall facilitates subsequent recall: A reappraisal. *Journal of Experimental Psychology: Human Learning and Memory, 4*, 210–221.

Tulving, E. (1967). The effects of presentation and recall in free recall learning. *Journal of Verbal Learning and Verbal Behavior, 6*, 175–184.

Tulving, E. (1985). Memory and consciousness. *Canadian Psychologist, 26*, 1–12.

Tulving, E., & Madigan, S. A. (1970). Memory and verbal learning. *Annual Review of Psychology, 21*, 437–484.

Watkins, M. J., & Gibson, J. M. (1988). On the relation between perceptual priming and recognition memory. *Journal of Experimental Psychology: Learning, Memory, and Cognition, 14*, 477–483.

Watkins, M. J., & Tulving, E. (1975). Episodic memory: When recognition fails. *Journal of Experimental Psychology: General, 104*, 5–29.

Weldon, M. S., & Roediger, H. L. (1987). Altering retrieval demands reverses the picture superiority effect. *Memory & Cognition, 15*, 269–280.

Wheeler, M. A., & Roediger, H. L. (1992). Disparate effects of repeated testing: Reconciling Ballard's (1913) and Bartlett's (1932) results. *Psychological Science, 3*, 240–245.

Whitehouse, W. G., Dinges, D. F., Orne, E. C., & Orne, M. T. (1988). Hypnotic hypermnesia: Enhanced memory accessibility or report bias? *Journal of Abnormal Psychology, 97*, 289–295.

Zaragoza, M., & Koshmider, J. W. (1989). Misled subjects may know more than their performance implies, *Journal of Experimental Psychology: Learning, Memory, and Cognition, 15*, 246–255.

Zaragoza, M., McCloskey, M., & Jamis, M. (1987). Misleading postevent information and recall of the original event: Further evidence against the memory impairment hypothesis. *Journal of Experimental Psychology: Learning, Memory, and Cognition, 13*, 36–44.

THE LONG-TERM RETENTION OF KNOWLEDGE AND SKILLS

Alice F. Healy
Deborah M. Clawson
Danielle S. McNamara
William R. Marmie
Vivian I. Schneider
Timothy C. Rickard
Robert J. Crutcher
Cheri L. King
K. Anders Ericsson
Lyle E. Bourne, Jr.

I. Introduction

For the last seven years we have been engaged in a research program aimed generally at understanding and improving the long-term retention of knowledge and skills. Our initial work (see Healy et al., 1992, for a summary) led us to propose that a crucial determinant of retention performance concerns the extent to which procedures acquired during study can be reinstated at test. That is, to demonstrate durable retention across a long delay interval, it is critical that the procedures used when acquiring the knowledge or skill are reinstated at a later time. Using this work as a foundation, we have tried to develop further general guidelines concerning training methods optimal for promoting superior long-term retention. As discussed below, the approach we have taken differs from that used in most earlier studies (see, e.g., Farr, 1987, for a cogent review).

THE PSYCHOLOGY OF LEARNING
AND MOTIVATION, VOL. 30

II. Features of Our Research Program

Five features of our program together distinguish it from earlier research on retention of knowledge and skills. First, we have been explicitly concerned with optimizing performance after a delay interval rather than inferring superior retention from optimized performance during acquisition (see Schmidt & Bjork, 1992, for a recent discussion of this issue). Toward this end, we are striving to find conditions of training that will enable performance to stand up over time, recognizing that efficiency of training is also a consideration (i.e., optimal training may be costly in terms of the time required). As real-life experience suggests, optimizing performance after a delay is crucial. In fields such as emergency care and the military (see, e.g., Wisher, Sabol, Sukenik, & Kern, 1991), people often have to assume their duties at short notice and with inadequate opportunities to refresh their skills before they are needed in a life-or-death situation. In this respect we have been guided by Bahrick's (1984) concept of *permastore*, a kind of memory that shows great durability over extended time periods as long as several decades. Our goal has been to identify conditions of learning or characteristics of learned material that differentiate between items that do or do not achieve permanency in memory.

Second, relative to most other empirical programs, we use longer retention intervals, usually including tests after several weeks or months, and in some cases including intervals up to one or two years.

Third, we employ a combination of structural and analytic experimental procedures. The structural approach aims to identify and describe the components of specific skills. Toward this end, existing experimental methods are refined and adapted to assess the retention characteristics of skill components after long periods of disuse. The analytic approach is concerned with the experimental investigation of factors influencing and promoting retention. This methodology is used to check hypotheses concerning the characteristics that distinguish between permanent and nonpermanent components of knowledge and skill.

Fourth, we have chosen to conduct comparable experiments over a wide range of different skills and paradigms, under the assumption that theoretical conclusions may rely heavily on the specific nature of the tasks under consideration and in order to capitalize on different processes crucial to retention that can be highlighted in different tasks. Our goal is to identify training guidelines that are either common (general over tasks) or idiosyncratic (specific to a particular task), but stable.

Fifth, we have used a nontraditional method to assess retention. In the traditional study, investigators require all subjects to achieve a fixed criterion of performance mastery in terms of accuracy. Retention is assessed by examining changes in the percentage of subjects who maintain that accuracy criterion as a function of delay. Farr (1987) criticized this traditional approach, suggesting that there are many other factors that can influence retention beyond reaching some mastery criterion (see Underwood, 1964, for another cogent discussion of this issue). For a variety of reasons, we have developed a method that differs in several important respects from the traditional approach. First, we provide training for subjects beyond the accuracy criterion. Second, especially when accuracy measures are near the ceiling, we monitor aspects of the skill that reveal performance changes beyond those evident by assessing accuracy alone, for example, component response time (RT) measures and verbal protocols. These measures provide us a means for defining overlearning without resorting simply to the number of trials after the accuracy criterion has been reached. These additional measures are used to assess retention performance as well as acquisition performance.

This research has led to the support or identification of several guidelines for improving long-term retention of skills. Initially we will state these ideas in general terms; then we will provide evidence for them in terms that are specific to particular experimental paradigms. Each of these guidelines should have application to a host of tasks, as is illustrated by the many different tasks studied in our research program. In this chapter, we focus on three classes of guidelines: those that relate to (1) optimizing conditions of training, (2) optimizing the learning strategy used, and (3) training to achieve automatic levels of processing.

In our earlier studies, we were impressed with the remarkable degree of long-term retention that subjects were able to achieve in a number of perceptual, cognitive, and motor tasks, including studies of target detection, data entry, and mental arithmetic (see Fendrich, Healy, & Bourne, 1991; Fendrich, Healy, & Bourne, 1993; Healy et al., 1992; Healy, Fendrich, & Proctor, 1990). Our more recent research has helped to clarify the limits of this durable-retention phenomenon, and we will present some evidence on those limitations before we discuss the optimization guidelines.

III. Specificity of Training

Two of the most significant questions one can ask about the effects of any training program are (1) how general and (2) how durable are these effects? Optimal training programs are those for which effects can be shown to be both general over a range of new situations within a given task domain and durable in the sense that performance suffers minimally over periods of disuse. In fact, however, training effects are often limited to the situations encountered during training and subject to significant forgetting in time (see Gick & Holyoak, 1987, for a discussion of this issue). Our evidence bearing on the reasons for these limitations also suggests certain steps that might be taken to overcome these limitations and to enhance transfer and retention of trained performance.

Our most pertinent evidence documenting these limitations comes from a task that requires mental arithmetic (Rickard, 1992). Subjects were trained extensively to perform simple, single-digit mental calculations (either multiplication or division). Training was limited to the subset of problems based on operand pairs of the digits 1–9, excluding squares, in a single operand order. For example, if $12 = 3 \times 4$ was one of the problems selected for training, $12 = 4 \times 3$ was not a part of the training series. Each training set consisted of 18 multiplication problems and 18 division problems. The subject was shown all problems within a training set (constituting a block of training trials) before any problem was repeated. Forty blocks of training occurred across three sessions, the last of which also included a posttest. In the posttest, subjects were given two blocks of problems, each containing four versions of each of the training problems. One of these versions was the same as that used in acquisition (e.g., $\_\_ = 4 \times 7$); the three others were tranformed versions, serving as tests of transfer. The manipulations used to create transfer versions of taining problems were (1) a change of operand order (e.g., $\_\_ = 7 \times 4$), (2) a change of operation (multiplication to division or division to multiplication; e.g., $28 = \_\_ \times 7$), and (3) both operand order and operation change (e.g., $28 = \_\_ \times 4$). Thus, the posttest consisted of all four versions of each problem. One month later, subjects were given a test of retention in which all four versions of each problem were presented on all four blocks of trials. The problems were presented on a CRT, and subjects typed their answers on the numeric keypad of the computer keyboard. They worked at their own pace, with a new problem appearing after feedback for the subjects' response to the preceding problem.

There are four points we wish to make about the limitations of training in this study. First, acquisition of skill during training might vary from totally specific to highly general. If training effects are general, then all problems within the same domain (single-digit operand problems) should benefit from practice on a subset of problems. On the posttest, performance should be roughly equivalent on all versions of the training problems. If transfer is specific, then only performance on trained problems should benefit from training. An intermediate position would suggest positive transfer effects to related arithmetic problems, such as problems with reversed operand order, but little or no effect to less related problems, such as those that involve a change of operation.

Our data show specific transfer of training. As shown in Fig. 1, which presents results only for test problems involving multiplication, any

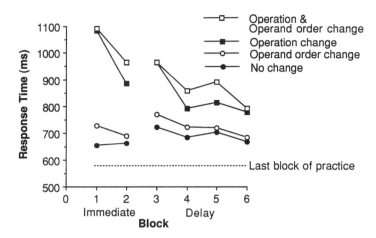

Fig. 1. Results of experiment by Rickard (1992) for test problems involving multiplication. Mean correct response time in milliseconds as a function of test time, block, and problem version. The mean for the last block of practice is also shown for comparison. (All means were calculated based on log response times and then transformed back to milliseconds by the anti-log function.)

change in problem format at the posttest had negative impact on performance. The degree of impact depended on the type of transformation made (operand order change versus operation change). But in all cases, performance was worse on transfer in contrast to training problems, suggesting that effects of training were specific to some extent to the problems used in training. We (Rickard, Mozer, & Bourne, 1992) are working on a simulation model based on interactive-activation principles, which is designed to account for the present transfer results as well as interference (i.e., priming and error) patterns that have been reported elsewhere in the mental arithmetic literature (see, e.g., the recent review by Ashcraft, 1992).

Second, the posttest constituted a condition of contextual interference (or variability; see Battig, 1979, and the section below on contextual interference in acquisition of logic rules). Problems practiced during training appeared in the posttest within the sequential context of other related problems. We would expect contextual variability to have a negative impact on performance during testing (although possibly leading to better retention on some later occasion, as we will discuss again shortly). In fact these interfering effects were reflected in the data comparing the no-change problems to the end of practice, causing roughly a 50- to 60-ms drop-off in average performance on problems practiced during training.

Third, performance on transfer problems provided a way to identify two processing components of the mental arithmetic task, both of which benefit from training. One of these components was more concrete or perceptually based, corresponding to the particular digits, in all of their characteristics including order, that comprise the problem. If any change in these perceptual characteristics was made between training and transfer, performance suffered. The second component of each task was more abstract or conceptual and related to the calculation required by the problem, in this case multiplication or division. A change between training and transfer in the operation required by the problem had a more substantial negative impact on performance than did a concrete operand order change.

Finally, the impact of a 1-month retention interval was more severe for the concrete, perceptible elements of the task than for the more abstract calculational elements. The only significant performance loss over the retention interval appeared in problems used in training (this effect was most salient for test problems involving division). All other problems, involving operand-order change, operation change, or both, showed little loss over the one-month retention interval. Thus, just as in language-based memory, as involved, for example, in sentence comprehension (e.g., Sachs, 1967), what is lost in time from the calculation task may be primarily surface information, such as operand order. The more abstract cognitive aspect, relating to an understanding of the material or the problem domain, may be highly resistant to the effects of disuse.

Overall, what these results suggest for training routines designed to optimize durability and transferabililty of training is that (1) problems used in training somehow must capture the variety of problems eventually to be encountered and (2) training should be focused on the abstract, understanding level of the task which, in contrast to more specific surface features, can be expected to be more durable over time.

IV. Guidelines for Improving Long-Term Retention

With these caveats in mind, let us discuss our research on the general optimization guidelines outlined earlier, starting with the class of guidelines concerning optimization of the conditions of training.

A. CONTEXTUAL INTERFERENCE IN ACQUISITION OF LOGIC RULES

Our work on optimizing training conditions includes a project on the acquisition and retention of logic rules (Schneider, 1991). This project pursues the contextual interference effect (Battig, 1979), defined as superior memory and greater intertask transfer for materials that are particularly difficult or presented under conditions of high interference. It has been shown that varying the processing requirements from trial to trial interferes with acquisition but aids retention and transfer (see, e.g., Battig, 1979; Carlson & Yaure, 1990). Presumably, items that have more contextual interference require more processing, and are thus learned more slowly, but if well learned initially will be retained as well as, or better than, the low-interference items. This finding is of clear importance to the study of long-term skill retention because it implies that the methods used to optimize performance during acquisition are not necessarily those that will optimize performance during subsequent retention tests.

The purpose of our study was to compare practice schedules in which different procedural rules were intermixed randomly or blocked together. We used a display meant to simulate a simplified aircraft instrument monitor consisting of four panels, only one of which was relevant (or operational) on any given trial. The relevant panels contained two lines of "X"s or "O"s in one of four combinations: XXX and XXX; XXX and OOO; OOO and XXX; OOO and OOO. The subjects' task was to decide whether or not the display in the relevant panel indicated an emergency. Each panel involved a different logical rule on which the decision was to be made. The four rules were: AND, OR, NAND, and NOR. For example, for the AND rule, an emergency was indicated only if both stimuli contained Xs (i.e., XXX and XXX).

Our first experiment included one group of subjects given blocked practice (in which all trials within a block involved the same rule, i.e., the same panel, although the particular stimulus configuration varied randomly) and a second group given random practice (in which both the rule and the stimulus varied randomly from trial to trial). All subjects started with an acquisition phase followed immediately afterward by two test blocks, one consisting of blocked rules and the other consisting of random rules.

The results of the acquisition phase in terms of correct log response time, $\ln(RT - 200 \text{ ms})$, showed that the random group yielded longer response times ($M = 6.691$) than did the blocked group ($M = 5.970$), in accord with previous findings that random practice leads to strong contextual interference.

Although blocked practice led to significantly shorter response times during the acquisition phase, it led to longer latencies on the test. There was a significant interaction of practice schedule and test type, so that subjects were slowest when exposed to the blocked practice schedule and given the random test (blocked practice, random test $M = 7.066$; blocked practice, blocked test $M = 6.192$; random practice, random test $M = 6.575$; random practice, blocked test, $M = 6.067$). These findings are in accord with predictions based on contextual interference.

In our second experiment we used a third practice schedule to examine whether the unpredictability of the rules in the random group, rather than the need to retrieve the rules, is at the heart of the contextual interference effect. This condition presented the rules in a fixed serial order (see Lee & Magill, 1983), so that the rules were predictable, but the rules changed from trial to trial, so that they had to be retrieved on each trial.

The second experiment included only a random test at the end of the acquisition phase, and this test was repeated after a delay interval, so that we could determine whether the contextual-interference effect would survive, disappear, or perhaps become magnified on a retention test. The retention intervals were one week and one month.

Results from the acquisition phase showed that the blocked-practice schedule yielded the shortest correct response times ($M = 5.593$), and the serial practice schedule ($M = 5.929$) yielded times midway between those of the blocked and random ($M = 6.402$) conditions, suggesting that both unpredictability and the need for rule retrieval contribute to contextual interference. Thus, blocked practice led to superior performance during acquisition.

In contrast, blocked practice led to inferior performance (i.e., longer response times) during both the immediate test (blocked $M = 6.505$, serial $M = 6.367$, random $M = 6.204$) and the long-term retention test (blocked $M = 6.488$, serial $M = 6.457$, random $M = 6.310$). This result was also found for proportion of correct responses (immediate test: blocked $M = .876$, serial $M = .948$, random $M = .977$; retention test: blocked $M = .946$, serial $M = .949$, random $M = .984$). Note that subjects given blocked practice made significantly fewer correct responses during the tests than subjects given random practice, even though they made more correct responses during training. Also note that there was no forgetting evident between the immediate and delayed tests; indeed, accuracy improved for the blocked condition on the retention test relative to the immediate test, perhaps because the subjects got practice at rule retrieval during the immediate test, in which the rules were presented in a random order. In sum, our findings support the principle that contextual interference promotes superior performance after training. This benefit seems attributable largely to the practice subjects received in retrieving the rules from memory. More generally, it seems crucial to match the conditions of training with the conditions required during subsequent tests.

B.   PART-WHOLE TRAINING IN MORSE CODE RECEPTION

In work on Morse code reception (Clawson, 1992), we considered the possibility that part-whole training procedures might enhance long-term retention. Specifically, we attempted to determine conditions under which independent training sessions on parts of the material would yield better acquisition and retention performance than would providing training on all the material from the beginning. In addition, we addressed a related question concerning whether any initial partial training should be restricted to the easiest material or to the most difficult material. A recently published visual discrimination study by Pellegrino, Doane, Fischer, and Alderton (1991) demonstrated that the most effective training started with the more difficult stimuli. This result could not be generalized straightforwardly to Morse code reception, of course, because Pellegrino et al.'s task was a simple visual-discrimination task, whereas Morse code reception is a difficult auditory-identification task. Therefore, we sought to determine whether the advantage for initially difficult training would also be found with Morse code training. Further, we were interested in whether this training advantage would also be evident on a delayed-retention test.

In our first two experiments subjects learned to receive Morse code signals and to translate them to their letter equivalents. For example, subjects would hear the series of beeps short-long-short (or di-da-di) and would be expected to respond by typing the letter "R" on a computer console. In our first experiment, subjects learned to receive 12 Morse code-letter pairs. We divided this set of pairs into two equal-sized subsets, one containing the easy items and the other containing the difficult items.

All subjects were given three sessions of training followed a month later by a retention session. During the first day of training, the subjects were divided into three groups. In the "easy-first" group, subjects received initial training on only the easy subset of code-letter pairs; in the "difficult-first" group, subjects received initial training on only the difficult subset; whereas in the "all-first" group, subjects received training on all the letters from the beginning. After the first session, training for all subjects involved the full set of 12 code-letter pairs. During each of the four sessions, the training period was preceded by a pretest and followed by a posttest. On all days including the first, these tests covered all 12 code-letter pairs.

The results are summarized in Fig. 2 in terms of proportion of correct responses on the pretests and posttests on each of the four sessions. Note that subjects in all three conditions showed similar levels of improvement across the first three days of training. However, the difference among the groups became evident immediately after the month-long retention interval, that is, on the retention pretest. Surprisingly, in light of the findings from Pellegrino et al. (1991), the difficult-first group showed a strong drop in performance at that point, whereas little forgetting was evident for the other groups.

To explore further this intriguing finding, we conducted a second experiment that included only the easy-first and difficult-first training groups with a substantially greater number of subjects in each group. Further, we altered our procedures to facilitate the recording of response times.

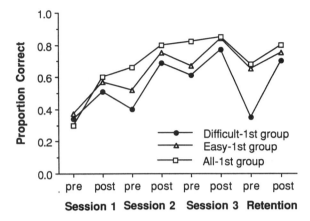

Fig. 2.   Results of Experiment 1 by Clawson (1992). Mean proportion of correct responses for pretests (pre) and posttests (post) as a function of initial training group and session.

As shown in Fig. 3, which summarizes the accuracy results broken down by the two types of letter pairs (easy and difficult), we found once again a larger drop in performance on the retention pretest for the difficult-first group than for the easy-first group, but in this case the difference between training groups was found only on the easy pairs.

Figure 4 shows the results in terms of mean correct response time, rather than accuracy. As for proportion of correct responses, we found worse

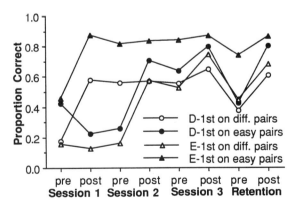

Fig. 3.   Results of Experiment 2 by Clawson (1992). Mean proportion of correct responses on easy and difficult (diff.) code-letter pairs for pretests (pre) and posttests (post) in the difficult-first (D-1st) and easy-first (E-1st) training groups as a function of session.

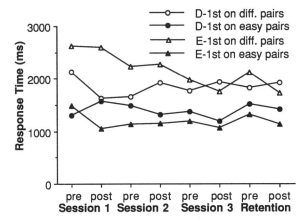

Fig. 4.   Results of Experiment 2 by Clawson (1992). Mean correct response time in milliseconds on easy and difficult (diff.) code-letter pairs for pretests (pre) and posttests (post) in the difficult-first (D-1st) and easy-first (E-1st) training groups as a function of session. (All means were calculated based on log response times and then transformed back to milliseconds by the anti-log function.)

performance (in this case, slower responding) for the difficult-first group than for the easy-first group on the easy pairs in the retention pretest. However, on the difficult pairs in that test, the difficult-first group was faster than the easy-first group. Despite this one advantage for the difficult-first group, in general, performance after training was inferior in our study when the difficult items were studied first. This finding contrasts to that of Pellegrino et al. (1991) who found that difficult-first training was superior. However, as we noted previously, there were many differences between our investigation of Morse code and Pellegrino et al.'s investigation of visual discrimination. We think the most crucial difference concerned the definition of the easy items. In our task the easy items were in fact quite challenging, performance on them being near 50% accuracy initially. In Pellegrino et al.'s task the easy items were truly easy, performance being at the ceiling during the initial training phase. When subjects must devote their initial training to very easy items, it is not surprising that they do not develop the strategies that would help them with more challenging material presented later.

The aim of our third experiment then was to localize the sources of difficulty for all the Morse code stimuli. Toward this end, we divided the Morse reception task into parts, not in terms of different stimuli to be learned, but rather in terms of subtasks to be performed.

All subjects in this experiment studied all 12 of the stimulus letters simultaneously, but there were three groups who studied them differently.

The code-to-letter group was trained in the normal reception task of hearing the codes and typing their corresponding letters; the code-to-dida group heard the codes and typed keys corresponding to "di" (short) and "da" (long), segmenting the auditory code into its elements; and the dida-to-letter group read simplified di-da patterns displayed on the CRT and translated the segmented signals into their corresponding letters, which they typed on the keyboard. In this experiment subjects were trained for two sessions with a pretest at the start of training, a posttest at the end of training, and a retention test two weeks later.

The results are summarized in Fig. 5 in terms of proportion of correct responses. Accuracy for the code-to-dida group was remarkably stable, showing only small (but significant) improvement as training progressed, whereas accuracy for the dida-to-letter and code-to-letter groups improved considerably across the acquisition sessions. Also, there was some forgetting across the two-week retention interval for the dida-to-letter and code-to-letter groups, but no forgetting for the code-to-dida group. The code-to-dida task involved a skill that was largely based on perceptual procedures, whereas both of the other tasks required the learning of paired associates. Our finding of no forgetting in the code-to-dida group but substantial forgetting in the other two groups is consistent with our previous observation that memory based on procedures, in contrast to memory for facts (or verbal associations), is highly resistant to forgetting over long delays (Healy et al., 1990, 1992).

Analyses of individual differences suggested that the code-to-dida group was more stable than were the other two groups across the three sessions.

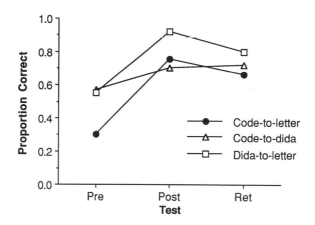

Fig. 5. Results of Experiment 3 by Clawson (1992). Mean proportion of correct responses for the three task groups on the pretest (Pre), posttest (Post), and retention test (Ret).

For subjects in the code-to-dida group, accuracy on the posttest and retention test was predictable from pretest scores, whereas for the other groups the correlations were all nonsignificant. This finding of stability for the code-to-dida group suggests that the processes involved in segmenting the auditory signal into elements may be the limiting factor leading to the failure of some students of Morse code to learn the reception task successfully. That is, individuals who are poor at the code-to-dida task may not be able to improve performance on the full code-to-letter task even with much practice.

In a post hoc analysis, we examined the extent to which separate performance on the component subtasks could predict performance on the whole Morse code reception task. For this analysis we computed a predicted accuracy level for the whole (code-to-letter) task based on the product of the observed accuracy levels for the two-part tasks. Although there was no difference between observed and predicted whole-task performance at the pretest (observed $M = .304$, predicted $M = .313$), observed whole-task performance tended (nonsignificantly) to exceed predictions at both the posttest (observed $M = .756$, predicted $M = .644$) and the retention test (observed $M = .661$, predicted $M = .576$), suggesting that subjects may develop effective strategies in the whole task to overcome problems encountered in the partial component tasks.

C. PART-WHOLE TRAINING OF TANK-GUNNER SKILLS

Whether acquisition and retention benefit from part-whole training was also a focus of our research with tank-gunner skills (Marmie & Healy, 1992). As in the first Morse code study, we examined whether there was superior transfer to the whole task from part- or whole-task training. As with the last Morse code study, we have broken down the whole task into sequential component subtasks.

In this study subjects were engaged in a realistic, goal-directed simulation exercise. The advantage of using this simulation exercise in part-whole training was threefold: First, it was a task that subjects generally found intrinsically motivating because of its similarity to an arcade video game. In contrast, for example, the important tests of part-whole training by Naylor and Briggs (1963) used training on a laboratory Markov prediction task, which seems less intrinsically motivating. Second, our division yielded clearly separable, meaningful, goal-directed subtasks (see Newell, Carlton, Fisher, & Rutter, 1989, who also recommended the use of natural subtasks). In contrast, for example, in a more recent study of part-whole training with a video game environment, Mane, Adams, and Donchin (1989) found it necessary to have subtasks be repetitive drills.

Third, and most important, the simulation exercises we used had separate
dependent measures that allowed us to examine the specific decay of task
components over a retention interval.

More specifically, in our study, stimuli were presented on TopGun Tank
Simulators. The simulators utilized color monitors mounted in an enclosed
sit-down unit, which was designed as a training machine for tank gunners.
Subjects in our experiment controlled tank gun-turret movements via hand
controls and aimed at threat targets with the aid of a sight. Two digitized
human voices played the roles of the commander and the loader, telling the
subjects where to lay on their sight, when they had ammunition loaded and
available for use, and when to fire. A schematic display of a target tank, as
viewed by subjects looking at the simulator monitor, is presented in Fig. 6.
Each session included a presentation of 100 target tanks divided into 10
blocks of 10 trials each, with each tank shown for a maximum of 20 sec.

The subjects' tank could not move, but the hand controls that moved
their sight allowed them 360° visibility. Subjects fired by pressing either of
two buttons under their index fingers. A threat tank was destroyed when a
shot struck its center of mass. The result was scored as a "kill." We
tabulated kills and two different response-time measures: time to make an
identification and time to fire (after an identification had been made). A
tank was considered identified when it entered the subject's field of view.
The identification (ID) measure reflected the search component of the
task, or how long it took the subject to find the target. The time-to-fire
measure reflected the combined subsequent components of sighting (or

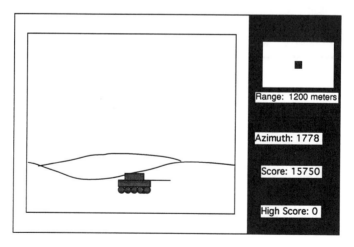

Fig. 6.   Schematic display of a target tank on the TopGun simulator monitor in the
experiment by Marmie and Healy (1992).

laying on the sight) and firing (or shooting at the tank). In general this measure reflected development of the sighting skill, which was the most difficult of the three components. Both of these measures were computed only for successful kills of the target tank.

Subjects were tested over four sessions. The first three sessions occurred during a single week, with the last session occurring four weeks later. The experiment employed two groups of subjects. During the first two sessions, the part-training group engaged in part-task training, practicing the sighting- and firing-task subcomponents (which are indexed by the time-to-fire measure). But training was not given on the search component (which is indexed by the ID measure); the simulators were programmed, using an optional function called "autoslew," to relieve the gunner of the requirement to ID the enemy threat (as occurs in a real tank when the commander assumes control of the ID task). The last two sessions involved the whole task, combining sighting and firing with searching. The whole-training group engaged in whole-task training and was trained on all three subcomponents of the task simultaneously throughout all four sessions.

Performance on the search component of the task is summarized in Fig. 7 in terms of mean time to ID in seconds. Note that because of the autoslew function, the first two sessions for the part-training group reflect the performance of the simulated commander, not that of the subjects. Although during the first two sessions the part-training subjects received no practice on the search component of the task, after the initial training they performed just as well as the whole-training group. Figure 8 shows mean time to fire. Note that the subjects given part training, which may have allowed

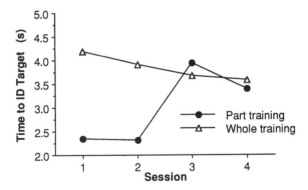

Fig. 7.   Results of the experiment by Marmie and Healy (1992). Mean time to identify (ID) target in seconds for successfully killed targets as a function of training group and session. (Session 4 is the retention session.)

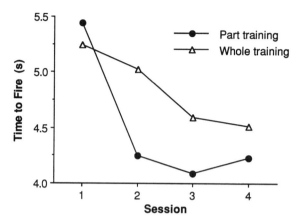

Fig. 8. Results of the experiment by Marmie and Healy (1992). Mean time to fire in seconds for successfully killed targets as a function of training group and session. (Session 4 is the retention session.)

them to concentrate on the sighting and firing subcomponents of the task initially, showed a large advantage in the second session of training, and that advantage was maintained after initial training, even during the retention test. Holding back on the training of the search subcomponent benefited the sighting and firing subcomponents with undistracted practice, and that benefit persisted even after the search subcomponent was introduced into the task.

Although it benefited response-time performance, part training did not appear to aid subjects in improving their accuracy on the task. Accuracy results are summarized in Fig. 9 in terms of mean proportion of kills. Note that during initial training, there was a substantial advantage for the part-training group because the commander efficiently took over the searching component of the task. After the initial training period, there was no difference between the two training groups.

The combined findings across the three different measures of performance indicate that part training does not hurt performance relative to whole training, and may in fact improve performance by allowing subjects to concentrate on one task at a time. By comparing this finding to that obtained in our initial Morse code experiment, which found a clear disadvantage for initial training on the difficult subcomponent, it is clear that any conclusions concerning part-whole training depend crucially on the nature of the whole task and the characteristics of the component part tasks. In particular, we attribute the disadvantage for the difficult-first condition in the Morse code study and the contrasting advantage for the (difficult-first)

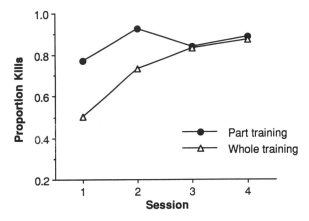

Fig. 9.   Results of the experiment by Marmie and Healy (1992). Mean proportion of kills as a function of training group and session. (Session 4 is the retention session.)

part-training condition in the tank-gunner study to the fact that the difficult items in the Morse code reception task could not be mastered within the time allotted, whereas the sighting and firing components of the tank-gunner task could be mastered during the initial training period. More generally, when training on only a part of a whole task, it seems crucial to focus on a component that is sufficiently complex to be engaging but not so complex as to be impossible to master in the time allowed.

D. A GENERATION ADVANTAGE FOR MENTAL ARITHMETIC AND VOCABULARY LEARNING

We have discussed some ways to manipulate the conditions of training in order to optimize long-term retention, including blocked/random and part/whole comparisons. Another powerful manipulation of training conditions is the comparison of reading and generating. The generation effect (see, e.g., Slamecka & Graf, 1978) refers to the finding that people show better retention of learned material when it is self-produced, or generated, than when it is simply copied, or read. The typical task used to investigate the generation effect has been one in which the subject is presented a series of paired associates in either a read or a generate format and is subsequently required to recall or recognize the second item of each pair. Thus, the subject's task is to recall the occurrence of a prior event or episode, in this case the prior occurrence of a paired associate. Previous studies of the generation effect have been limited almost exclusively to examinations of memory for episodes or events (see, e.g., Crutcher & Healy, 1989). In contrast, our recent work (McNamara & Healy, 1991) extended this finding to memory for facts and skills, including multiplication skill. In accordance with our procedural reinstatement framework (see Healy et al., 1992), we proposed that a critical factor leading to a generation advantage for skill training is that stable and efficient cognitive strategies be developed during the training process. Multiplication is a skill for which most college students have already developed some cognitive strategies. For simple single-digit operand problems, we would expect no change in these strategies as a function of training because they are extremely well entrenched. In fact, answer retrieval might be or become automatic (see the section below on direct and mediated retrieval in mental arithmetic). In contrast, most college students have not developed stable cognitive strategies for more difficult multiplication problems with operands greater than 12. Thus, only for these difficult problems would a generation advantage be expected because the generate condition would be more apt than the read condition to promote the formation of new cognitive strategies.

We tested this prediction by comparing read and generate conditions of training on both easy (e.g., $40 \times 9 = 360$) and hard (e.g., $14 \times 9 = 126$) multiplication problems. Subjects were given a pretest, training in either the read or generate condition, and a posttest, all on multiplication problems. In the read condition, subjects were presented the multiplication problem and answer on the computer screen (e.g., $40 \times 9 = 360$). They copied the problem and answer by typing them on the number pad. In the generate condition, subjects were presented the problem on the computer screen (e.g., $40 \times 9 = \quad$). They then typed the problem and the answer that they generated.

The results of this study are summarized in Fig. 10 for proportion of correct responses. In accord with predictions, a generation advantage was found only on the hard problems in the posttest.

The arithmetic material studied in this experiment was already familiar to the subjects before training. Of great interest would be the extension of this investigation to situations in which individuals are learning new material. Such a question has important implications for the many training situations that involve teaching new material, rather than improving the efficiency with which old material is retrieved.

Therefore, in our next experiment we had subjects learn word-nonword associations. The findings from our last experiment suggested that the use of cognitive strategies aids learning and retention. However, we did not directly assess strategy use in that study. Hence, in the present experiment we directly examined the strategies used by the subjects. The most probable relevant cognitive strategies in this case were mnemonic codes linking the word and nonword components of each pair. We expected subjects in

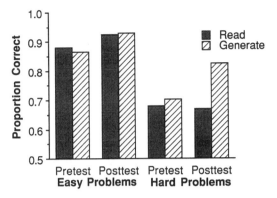

Fig. 10. Results of Experiment 1 by McNamara and Healy (1991). Mean proportion of correct responses on the pretest and posttest as a function of training condition and problem difficulty.

the generate condition to develop more mnemonic codes than subjects in the read condition and, therefore, to show superior learning and retention of the word-nonword pairs. We further expected that subjects in the read condition who developed mnemonic codes would show a level of performance comparable to that of subjects in the generate condition. To assess the extent of mnemonic coding, we administered a retrospective questionnaire asking the subjects to report their use of mnemonic codes for each word-nonword pair.

Subjects were given a list of 30 word-nonword pairs to study for 10 min before training began. They were then administered a pretest, followed by training, and then a posttest. To evaluate the long-term impact of both training and mnemonic coding, we included a retention test after a one-week delay.

As expected, the generation advantage was evident only after training, that is, on both the posttest and the retention test. Specifically, on the pretest there was no advantage in terms of the proportion of correct responses for the generate condition ($M = .297$) relative to the read condition ($M = .353$), whereas on the posttest the generate condition ($M = .956$) was superior to the read condition ($M = .833$). Likewise, on the retention test, the generate condition ($M = .756$) showed higher accuracy than the read condition ($M = .658$).

In order to pinpoint the locus of the generation advantage, we categorized the subjects in each training condition into those with a relatively high and those with a relatively low average mnemonic score on the basis of the retrospective questionnaire. Figure 11 presents the proportions of

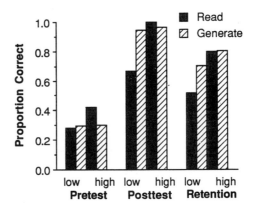

Fig. 11. Results of Experiment 2 by McNamara and Healy (1991). Mean proportion of correct responses for the subjects with low and high average mnemonic scores on the pretest, posttest, and retention test as a function of training condition.

correct responses separately for low and high mnemonic subjects. As predicted, subjects in the read condition who used mnemonic coding showed a level of performance on the posttest and retention test comparable to that shown by subjects in the generate condition.

Did the likelihood of recalling a particular nonword depend on whether subjects employed a mnemonic strategy to encode it? Figure 12 shows that the overall proportion of correct responses was highest for the items given

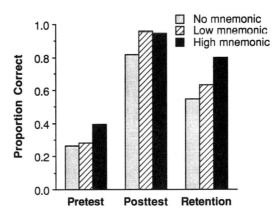

Fig. 12. Results of Experiment 2 by McNamara and Healy (1991). Mean proportion of correct responses for the items given no mnemonic, a low mnemonic, or a high mnemonic score on the pretest, posttest, and retention test.

high mnemonic scores and lowest for the items with no mnemonics. Crucially, forgetting across the retention interval was least for items given high mnemonic scores. This finding suggests that a mnemonic strategy aids not only coding but also long-term retention of information. More generally, this finding indicates that to maximize long-term retention it is crucial to optimize not only the conditions of training but also the learning strategy used by the subjects.

E. DIRECT AND MEDIATED RETRIEVAL IN MENTAL ARITHMETIC

Facts can be retrieved from memory in one of two ways, either automatically (by direct access to a fact network) or indirectly (by some mediated route). In the latter case, retrieval is deliberate, conscious, and effortful, whereas in the former case it occurs effortlessly.

Direct access is not a characteristic of tasks but rather of facts or skill components of a task. Within any particular task domain, direct access co-exists with mediated retrieval. For example, we have shown in a mental arithmetic task that sometimes answers are achieved directly and at other times indirectly (Bourne & Rickard, 1991). Note that mental arithmetic is a skill that most adults will claim already to have. Here we are interested in the effects that further practice has on a known skill. As we will see, performance is based partly on direct and partly on mediated answer retrieval, and a transition from indirect to direct retrieval may be an important consequence of further training that might have major implications for long-term memory.

In one study, we gave subjects two 1-hr sessions of practice on 25 selected single-digit multiplication problems. These problems were presented to subjects one at a time in blocks. Each of the two sessions consisted of 30 blocks of 25 problems each. In the first two blocks of each session subjects were asked, after responding to each problem, whether the answer popped into mind directly or had to be retrieved through one or more consciously mediated steps. An example of mediated performance is based on an anchor-and-adjust strategy: Asked to provide an answer to 8×6, the subject retrieves $8 \times 5 = 40$ (anchor) and adds 8 (adjust).

About 18% of the problems in the first two blocks were solved by mediation. There was some variability among subjects, who ranged from no mediation (all direct retrievals, by self-report) to about 60% mediation. We observed both intrasubject and intraproblem stability in these data. That is, if a subject reported mediation on Block 1 of Session 1, he or she was also likely to report mediation on Block 2 of Session 1. Likewise, if a particular problem was mediated on Block 1, it was likely to be mediated on Block 2 as well. It will come as no surprise that, when mediation was reported, the subject was slower to respond with the correct answer. Figure 13 shows response time on the first two blocks of Session 1 for problems that were mediated on both occasions (Both Other), on only one occasion (Other 1 and Other 2), or on neither occasion (Both Direct). The data of subjects who never reported mediation (All Direct) are also included for comparison. Somewhat more interesting is the fact that the effects of mediation persisted throughout the entire experiment. In Fig. 14, we show response time on all 60 blocks of practice (Session 1 and Session 2) for problems identified as direct or other on the first two blocks of Session 1. We interpret the fact that response time differences persisted to suggest that if a problem was mediated early in the training session, it had a high probability of continuing to require mediation throughout the remaining blocks of training. Supporting this argument are the data from Blocks 1 and 2 from Session 2. Approximately the same number of problems (16%) required mediation on the second session as on the first session. Moreover, there was a strong correspondence between subjects reporting mediation and between problems requiring mediation in the two sessions. Although subjects became faster with training, it thus does appear that the method by which a given subject solved a given problem remained stable over a large number of repetitions. This finding may pose a challenge for Logan's (1988) influential instance theory of automatization, which suggests that increased learning leads to a transition from mediated to direct

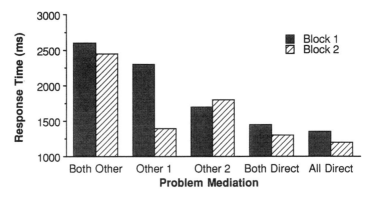

Fig. 13.   Results of experiment by Bourne and Rickard (1991). Mean correct response time in milliseconds on the first two blocks of Session 1 as a function of problem mediation. (All means were calculated based on log response times and then transformed back to milliseconds by the anti-log function.)

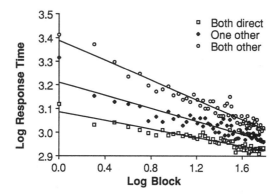

Fig. 14. Results of experiment by Bourne and Rickard (1991). Mean correct response time in log milliseconds for all 60 blocks as a function of log block and problem mediation on the first two blocks of Session 1.

retrieval. Further investigations with more extensive practice are needed to resolve this issue.

F. DIRECT AND MEDIATED RETRIEVAL IN VOCABULARY ACQUISITION

In order to study the transition from mediated to direct retrieval under controlled practice conditions, it may be preferable to study the acquisition of new knowledge and then to study changes in retrieval as a function of extended practice. A particularly attractive task domain to study retrieval of new knowledge is the learning of vocabulary items in a foreign language. We have in several studies instructed subjects to learn Spanish vocabulary items with the key-word method (see, e.g., Crutcher, 1990, 1992; Healy et al., 1992).

In the key-word method, the Spanish word (e.g., *doronico*) is first related to a key word, a concrete English word similar in sound to the Spanish word (e.g., *door*). The key word is then associated to the English equivalent (*leopard*) by forming an interactive image (e.g., a leopard walking through a door). This method of learning provides a great deal of control over mediational processes, thus assuring a similar encoding structure across all subjects.

We have shown that retrieval of English equivalents after original acquisition was virtually always mediated by retrieval of the key word in working memory, based on three sources of information (Crutcher, 1992).

First, the retrieval times for the English equivalent of the Spanish word, the Vocabulary Task, were substantially slower ($M = 2,041$ ms) than those for the two subtasks, the Key Word subtask ($M = 1,653$ ms), which involves responding with the similar-sounding English key word given the Spanish word as a cue, and the English subtask ($M = 1,633$ ms), which involves responding with the English translation given the key word as a cue.

Second, retrieval accuracy for the English equivalent of the Spanish word after a delay of a week, a month, or a year was a direct function of accuracy on the two subtasks. That is, accurate retrieval of the English equivalent was observed virtually only when both subtasks were accurately performed at the retention test.

Third, retrospective verbal reports after successful retrievals revealed that subjects reported accessing the key word prior to accessing the English equivalent. Indeed, when subjects reported retrieving the English equivalent directly, the retrieval time was over 500 ms faster. Hence, we can conclude that retrieval after original learning was mediated.

We have also studied the effects on retrieval of 80 additional retrieval trials with each item in several sessions spread out over two weeks. After initial acquisition and test, subjects practiced the Vocabulary Task (full practice) for half of the items and the subtask of retrieving the English equivalent using the key word (subtask practice) for the other half of the items. The retrieval times for the initial test and the final test after extended practice are shown in Fig. 15; note that the tests included both tasks (Vocabulary Task and English subtask) for all items.

At the initial test the Vocabulary Task was reliably slower than the English subtask, which replicated the earlier finding of mediated retrieval following acquisition. At the final test after practice, a reliable cross-over interaction was found, in which the items in the full-practice condition were retrieved faster with the Vocabulary Task than with the English subtask, with the opposite result for items in the subtask-practice condition. An analysis of retrospective reports for only the Vocabulary Task revealed that at the initial test, subjects reported retrievals involving the mediation of the key word for both the subtask-practiced items ($M = 86.7\%$) and the full-practiced items ($M = 83.8\%$), but at final test most retrievals for full-practiced items involved no reported mediation ($M = 15.6\%$), although most retrievals for subtask-practiced items continued to involve reported mediation ($M = 87.0\%$). We are currently analyzing data from a one-month retention test of these subjects.

These results clearly showed that after extended practice retrieval was no longer a sequential process involving access of the key word in working memory. One possibility is that a genuinely different association was

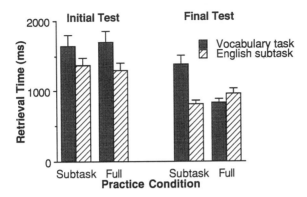

Fig. 15. Results of experiment by Crutcher (1992). Mean correct response time in milliseconds for the Vocabulary Task and the English subtask on the initial and final tests as a function of practice condition. (All means were calculated based on log response times and were then transformed back to milliseconds by the anti-log function.) Standard errors of the mean shown as bars.

formed between the Spanish word and its English equivalent. Another possibility is that retrieval still involved the key word but that with extended practice access involved covert mediation of the key word through spreading activation. In support of the latter interpretation we showed in a new experiment that learning a new association to an old key word interfered with subsequent retrieval of the original Spanish-English pair, even when that original pair had been extensively practiced. In agreement with an earlier study on the effects of extensive practice (Pirolli & Anderson, 1985; see also our own research with mental multiplication, Bourne & Rickard, 1991), we demonstrated in this study that the original encodings with their mediators continued to exert their influence after extensive practice even when the observable characteristics of the retrieval process suggested direct retrieval.

G. AUTOMATIC PROCESSING IN COLOR-WORD INTERFERENCE

Much of our initial work on the long-term retention of skills (see, e.g., Healy et al., 1992) was guided by a hypothesis relating superior retention, or entry into permastore, to the achievement of automatic processing, or direct retrieval, during acquisition. We attempted to test this hypothesis in two different domains, the first involving target detection and the second involving mental multiplication (see Healy et al., 1990, 1992; Fendrich et al., 1993). We did find superior long-term retention in both of those studies, but we have as yet been unable to establish conclusively that automaticity was achieved by our subjects and, therefore, whether there was a clear relationship between automatic processing and long-term retention. We propose that the task that might hold the key to resolving this issue is the familiar Stroop color-word interference task. In the Stroop task, subjects are asked to name the color of the ink in which color words are printed. The ink color and word do not correspond. For example, given the word *purple* printed in red ink, the appropriate response is "red." This task has been widely accepted as demonstrating that word reading is automatic and hence interferes with the nonautomatic task of color naming (see, e.g., MacLeod, 1991, for a recent review of research on the Stroop effect). Our proposed study involves the training of the color-naming task to the point of automaticity so that no interference would be evident. Some of us (Clawson, King, Healy, Ericsson, & Marmie) are training subjects in two different color-naming situations. The first training condition involves practice in simply naming color patches. The second training condition involves practice in naming the colors of incongruent color words. Examining the effects of training on performance in the Stroop task should enable us to resolve the issue of interest concerning long-term retention, and should also allow us to disentangle the competing theories that have been proposed as explanations for the Stroop effect (see MacLeod, 1991).

The results from two pilot subjects are shown in Fig. 16. One subject was given training only on the color-patches task (shown on the left of Fig. 16), and the second subject was given training only on the Stroop task itself

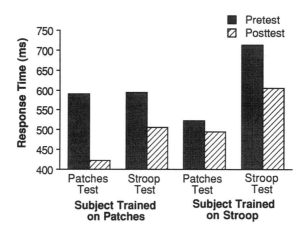

Fig. 16. Results of pilot experiment by Clawson, King, Healy, Ericsson, and Marmie. Mean corrrect response time in milliseconds for the patches and Stroop tests on the pretest and posttest as a function of training condition.

(shown on the right of Fig. 16). These preliminary subjects were given a pretest on one day, a single hour of training the next day, and then a posttest the following day. The pretests and posttests included both color patch naming and Stroop tests. Note that despite the fact that these pilot subjects were given only one hour of training, as opposed to the 12 hours of practice planned for the full experiment, we found substantial decreases in response times from the pretest to the posttest on both tasks for both subjects, suggesting that indeed training will prove to have profound effects and will lead to automatic color-naming responses. Hence, we are encouraged that this study will allow us to elucidate the relationship between automatic processing and long-term retention.

V. Summary and Conclusions

In closing, we will review the three classes of guidelines we found to optimize long-term retention (see Table I for a summary). The first class of guidelines concerned ways to optimize the conditions of training. We discussed three general guidelines in this class. The first concerned the

TABLE I

GUIDELINES FOR OPTIMIZING LONG-TERM RETENTION

Guideline	Article section	Topic
1. Optimize conditions of training.		
A. Promote contextual interference.	IV,A	Acquisition of logic rules
B. Focus initially on maximally trainable component.	IV,B	Morse code reception
	IV,C	Tank-gunner skills
C. Encourage generation during practice.	IV,D	Mental arithmetic and vocabulary learning
2. Optimize the learning strategy used.	IV,D	Vocabulary learning
3. Achieving automaticity is difficult but may have a unique retention advantage.	IV,E	Mental arithmetic
	IV,F	Vocabulary acquisition
	IV,G	Color-Word interference

contextual interference found, for example, with random sequences of tasks as opposed to fixed or predictable sequences. Although random sequences did suppress performance during acquisition, they promoted superior performance after training. We attribute this benefit in large part to the practice subjects received in retrieval from memory of the appropriate response preparation procedures and to the necessity to match the conditions of training with the characteristics of the desired target performance. The second general guideline in this class concerned training parts of a task versus the whole task. We conclude from our findings that it is best to focus initially on a maximally trainable component of the task, that is, to avoid wasting time on either a trivial component or a component that cannot be adequately mastered within the constraints of the training period. The third general guideline in this class concerned the distinction between generating and reading. We conclude that the well-known generation advantage can be extended from memory for episodes to memory for facts and skills.

The second class of guidelines concerned ways to optimize the strategies used. We found that in tasks that require deliberate retrieval from memory, training that promotes efficient encoding strategies maximizes long-term retention.

The third class of guidelines concerned ways to attain direct access, or automatic retrieval, from memory. We found in several domains that achieving automaticity requires extensive practice. It is surprising that even after vast amounts of practice there is still mediated retrieval for a small subset of items. Further, even when retrieval appears automatic after extensive practice, mediators may still continue to exert their influence. Finally, we are in a position now to test our original hypothesis that there is a unique retention advantage for items that have achieved the status of automatic retrieval.

We started this chapter by summarizing some of our work demonstrating the specificity of improvement in performance. That is, training on specific items showed little or no transfer to related items. The specific characteristics of the training context seemed to have a profound influence on immediate transfer to other contexts. Hence, we now need to focus more on the transfer of training to new skills and on optimizing the generalizability of training. Our task had been to examine the optimization of long-term retention, but we have learned that optimizing retention does not guarantee generalizability, and it is even possible that there is a trade-off between durability and generalizability. Our horizons have, thus, now broadened; therefore, what we intend for the future is to explore conditions of training and strategy utilization that will simultaneously maximize both generalizability and long-term retention.

ACKNOWLEDGMENTS

This research was supported by Army Research Institute Contract MDA903-90-K-0066 to the Institute of Cognitive Science at the University of Colorado. Robert J. Crutcher is now at the University of Illinois, Chicago; K. Anders Ericsson is now at Florida State University, Tallahassee. We are grateful to Douglas Medin and Evan Heit for helpful comments concerning an earlier version of this chapter.

REFERENCES

Ashcraft, M. H. (1992). Cognitive arithmetic: A review of data and theory. *Cognition, 44,* 75–106.

Bahrick, H. P. (1984). Semantic memory content in permastore: Fifty years of memory for Spanish learned in school. *Journal of Experimental Psychology: General, 113,* 1–29.

Battig, W. F. (1979). The flexibility of human memory. In L. S. Cermak & F. I. M. Craik (Eds.), *Levels of processing in human memory* (pp. 23–44). Hillsdale, NJ: Erlbaum.

Bourne, L. E., Jr., & Rickard, T. C. (1991, July). *Mental calculation: The development of a cognitive skill.* San Jose, Costa Ríca: Inter-American Congress of Psychology.

Carlson, R. A., & Yaure, R. G. (1990). Practice schedules and the use of component skills in problem solving. *Journal of Experimental Psychology: Learning, Memory, and Cognition, 16,* 484–496.

Clawson, D. M. (1992). *Acquisition and retention of Morse code reception skills.* Unpublished master's thesis, University of Colorado, Boulder.

Crutcher, R. J. (1990). *The role of mediation in knowledge acquisition and retention: Learning foreign vocabulary using the keyword method* (Tech. Rep. No. 90-10). Boulder, CO: University of Colorado, Institute of Cognitive Science.

Crutcher, R. J. (1992). *The effects of practice on retrieval of foreign vocabulary using the keyword method.* Unpublished doctroral dissertation, University of Colorado, Boulder.

Crutcher, R. J., & Healy, A. F. (1989). Cognitive operations and the generation effect. *Journal of Experimental Psychology: Learning, Memory, and Cognition, 15,* 669–675.

Farr, M. J. (1987). *The long-term retention of knowledge and skills: A cognitive and instructional perspective.* New York: Springer-Verlag.

Fendrich, D. W., Healy, A. F., & Bourne, L. E., Jr. (1991). Long-term repetition effects for motoric and perceptual procedures. *Journal of Experimental Psychology: Learning, Memory, and Cognition, 17,* 137–151.

Fendrich, D. W., Healy, A. F., & Bourne, L. E., Jr. (1993). Mental arithmetic: Training and retention of multiplication skill. In C. Izawa (Ed.), *Cognitive psychology applied* (pp. 111–133). Hillsdale, New Jersey: Erlbaum.

Gick, M. L., & Holyoak, K. J. (1987). The cognitive basis of knowledge transfer. In S. M. Cormier & J. D. Hagman (Eds.), *Transfer of training: Contemporary research and applications* (pp. 9–46). New York: Academic Press.

Healy, A. F., Fendrich, D. W., Crutcher, R. J., Wittman, W. T., Gesi, A. T., Ericsson, K. A., & Bourne, L. E., Jr. (1992). The long-term retention of skills. In A. F. Healy, S. M. Kosslyn, & R. M. Shiffrin (Eds.), *From learning processes to cognitive processes: Essays in honor of William K. Estes* (Vol. 2, pp. 87–118). Hillsdale, NJ: Erlbaum.

Healy, A. F., Fendrich, D. W., & Proctor, J. D. (1990). Acquisition and retention of a letter-detection skill. *Journal of Experimental Psychology: Learning, Memory, and Cognition, 16,* 270–281.

Lee, T. D., & Magill, R. A. (1983). The locus of contextual interference in motor-skill acquisition. *Journal of Experimental Psychology: Learning, Memory, and Cognition, 9,* 730–746.

Logan, G. D. (1988). Toward an instance theory of automatization. *Psychological Review, 95,* 492–527.

MacLeod, C. M. (1991). Half a century of research on the Stroop effect: An integrative review. *Psychological Bulletin, 109,* 163–203.

Mane, A. M., Adams, J. A., & Donchin, E. (1989). Adaptive and part-whole training in the acquisition of a complex perceptual-motor skill. *Acta Psychologica, 71,* 179–196.

Marmie, W. R., & Healy, A. F. (1992). *The long-term retention of a complex skill: Part-whole training of tank gunner simulation exercises.* Unpublished manuscript.

McNamara, D. S., & Healy, A. F. (1991, November). *A generation advantage for multiplication skill and nonword vocabulary acquisition.* Paper presented at the 32nd. Annual Meeting of the Psychonomic Society, San Francisco, CA.

Naylor, J. C., & Briggs, G. E. (1963). Effects of task complexity and task organization on the relative efficiency of part and whole training methods. *Journal of Experimental Psychology, 65,* 217–224.

Newell, K. M., Carlton, M. J., Fisher, A. T., & Rutter, B. G. (1989). Whole-part training strategies for learning the response dynamics of microprocessor driven simulators. *Acta Psychologica, 71,* 197–216.

Pellegrino, J. W., Doane, S. M., Fischer, S. C., & Alderton, D. (1991). Stimulus complexity effects in visual comparisons: The effects of practice and learning context. *Journal of Experimental Psychology: Human Perception and Performance, 17,* 781–791.

Pirolli, P. L., & Anderson, J. R. (1985). The role of practice in fact retrieval. *Journal of Experimental Psychology: Learning, Memory, and Cognition, 11,* 136–153.

Rickard, T. C. (1992). *Acquisition and transfer of mental arithmetic skill.* Unpublished master's thesis, University of Colorado, Boulder.

Rickard, T. C., Mozer, M. C., & Bourne, L. E., Jr. (1992). *An interactive activation model of arithmetic fact retrieval* (Tech. Rep. No. 92-15). Boulder, CO: University of Colorado, Institute of Cognitive Science.

Sachs, J. S. (1967). Recognition memory for syntactic and semantic aspects of connected discourse. *Perception & Psychophysics, 2,* 437–442.

Schmidt, R. A., & Bjork, R. A. (1992). New conceptualizations of practice: Common principles in three paradigms suggest new concepts for training. *Psychological Science, 3,* 207–217.

Schneider, V. I. (1991). *The effects of contextual interference on the acquisition and retention of logic rules.* Unpublished doctoral dissertation, University of Colorado, Boulder.

Slamecka, N. J., & Graf, P. (1978). The generation effect: Delineation of a phenomenon. *Journal of Experimental Psychology: Human Learning and Memory, 4,* 592–604.

Underwood, B. J. (1964). Degree of learning and the measurement of forgetting. *Journal of Verbal Learning and Verbal Behavior, 3,* 112–129.

Wisher, R. A., Sabol, M. A., Sukenik, H. K., & Kern, R. P. (1991). *Individual ready reserve (IRR) call-up: Skill decay* (Research Report No. 1595). Alexandria, VA: U.S. Army Research Institute.

A COMPREHENSION-BASED APPROACH TO LEARNING AND UNDERSTANDING

Walter Kintsch
Bruce K. Britton
Charles R. Fletcher
Eileen Kintsch
Suzanne M. Mannes
Mitchell J. Nathan

I. Introduction

In this paper we outline a theory of how people understand texts, remember them, and learn from them. The theory is the model of discourse comprehension that was developed in Kintsch and van Dijk (1978), van Dijk and Kintsch (1983), and Kintsch (1988). We then describe a number of experiments derived from this theory and their instructional implications. All of this work has been published previously.[1] The reason for reviewing it here is twofold. First, we want to compare and contrast this theory with alternative approaches. Secondly, we shall attempt to give a broader picture of how research in text processing can inform educational practice, and how application can guide the development of a theory. The relation between theory and instructional implications is clear enough in each of

---

[1] The experimental work is reported in Bloom, Fletcher, van den Broek, Reitz, and Shapiro (1990); Britton, van Dusen, Glynn, and Hemphill (1990); Britton and Gulgoz (1991); Fletcher, Hummel and Marsolek (1990); E. Kintsch (1990); Mannes and Kintsch (1987); and Nathan, Kintsch, and Young (1992).

165

the original papers, but it is always a relation between one specific aspect of the theory and some specific instructional consequence or recommendation. From individual studies it is difficult to obtain a picture of the full scope and potential of the theory, and it is hard to see how much the development of the theory was actually driven by a concern for its pedagogical utility. Here, we present a review that highlights a variety of applications and that contrasts them with other psychological theories that are currently of importance in educational research. This paper is, therefore, not a general review of the field of discourse comprehension, but of a particular approach to this problem and its educational implications.

The problems investigated in these studies are still laboratory problems that so far have no direct instructional applications. However, this research can provide a basis for future instructional projects because of the implications it has for a number of important issues that arise when texts are employed for instructional purposes. Specifically, we are concerned here with three problems. First, it has often been claimed that the reader–text interaction is the crucial factor in comprehension and learning. The problem has been to specify concretely just what this interaction consists of. We show that the ability to model this interaction in concrete detail allows us to gain more control over the outcome of reading episodes. Secondly, we contrast our approach with theories that conceive of reading as essentially a passive process of assimilating information. We show what role active inferencing and knowledge elaboration play in learning from text, but also point out a number of constraining factors that need to be understood in order to guide the reader's activities into educationally fruitful directions. Finally, we consider ways to overcome the problems that occur when the mental representation that readers form on the basis of a text are insufficiently connected with their mental representation of the world itself. How can we help readers to form mental representations that are situated, that is, integrated with their mental models of the real world, rather than being abstract textual structures of their own? These are broad issues of major importance, and the few studies reported here fall far short of providing definitive answers. However, they show that by embedding these questions into the context of a general theory of discourse comprehension, such questions can at least be approached in a productive manner.

II. A Psychological Process Model of Discourse Comprehension

Traditionally, the study of language has been divided into syntax, semantics, and pragmatics, with the first two comprising the principal concern of linguists, and the third of greatest interest for the psychologists. In an alternative, more process-oriented view, we can structure our investigations according to the level of the psychological processes involved, from perception (which by itself comprises many levels), word identification, sentence parsing, meaning construction, and global understanding of a text, to the building of a mental model, and beyond that, to reasoning and problem solving on the basis of that model, and to thinking about the text.

Of these many levels, we have focused on the processes involved in understanding a text and in forming models of the situation described by the text. Understanding, in our view, implies forming mental representations. The two representations that we shall be most concerned with here are the *propositional textbase,* which has both a local and a global component, and the *situation model.* The textbase is a representation of the semantic structure of the text, including its rhetorical structure. The situation model, which represents the situation or event described by the text, integrates previous information from the reader's long-term memory with that contributed by the text.

The Kintsch and van Dijk theory provides a computational account of how these mental representations are formed when reading a text, or listening to it. That is, the theory specifies the sequence of computations that are involved in human text understanding. By implementing these computations with a computer, it is possible to investigate implications of the theory, such as (1) which computations lead to desirable outcomes and which do not, (2) which computations are difficult and resource demanding, and (3) what are the characteristics of the text representations created by these computations.

COHERENCE AND THE PROPOSITIONAL TEXTBASE[2]

Consider first the propositional textbase—the mental representation of the meaning of the text. This representation consists of a network of concepts (like "John" and "book") and propositions that tie together several concepts as arguments of a proposition by means of a predicate (like "John gives Mary a book" or "Mary reads the book"), as illustrated in Fig. 1. The relations among propositions (such as the relation between "give" and "read" here) may be any one of many different semantic relations, such as causal, prerequisite, consequence, part, class inclusion and the like. Frequently, however, it is convenient to approximate these relations simply by means of argument overlap: read and give are related because

---

[2] It is not possible to present the construction–integration theory of comprehension in adequate detail here. Further information can be found in the papers already mentioned, as well as in Kintsch (1992), Kintsch and Welsch (1991), Mannes and Doane (1991), and Mannes and Kintsch (1991).

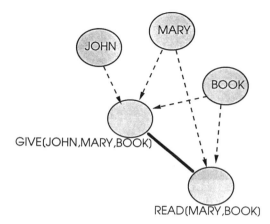

JOHN

MARY

BOOK

GIVE(JOHN,MARY,BOOK)

READ(MARY,BOOK)

Fig. 1.   Example of a propositional textbase, John gives Mary a book. Mary reads the book. A number of different relationships exist between the GIVE and READ propositions, such as argument overlap, temporal sequence, and entailment.

they share the common arguments Mary and book. This is a crude approximation, and it is often necessary to be more precise, for example, to analyze the causal relations in a story. However, for some purposes argument overlap is a very useful default because it provides a simple and objective index of semantic relatedness.

   Texts are read word by word and sentence by sentence. Hence understanding must take place sequentially. Since readers cannot keep in active working memory the whole mental representation they create for a long text, a theory of comprehension must explain how a reader is nevertheless able to form a coherent representation of the text. The Kintsch and van Dijk (1978) model postulates the following process. Only a small segment of the text, perhaps a sentence, is actively processed at any time. The previously read text, except for a few important propositions, is stored in long-term memory. The important propositions are kept in the working memory buffer, in the hope that they will provide a link between the previous text and new, incoming text.[3] This process is indicated schematically in Fig. 2. Long-term memory contains the trace resulting from the processing of previous sentences. A few elements of this trace—the ones most highly activated on the last processing cycle (Kintsch, 1988)—are

---

[3] List-learning models of memory, such as Atkinson and Shiffrin (1968), employ a buffer in a similar manner to maintain information temporarily in a short-term store, but since all the items in a list are more or less equal, the to-be-maintained items can be selected probabilistically, whereas with text the differing importance of the various text elements must be considered.

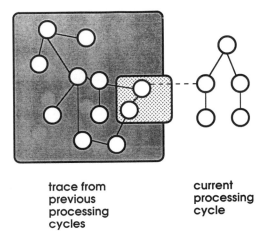

trace from   current
previous   processing
processing   cycle
cycles

Fig. 2.   The cyclical nature of text processing: traces from previous cycles form a network
in long-term memory (shaded area); only a small number of these propositions are maintained
in the focus of attention (cross-hatched area) and linked to the current input.

still in the focus of attention (i.e., active in working memory), where they
may be combined with the new sentence material, thus forming a link
between the already generated structure in long-term memory and the
current input.

It is, of course, not necessarily the case that the most active propositions
from the previous cycle have any relationship at all to the next sentence,
as, for example, when a topic-shift occurs. If there is a relationship,
coherence is maintained. If not, a break in coherence occurs, which results
in one of the following outcomes: The reader may bridge the coherence gap
either by searching long-term memory for a linking proposition and rein-
stating it in working memory or by generating a linking proposition via an
inference. When this happens, reading times typically increase (e.g., Lesgold, Roth, & Curtis, 1979). Alternatively, the coherence gap may be
unresolved, resulting in immediate comprehension problems and difficulties later in retrieving the information. Thus, breaks in coherence are
important. They demand extra work during comprehension and, if left
unresolved, they may cause problems later.

At this point, our sketch of the comprehension theory is still incomplete.
Specifically, we have not yet considered how readers bring their own
knowledge to bear in understanding a text and how they integrate what
they learn from the text with what they already know. We shall return to
these questions later, but first two issues will be discussed that set apart
the present approach from other theories of discourse comprehension. In
comparing and contrasting the implications of the theory described here

with well-known alternatives we hope to clarify the essential features of each.

The first issue concerns the ancient puzzle of where the meaning of a text resides: in the text? in the mind of the reader? or in the interaction between reader and text? The strong and weak points of these positions have long been known and continue to be vigorously debated (e.g., Rosenblatt, 1978). The third alternative has been regarded favorably by many participants in that debate—except for its vagueness. A model such as the present one removes this vagueness and specifies precisely what the interaction between reader and text consists of. This point is made in Section III, in which we contrast a position based on a deep linguistic, structural analysis of narratives (Trabasso & Sperry, 1985) with our process-oriented view.

The present approach also has implications for the second issue we address in Section III: What features make a text understandable, readable, and memorable? Once again, we shall show that it is not just a matter of text properties. Instead, only a direct consideration of the nature of the reader–text interaction can provide a satisfactory answer to this age-old question. Thus, in both cases, our answers are derived from the computational mechanisms postulated by the model of comprehension: If, indeed, people employ analogous computations in comprehension, then our conclusions follow about which features of a text are most significant and which less so, and about what can be done to improve the readability of text.

III.   Text Structure: On the Page or in the Head?

What is the structure of a text? Is it a property of the text, or is it a mental representation that is the result of a particular reader–text interaction? The theory sketched above has specific, detailed, and testable implications vis-à-vis these long-standing controversial issues.

When a discourse linguist analyzes a text, he or she attempts to identify all of the relationships among its constituent statements (see e.g., Halliday & Hasan, 1976; van Dijk, 1972). Some controversy exists over exactly what kinds of relationships are possible and the criteria one should use to identify them. Nevertheless, two important points of agreement are clear: First, each text has a *structure* that can be discerned through careful analysis. Second, the types of relationships that constitute that structure vary from one genre of text to another.

A reader's task in some ways is like that of a discourse linguist. In order to understand a text he or she must determine the structure of the portion of the text currently being read and how each new statement is related to those that preceded it. We have noted above that this process is constrained both by the semantic and rhetorical structure of the text and by the limitations of the reader's information-processing system and background knowledge. In response to these constraints, readers develop comprehension strategies that permit them to discover as much of a text's structure as needed or as is possible with a minimum expenditure of cognitive resources. These strategies provide the reader with a mental representation that (except for the simplest texts) includes only a subset of the relationships among statements that would be part of the text linguist's analysis. Not surprisingly, the kinds of comprehension strategies that psychologists have proposed differ from one genre of text to another (cf. Clark, Stephenson, & Rutter, 1986; Fletcher & Bloom, 1988; Kintsch & Greeno, 1985; Spilich, Vesonder, Chiesi, & Voss, 1979). This is due, at least in part, to the fact that the types of relationships that provide coherence and structure to a text differ across genres.

A. THE STRUCTURE OF NARRATIVE TEXTS

The best-understood type of text—for readers and researchers alike—is, without doubt, the narrative. Narratives have received far more attention than any other genre. Most authors agree that narrative content is held together by causal and enabling relationships (see e.g., Black & Bower, 1980; Schank, 1975). This claim is consistent with our intuition that we as readers understand a statement from a narrative when we know what caused or enabled it, and that we understand the narrative as a whole when we can find a sequence of causal and enabling relationships that connect its opening to its final outcome.

Trabasso and Sperry (1985) have refined this notion by proposing that two statements from a narrative are semantically related if, in the circumstances described by the text, one of them (the consequence) would not have occurred had the other (the antecedent) not occurred. This single criterion, which they call "necessity in the circumstances," allows them to identify both causal and enabling relationships. As an example of how this criterion is applied, consider the first sentence of "Danny's New Bike" (Table I). In the circumstances described by the text, Danny would not have wanted the bike (Statement 1) if he hadn't seen it in the shop window (Statement 2). Therefore, a semantic link exists in the text *from* Statement 2 *to* Statement 1. When we analyze the entire text in this fashion, the result is the network shown in Fig. 3. The nodes in this network represent individual states and events in the world described by the text. The links represent the causal and enabling relationships among

TABLE I

Danny's New Bike

Sentence	Statement	
1	1	Danny wanted to have the red bike
	2	that he saw in the window of the neighborhood bike shop.
2	3	Danny knew that first he had to have $50
	4	to buy the bike.
3	5	He asked his parents if they would give him the money.
4	6	His parents denied his request.
5	7	They suggested that Danny earn the money himself
	8	by getting a job.
6	9	Danny was mad at his parents
	10	for not giving him the money,
	11	but he was determined to get the $50 somehow.
7	12	He knew he would have to find a job,
	13	so he called the newspaper
	14	and asked for the paper route.
8	15	He started delivering papers in his neighborhood the next week
	16	and earned $10 a week.
9	17	With this job,
	18	Danny had $50 within a few weeks.
10	19	He took his hard-earned money to the shop,
	20	bought the bike,
	21	and rode home happily.

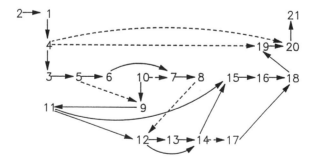

Fig. 3. The structure of "Danny's New Bike." Each node corresponds to one of the numbered statements in Table I. Solid links show causal or enabling relationships that are easily detected by a reader. Dashed links show relationships that can be discovered only through a reinstatement search. From Bloom et al., 1990, *Memory & Cognition, 18,* 65–71. Reprinted by permission of the Psychonomic Society, Inc.

them. Trabasso and his colleagues (e.g., Trabasso & Sperry, 1985; Trabasso & van den Broek, 1985) have presented compelling evidence for the correctness of this structural analysis. However, we still need to explain how a reader actually makes use of these semantic links in comprehending a story.

B. COMPREHENSION AND LIMITATIONS OF THE HUMAN INFORMATION-PROCESSING SYSTEM

According to the theory outlined above, when a reader encounters a sentence, he or she must retrieve the meaning of each word from long-term memory, assemble those meanings into individual propositions, assemble the propositions into discrete states and events, and then identify the relationships among the states and events. If the sentence is part of a longer text, the reader must also determine how the states and events within the sentence are related to the preceding text. This determination is problematic, first of all, because a relationship between two parts of a text can be detected only if both are simultaneously available in working memory, and secondly, because working memory has a limited capacity. The general solution to this problem has been described above. At the end of each sentence the reader focuses his or her attention on the most highly activated elements of the text, usually a single state or event. That state or event remains active in short-term memory while the following sentence is read. If all goes well, the selected information provides a semantic link between the new sentence and the earlier text. Exactly which portions of the current sentence will be most activated will depend on the reader's comprehension strategies, which, in turn, are genre specific. Thus, in a narrative, one expects readers to emphasize causal relations, and hence causally significant events are likely to become most strongly activated in working memory.

For hurried, careless, or poor readers this may represent the end of the comprehension process (see, e.g., McKoon & Ratcliff, 1992), but more careful readers will recognize that too much of a text's structure is overlooked by this process. As a result, if reading goals demand a more careful analysis, and the resources (time, effort) are available, a reader will search through a text, or its representation in long-term memory, for earlier statements that are semantically related to the sentence he or she is attempting to understand and will construct a more faithful representation of the text.

C. COMPREHENSION STRATEGIES FOR NARRATIVE TEXTS

Fletcher and his colleagues have explored these narrative comprehension strategies in detail (Bloom et al., 1990; Fletcher & Bloom, 1988; Fletcher et et al., 1990). In keeping with previous research (especially van Dijk & Kintsch, 1983; Trabasso & Sperry, 1985) they began by assuming: (1) that a reader's short-term memory can hold only the current sentence plus the propositions corresponding to a single state or event from earlier in the text, and (2) that a reader understands a narrative by discovering its causal structure. They then examined several candidate short-term memory-management strategies and found that a reader can maximize the proportion of a text's causal structure that he or she discovers by always focusing attention on the most recent state or event with antecedents earlier in the text. At any given point in a narrative, this represents the most likely causal antecedent to the following sentence. It also remains in short-term memory each time the reader begins a new sentence.

As an example of how this strategy works, consider Fig. 4, which illustrates the sentence-by-sentence processing of "Danny's New Bike." For each sentence the figure shows: (1) the subset of the larger text structure (Fig. 3) detected by the reader, and (2) the individual state or event that (according to the strategy) remains in short-term memory while the following sentence is read (these are underlined). It is important to note

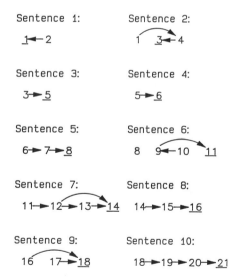

Fig. 4. Sentence-by-sentence processing of "Danny's New Bike." The statement that becomes the focus of attention at the end of each sentence is underlined. A coherence break in Sentence 6 is indicated by the absence of a link connecting Statement 8 (the focus of attention at the conclusion of Sentence 5) to the new sentence (composed of Statements 9, 10, and 11). From Bloom et al., 1990, *Memory & Cognition, 18,* 65–71. Reprinted by permission of the Psychonomic Society, Inc.

TABLE II

EXAMPLE OF MATERIALS FROM THE EXPERIMENT BY FLETCHER,
HUMMEL, & MARSOLEK (1990)[a]

1. Kate was having some friends over for her boyfriend's birthday and she wanted to serve a birthday cake.
2. She took out the ingredients she had bought and began to make a chocolate cake.
3. As she was mixing the batter, her sister came home and told her the oven was broken. (*critical sentence containing the test word*)
4a. Her sister had tried to use the oven earlier but discovered that it would not heat up. (*antecedent version*)
4b. Since she had the cake batter all ready she thought that she would use the neighbor's oven. (*consequence version*)
5. *** TOLD ***

[a] The antecedent version of this text includes sentence 4a, while the consequence version includes sentence 4b instead.

that a reader employing this strategy would discover 20 of the 26 possible causal and enabling links in this text without performing any reinstatement searches. These links are shown in both Fig. 3 and Fig. 4. The six links requiring additional processing effort are indicated by dashed arrows in Fig. 3.

Fletcher et al. (1990) performed the following experiment to test the psychological validity of this short-term memory-management strategy. College student subjects were presented with brief narratives on a computer screen, such as the one shown in Table II. Each text was shown one sentence at a time, and each sentence remained on the screen just long enough for subjects to read it. At some point, a probe word was presented instead of another sentence. Readers were required to decide as quickly as possible whether this probe word had occurred earlier in the text and to indicate their decision by pressing one of two buttons. Probes for which a "yes" response was appropriate were always taken from the sentence immediately preceding one of two alternative intervening sentences. In one condition of the experiment (the antecedent condition), the intervening sentence contained a causal antecedent to the statement that included the probe word (4a). Under these circumstances, the proposition containing the probe word should remain in the reader's short-term memory because the reader's attention remains focused on the current state. As a result the probe should be recognized quickly and accurately. In the other condition (the consequence condition) the intervening sentence contained a causal consequence of the critical statement (4b). Under these circumstances, the proposition containing the probe word should (theoretically) not remain in the reader's short-term memory and would need to be retrieved from long-term memory. As a result, the probe should be recognized less quickly and less accurately than probes from the antecedent condition. These predictions were confirmed by Fletcher et al. (1990), thus demonstrating that the causal relations in a narrative text play a crucial role in determining where the reader's attention is focused during comprehension.

The occurrence of reinstatement searches during narrative comprehension was investigated by Bloom et al. (1990). They found that readers are most likely to reinstate an idea when they encounter a coherence break—a situation in which the state or event held over in short-term memory has no causal or enabling links to the sentence being read. In "Danny's New Bike" the only coherence break occurs in the sixth sentence (Statement 9: "Danny was mad at his parents"). Readers are required to reinstate Statement 5 ("He asked his parents if they would give him the money") to preserve the coherence of the text (see Fig. 3). As predicted, all of the participants in their experiment showed marked increases in reading time when they encountered such breaks. The authors assume that the extra time reflects time needed to retrieve information from long-term memory.

The research on narrative comprehension by Fletcher and his colleagues illustrates several important points. The structure of a text, as analyzed by the linguist, is important, but what really matters is how the reader interacts with that structure. Exactly how the text structure will be represented in the reader's memory depends on the information-processing constraints of the human system. Expressed in such general terms, this is nothing but a truism. However, the studies described above specify the mechanism that computes the structure in the head for a given text. It is useful to think of a text's linguistic structure (the structure on the page) as an ideal that readers strive toward. Because of the limitations of the human-information processing system, readers typically end up with a mental representation of a text (the structure in the head) that falls short of that ideal. A reader's skill and motivation may well determine how closely he or she approaches the ideal representation.

The instructional implications of these findings have not yet been explored. Nevertheless, it appears likely that instruction could make use of this knowledge about how structure moves from the page into the reader's head. Less skilled readers, whose resources are taken up by other aspects of the reading process, probably lack the short-term memory capacity needed to carry over enough information from cycle to cycle so that a coherent text representation is achieved. This may be the case even if they possess the right strategies (i.e., knowledge about the causal relations in a story, which is apparently acquired very early, e.g., Poulsen, Kintsch,

Kintsch, & Premack, 1979). Thus, the instructor could guide such readers to perform reinstatement searches at crucial points in the text. Knowing what should happen in comprehending a story could help the teacher make it happen.

IV. Diagnosing and Circumventing Comprehension Problems

We now turn to another issue in which a comprehension model that focuses on the reader–text interaction can be contrasted with traditional approaches that emphasize either text or reader characteristics in isolation. Many years of research have been devoted to readability questions: What are the features that make a text easy or difficult to read and remember? How can instructional texts be improved? We cannot review the huge literature concerned with readability (see Britton, Gulgoz, & Glynn, 1993, and Weaver & Kintsch, 1990, for a discussion of this field from the present perspective), but the outcome of this research was ultimately disappointing. Controlled studies of the effects of readability (including Coleman, 1962; Duffy & Kabance, 1982) have yielded very small effects or none at all. Another approach to improving instructional texts consisted in the compilation of various lists of expert recommendations for good writing. The trouble with this approach is that it yields pitifully low agreement (Britton, 1986): Different features of a text are considered important by different authors.

What sort of alternatives does our model of comprehension suggest? For one, we know that coherence is important for a text to be understood, and that readers must make bridging inferences (Haviland & Clark, 1974) where the text is not sufficiently explicit. We also know that under many conditions normal readers do not always make the necessary inferences (McKoon & Ratcliff, 1992). Hence, if we know where in a text readers must infer information that has been left implicit by the author, we should be able to locate readability problems and alter the text to avoid them.

A. PREDICTING RECALL FROM COMPREHENSION BREAKDOWNS

In the previous section we argued that text structure is but one determinant of the text representation achieved by the reader, and of the ease with which it is constructed. Other determinants include the reader's own strategies, knowledge, and resource limitations. The reader must have sufficient memory capacity to perform the reinstatement searches that link the present text with what was read before. In addition, a text relies to a greater or lesser extent on the reader's knowledge of the domain to fill in gaps in the meaning via inferences. These bridging inferences are generated quite automatically when one is dealing with a familiar topic. However, they can be resource consuming and require a great deal of problem solving when one is reading about a less familiar domain. A failure to generate bridging inferences may even lead to a breakdown in comprehension.

The notion that certain cognitive processes are resource limited is a very common one in cognitive psychology (e.g., Norman & Bobrow, 1975). If one process, or one component of a process, demands a large part of a person's cognitive resources (short-term memory capacity, attention, etc.) other processes that have to be performed at the same time will suffer, unless they are fully automated, that is, not resource demanding. Thus, if a reader must devote too many resources to decoding, comprehension will suffer (Perfetti, 1985; 1989). If bridging inferences are too demanding, for example, because the relevant knowledge is not readily available, similar comprehension deficits result.

Not only are reinstatement searches and inferences major sources of reading difficulty (Bloom et al., 1990; Kintsch & Vipond, 1979; Miller & Kintsch, 1980), they also predict what subjects are able to recall from a text. Memory encoding is affected if too high a proportion of the reader's cognitive resources must be devoted to the establishment of coherence, because other components of the comprehension process may thereby be neglected. Retrieval problems result when readers fail to construct a coherent textbase during encoding by not engaging in the necessary inferencing and memory searches, because retrieval depends on the availability in long-term memory of a richly interlinked network of information.

Britton and his colleagues performed a series of studies that showed how texts could be improved by taking into consideration the factors discussed above. In their first study (Britton et al., 1990) eight high school history texts, 600–1000 words long, were analyzed for coherence breaks. Each text was propositionalized, and the sequence of comprehension cycles was simulated according to the model of Miller and Kintsch (1980). When coherence failed for the model, that is, when there was no argument overlap between the propositions kept in the buffer and the propositions of the next cycle, the program stopped. At this point, either an old proposition not available in the buffer was found that reestablished coherence, or a proposition was added that created the required linkage. In the first case, a reinstatement was counted, in the second an inference. The simulation was then restarted and the processing cycles continued until another break occurred or until the whole passage had been processed.

Each text was read and recalled by 24 undergraduates. Table III shows the percentage of immediate free recall by these subjects for the eight texts and the number of gap-filling inferences required to establish coherence, according to the theoretical analysis. The correlation between these two sets of scores in Table III is $-.89$. Table IV shows similar correlations between free recall as well as a short-answer test, both immediate and delayed, for reinstatements and inferences. (The data shown in Table III provided the correlation in the first cell in Table IV.) The number of reinstatements and the number of bridging inferences required for processing a text are good predictors of both recall and performance on a short-answer test.

B. REVISING A TEXT TO PREVENT COMPREHENSION BREAKDOWNS

Clearly, there are differences in the quality of written texts, and a poorly written text can be greatly improved by an expert writer. Even though experts can describe what they are doing in general terms and can enunciate some principles of good writing, which may help to a greater or lesser extent, revising a text is certainly more of an art than it is a well-understood algorithmic process. Our comprehension model provides an alternative approach that makes it possible to diagnose problem spots in the processing of text: By pinpointing the gaps in coherence requiring a reinstatement or inference, the text can be rewritten to circumvent these problems. Thus, a principled, theory-based revision of the text can be obtained, and its effectiveness can be empirically evaluated and compared with that of an intuitive revision by an expert writer.

TABLE III

RECALL AND INFERENCE CALLS FOR TWO TEXTS, EACH IN FOUR DIFFERENT VERSIONS

Passage	Rewriters	Immediate recall (%)	Inference calls
Vietnam	Composition instructors	28	3
Korea	Composition instuctors	25	3
Vietnam	Discourse researchers	23	4
Vietnam	Original	22	4
Korea	Discourse researchers	20	8
Vietnam	Time-Life	20	8
Korea	Original	14	8
Korea	Time-Life	13	13

TABLE IV

CORRELATIONS BETWEEN INFERENCE CALLS,
REINSTATEMENTS, AND RECALL

	Free recall		Short answer	
	Immediate	Delayed	Immediate	Delayed
Inference calls	−.89	−.85	−.78	−.76
Reinstatements	−.80	−.75	−.71	−.70

Accordingly, Britton and Gulgoz (1991) selected a 1,030-word text on the air war in North Vietnam from a document on Air Force history. They simulated comprehension of this text by putting it sentence by sentence through the computer model of Miller and Kintsch (1980), and by noting potential problems in establishing coherence. Such problems occur when there is no explicit relation between the propositions carried over in the short-term memory buffer from the previous cycle and the propositions derived from the current sentence. Whenever the simulation broke down, because of lack of overlapping arguments among the propositions, Britton and Gulgoz rewrote the text so as to circumvent the problem. The beginning of the original text follows:

Air War in the North, 1965
By the fall of 1964, Americans in both Saigon and Washington had begun to focus on Hanoi as the source of the continuing problem in the South.

The inferences necessary for comprehension that were added to the original text are shown in parentheses:

Air War in North (Vietnam), 1985
By the fall of 1964 (causing events in 1965), Americans in both Saigon and Washington had begun to focus on Hanoi (capitol of North Vietnam) as the source of the continuing problems in the South.

North is identified as *North Vietnam,* the relation between *1965* in the title and the events of *1964* is explicated, and *Hanoi* is identified as the *capitol of North Vietnam.* Propositions corresponding to these ideas were added to the original text propositions, so that the model was able to generate a coherent textbase. Finally, the text was rewritten, incorporating these inferences:

Air War in North Vietnam, 1965
By the beginning of 1965, Americans in both Saigon and Washington had begun to focus on Hanoi, capitol of North Vietnam, as the source of the continuing problems in the South.

There were a total of 40 such coherence problems in the original text. (Further changes were made to the sentence shown here to make it coherent with the sentences following it). The result was a principled revision of the original text. Note that only co-reference was explicitly considered in revising this text; one could, of course, also consider coherence in terms of causal or other semantic relations, as was done in the studies on narratives. A heuristic revision was also constructed by an expert writer who used general principles for good writing. This heuristic revision was thought of as an upper bound for the principled revision, showing what could be done if an expert had complete freedom to rewrite the text in the best way known. Britton and Gulgoz then gave each version of the text to 22 undergraduate students to read at their own rate and to recall. The results are shown in Table V.

The principled revision was longer than either the original text or the heuristic revision. However, subjects read the principled revision at a faster rate than the other two versions of the text, and most importantly, recalled significantly more from the principled revision than from the original text. Indeed, the principled revision produced a higher recall score (though non-significantly) than even the heuristic revision. In terms

TABLE V

READING TIMES AND RECALL FOR THE ORIGINAL
AND REVISED VERSIONS OF THE AIR FORCE TEXT

	Original version	Principled revision	Heuristic revision
Length (words)	1030	1302	1027
Reading time (min)	10	12	10
Reading rate (words per min)	112	121	114
Recall (number of propositions)	36	59	56
Propositions recalled per min	3	5	6

of an efficiency measure, propositions recalled per minute of study time, the revised texts were almost twice as efficient as the original text.

Not only was the quantity of recall improved but also the quality of the information acquired by reading the text. This result was achieved in the following way. Britton and Gulgoz first determined how the author thought about the relations among several key terms in his original article by having him indicate how closely related these terms were. Then they had the readers of the article do the same thing. A comparison of the structures generated by the author and by his readers indicates how closely readers have adopted the author's viewpoint. If the author was completely successful, his readers should have adopted the same situation model, as indexed by their ratings of the relatedness of key terms from the article, that he tried to impart to them. This procedure was designed to elicit what readers knew about the air war in Vietnam. That is, Britton and Gulgoz were not interested just in whether the subjects remembered what they had read, but in whether they also formed a correct situation model about the air war in Vietnam.

Specifically, Britton and Gulgoz selected 12 terms from the article. These 12 key words form 66 pairs. Subjects were asked to rate the strength of the relationship between the two words in each pair on a 7-point scale. The author of the original article produced one set of such ratings. A panel of seven experts (two military historians, a former ambassador, etc.) who had read the original text produced another set of ratings. Finally, 40 Air Force recruits rated the word pairs after reading one of the three versions of the text. The ratings correlated only .08 (not significantly different from 0) with the ratings of the author among the recruits who had read the original version, but the correlations with the author were significant, $r = .52$ and $.61$, respectively, among those who had read the principled revision or the heuristic revision. The results were about the same when the ratings of the recruits were compared, not with the author's own understanding of his text, but with those of the seven experts. Figure 5A shows the "knowledge map" that was computed by a scaling method called *Pathfinder* (Schvaneveldt, Durso, & Dearholt, 1989) for the seven experts. The concept *graduated response strategy* is central, just as it was in the original paper, and the other concepts are arranged in a reasonable way around it. The article didn't say much about the military (it focused on Johnson's civilian advisors), and the strategy was far from successful; these facts are reflected in the experts' map. Figure 5B shows the knowledge map for subjects who read the principled revision. Here also, most of the links are reasonable. However, the subjects who read the original version of the text, shown in Fig. 5C, provided a rather different picture: Most importantly, these

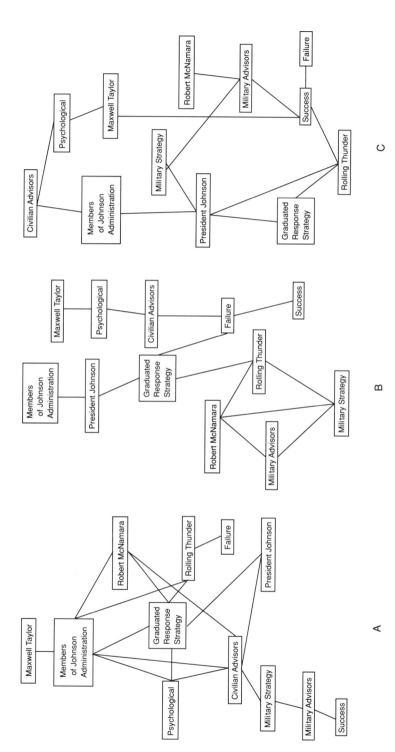

Fig. 5. Twelve key concepts and their interrelationships (A) from subject matter experts who read the Air Force text, (B) from Air Force recruits who read the principled revision of the Air Force text, and (C) from Air Force recruits who read the original version of the Air Force text. From B. K. Britton & S. Golguz, "Using Kintsch's computational model to improve instructional text: Effects of repairing inference calls on recall and cognitive structures," *Journal of Educational Psychology, 83*, 329–345. Copyright 1991 by The American Psychological Association. Adapted by permission.

subjects have associated operation Rolling Thunder, the dismal product of this strategy, with success.

These qualitative results are even more revealing than the quantitative differences in the amount recalled after reading the original and the revised text. For the undergraduate students and Air Force recruits, the original text was a failure: Not only did they not remember much of the information, but what they learned from it about the air war in North Vietnam—the situation model they constructed, partly from the text, partly from what they already knew—was simply incorrect in the sense that it differed from what the author intended and from the way experts understood the text.

This is quite an interesting finding. We have a text that unknowledgeable readers cannot handle. They cannot recall it, and they misunderstand the content. Comprehension theory provides us with the means to rewrite that text in a principled manner, making it easier for such readers to establish a coherent textbase. The revision significantly improved the quantity of recall as well as the accuracy of the information that readers acquired. It is worth noting here that these improvements were achieved with a very simple model—indeed, an oversimplified view of coherence, for coherence involves certainly more than argument overlap—yet even with such an oversimplification one can achieve results with practical consequences. Our strategy here may be compared to that of an engineer who uses an approximation to a complex physical system that neglects a lot of relevant factors, but is still workable. That this is possible is good news, indeed, for it shows that in order to achieve educationally significant results, we do not need to know everything.

Yet surely there is more to comprehension than coherence, whether measured in terms of argument overlap at the surface level (Britton & Gulgoz), or in terms of the causal links in the semantic structure (Fletcher et al.). Nevertheless, as Britton and Gulgoz have shown, facilitating the task of the reader in just this one respect can have strong beneficial consequences. Writing texts that relieve the students of inferencing and that help them to avoid memory searches can significantly improve their ability to understand and reproduce a text.

In Sections V and VI we discuss two other research projects that stem from the same theoretical background but that are concerned with different aspects of the theory. In Section V we focus on the role of macrostructures in comprehension and the process by which they are constructed. This study makes an interesting and important contrast to the Britton and Gulgoz work. Then in Section VI we shall return to the distinction between textbase and situation model, or between remembering the text and learning from the text—an issue that we have slighted so far, but that is of central importance in educational research and instruction.

V. The Role of Active Inferencing in the Construction of Text Meaning

We have described a theory of discourse comprehension and contrasted it with other approaches, focusing on the importance that is assigned to the reader–text interaction by the theory. However, so far we have described this interaction as a fairly passive process, with the reader mainly absorbing textual information and completing it inferentially as required. We now want to contrast our theory with alternative approaches to discourse comprehension along an activity dimension. Theories of discourse comprehension have traditionally assigned the reader a more or less passive role, as we have done above. The reader in some sense copies what is found in the text into a mental representation, a process that may require some bridging inferences, but that is basically one of information assimilation. Early theories of discourse comprehension, including our own, were typically of this form (e.g., Frederiksen 1975; Kintsch, 1974; Meyer, 1975). Later, this picture was elaborated to allow for schema-based reconstruction processes (Anderson, 1984; Schank & Abelson, 1977). The schema, however, was thought of as a prefabricated memory structure that needed only to be retrieved from long-term memory, leaving the reader still in a passive role—copying from both text and schema. Superior comprehension and recall were attributed to the existence of more completely elaborated schemata in long-term memory into which incoming information could be incorporated.

In contrast, the present model assigns the reader a much more active role in the construction of meaning from text. We first discuss two experimental results that help us to specify just what this activity consists of. We then show how this active reader can be conceptualized within the present theory, and contrast this approach with various alternatives.

First, however, let us again consider the results of Britton and Gulgoz, as there are limiting conditions on their generality that should be made explicit. It is not always the case that inferences and reinstatement searches interfere with text comprehension and memory—that occurs only when these activities are not done, or are not done correctly. Typically this happens when readers lack efficient strategies and resources (Perfetti, 1985), or the requisite domain knowledge (Perfetti & Mc-Cutchen, 1987). On the other hand, readers with good strategies and resources, or those with considerable knowledge of the domain, often have no trouble making simple bridging inferences themselves—and, as we shall see below, there may be beneficial consequences of these activities.

Let us consider what happens when different kinds of readers are confronted with an inconsiderate text—one in which the normal coherence relationships are disrupted and in which linguistic cues to the appropriate bridging inferences are lacking.

A.   THE DEVELOPMENT OF SUMMARIZATION SKILL

E. Kintsch (1990) used the theory of comprehension to gain a detailed picture of developmental differences in the ability to summarize expository text. In her study 96 students from three age groups were given a one-page, single-spaced text to read and summarize in writing. The students were normal readers from Grades 6, 10, and college.

Two texts were written at a sixth-grade reading level. They compared two relatively unfamiliar foreign countries with respect to three global factors that would influence their future development: the geographic features of the countries, their economies, and their cultures. However, these factors were not mentioned explicitly in the texts and had to be inferred by the reader. In addition, the texts were written at a very concrete level in order to maximize opportunities to form generalizing inferences or macropropositions.

The difficulty of the texts was manipulated at both the microstructure and the macrostructure processing levels, resulting in four versions of each text: (1) good macrostructure—good microstructure, (2) good macrostructure—poor microstructure, (3) poor macrostructure—good microstructure, and (4) poor macrostructure—poor microstructure. Processing at the microstructure level was made more difficult by eliminating many sentence connectives (e.g., "in contrast," "therefore," "however," and the like) and by using harder words and sentence structures. Macrostructure processing was made difficult by disrupting the topic structure, without, however, destroying the local connections between propositions. For example, instead of comparing two countries on the basis of each attribute in order, a paragraph containing facts about agriculture, social problems, and exports of one country was followed by a paragraph describing education, farming, and climate of the other country. Each subject received one version of a single text to summarize.

The results of this study revealed major changes with age in constructive (or inferential) processing and in the mental representation of the textual material. In general, collapsing across text versions, the summaries of the three subject groups did not differ significantly in the number of text propositions they contained. However, there were significant differences across the three age groups in the amount of inferred material (generalizations, elaborations, and reorderings). The summaries of the younger students consisted largely of propositions from the original text, with very few inferences of any kind, while the amount of inferential processing increased gradually across the other two grade levels. The increase in the number of generalizations, elaborations, and reorderings is shown as a function of age in Fig. 6.

The tendency with age to reformulate the content of the text in more general terms was accompanied by a corresponding decrease in the amount of text details. This showed up both in the number of generalization inferences that occurred in the students' summaries and in the level at which text-based statements occurred in the summaries. The ideal

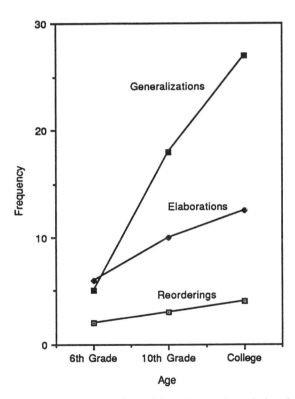

Fig. 6.   The frequency of generalizations, elaborations, and reorderings in the subjects' summaries as a function of age.

macrostructure for these texts formed a hierarchy with a general topic statement at the top and various levels of subtopics. The few macropropositions that occurred in the younger students' summaries were typically top-level statements about the topic. The bulk of their compositions consisted of an assortment of details from the text. In contrast, the high school and college students' summaries included macrorelevant statements at all levels of the hierarchy, a result suggesting a meaning representation that differentiates the ideas into several levels of importance. This structure was similar to the one used by the author.

In summary, more mature readers were characterized not so much by a better ability to reproduce the text (there were no real differences in this respect among the three age groups), but in the quantity and quality of the inferences they made in reading the text. Unlike 6th graders, 10th graders and especially college students made a large number of generalizations, and were more likely to elaborate what they read from their own knowledge (Fig. 6). As a consequence of this active processing, they generated macrostructures that more adequately reflected the intended hierarchical structure of the text, and hence were able to write better summaries. Thus, the use of active processing strategies in reading differentiates young and experienced readers. However, E. Kintsch also showed in her study that certain features of a text may stimulate active processing—with beneficial results, but only under some conditions.

B. EFFECTS OF POOR MACROSTRUCTURE

Text version affected comprehension differentially in the three age groups. Older students were more successful at dealing with comprehension difficulties at both the macrostructure and the microstructure level. The results for the macrostructure-level analysis are shown in Fig. 7, in which the percentage of statements in the summaries that expressed macropropositions is shown for the three age groups. (In the ideal summary, all statements would be macrorelevant.) Less than a third of what sixth-grade students put into their summaries consisted of macrostatements when the students read the good text, the remainder being detail statements from the text that do not belong in a summary. Furthermore, for the text with poor macrostructure this percentage dropped by almost one half. Thus, while sixth graders do not write very good summaries of even a well-organized text, a poorly written text greatly interferes with their ability to include macrorelevant information.

Tenth graders, on the other hand, had a higher overall percentage of macrostatements in their summaries, as one would expect, but, more

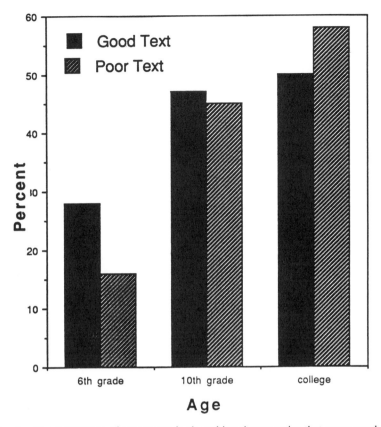

Fig. 7. The percentage of statements in the subjects' summaries that corresponded to macropropositions as function of age for both versions of the text.

importantly, this percentage was not affected by whether they read the good or the poor text version. Interestingly, college students wrote better summaries (in the sense that the percentage of macropropositions was higher) when they read the poorly written text than when they read the good text. Thus, difficulties with the coherence structure of the text seems to have interfered with the younger readers' comprehension, perhaps because of knowledge deficiencies or because their ability to generate even lower-level bridging inferences was not sufficiently automatic (cf. Perfetti, 1985), or both. In contrast, the poorly organized passages resulted in more constructive effort on the part of the oldest group of students, who responded to the challenge by writing better and more generalized summaries.

This rather surprising result[4] has some important educational implications which, however, pose a difficult challenge when it comes to designing appropriate kinds of instruction. On the one hand, less skilled readers and those with little background knowledge in a domain need maximum support. One way to provide this would be to construct very explicit, coherent texts which reduce the amount of gap-filling inferences needed to form a coherent representation of the content, as Britton and Gulgoz did in their study. On the other hand, readers with adequate literacy skills who are moderately familiar with the domain might benefit a great deal from having to work harder to get the meaning. By breaking down easy, automatic processing and increasing the amount of active, constructive effort needed to understand a text, the writer forces learners to engage in more problem-solving activities. These, in turn, may help the readers to achieve a deeper understanding of what they are reading. Taken together, the findings of Britton and Gulgoz and of E. Kintsch suggest that students may be better served by an instructional approach that is sensitive to the interactions of text quality and individual differences in readers, but one that helps students do their own thinking, rather than doing it for them.

In the study just described, active processing was achieved by making the text just difficult enough so that it stimulates readers to make their own inferences. In Section VI we describe how a similar effect is obtained by presenting a text in such a way that it still activates relevant knowledge, but so that there is a mismatch between the reader's knowledge structure and the text structure. For learning from text, such a discrepancy can be an advantage rather than a hindrance.

VI. Learning from Text

The studies reported so far have been concerned primarily with text comprehension and memory. In terms of the comprehension theory, the relevant level of knowledge representation is the textbase—the mental representation of the text itself upon which such behaviors as text recall and summarization are usually based. There is, however, another level of representation that is pedagogically important—the situation model. Here, we are not primarily concerned with how well a reader can reproduce or summarize a text, but with how well the content of the text

---

[4] Parallel results have sometimes been reported in the list-learning literature, where it was found that higher cognitive effort under some circumstances actually improves learning (e.g., Ellis, Parente, and Walker, 1974; Tyler, Hertel, McCallum and Ellis, 1979).

has been understood and assimilated into the reader's general store of knowledge. In other words, the distinction we are making is between *memory for a text* and *learning from a text.*

This distinction has not always been observed in the literature, though there are some exceptions. For example, Perfetti (1989) distinguishes two types of comprehension: the meaning of a text, which is restricted to the text and primarily non-inferential, and the interpretation, which is less text based and which contains more inferential material. Meaning of a text is constructed with a relatively small amount of prior knowledge, whereas interpretation depends heavily on prior knowledge. In the van Dijk and Kintsch theory, text meaning corresponds to the textbase, and interpretation to the situation model. What really distinguishes the two levels of representation, Perfetti claims, is the richness of inference.

In order to explore this distinction, Mannes and Kintsch (1987) gave two groups of subjects a preorganizer to study before reading a target, or to-be-learned, text. The text was about the use of microbes in industry, that is, how bacteria and other microbes are used to make things, for example, insulin, in industrial settings. One group of subjects received a preorganizer that prepared them for this text. It took the form of an outline that structured the information similarly and represented a point of view similar to the target text. This constitutes the *consistent outline.* This preorganizer is much like those traditionally used in advance organizer research. It provides for the reader an appropriate framework into which the content of the target text can be assimilated (Mayer, 1979) or subsumed (Ausubel, 1968).

The other group of subjects also received an outline preorganizer, which contained exactly the same information as the first outline but organized in a different manner. It is called the *inconsistent outline,* although only its structure and perspective, not its content, were inconsistent with the text. This outline closely followed an encyclopedia entry on microbes, emphasizing their characteristics and describing how these characteristics could be used to classify microbes as of one type or another. Figure 8 shows an example of how the same topic—types of microbes—was embedded in two different contexts in the two outlines.

Subjects studied either one or the other outline for about a half an hour and answered questions on the outline information. Then they read the target text, which was taken from a *Science 85* magazine article entitled "Industry in Ferment." After reading the text some subjects were asked to complete a variety of tasks immediately, and others performed them after a delay of two days. The tasks included summarization, true-false sentence verification, and cued recall. Here, we report on a relevant subset of the results.

I. BACTERIA ARE REGARDED AS THE SIMPLEST FORMS OF YEAST AND MOLD
   CONTAINING NO CHLOROPHYLL
II. BACTERIA CAN BE CLASSIFIED ACCORDING TO FOUR CHARACTERISTICS
   A. MICROSCOPIC APPEARANCE AND STAINING REACTION (MORPHOLOGY)
      1. MOST BACTERIAL FORMS RANGE IN SIZE FROM .5 TO 10 MICRONS IN
         LENGTH. A MICRON = .001 MILLIMETER
      2. MORPHOLOGICALLY (IN FORM AND STRUCTURE), BACTERIA FALL INTO
         FOUR CATEGORIES:
         a. *APPROXIMATELY SPHERICAL—COCCUS*
         b. *ROD OR CYLINDRICAL BACILLUS*   CHARACTERISTICS
         c. *RIGID COILED ROD—SPIRILA*   OUTLINE
         d.*FLEXIBLE HAIR-LIKE—SPIROCHETE*
      3. COLONIES OF BACTERIA MAY BE TRANSLUCENT (CLEAR), OR OPAQUE;
         WHITE, VIOLET, YELLOW, OR COLORLESS; SHINY OR DULL; AND VISCOUS,
         PASTY, OR CRUMBLY IN CONSISTENCY

---

1. FORTUNATELY, DIFFERENT-SIZED MICROBES ARE SEPARABLE; SMALL MI-
   CROBES GET CAUGHT IN HOLES WHICH LARGER, DIFFERENT-SHAPED ONES
   DON'T. MOST BACTERIA RANGE IN SIZE FROM .5 TO 10 MICRONS IN LENGTH. A
   MICRON = .001 MILLIMETER AND MORPHOLOGICALLY (IN FORM AND STRUC-
   TURE), BACTERIA FALL INTO 4 CATEGORIES:
   a. *APPROXIMATELY SPHERICAL—COCCUS*
   b. *ROD OR CYLINDRICAL—BACILLUS*   INDUSTRY
   c. *RIGID COILED ROD–SPIRILA*   OUTLINE
   d. *FLEXIBLE HAIR-LIKE—SPIROCHETE*
2. IN ARTIFICIAL SITUATIONS, COLONIES OF WORKING BUGS LIVE IN PORES OF
   PERMEABLE TUBES AND GROW THERE. THESE MICROBES WILL SOON FILL ALL
   AVAILABLE CREVICES IN THE POROUS TUBES IN WHICH THEY LIVE AND GROW.

Fig. 8.   Information about microbes is presented in two different ways. The Industry Outline corresponds to the organization of the target text.

Subjects' performance on the cued recall task for a particular paragraph from the text conformed quite well to expectations. By and large,
all recall protocols showed a levels effect. That is, the subjects recalled
the more important things in the paragraph more often than detail items,
with those receiving an inconsistent outline and those tested after a delay
producing slightly fewer propositions overall. It thus appears that all
subjects, regardless of condition, had formed an appropriate memory
representation of the text.

Subjects in both outline groups also showed the traditional levels effect when asked to summarize the text immediately. They produced a
fair amount of material and produced more propositions from the higher
levels of the text hierarchy than from the lower, detail levels. In contrast,
following a delay, those who had received an inconsistent outline produced propositions from all levels of the text hierarchy, almost without
regard for their level of importance in the text, whereas the subjects who

had received a consistent outline still produced summaries exhibiting a levels effect. It appears that the inconsistent outline interfered with the subjects' ability to distinguish between information that is important to the text and that which is merely a textual detail.

The poor performance on the summarization task with the inconsistent outline contrasts with the results from the true–false verification task because the inconsistent outline enhanced performance on this task. In the true–false task subjects were shown sentences that were of one of three types: verbatim statements taken directly from the text; meaning-preserving paraphrases of statements from the text; or inferences that did not occur in the text at all but that required subjects to put together information from different parts of the text to make their judgments. These sentences, mixed within a series of appropriate distractor items, were shown to subjects. Subjects' performance on this task shows a surprising interaction of statement type and outline consistency. Those who received a consistent outline, one structured and presented from the same point of view as the text, did quite well on the statements that were taken verbatim from the text. However, as Fig. 9 shows, these subjects verified correctly only about a quarter of the inference statements.

The inconsistent group however showed quite a different pattern of results. In fact their performance on the verbatim statements was comparatively poor, but they did rather well on verifying the inferences. These inference questions require a certain type of problem solving or knowledge integration, rather than pure memory retrieval. Fig. 9 shows this interaction of outline and problem-statement type.[5]

Clearly what is happening here is that the mental representation of the text that is formed consists of a combination of the readers' pre-knowledge—the outline they have read—and the target text. When the two are congruent, a good, well-ordered textbase results; when they are incongruent, the textbase suffers, but a richer, more useful situation model is obtained. This finding is congruent with the assimilation theory of Mayer (1979): Because advance organizers provide a meaningful context to encourage the integration of old and new ideas, the reader's situation model should improve and allow transfer to novel tasks, although this change entails a loss of detail. However, assimilation theory does not explicitly describe why different organizers, which contain the same content and thus should activate the same knowledge structures in memory, produce different patterns of results. According to our comprehension theory the answer to this question has to do with how prior knowledge and text interact. So far, our discussion of the theory has not addressed this point. It is, however, a central issue in the study of text

---

[5] For related results, see Mayer, Cook and Dyck (1984) and McDonald (1987).

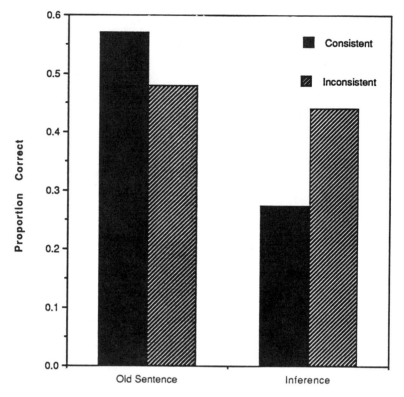

Fig. 9.   Proportion of correct responses on a sentence verification test for old statements (verbatim from the text) and inference statements.

comprehension, which has far-reaching implications. Below we briefly describe an expansion of the comprehension theory that deals with this important aspect of comprehension. We shall then return to the question of how this expanded theory is able to account for the Mannes and Kintsch results.

A.   THE CONSTRUCTION–INTEGRATION MODEL

Comprehension always involves an interaction between what is already known and the new information provided by the text. In order to form the propositional textbase, knowledge of the syntax and semantics of the language is required. Situation models involve all kinds of general world knowledge, as well as personal experience. The construction–integration (CI) theory of Kintsch (1988) describes how this knowledge is used in comprehension.

Someone reading a text typically thinks of, or activates in memory, things that are relevant to understanding the content in the present context, and not of the myriad other things that are related but irrelevant in this context. People who build intelligent systems know that such selective memory retrieval poses an almost insurmountable problem, yet the human mind solves it elegantly and typically so effortlessly that we are hardly aware of the dimensions of the difficulty.

Other theories have tried to account for contextually sensitive knowledge activation by postulating sophisticated and powerful prediction rules by means of which knowledge is activated—rules smart enough to always give the reader only what is relevant. The concept of a schema in its various versions (frames, scripts) has been used to formulate such rules. Schema theory assumes that knowledge in long-term memory is organized into schematic structures that guide and control the processes of knowledge activation. Thus, during comprehension only knowledge that is "appropriate" to the currently active schema becomes activated. However, it is not easy to make schemata work with enough flexibility and context sensitivity to effectively guide knowledge activation in AI systems, and there are psychological problems with this notion as well (see Kintsch, 1988, and Mannes & Doane, 1991, for details).

The CI model suggests an alternative to schematic knowledge activation. Mental representations need not exist as preformed structures in memory, but can be constructed via weak rules. Inferencing via knowledge activation is not smart, not guided by powerful schemata, but careless and promiscuous. The activation process is a probabilistic one, in which all knowledge that is related to the input (e.g., associatively, via argument overlap or semantic relations) has some opportunity to become active. Thus, the context activates much knowledge, allowing many irrelevant and even contradictory elements to be activated. However, the text elements themselves and the knowledge elements that have been activated in such an unguided manner are not unrelated but are richly interrelated via semantic as well as experiential links. Thus, the *construction phase* of the CI model results in a network that includes both the textual material and the knowledge that has been activated, only some of which is relevant. This network has the ability, however, to deactivate those portions of itself that are irrelevant or contradictory. This takes place during the *integration phase* of the model. In this phase activation is allowed to flow through the network until it finds a stable state. Activity collects in those parts of the network that are most richly and most strongly interconnected and flows away from isolated nodes that are not well linked to the total structure, or from nodes with inhibitory connections (for example, where there are contradictions between propositions).

The CI model achieves this process of contextual integration by means of a spreading activation process. Related approaches have been developed within the parallel distributed processing paradigm. For example, Rumelhart, Smolensky, McClelland, and Hinton (1986) describe a model that determines what type of room is being described by a particular set of characteristics. These characteristics might include things like a couch, lamp, sink, and television. The fact that three of these items are typically found in a living room, and thus are related to one another, serves to reinforce their activity during an integration phase, while the concept of sink becomes deactivated because it is not related to the other three.

Figure 10 sketches the main elements of the construction–integration theory. First, during the construction phase, a set of production rules

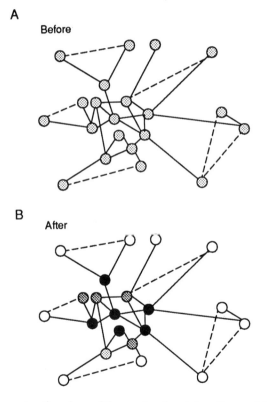

Fig. 10.   In the construction phase of the construction–integration model (A), a network of propositions is generated with positive (solid lines) and negative links (broken lines); all nodes are equally activated. In the integration phase (B), positively interlinked nodes become more strongly active, while outliers and inhibited nodes are deactivated.

generates a propositional textbase from the words and sentences of a text, and other production rules spuriously and promiscuously activate knowledge that is associated with the textbase propositions. The result is a network such as that shown in Fig. 10A with facilitatory and inhibitory connections, but with a core of richly interconnected items. In the integration phase, items with many positive interconnections strengthen each other, while activation flows away from sparsely connected areas of the network as well as from inhibited nodes. The result is an integrated text representation, consisting of both the major elements of the textbase and contextually relevant knowledge that has been activated, while irrelevant and contradictory nodes have lost their activation (Fig. 10B).

Thus, weak, associative rules for the activation of knowledge can nevertheless generate a highly context-sensitive text representation in which textual elements and preknowledge are integrated, yielding controlled, but flexible behavior. The advantage of this scheme is that one need not assume fixed schemata that never quite fit a given context. Instead, a new structure is generated in a context-sensitive manner. Schemata, frames, and scripts are regarded not as fixed memory structures that just need to be called up and filled in, but as emergent structures that are formed from local associative relations in the context of a specific situation, specific goals, and task demands. This is not to say that schemata play no significant role in comprehension and problem solving—only that they cannot be pulled, fixed and ready to use, from the drawer of memory. Rather, they need to be put together first from local building blocks, respecting whatever dynamic constraints the context imposes.[6]

B. UNDERSTANDING THE EFFECTS OF CONSISTENT AND INCONSISTENT PREORGANIZERS

How can the CI model help us to understand the Mannes and Kintsch results? According to the model, as a text is read, a mental representation of that text is developed. Our interpretation of the results suggests that the representations built by subjects in the two different outline conditions are quite different.

All texts and everything we experience is interpreted with respect to what we already know. Because the subjects in the Mannes and Kintsch (1987) experiment were selected so that students with a biology background were eliminated, each subject's preknowledge of the content domain was essentially limited to what he or she learned from the outline in question. When the subjects who had received a consistent outline en-

---

[6] Compare the notion of scripts as stable memory structures in Schank and Abelson (1977) with the notion of Memory Organization Packets (MOPs) as building blocks in Schank (1982).

countered a text on the industrial uses of microbes, they found the topic familiar; the text simply expanded upon what they had already learned from the outline. The other group, who had studied an inconsistent outline, had a different experience when they read the text. Although they realized that the text was about microbes, the two texts appeared quite different because one emphasized the characteristics of microbes while the other focused on how microbes are used. Although the informational content of the two outlines was exactly the same, the perspective from which that information was presented was different.[7]

So, too, were the meaning representations constructed by the two groups of subjects. For subjects for whom the text was consistent with their preknowledge, reading the text was easy. They were able to encode the material with little difficulty, and they had sufficient resources to concentrate on encoding the individual sentences and words. That is, they had already developed a situation model that was consistent with the macrostructure of the incoming text. The importance relationships between ideas were the same in both cases, and subjects could spend their time making sure that they had a robust and relatively permanent textbase. It was probably organized hierarchically, as were the text and outline, and the perspective about what was important and what was not was reinforced by both documents.

The subjects for whom the text appeared to be different from what they had already learned, those who had received an inconsistent outline, had to spend a lot of time figuring out what this text had to do with the outline they had read and trying to reconcile this new information with what they already knew. The text appeared to be emphasizing as important different ideas from those emphasized on their outline. They had little time to pay attention to the exact words in the text or to try to encode them permanently. Instead, they spent more effort trying to reconcile their newly emerging situation model with the old one derived from the outline. Thus, they came away from the reading episode with a situation model of the domain contents that reflected accurately neither of the original text structures, but which contained elements of each with various links among related concepts. This representation would be more like a network, with each concept having a variety of links to other concepts. Multiple ties to other concepts were created because many of the learned concepts occurred in different contexts and were associated with different concepts in the text and outline. The cost of deriving this more complicated structure was that it made it more difficult to achieve a durable textbase representation.

---

[7] Perspective effects in text comprehension are well documented in the literature; see for example Anderson and Pichert (1978) and Sulin and Dooling (1974).

Thus, when the text and the outline are organized in the same way, each idea unit will be well encoded, but there will be relatively fewer links among the units. When the text and the outline are structured in different ways, there will be more, though weaker links among the elements of the network. These differences in subjects' knowledge representation are reflected in the performance differences that were observed and can be accounted for by the CI model as follows.

When a sentence to be verified is encountered, nodes or concepts in the network become activated. In the case of the consistent outline a neat, hierarchically organized representation results with a strong textbase component. Activity flows in an orderly manner, and the network settles quickly. When the network has settled, the nodes representing the concepts in the statement to be verified have maintained a high level of activity, thus allowing for excellent verbatim sentence verification.

In the case of the inconsistent outline, when a sentence is presented for verification, activity flows through the network in a less constrained manner. It activates related concepts in both the outline and the text, and secondary activation flows to concepts to which they, in turn, were associated. Thus, the spread of activity reaches farther, and as a result, when the network settles, many concepts are slightly active. This makes it difficult to verify specific statements with a high degree of confidence but has a beneficial side effect. When subjects are asked to verify inferences, there is a better chance that the concepts mentioned in the inference both have some degree of activity and are accessible to the subject. Thus, although no one statement is particularly active, many have the chance to become combined in new ways. Hence, the subjects with the more network-like representation, containing a rich set of links, have relatively more trouble verifying verbatim statements, but when their inference-verification ability is compared to that of the other group, they do much better.

In summary, it appears that varying perspectives in a domain will help students to solve novel problems and to think on their own, as evidenced by their superior inferencing, even though this ability might not show up on standard memory-retrieval tests. Of course these beneficial effects will depend on whether the student is willing to make the necessary cognitive effort and has sufficient cognitive resources available.

C. COMPREHENSION AS THE ACTIVE CONSTRUCTION OF MEANING

The point that the two previous studies make is that there is much more to text comprehension than being able to reproduce the text in some form or another. Text comprehension does not have to be merely the passive absorption of information, and knowledge use is not necessarily restricted to the application of static memory schemata. Active strategies for the construction of situation models lead to deeper forms of under-standing—understanding of the conceptual structure of a domain, rather than merely the text itself. Novel knowledge structures can emerge in the construction of meaning—structures that are not static schemata, but that are dynamically generated in the context of a comprehension epi-sode. Thus, the CI theory shows how people learn from texts, not by memorizing the text, but by understanding new situations. In this sense the theory pushes the limits of the domain of comprehension far into the territory of problem solving and thinking. Deep understanding is, indeed, a form of problem solving and thinking.

The CI theory thus changes the psychological landscape. It points to a continuity between comprehension and problem-solving processes, and thus distinguishes itself both from traditional views of compre-hension that were entirely focused on the text itself (Frederiksen, 1975; Kintsch, 1974; Meyer, 1975) and theories of thinking and problem solv-ing that have little use for the concept of comprehension (Anderson, 1983; Newell, 1990; Newell & Simon, 1972; "comprehension" is not an index entry of its own in either of these books). These theories approach their subject matter in an entirely different way, based upon the para-digm of problem solving as a search process rather than of constraint satisfaction. We do not deny that search processes are important, but we want to draw attention to the fact that the scope of comprehension processes can be much greater than has been assumed traditionally, and that some of what has been discussed under the label of thinking can fruitfully be regarded as an issue of comprehension.

VII.   A Tutor for Word Algebra Problems

Although the studies described so far have implications for instruction, they do not deal with instruction directly. For this work, we need more than a model of how students comprehend, remember, and learn. We also need, first of all, a theory of instruction, and secondly, research in instructional settings to develop and evaluate the notions derived from laboratory studies. Below we describe in some detail a study that illus-trates the first of these steps. We show how our understanding of the psychological processes involved in solving word algebra problems can lead to the development of a computer tutor for such problems, within a specific instructional framework. We have, as yet, not undertaken Step 2, the evaluation of this tutor in an actual classroom, but only in a laboratory setting. However, although we cannot offer more than tentative conclusions, we feel it worthwhile, nevertheless, to trace, at least part way, the long path from psychological theory and laboratory experiments to actual instructional use.

In principle, psychological-processing theory could be combined with any kind of instructional theory to yield a program for instruction. Thus, one could imagine, for example, an instructional program in which specific processing steps (specified by the psychological theory) are differentially reinforced according to the principles of reinforcement theory. Instead, we choose for our purposes a popular contemporary instructional theory—the framework derived from Vygotsky, as it has been described by Bereiter and Scardamalia; Brown and Palincsar; and Collins, Brown, and Newman—all in Resnick (1989)—to name a few representative examples.

We are not going to describe this framework here in any detail. That would be beyond the scope of the present article, which focuses on issues of comprehension, not of instruction. Neither do we make any original contributions to this framework. We are merely using for our purposes a set of instructional principles that others have developed. The reader must, therefore, be referred to the original sources regarding Vygotskyan instructional theory. We would, however, like to emphasize a core idea from that theory that intersects in many ways with the theory of comprehension presented here. This is Vygotsky's notion that learning can take place only in certain restricted zones of development ("the zone of proximal development"), where the student has only incomplete knowledge or skill, but knows enough to make further learning possible. The role of instruction is to help the student to progress from what is known to the unknown by means of temporary supports (scaffolding, procedural facilitation).[8]

The logic of the enterprise is therefore as follows. The comprehension theory described above is used as a tool for the analysis of the process involved in understanding and solving a word algebra problem. Points of difficulty are located within this process. Temporary crutches are designed by means of which the student can overcome these difficult steps in the process of problem solving. Eventually the student can understand the problem without help and proceeds to new horizons.

Nathan, Kintsch, and Young (1992) have developed a tutor that helps students to comprehend word algebra problems and thereby supports their problem solving. This is a serious practical issue, because word

---

[8] Reusser (1992) provides a detailed description of the various kinds of instructional supports that are available for mathematical word problems.

problems are notoriously difficult for students at all levels. Schools often do not really teach students how to solve such problems, but let them figure it out by themselves. The reason for this is that it is not clear what to teach.

Psychological theory can be of use here, by specifying what sort of mental representation the student needs to construct in order to solve a word problem, and what operations must be performed to achieve a solution. In the case of algebra word problems, what to teach involves more than just the algebraic operations. Often, students have no trouble with those. The real difficulty lies in the conceptual operations necessary to construct a solvable, formal problem representation upon which the algebraic operations can be brought to bear. Thus, the comprehension theory can be used to provide a detailed cognitive analysis of the task demands so that instruction can target those areas where processing breakdowns are likely to occur.

The word algebra tutor proposed by Nathan et al. (1992) is an extension of the earlier work of Kintsch and Greeno (1985) in which the comprehension theory was applied to first- to third-grade arithmetic problem solving. In that study a detailed model of how children understand and solve word problems was worked out. This model was expressed as a computer simulation, and a series of experimental investigations were performed to evaluate its empirical adequacy (Cummins, Kintsch, Reusser, & Weimer, 1988). As a result, an explicit and proven model was available for inclusion as a component of an instructional system for teaching word arithmetic problems in the early grades of school (Reusser, Kämpfer, & Stüssi, 1990).

For the domain of algebra word problems, however, this approach was not feasible. Although it was fairly obvious how the Kintsch and Greeno approach could be extended to this domain, it was not possible to construct a computer simulation. This could be done for arithmetic, because relatively little general world knowledge is required to understand these problems. The necessary knowledge proved to be fairly restricted and not too difficult to incorporate into the simulation. For college algebra word problems, on the other hand, the requisite world knowledge is essentially unbounded. As yet no one in psychology or in artificial intelligence knows how to simulate such a huge knowledge base. Hence, no simulation could be performed for algebra problems, nor was it possible to provide a direct empirical test of the model. The strategy we chose instead was to further develop the theory, incorporate it into a computerized instructional system, and then test empirically the adequacy of that system.

According to the instructional principles mentioned above, the purpose of a tutoring system should be to help students understand word problems at a conceptual level and therefore be able to solve them. Rather than leading the student repeatedly down the correct solution path, as in some traditional instruction and in intelligent tutoring, the algebra tutor allows students to work out for themselves the underlying problem representation. It enables them to do so by supporting their problem solving in various ways: For example, mental operations that otherwise remain implicit are made explicit by a graphical representation of the problem model, memory loads are lightened by making relevant information available in an accessible form, calculations are supported through immediate error correction, and a bridge is provided between the abstract algebraic formulation of the problem and the naive situational understanding that students have about the problem. In this system, it is not necessary for the computer to understand the problem or to solve it; nor does it need to know anything about the student. Yet we believe that even a fairly unintelligent tutor can help the student. Hence, our approach has been to exploit the intelligence of the student. Rather than being itself intelligent, the function of the system would be to make it possible for the student to behave intelligently, and in so doing to gain the conceptual understanding of such problems that is needed to solve them in all their various guises.

The tutor joins these instructional principles with implications from the theory of text processing in the following way. First, we know that some relations that are needed to properly specify the mathematical solution are based on aspects of the situation that the author of the problem leaves unstated. Thus, they may also be absent from the reader's textbase. These relations need to be inferred by the reader, drawing upon the prior knowledge of the situation—the situation model. As we have seen above, such inferences can make large demands on the reasoning and memory of a problem solver. When the reader fails to make these inferences, a poor representation of the text results, one that may not maintain global coherence (examples have been provided above in the discussion of the work of Britton and Fletcher). When an inadequate representation is used as the basis for problem solving, unstated, though critical information will tend to be omitted. As a consequence, the associated equations will be omitted from the solutions or will be replaced by ones that correspond to the false, usually oversimplified text representation (Cummins et al., 1988). Hence instructional interventions must concentrate on encouraging situation-based reasoning in understanding word-problem texts, that is, on providing a framework that allows students to generate the situational inferences necessary for the comprehension and solution of the problem.

A. THE ANIMATE TUTOR

In this section we first outline how the Kintsch and Greeno (1985) model of word-arithmetic problem solving can be extended to the domain of algebra word problems. Then we describe the computer tutor that was designed to test the assumptions outlined above and briefly indicate the results of our evaluation of the system in a training study.

Consider a typical word algebra problem:

> *Problem 1.* A plane leaves Denver traveling west at 200 miles per hour. Three hours later a second plane leaves Denver on a parallel course and travels west at 250 miles per hour. How long will it take the second plane to overtake the first?

As with any other text, a surface-level representation, a textbase and a situation model will be formed in comprehending this text. As noted, the textbase represents the semantics of the text, the meaning of the discourse. A model of the situation described by the passage governs inferencing and elaborations in a manner consistent with the reader's experiences and long-term store of knowledge. There is much unstated information that is important to support true understanding of the text; for example, the realization that the point of "overtake" is when the two vehicles have traveled the same distance away from the place of origin.

In addition to these three levels of representation—the linguistic surface level, the semantic textbase, and the situation model—it is useful to introduce a fourth type of representation, the problem model, which captures information about the formal relations and quantities in the passage and which is used by readers when they are put in a problem-solving context. In a manner analogous to the representation of long-term knowledge in the situation model, the problem model serves to represent information relevant to problem-solving behavior (Kintsch & Greeno, 1985): Schemata for organizing quantities and relations are constructed, and the reader's attention is directed to numbers and initial and final conditions.

These two levels of representation, the situation model and the problem model, appear to be the locus of the difficulties in solving word problems. Greeno (1989), Larkin (1983), Schoenfeld (1985), and a number of others have suggested that these two representations cannot exist in isolation from each other and still support competent problem solving. Rather, information from the problem model and from the situation model must mutually constrain each other, forcing a mental representation that describes a problem that is at once physically, or situationally, plausible and mathematically solvable. Furthermore, they must be in correspondence so that the abstract relations and quantities of the underlying formal problem model are meaningful to the student in the context of the cover story (Greeno, 1989).

Consequently, we draw on this analysis at the level of mental representations to hypothesize a necessary criterion for problem comprehension. Problem comprehension, we suggest, occurs to the degree that students relate the representation of the problem model to their model of the situation depicted in the problem text. This process is summarized in Fig. 11, which depicts the representations readers form when reading a word problem (about a helicopter converging on a giant ant) and shows

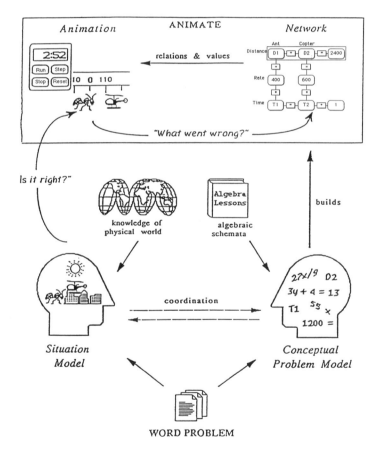

Fig. 11. The coordination between situation model and problem model in solving a word algebra problem. Reprinted from Nathan, Kintsch, & Young (1992) with permission from Lawrence Erlbaum.

how the correspondence between the problem model and situation model is highlighted by the computer tutor.

We argue that the comprehension-based difficulties for solving word problems can be addressed by facilitating the correspondence between the reader's understanding of the situation and the activated problem information. How can this correspondence be imparted to the student? How can problem comprehension be taught? An instructional technique for fostering learning of procedural information is to make the goals of the task explicit to the student and then to engage the student in completing the task (Anderson, Boyle, Farrell, & Reiser, 1987; Scardamalia, Bereiter, McLean, Swallow, & Woodruff, 1989). What our tutor does is to make the correspondence between the two representations explicit to the student. We do this by providing the students with external correlates of the two representations—the situation model and the problem model—and having them assess the correlation between them. For the situation model of many algebra story problems, a logical correlate is to provide pictures or animations that move through the states described and implied by the problem text. To this end, we provide the student with the means of constructing simple computer animations that can be easily directed by mathematical equations and altered until the appropriate mapping of problem model to situation model is achieved. For the problem model, we have developed a graphic representation of the algebraically relevant entities and schemata mentioned in a problem. The important constraints are that (1) this scheme express those relations that the theory claims are important, and (2) students find this kind of representation natural and easy to work with (Weaver & Kintsch, 1992). The representation of the problem model for the two-planes problem (Problem 1) is shown in Fig. 12.[9]

The computer tutoring environment, called ANIMATE, was designed to focus attention on the correspondence between the situational information and the formal problem information of a story problem. Specifically, the student builds computer animations by specifying the quantities and relations of the formal problem model. The rates, travel times, and delays are extracted from the problem model and are used to drive the computer animation. The student may run the animation, which acts only as the problem model allows. We then rely on the student's understanding of the situation described by the problem text as a means of

---

[9] The reader familiar with the history of mathematics instruction will realize that what we are doing here is quite similar to a number of previous schemes that were developed for the same purpose. As so often, practical genius has anticipated scientific developments. Yet what the latter has achieved is to explain *why* such schemes are useful.

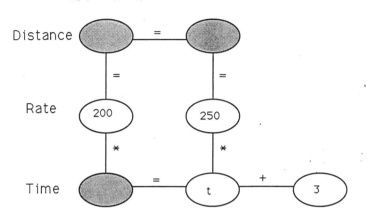

Fig. 12. The representation of the conceptual structure of a word algebra problem in terms of interacting distance-rate-time schemata.

assessing the animation. If the animation is consistent with the student's expectations, the problem model is describing the situation in an appropriate manner. However, if the animation acts contrary to the student's expectations (i.e., contrary to the situation model), then the problem model must be corrected. The manner in which the animation deviates from its expected behavior helps students to constrain their diagnosis of the problem model, thus giving the formal quantities meaning and context, as well as further strengthening the correspondence between the two representations. This arrangement takes advantage of the fact that students are poor at assessing formal relations (Larkin, 1983; Greeno, 1989) but have a good understanding of situational information. Figure 13 shows the computer screen for a problem in which a giant ant and a helicopter are on a collision course. The tools available to the student are at left. The problem model that was generated is shown at right, and the animation at the top.

B. EVALUATION OF ANIMATE

How do students perform with ANIMATE, and does good problem comprehension transfer to settings in which the student has no animation? In order to assess the effectiveness of our tutor, we compared three groups of students. One group used the complete ANIMATE tutor with animation and graphic problem model. The second group used a tutor identical in every way except for the absence of any animation (our situation-model correlate), while the control group used only equations to solve the problems. There were marked differences in problem solving perfor-

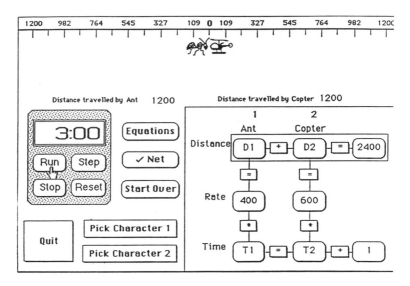

Fig. 13.   A picture of the screen of the ANIMATE tutor for a collision problem. Reprinted from Nathan, Kintsch, & Young (1992) with permission from Lawrence Erlbaum.

mance of the ANIMATE group that transferred to test settings without the tutor. On training tasks (tasks performed with either the ANIMATE tutor, the non-animation tutor, or the traditional equation-based method) Nathan et al. (1992) found that the ANIMATE group performed significantly higher than either the non-animation or the control group who received conventional algebra instruction. When subjects were tested on novel problems without the use of the tutor, we found that gain scores, as measured by the difference between posttest and pretest performance, were in line with the above results. All groups improved significantly, yet ANIMATE subjects improved far more than both non-animation subjects and equation subjects.

ANIMATE is our effort to bridge the gap between basic research in comprehension and educational application. It has recently been expanded in scope (Nathan, 1991), but it has not yet been tested in a classroom setting. Nevertheless, as a prototype system, it shows one way in which basic research on comprehension can have a direct impact on instructional practices. Many other projects could be attempted today along these lines. ANIMATE also shows, however, that the path from psychological theory to instruction is long and not unproblematic. Not only must we get the theory right, we also need the right instructional principles, and even then success or failure will be determined equally by how skillfully theory and principles become translated into instruction.

VIII. Conclusion

We have reviewed here the educational implications of a psychological process model of discourse comprehension. We have indicated the place of this model among other contemporary approaches to discourse comprehension in cognitive science by emphasizing three global contrasts. First, we have contrasted our approach with others along a dimension that ranges from a concern with the text as an autonomous object to an emphasis on the processor, the subject of comprehension. Much of the work on text comprehension in linguistics and psychology can be located at one end of this dimension, the structural analysis of text, while some literary scholars focus primarily on the other end, the reader's reactions. A middle position, emphasizing the reader–text interaction, has often been advocated by researchers in various fields (see the discussion of this issue in Rosenblatt, 1978). The present approach goes beyond mere advocacy, because we are able to specify in computational detail just what this interaction entails. We have used our analyses to explore two questions here: What is the relationship between the structure of a text and the structure of the mental representation formed from that text? How can we help students to understand a difficult text?

The second dimension that we have used to differentiate our approach from others is one that ranges from reading as passive absorption of information from the text to reading as an active construction of meaning. Most traditional process theories of comprehension can be located at the passive end of this dimension. Even schema theory assigns the reader a fairly passive role: Once an appropriate schema has been retrieved, it provides the default information to fill in gaps that were left implicit in the text. In contrast, the present approach, like other current theorizing about the formation of mental models, emphasizes the active construction of meaning from the text—not merely the copying of information from the text or from pre-existing memory schemata, but the generation of new structures in a dynamically changing context. We have shown that this kind of approach can provide new insights relative to some old problems: When is inferential work on the part of the reader helpful, and when is it harmful? Just what is the difference between remembering a text and learning something from that text?

The final problem addressed is that the mental representations that are formed on the basis of reading a text must be related to and embedded in the reader's understanding of the real-world situation described by the text. By working through an example, we have shown how basic research on comprehension can be turned into a useful practical technology. We were able to improve students' conceptual understanding of algebra word problems by using our theoretical understanding of the comprehension processes involved.

These projects demonstrate the feasibility of theoretically motivated projects in education. This has been tried often enough before, not always successfully, because the psychological theories used were too simplistic and could not provide adequate accounts of complex behaviors. The studies described here show that in the domain of text comprehension it is now possible to forge direct links between research in cognitive science and educational practice.

The goal of the work reported here is not just to improve instruction in a global sense, but to do so on the basis of an explicit theoretical understanding of the problem solving and learning processes involved. Why is it desirable to derive instruction from a serious theoretical foundation, rather than to rely on experience and intuition? Expert intuitions about how to instruct or how to revise a text to make it more comprehensible are notoriously difficult to pin down and to explain to others. Basing our educational interventions on well-formulated principles of comprehension and learning enables us to understand what we are doing and why it works. In all science it is good theory that produces an effective technology. There will always be a role for experience and intuition in education, but, in addition, comprehension theory is mature enough today to systematically explore its potential for instruction.

Finally, it should not be overlooked that this educationally motivated research has contributed a great deal to the further development and refinement of the theory of comprehension. It would have been all too easy to focus on a few narrow laboratory problems and to neglect the difficult but important questions that our concern with education forced us to address. The significance of forming adequate situation models, of learning from a text rather than remembering it, the situated nature of comprehension, are all issues arising from the educational perspective that we have taken. This perspective, therefore, has been a major determinant of the direction that comprehension theory has taken in recent years. The planned expansion of our educational research beyond the laboratory into the domain of classroom instructional studies will no doubt provide a further impetus for theory development, and will help to keep it focused on real-life problems.

References

Anderson, J. R. (1983). *The architecture of cognition*. Cambridge, MA: Harvard University Press.

Anderson, J. R., Boyle, C. F., Farrell, R., & Reiser, B. (1987). Cognitive principles in the design of computer tutors. In P. Morris (Ed.), *Modelling cognition* (pp. 93–134). New York: Wiley.

Anderson, R. C. (1984). Role of the reader's schema in comprehension, learning, and memory. In R. C. Anderson, J. Osborn, & R. B. Tierney (Eds.), *Learning to read in American schools* (pp. 243–258). Hillsdale, NJ: Erlbaum.

Anderson, R. C., & Pichert, J. W. (1978). Recall of previously unrecallable material following a shirt in perspective. *Journal of Verbal Behavior and Verbal Learning, 17,* 1–12.

Atkinson, R. C., & Shiffrin, R. M. (1968). *Human memory: A proposed system and its control processes.* New York: Academic Press.

Ausubel, D. P. (1968). *Educational psychology: A cognitive view.* New York: Holt, Rinehart & Winston.

Bereiter, C., & Scardamalia, M. (1989). Intentional learning as a goal of instruction. In L. B. Resnick (Ed.), *Knowing, learning, and instruction: Essays in honor of Robert Glaser* (pp. 361–392). Hillsdale, NJ: Erlbaum.

Black, J. B., & Bower, G. H. (1980). Story understanding as problem solving. *Poetics, 9,* 223–250.

Bloom, C. P., Fletcher, C. R., van den Broek, P., Reitz, L., & Shapiro, B. P. (1990). An on-line assessment of causal reasoning in comprehension. *Memory & Cognition, 18,* 65–71.

Britton, B. K. (1986). Capturing art to improve text quality. *Educational Psychologist, 21,* 333–356.

Britton, B. K., & Gulgoz, S. (1991). Using Kintsch's computational model to improve instructional text: Effects of repairing inference calls on recall and cognitive structures. *Journal of Educational Psychology, 83,* 329–345.

Britton, B. K., Gulgoz, S., & Glynn, S. (1993). Impact of good and poor writing on learners: Research and theory. In B. K. Britton, A. Woodward, & M. Binkley (Eds.), *Learning from textbooks.* Hillsdale, NJ: Erlbaum.

Britton, B. K., Van Dusen, L., Glynn, S. M., & Hemphill, D. (1990). The impact of inferences on instructional text. In A. C. Graesser, & G. H. Bower (Eds.), *Inferences and text comprehension* (pp. 53–70). New York: Academic Press.

Brown, A. L., & Palincsar, A. S. (1989). Guided, cooperative learning and individual knowledge acquisition. In L. B. Resnick (Ed.), *Knowing, learning, and instruction: Essays in honor of Robert Glaser* (pp. 393–451). Hillsdale, NJ: Erlbaum.

Clark, N. K., Stephenson, G. M., & Rutter, D. R. (1986). Memory for complex social discourse: The analysis and prediction of individual and group recall. *Journal of Memory and Language, 25,* 295–313.

Coleman, E. B. (1962). Improving comprehensibility by shortening sentences. *Journal of Applied Psychology, 70,* 109–118.

Collins, A., Brown, J. S., & Newman, S. E. (1989). Cognitive apprenticeship: Teaching the crafts of reading, writing, and mathematics. In L. B. Resnick (Ed.), *Knowing, learning, and instruction: Essays in honor of Robert Glaser.* (pp. 453–494). Hillsdale, NJ: Erlbaum.

Cummins, D. D., Kintsch, W., Reusser, K., & Weimer, R. (1988). The role of understanding in solving word problems. *Cognitive Psychology, 20,* 405–438.

van Dijk, T. A. (1972). *Some aspects of text grammars.* The Hague: Mouton.

van Dijk, T. A., & Kintsch, W. (1983). *Strategies of discourse comprehension.* New York: Academic Press.

Duffy, T., & Kabance, P. (1982). Testing a readable writing approach to text revision. *Journal of Educational Psychology, 74,* 733–748.

Ellis, H. C., Parente, F. J., & Walker, C. W. (1974). Coding and varied input versus repetition in human memory. *Journal of Experimental Psychology, 102,* 284–290.

Fletcher, C. R., & Bloom, C. P. (1988). Causal reasoning in the comprehension of simple narrative texts. *Journal of Memory and Language, 27,* 235–244.

Fletcher, C. R., Hummel, J. E., & Marsolek, C. J. (1990). Causality and the allocation of attention during comprehension. *Journal of Experimental Psychology: Learning, Memory, and Cognition, 16,* 233–240.

Frederiksen, C. H. (1975). Representing logical and semantic structure acquired from discourse. *Cognitive Psychology, 7,* 371–458.

Greeno, J. G. (1989). Situations, mental models, and generative knowledge. In D. Klahr, & K. Kotovsky (Eds.), *Complex information processing* (pp. 285–318). Hillsdale, NJ: Erlbaum.

Halliday, M. A. K., & Hasan, R. (1976). *Cohesion in English.* London: Longman.

Haviland, S. E., & Clark, H. H. (1974). What's new? Acquiring new information as a process in comprehension. *Journal of Verbal Learning and Verbal Behavior, 13,* 512–521.

Kintsch, E. (1990). Macroprocesses and microprocesses in the development of summarization skill. *Cognition and Instruction, 7,* 161–195.

Kintsch, W. (1974). *The representation of meaning in memory.* Hillsdale, NJ: Erlbaum.

Kintsch, W. (1988). The use of knowledge in discourse processing: A construction–integration model. *Psychological Review, 95,* 163–182.

Kintsch, W. (1992). How readers construct situation models for stories: The role of syntactic cues and causal inferences. In A. F. Healy, S. M. Kosslyn, R. M. Shiffrin (Eds.) *From learning processes to cognitive processes: Essays in honor of William K. Estes* (Vol. 2, pp. 261–278). Hillsdale, NJ: Erlbaum.

Kintsch, W., & van Dijk, T. A. (1978). Towards a model of text comprehension and production. *Psychological Review, 85,* 363–394.

Kintsch, W., & Greeno, J. G. (1985). Understanding and solving word arithmetic problems. *Psychological Review, 92,* 109–129.

Kintsch, W., & Vipond, D. (1979). Reading comprehension and readability in educational practice and psychological theory. In L. G. Nilsson (Ed.), *Perspectives of memory research* (pp. 325–366). Hillsdale, NJ: Erlbaum.

Kintsch, W., & Welsch, D. (1991). The construction–integration model: A framework for studying memory for text. In W. E. Hockley & S. Lewandowsky (Eds.), *Relating theory and data: Essays on human memory in honor of Bennet B. Murdock* (pp. 367–385). Hilllsdale, NJ: Erlbaum.

Larkin, J. H. (1983). Expert and novice differences in solving physics word problems. In D. Gentner, & A. L. Stevens (Eds.), *Mental models* (pp. 75–98). Hillsdale, NJ: Erlbaum.

Lesgold, A. M., Roth, S. F., & Curtis, M. E. (1979). Foregrounding effects in discourse comprehension. *Journal of Verbal Learning and Verbal Behavior, 18,* 291–308.

Mannes, S. M., & Doane, S. M. (1991). A hybrid model of script generation: Or getting the best of both worlds. *Connection Science* 3(1), 61–87.

Mannes, S. M., & Kintsch, W. (1987). Knowledge organization and text organization. *Cognition and Instruction, 4,* 91–115.

Mannes, S. M., & Kintsch, W. (1991). Planning routine computing tasks: Understanding what to do. *Cognitive Science, 15,* 305–342.

Mayer, R. C., Cook, L. K., & Dyck, J. L. (1984). Techniques to help readers build mental models from scientific texts: Definitions, pretraining, and signaling. *Journal of Educational Psychology, 76,* 1089–1105.

Mayer, R. E. (1979). Twenty years of research on advance organizers: Assimilation theory is still the best predictor of results. *Instructional Science, 8,* 133–167.

McDonald, D. R. (1987). *Drawing inferences from expository texts.* Unpublished doctoral dissertation, New Mexico State University.

McKoon, G., & Ratcliff, R. (1992). Inference during reading. *Psychological Review, 99*(3), 440–466.

Meyer, B. J. F. (1975). *The organization of prose and its effect on memory.* Amsterdam: North Holland.

Miller, J. R., & Kintsch, W. (1980). Readability and recall of short prose passages: A theoretical analysis. *Journal of Experimental Psychology: Human Learning and Memory, 6,* 335–354.

Nathan, M. J. (1991). A theory of word algebra comprehension and its implications for the design of computer-based learning environments. Unpublished doctoral dissertation., University of Colorado.

Nathan, M. J., Kintsch, W., & Young, E. (1992). A theory of word algebra problem comprehension and its implications for the design of learning environments. *Cognition and Instruction, 9*(4), 329–389.

Newell, A. (1990). *Unified theories of cognition.* Cambridge, MA: Harvard University Press.

Newell, A., & Simon, H. A. (1972). *Human problem solving.* Englewood Cliffs, NJ: Prentice-Hall.

Norman, D. A., & Bobrow, D. (1975). On data limited and resource limited processess. *Cognitive Psychology, 7,* 44–64.

Perfetti, C. A. (1985). *Reading ability.* New York: Oxford University Press.

Perfetti, C. A. (1989). There are generalized abilities and one of them is reading. In L. B. Resnick (Ed.), *Knowing, learning, and instruction: Essays in honor of Robert Glaser* (pp. 307–335). Hillsdale, NJ: Erlbaum.

Perfetti, C. A., & McCutchen, D. (1987). Schooled language competence: Linguistic abilities in reading and writing. In S. Rosenberg (Ed.), *Advances in applied psycholinguistics* (pp. 105–141). New York: Cambridge University Press.

Poulsen, D., Kintsch, E., Kintsch, W., & Premack, D. (1979). Children's comprehension and memory for stories. *Journal of Experimental Child Psychology, 28,* 379–403.

Resnick, L. B. (Ed.) (1989). *Knowing, learning, & instruction: Essays in honor of Robert Glaser.* Hillsdale, NJ: Erlbaum.

Reusser, K. (1993) Tutoring systems and pedagogical theory: Representational tools for understanding planning and reflection and problem solving. In S. Lajorie & S. Derry (Eds.), *Computers as cognitive tools.* Hillsdale, NJ: Erlbaum.

Reusser, K., Kämpfer, A., & Stüssi, R. (1990). HERON: Ein adaptives tutorielles System zum Lösen mathematischer Textaufgaben. In A. Reuter (Ed.), *Informatik auf dem Weg zum Anwender.* Berlin: Springer.

Rosenblatt, L. M. (1978). *The reader, the text, the poem.* Carbondale, IL: Southern Illinois University Press.

Rumelhart, D. E., Smolensky, P., McClelland, J. L., & Hinton, G. E. (1986). Schemata and sequential thought processes in PDP models. In J. L. McClelland, D. E. Rumelhart, & the PDP Research Group, (Eds.), *Parallel distributed processing. Vol. 2: Psychological and biological models* (pp. 7–57). Cambridge, MA: Bradford.

Scardamalia, M., Bereiter, C., McLean, R. S., Swallow, J., & Woodruff, E. (1989). Computer supported intentional learning environments. *Journal of Educational Computing Research, 5,* 51–68.

Schank, R. (1975). The structure of episodes in memory. In D. G. Bobrow & A. M. Collins (Eds.), *Representation and understanding: Studies in cognitive science* (pp. 237–272). New York: Academic Press.

Schank, R. C. (1982). *Dynamic memory.* New York: Cambridge University Press.

Schank, R. C., & Abelson, R. P. (1977). *Scripts, plans, goals, and understanding*. Hillsdale, NJ: Erlbaum.

Schoenfeld, A. H. (1985). *Mathematical Problem Solving*. Orlando, FL: Academic Press.

Schvaneveldt, R. W., Durso, F. T., & Dearhold, D. W. (1989). *Pathfinder: Scaling with network structures* (Tech. Rep. No. MCCS-85-9). Las Cruces: New Mexico State University.

Spilich, G. J., Vesonder, G. T., Chiesi, H. L., & Voss, J. F. (1979). Text processing of domain related information for individuals with high and low domain knowledge. *Journal of Verbal Learning and Verbal Behavior, 18*, 275–290.

Sulin, R. A., & Dooling, D. J. (1974). Intrusion of a thematic idea in retention of prose. *Journal of Experimental Psychology, 103*, 255–262.

Trabasso, T., & van den Broek, P. (1985). Causal thinking and the representation of narrative events. *Journal of Memory and Language, 24*, 612–630.

Trabasso, T., & Sperry, L. L. (1985). Causal relatedness and importance of story events. *Journal of Memory and Language, 24*, 595–611.

Tyler, S. W., Hertel, P. T., McCallum, M. C., & Ellis, H. C. (1979). Cognitive effort and memory. *Journal of Experimental Psychology: Human Learning and Memory, 5*, 607–617.

Weaver, C. A. III, & Kintsch, W. (1990) Expository text. In R. Barr, M. L., Kamil, P. B. Rosenthal, & P. D. Pearson (Eds.), *Handbook of reading* (pp. 230–245). New York: Longman.

Weaver, C. A. III, & Kintsch, W. (1992). Enhancing students' comprehension of the conceptual structure of word algebra problems. *Journal of Educational Psychology, 84*(4), 419–428.

SEPARATING CAUSAL LAWS FROM CASUAL FACTS: PRESSING THE LIMITS OF STATISTICAL RELEVANCE

Patricia W. Cheng

I. Introduction

The problem of causal induction, as Goodman (1954/1983 p. 19) put it, is "to distinguish accurately between causal laws and casual facts." What is the criterion by which people judge some sequences to be causal and reject others as accidental? One proposal is that this criterion is, at least in part, based on *statistical relevance* (e.g., Anderson, 1990; Cartwright, 1983, 1989; Cheng & Novick, 1990a, 1992; Jenkins & Ward, 1965; Kelley, 1967, 1973; Salmon, 1971, 1984).[1] Proponents of this view attempt to formulate this component of the criterion in terms of some variant of the difference between the probability of the effect in the presence of the cause and that in its absence. This view has its roots in the notion of regularity first proposed by Hume (1739/1987), who argued that people infer causal relations by observing the constant conjunction of cause and effect. Deterministic criteria for causality (e.g., Mackie, 1974) may be regarded as special extreme cases of the statistical-relevance view. For my purpose here of studying everyday causal induction, I will regard this view as claiming that statistical relevance provides evidence for the causal structure of the

[1] The term *statistical relevance* originates from Salmon (1971), who proposed a specific model of the statistical-relevance basis of scientific explanation. I use the term here broadly to denote the approach rather than his specific theory.

215

world.[2] Many criticisms have been raised against this relevance view by proponents of a view that has been more popular within psychology, which I will call the *power* view. This view, in its psychological variants (e.g., Bullock, Gelman & Baillargeon, 1982; Michotte, 1946/1963; Shultz, 1982; Turner, 1987; White, 1989), claims that instead of statistical relevance, the critical criterion for distinguishing between causal and accidental sequences is the perception or knowledge of a causal power, a causal impression, the knowledge of a mechanism, or the knowledge of the transmission of some generative source. For example, according to White (1988, p. 48) the computation of statistical relevance "appears to be a relatively late and imperfect development, at least in causal processing, and seems not to be basic to causal processing." And Shultz (1982, p. 46) concludes in his monograph, "In contrast to research focusing on Humean or neo-Humean rules (e.g., regularity of succession, temporal and spatial contiguity, covariation, conditionship), the present studies have touched more directly on what can arguably be called the essence of causal reasoning (namely, knowledge of the generative or productive nature of causation)."

As I read the debate between the two views, I often have the feeling that it is not really a debate at all, but simply an illusory interchange created by the superimposition of halves of separate debates—each on issues that bear identical or similar labels, but that are actually quite independent. The points made on each side hit the opponent occasionally, but seemingly more by accident than by intent, given where the debaters think their opponents stand. As I will try to show, one of two main issues for the power side of the debate is, Given the causal knowledge that people typically have, do we use this knowledge to interpret novel relations as instances of known causal relations? This type of inference clearly shows a direct top-down influence of prior causal knowledge; our understanding of a cause, or a particular type of cause, plays a central role. A second issue for the same side is, Are there specific, probably innate, processes that yield inferences to various specific types of causality? Some of our causal knowledge could have an innate basis, but presumably a substantial part is acquired. For the statistical-relevance side, the main issue is, How do we discover causal relations? That is, for acquired causal relations, how do we first come to judge that they are causal? Knowledge of a superordinate causal relation is not treated as a given. Like the first issue, the third

---

[2] Although Hume was skeptical about the existence of causal relations in the world, arguing that they exist only in our minds, ordinary people without the luxury of philosophical training are evidently safe from this perhaps disorienting worry. As a psychologist concerned with everyday reasoning, I assume that people believe that causal powers exist in the world. To my knowledge, no theorist of everyday inference has assumed otherwise. Skepticism concerning the existence of causal powers in the world is a philosophical issue that I will not address.

concerns a process that is general across different types of causal relations. However, unlike the first issue, the third involves a bottom-up inductive aspect, an aspect that is essential, albeit insufficient, for the discovery of causes.

A. WHY BOTHER TO EVALUATE THIS DEBATE?

Each of these three issues is interesting in its own right. For a typical adult, truly novel causal relations that do not fit into any previously acquired types of causal relations are probably rare. Many of the causal inferences we make in our everyday life, as power theorists point out, are influenced by our top-down causal knowledge. Understanding how this knowledge is integrated with new information is therefore critical in understanding everyday causal inference. Moreover, there are indefinitely many candidate causal factors, which are certainly beyond our computational capacity to test exhaustively. There must, therefore, be constraints on how to select or construct candidates. Top-down knowledge and specific innate criteria play this crucial role. However, there remains the issue of how the acquired top-down knowledge first gets to be there. One goal of the third line of inquiry is to trace the origin of how sequences of events come to be viewed as accidental (e.g., a red car entering a parking lot before a blue car leaves it), as noncausal despite their apparent regularity (e.g., sunrise following a rooster's crowing for a farm child), or as causal (e.g., the striking of a match followed by its lighting). A closely related goal is to explicate what makes disparate types of specific causal relations all causal. Without an element that is common across such processes, it is not clear why they all give an output that instantiates the concept of causality.

More generally, all of these topics are important in that causal regularities support explanation and prediction, whereas accidental sequences do not. In the examples above, we would not explain the blue car's leaving by the red car's entering, nor would we explain sunrise by the rooster's crowing, whereas we *would* explain the match's lighting by its being struck. From past experience telling us that butter melts when heated to 150 °F, we would be willing to make the (fallible) prediction that the next piece of butter heated to the same temperature would also melt, as Goodman (1954/1983) pointed out. However, from past experience telling us that all coins in Goodman's pocket on VE day[3] are silver, we might be quite unwilling to predict that the next coin to go into his pocket that day would also be silver. Accidental regular sequences only support prediction if there is a mediating causal relation, without which they do not support prediction at all. For example, although a drop in the barometric reading is

[3] Victory in Europe, World War II.

regularly followed by a storm, and we would ordinarily be willing to predict an approaching storm from a drop in the reading, we would be unwilling to do so if, say, the drop is known to be the result of mercury being removed from the barometer. The mediating cause—a drop in the atmospheric pressure—is missing. Thus, a drop in the reading per se does not support the prediction of an approaching storm. It certainly does not explain the occurrence of a storm.

One might think that it is the level of generality that determines whether a relevance relation is causal. Goodman's pocket on VE day is a particular object at a particular time on earth, whereas butter refers to a substance anywhere, anytime. The story does not seem so straightforward, however. Consider the following regularities that apparently are at the same level of generality (Salmon, 1989, p. 15):

> No gold sphere has a mass greater than 100,000 kg.
> No enriched uranium sphere has a mass greater than 100,000 kg.

Because the critical mass for enriched uranium is only a few kilograms, the second regularity should be considered lawful. One might think of the nature of enriched uranium as causing the sphere's mass to be smaller than a certain criterion. Assuming the truth of the regularity regarding gold spheres for the sake of argument, we see that being gold does not have the analogous effect. Yet these regularities have identical scope and form.

A related property that differs between causal and accidental regularities is that causal regularities lead to acceptable counterfactuals, whereas accidental ones do not. For example, whereas we would conclude that if this solid piece of butter had been heated to 150 °F, it would have melted, we would not conclude that if this copper coin had been in Goodman's pocket, it would have been silver. Similarly, whereas we would conclude from the regularity about enriched uranium that if something were a sphere with mass greater than 100,000 kg it would not be composed of enriched uranium, we would not conclude from the regularity about gold that if something were a sphere with mass greater than 100,000 kg it would not be composed of gold. Note that the issue is not whether these predictions will turn out to be true. Given that predictions are empirically based, they are inevitably fallible. The issue is whether they are intuitively plausible.

Separating causes from accidental sequences is a task that people clearly perform, from infancy on in the case of the perception of causes for some kinds of motion (Leslie, 1984; Leslie & Keeble, 1987). Causal inferences become increasingly systematic as we approach adulthood, as psychological research (Bullock, 1985; Cheng & Novick, 1992; Shultz &

Kesterbaum, 1985) and our intuitions tell us. Even rats and pigeons in Pavlovian conditioning experiments appear to behave like humans inferring causes (Rescorla, 1988; Shanks & Dickinson, 1987). Rescorla (1988) writes,

> in teaching undergraduates, I favor an analogy between animals showing Pavlovian conditioning and scientists identifying the cause of a phenomenon. If one thinks of Pavlovian conditioning as developing between a CS and a US under just those circumstances that would lead a scientist to conclude that the CS causes the US, one has a surprisingly successful heuristic for remembering the facts of what it takes to produce Pavlovian associative learning. (p. 154)

The problem of this basic task of causal induction was posed by Hume (1739/1987) more than two and half centuries ago. He convincingly argued that there is no logical way to prove that *"those instances, of which we have had no experience, resemble those, of which we have had experience"* (p. 89). Because the prediction of the occurence of an effect based on the occurrence of its cause does not have any deductive logical justification, there must be an empirical criterion governing such inferences. What this criterion is remains unresolved today.

B. GOALS

Because the debate in the psychological literature on causal reasoning concerns intriguing issues, it may be worthwhile to clarify and understand the confusion. A cause of the confusion, I think, is that some assumptions held by the participants have been left implicit—in particular, the "givens" in the first and third issues are almost never explicitly stated. Although both sides of the debate are concerned with how people make causal judgments, the power side begins its answer given directly relevant prior causal knowledge, whereas the statistical-relevance side begins without such knowledge. Because second-guessing what other investigators have in mind (at times despite what they write) is not a fruitful activity, I will not attempt to do so. Instead, I will try to evaluate the evidence and arguments with respect to more explicitly formulated assumptions, with the goal of seeing where the diverse lines of evidence on which investigators base their arguments fit in a coherent picture. This effort will sometimes require separating the evidence from the points originally made with that evidence. I think the resulting picture is far less discordant than what the rhetoric suggests.

Although I will interpret evidence from both sides, my evaluation will focus on the status of the bottom-up component. I will not aim at a comprehensive review of the evidence and arguments against the statistical-relevance view, but rather will aim at illustrating and clarifying some common confusions in the psychological literature.

I will argue that the type of statistical relation that best characterizes this criterion in everyday reasoning is not constant conjunction, as proposed by Hume; nor is it covariation (Kelley, 1967), as can be traced to J. S. Mill (1843/1973); nor is it contingency or contrast per se (Jenkins & Ward, 1965; Rescorla, 1968), which is a probabilistic generalization of covariation. A component of this criterion does, however, appear to be a generalized concept of contrast–*conditional contrast* (cf. Cartwright, 1983, 1989; Reichenbach, 1956; Salmon, 1980; Suppes, 1970). Instead of being estimated on the basis of the universal set of experienced events, contrast is estimated conditional on some privileged subset of events. I will try to show that many of the problems that have been raised against constant conjunction, covariation, and contingency can be solved by this broader conception of statistical relevance. A second goal of this article, then, is to review and discuss evidence supporting the role of conditional contrast in causal judgments.

Although conditional contrast can overcome some of the problems that defeat unconditional contrast as the criterion for the discovery of causes, it by no means provides the entire solution. My third goal is to discuss some unsolved problems and limitations of conditional contrast. One critical unsolved problem is the constraints on conditionalization–the issue of how the privileged subsets are determined. A second problem is the level of abstraction at which a cause is defined, a recurring issue in many applications of contrast, as I will illustrate. I will discuss some potential solutions to these problems. Nonetheless, after relevance in the form of conditional contrast does its best, a daunting gap in our knowledge still remains. Many psychologists who see the shortcomings of constant succession, covariation, or contingency resort to some variant of the power view. I believe that in doing so, they are not only rejecting an answer but also switching the question. Although the knowledge of power is clearly important to causal judgments on novel instances when we have that knowledge, it leaves unanswered the issue of how acquired causal knowledge, such as the power in question, is first established. The gap left by statistical relevance is not filled by the notion of power.

To summarize, my goals are to separate the issues in the debate, review what statistical relevance as defined by conditional contrast can explain, consider some outstanding problems that do not seem hopeless within the concept of statistical relevance, and sketch a remaining gap of knowledge that clearly lies outside the realm of this concept.

II. Evaluating Criticisms of Statistical Accounts

A. HUME'S PROPOSAL ON THE RELATIONSHIP BETWEEN REGULARITY AND POWER

Because the debate has its origin in Hume's problem and his solution, considering his position on the issue might be a good place to start. As is well known, Hume (1739/1987) identified three properties that are jointly required for an inference to a cause of an effect: contiguity (spatial and temporal), priority of the cause in time, and constant conjunction. In the "Abstract" of *A Treatise on Human Nature* (1740/1987; pp. 649–650), he writes,

> Here is a billiard-ball lying on the table, and another ball moving toward it with rapidity. They strike; the ball which was formerly at rest, now acquires a motion. This is as perfect an instance of the relations of cause and effect as any which we know, either by sensation or reflection. Let us therefore examine it. 'Tis evident, that the two balls touched one another before the motion was communicated, and that there was no interval betwixt the shock and the motion. *Contiguity* in time and place is therefore a requisite circumstance to the operation of all causes. 'Tis evident likewise, that the motion, which was the cause, is prior to the motion, which was the effect. *Priority* in time, is therefore another requisite circumstance in every cause. But this is not all. Let us try any other balls of the same kind in a like situation, and we shall always find that the impulse of the one produces motion in the other. Here therefore is a *third* circumstance, viz. that of *constant conjunction* betwixt the cause and the effect. Every object like the cause, produces always some object like the effect. Beyond these three circumstances of contiguity, priority, and constant conjunction, I can discover nothing in this cause.

What Hume was unable to find is at least as notable as what he did find. He was unable to find any power, necessity, connection, productive quality, efficacy, force, energy, or any of a number of such notions that he took to be nearly synonymous with each other. He did not deny, however, that we have the intuition of a cause as having a necessary connection to its effect. In fact, in the *Treatise,* after proposing the characteristics of contiguity and priority, he noted that "An object may be contiguous and prior to another, without being consider'd as its cause", and that "there is a NECESSARY CONNEXION to be taken into consideration" (p. 77). He set it as his goal "to discover the nature of this necessary connexion." He concluded that he could not discover it in any single instance of the occurrence of a cause and its effect. However, the constant conjunction of objects like the cause with objects like the effect observed in multiple instances "constitutes the very essence of power or connexion, and is the source, from which the idea of it arises'' (p. 163).[4] What he did deny was that we infer a causal relation based on the knowledge of a power or necessary connection; rather, he argued that "the necessary connexion depends on the inference, instead of the inference's depending on the necessary connexion" (p. 88). In other words, power is not the solution to the problem of how we come to infer a causal relation, but rather a consequence of the solution.

One might expect that how we come to judge that a factor is a cause is based on our understanding of a cause. However, it is possible that the criterion used in the induction process is distinct from our explicit understanding of a cause, which is the output rather than the basis of the process. We may have conscious access only to the output but not to the process itself. In particular, our explicit understanding seems to be that a cause has the power to produce its effect, whereas a key component in the criterion, of which people probably have only tacit knowledge, seems to be relevance based.

B.   VARIANTS OF STATISTICAL ACCOUNTS

Many psychologists have raised criticisms against statistical accounts (e.g., Bullock et al., 1982; Koslowski, Okagaki, Lorenz, & Umbach, 1989; Michotte, 1963; Shultz, 1982; Turner, 1987; White, 1992). I will review some of their arguments and evidence. Because the criticisms were raised against different variants of these accounts, let me first list three frequently criticized versions, and a fourth that may be regarded as normative (or at least as the most normative of the ones proposed), but that has seldom been considered in psychology. The first one has already been mentioned above, namely, Hume's criterion of the *constant conjunction* of the cause and the effect, where the cause precedes the effect and is temporally and spatially contiguous to it. The second is Kelley's (1967, p. 194) *covariation principle,* which states, "The effect is attributed to that condition which is present when the effect is present and which is absent when the effect is absent.'' This principle can be traced to Mill's (1843/1973) "joint method of agreement and difference.'' Kelley (1967) further proposed an interpretation of the covariation principle for explaining human behavior in terms of an analogy to the analysis of variance (ANOVA) with the dimensions of persons, stimuli, and time as its independent variables.

Both the constant conjunction and the covariation principles are deterministic. It has been noted, however, that many relations in our everyday

---

[4] Some psychologists have attributed a fourth criterion of causality to Hume—the similarity between a cause and its effect. This is erroneous. The similarity that Hume referred to is that among instances of the cause or that among instances of the effect, not that between an instance of the cause and an instance of the effect.

life and in science that we consider causal are probabilistic (e.g., Einhorn & Hogarth, 1986; Salmon, 1965; Suppes, 1970). For example, no one has trouble understanding "icy roads cause car accidents," even though not all cars driving on icy roads have accidents, nor do accidents happen only when there are icy roads. The remaining variants of statistical accounts that I will consider are probabilistic. The third variant is *unconditional contrast,* as defined by the difference between the probability of a target effect E given the presence of a potential causal factor C and its probability given the absence of the factor. If this difference is noticeably greater than 0 [i.e., $P(E \mid C) - P(E \mid \bar{C}) > 0$], C is inferred to be a facilitatory cause of E (Jenkins & Ward, 1965; Rescorla, 1968). These probabilities are typically (although not necessarily) assumed to be estimated by frequencies. The set of events over which this contrast is defined is by default assumed to be the universal set, which for an experiment is taken to be the entire set of events presented in it. Kelley's covariation principle is equivalent to the special case in which contrast equals 1 [$P(C \mid E) = 1$ and $P(C \mid \bar{E}) = 0$ in conjunction imply $P(E \mid C) = 1$ and $P(E \mid \bar{C}) = 0$].

Besides being probabilistic, unconditional contrast differs from constant conjunction in that it considers what occurs in the *absence* of the cause in addition to an association betwen the occurrence of the cause and of the effect. The importance of this distinction can be illustrated by an example about John Jones, a man who faithfully consumed his wife's birth-control pills and did not become pregnant (Salmon, 1971). By the criterion of constant conjunction, because any man who regularly takes oral contraceptives will avoid becoming pregnant, Jones' consumption of contraceptives would be a cause of his success at avoiding pregnancy. This inference does not follow from contrast, however, because any man who does not regularly take oral contraceptives will also avoid pregnancy. Whereas constant conjunction does not incorporate the notion of *relevance,* contrast and the other variants of the statistical approaches I discuss do incorporate the idea.

The fourth variant, *conditional contrast,* is a generalization of the third. A rough characterization of this variant is that contrast for C with respect to E is computed within sets of events in which alternative causal factors K_i are kept constant: If $P(E \mid C \cdot K_1 \cdot K_2 \cdot \ldots K_n) - P(E \mid \bar{C} \cdot K_1 \cdot K_2 \cdot \ldots K_n)$ is noticeably greater than 0, C is inferred to be a facilitatory cause of E (cf. criterion CC in Cartwright, 1983, 1989; Salmon, 1980; Suppes, 1970).[5] An isolated period denotes "and." Each K_i denotes a definite choice between the presence and the absence of the factor. The difference in conditional

---

[5] An exception is when there is a ceiling effect due to the presence of an alternative cause, or a floor effect due to the absence of a component of the cause, in which case the conditional contrasts for a causal factor need not all differ from 0.

probabilities is ideally computed for every combination of the presence and absence of alternative causes. Moreover, the ideal set of conditionalizing factors would include all those and only those that are actually causal. Given the limitations of knowledge, however, the best that people could do is to select as conditionalizing factors those that they currently *believe* to be plausible causes. Even among these choices, information and processing limits may lead to the selection of some conditionalizing factors over others. Computing conditional contrasts is analogous to using control conditions in standard experimental design, in which extraneous variables are kept constant.

The key reason for the generalization to conditional contrasts is that they provide a way of distinguishing between genuine and spurious causes. For example, the total of sales of ice cream covaries with (i.e., is statistically relevant to) crime rate. Despite this relevance relation, one would not draw the conclusion that ice cream sales cause crime or vice versa. According to conditional contrasts, when the contrast for ice cream sales with respect to crime rate is computed conditional on a genuine cause, air temperature in this case, the rate of ice cream sales no longer covaries with crime rate. It is a spurious cause, which is "screened off" from crime by air temperature.

The above definitions assume that events, causes, and effects can be represented discretely. An additional assumption is that the cause temporally, or psychologically, precedes its effect. I assume that a cause is psychologically prior to an effect if the cause is the entity that can be more directly manipulated.

C.   CRITICISM 1: CAUSAL INFERENCES ORIGINATE IN THE DIRECT PERCEPTION OF CAUSALITY

Michotte's (1946/1963) findings about the perception of the cause of motion have often been interpreted as a definitive refutation of Hume's criterion of constant conjunction, or more generally of regularity theories. In the basic version of his often-cited "launching" experiments (Experiment 1), an object (B) is at the center of the screen, and another object (A) is 40 mm to its left. The subject fixates on Object B. At a given moment, A sets off and moves toward B at a constant speed of 30 cm/sec. It stops at the moment it comes into contact with B, while B then starts and moves to the right away from A, either at the same speed, or more slowly. (Other launching experiments used variants of this basic procedure, which bears some resemblance to Hume's billiard-ball example.) Describing his results when the collision satisfies some fairly strict spatio-temporal constraints (e.g., B has to start moving within a few tenths of a second of the collision),

Michotte writes, "The impression is clear: it is the blow given by A which *makes B go,* which *produces* B's movement" (p. 20). The bump by A is often perceived to "send B off" or to "launch" B. He regards his findings as refuting Hume's (1748/1975, Section VII, part ii, p. 74) claim that "we never can observe any tye between" a cause and an effect. The cause or power that produces motion can be "directly experienced" (Michotte, 1946/1963, p. 21) in a single instance. Therefore there is no need for repeated experience of the conjunction of the cause and the effect. He concludes (p. 256):

> If Hume had been able to carry out experiments such as ours, there is no doubt that he would have been led to revise his views on the psychological origin of the popular idea of causality. He would probably have appealed in his explanation to the "causal impression" rather than to habit and expectation.

Other researchers have agreed with Michotte's interpretation that there is direct perception of causality and that constant conjunction is unnecessary (Leslie, 1982; Shultz, 1982; White, 1992).

1. Does Perceptual Causality Refute the Necessity of the Criterion of Contrast?

One might likewise conclude from Michotte's findings that statistical relevance is not necessary for the perception of causality. It is obvious that the collision occurs only once in a trial in Michotte's experiment. Moreover, it is true that from a single event involving the presence or absence of the cause and the presence or absence of the effect, none of the statistical criteria could yield a causal inference. What may not be so obvious, however, is that a single trial does contain information about multiple events that enables the computation of contrast. I will show that if, instead of constant conjunction, a relevance criterion such as contrast is considered, then Michotte's findings actually support a criterion that is a special case of relevance.

Michotte (1946/1963) reported many findings clearly showing that contrast is not sufficient to produce the perception of causality. For example, when the speed of B after the collision is noticeably greater than that of A before the collision, there was no perception of launching in adults (Experiment 40). Similarly, modifying Experiment 1 by introducing a temporal delay of 1/5 sec or more between A arriving at the center and the B starting to move destroys the launching effect (Experiment 29). An infant analogue of this finding was reported by Leslie and Keeble (1987). The question I raise does not concern the sufficiency of contrast, which has been soundly refuted, but rather its necessity.

The interpretation that relevance is unnecessary for the perception of causality rests on the assumption that a trial in Michotte's experiments contains one single event, within which the cause is either present or absent and the effect is either present or absent. Under this assumption, the entire sequence of the movement of A in a collision trial up to and including the collision would be represented as the presence of the potential cause. However, depending on the temporal scope of what is considered the cause, there can be more than one event in a single trial. For example, if the potential causal factor is defined as the Colliding of Moving Object A into Object B, then a trial also contains an event (or events) in which that factor is absent. Because only factors prior to the occurrence of the effect (B moving away) are potential causal factors, let us consider the status of the potential cause, collision by Moving Object A, before B moves away. We see that when A collides with B (i.e., in the presence of the potential cause), the effect occurs; but before the collision (i.e., in the absence of the potential cause), the effect does not occur. Therefore, the information in a single trial yields a positive contrast.

The scope of the definition of a cause clearly should not be left arbitrary in a statistical-relevance theory. For the purpose of interpreting Michotte's findings, it seems that defining the cause as *collision by a moving object* accords better with our phenomenological experience, and on that basis alone is at least as justifiable as defining it as the entire sequence of the movement of A, which corresponds to whatever is defined by the experimenter as a "trial." But, of course, there is the deeper issue of what determines the scope of the cause that we experience. I will return to a discussion of a solution to this problem when we have seen the problem in various guises. However, first let me give some justification for the definition that I gave above.

Two of Michotte's experiments show that the impression of causality is critically dependent on how B moves *before* A collides with it. In Experiment 21 (Michotte, 1946/1963) which is otherwise the same as Experiment 1, B moves to and fro before A begins to move. A collides with B at the center of the screen just as B comes to a rest and is about to change direction. A stays, and B changes direction as before. There is no launching effect when observers view the situation as a whole: B's movements "seemed entirely independent of the movement performed by A" (p. 74). Thus, in comparison with the results of Experiment 1, we see that the occurrence of the effect (B moving away) prior to the collision eliminates the impression of launching otherwise produced by its occurrence after the collision. Because the movement of B before and after the collision has opposite influences on this impression, time prior to the collision and the collision itself cannot together be represented by a single theoretical entity; that is, the representation of the entire movement of A up to and including the collision as "the presence of the cause" is too coarse-grained to reflect the dependencies observed. Considering *collision by moving object A* as the cause instead, we see that when the effect (B's movement or pattern of movement) occurs both in the presence of the cause (the collision) and in its absence, there was no perception of causality. This definition yields an interpretation of the results consistent with contrast as a necessary criterion.[6]

In Experiment 17, objects A and B begin to move simultaneously in the same direction. A moves at a speed of 29 cm/sec, and B moves at one of 5 speeds ranging from 7 to 27 cm/sec. A stops after coming into contact with B, but B continues to move, changing to a speed of 40 cm/sec. Michotte reported that for conditions in which B moved at a slow rate (15 or less cm/sec), the impression of launching is "quite as good" as in the case when B is still. However, for conditions in which B moved at a relatively fast rate (25 and 27 cm/sec) prior to the collision (i.e., in the absence of the cause), as in the presence of the cause (40 cm/sec), there was no perception of causality. When B moved at an intermediate speed, the impression of causality was only sometimes obtained. Here, an analysis in terms of a counterpart of contrast for continuous variables representing the potential causal factor and the effect would be more appropriate. Nevertheless, using contrast as an approximation and, as before, defining "collision by A" as the cause, we can see that if the effect is "B moving at a speed within a certain range of 40 cm/sec," say 40 ± 15 cm/sec for most subjects, then contrast would explain the impression of launching in these conditions. In the conditions in which B is slow before the collision, the effect does not occur in the absence of the cause but does occur in its presence. The positive contrast yields a prediction of the impression of launching. To the contrary, in the conditions in which B moves at a high speed prior to the collision, the effect occurs both in the absence of the cause and in its presence; contrast therefore predicts no impression of launching. When B moves at an intermediate speed, that speed might fall within the range of the effect for some subjects but outside that range for others, predicting that the impression of launching sometimes obtains. Like Experiment 21, Experiment 17 shows that (1) how B moves prior to the collision relative to how it moves after the collision critically influences the perception of

[6] Michotte noted that concentration on the point of collision "can produce isolation of the last phase" (p. 74)—the final movement of B to the right—and the launching effect reappears. If the focussing causes the to-and-fro movement of B to be ignored, and the effective input for B is such that its movement changes from the period before the collision to that after the collision, then the attendant reappearance of launching is consistent with a criterion of contrast.

causality, and (2) when there was no noticeable change in the movement of B before and after collision by A, there was no perception of launching. The results are consistent with contrast as a necessary criterion of causality.[7]

Results from Michotte's Experiment 12 corroborate the appropriateness of the definition of the cause as collision by a moving object, rather than as the entire sequence of movement of A. (Note that according to contrast, the defined duration of the cause should not be too short either. If this defined duration is made arbitrarily short, the probability of the effect given the presence of the cause, and hence its contrast, can be made arbitrarily small.) This experiment shows that to produce the launching effect, it is necessary for A to travel only a very short distance. As in Experiment 1, B appears stationary at the center and A appears on the side. The only difference from Experiment 1 is that Object A travels various distances, ranging from 95 mm to 5 mm, before reaching B. At the distance of 5 mm, the launching effect was reported to be "almost as good as it is when the distances were greater" (p. 57). Moving object A obviously has to be present for a non-zero amount of time for its collision with B to be perceived as the cause of B's movement. Michotte concluded, "it would not be far wrong to say that a causal impression must appear as soon as the threshold is passed beyond which a movement of A in the direction of B is clearly perceptible" (p. 57). Thus, before this critical period, the cause should be represented as absent, regardless of whether Moving Object A is actually present.

Schlottmann and Shanks (1992) reported some results concerning variations of Michotte's launching procedure that might appear to challenge the necessity of contrast for the impression of launching. They claimed that manipulating the value of contrast (*contingency* in their terms) affects judgments of how necessary collisions were in order for Object B to move (across many trials), but that contrast does not affect the perception of causality on any single "collision" trial. Like the common interpretation of Michotte's findings, however, Schlottmann and Shanks' definition of contrast—and hence their conclusion—rests on the assumption that a trial that produces the impression of launching consists of a single event in which the cause is present.

In the experiment that presents the most direct evidence for their conclusion (Experiment 2), Schlottmann and Shanks (1992) attempted to examine the effect of varying contrast on two kinds of causal ratings. Con-

---

[7] Experiments 17 and 21 may be considered the perception-of-causality analogs of the conditions in Rescorla's (1968) experiment on Pavlovian conditioning in which the unconditioned stimulus occurs with various probabilities in the absence of the conditioned stimulus.

trast was varied by interspersing trials on which a collision occurred and B moved (the typical launching procedure) with trials on which A remained stationary on the edge of the display—so that no collision occurred—and B either moved or did not move. In the "contingent" condition, B remained stationary on trials in which A was stationary. In the "noncontingent" condition, B moved on such trials. On selected collision trials, adult human subjects were asked to rate their natural perception of the relationship between cause and effect for that specific collision. They were also given another rating task in which they were encouraged to treat the cause–effect relationship as an arbitrary one and were instructed to rate "how necessary collisions are for making" B move based on "many events" in which B "may or may not move with or without a collision" (Schlottmann & Shanks, 1992, p. 335). The instructions were repeated and clarified if a subject indicated that collisions were necessary in a noncontingent example series with multiple trials.

Schlottmann and Shanks reported that the intuitive causal perception ratings did not differ across the contingent and noncontingent conditions, whereas the arbitrary necessity judgments were much higher for the contingent than for the noncontingent condition, leading the investigators to conclude that varying contrast affects necessity judgments but does not affect the perception of causality. Alternatively, however, this pattern of results can be explained by the assumption that the subjects, unlike the investigators, defined the scope of a cause differently for the two types of ratings, thereby obtaining different conditional probabilities and contrast values. Subjects may have naturally represented a single trial as a multiple-event series in order to make the perception ratings; whereas because of the experimenters' instructions, subjects may have re-represented an entire trial as a single event in order to make the arbitrary necessity judgments.

The perception ratings referred to single-collision trials. Such trials were identical across conditions. If each collision trial is split into events in which the potential cause (collision by Moving Object A) is first absent and then present, as explained earlier, then the contrast for the cause is 1. Therefore, the hypothesis that contrast is a necessary component of the criterion predicts that if other necessary conditions such as spatiotemporal contiguity are present, then perception ratings should be equally high across the contingent and noncontingent conditions.

The necessity ratings were explicitly based on multiple trials. The instructions for such ratings encouraged considering the entire trial as a single event in which the potential cause (the entire sequence of the movement of A up to the collision) is either present or absent. Across trials for the contingent condition, then, the probability of B moving, given that

A did not move, was 0: B moved on trials in which A moved, and it did not move on trials in which A did not move. Necessity defined across trials-as-single-events therefore predicts that the necessity ratings should be high. Recall that the probability of B moving given a collision was 1 for both conditions, and only the probability of B moving given no collision varied across conditions. It follows that contrast and the necessity of the collision for B's movement, defined across trials, make the same predictions.

For the noncontingent condition, B moved on trials in which A moved, but it also moved on trials in which A did not move. The probability of B moving given that A did not move on a trial was 1, and the contrast for A's movement was 0. These values differ from the corresponding values for the potential cause defined within a trial. Therefore we would expect the necessity judgments, unlike the perception ratings, to be low. Thus for both types of ratings for both conditions, subjects' responses were consistent with the respective conditional probabilities and contrast values based on differing representations of the potential causes.

To summarize, Michotte's and related findings clearly refute the necessity of the criterion of constant conjunction of the cause and the effect. Whether these results refute the necessity of relevance as defined by contrast, however, is questionable. From the fact that the cause and the effect occur only once on a trial, it does not necessarily follow that the causal inference drawn is based on a single event; it may in addition be based on events that occur during those parts of the same trial in which the cause was absent.[8] These findings do not show, as has been commonly assumed, that satisfying some specific spatiotemporal criterion at and after the collision is sufficient to produce the perception of causality—there are event sequences that satisfy these constraints but that are not perceived as causal. An additional requirement is contrast. Converging experimental results show that *when there is evidence that B does not change its movement in the presence versus the absence of the cause, there is no perception of causality.*

Visible mechanical causality is one among many types of causal relations. Different types of causal relations clearly have different spatiotemporal constraints. Compare the spatiotemporal constraints in the launching phenomenon, in the effects of a magnet, and in the effects of the HIV virus. Such constraints for specific relations may be regarded as specific supplements to contrast, which is general across types of causal relations.

---

[8] This point similarly applies to Garcia, McGowan, and Green's (1972) well-known result showing that a single pairing of novel-tasting water and illness can induce an aversion to water with the same or similar taste.

2. The Role of Replications

Even though the launching effect is consistent with the criterion of contrast, a salient feature that distinguishes it from many other causal inferences is that its emergence seems to require only one or at most a few
trials. What role do replications play? It is standard to assume that the
reliability of the estimates of each of the two probabilities in a contrast
increases with the frequency of events. Michotte reported that the causal
impression sometimes does not appear at the first presentation of the
experiment, especially for subjects who were not accustomed to observing
presentations in his laboratory (Michotte, 1963, p. 20, footnote 25). He
reported that when the presentation is repeated a few times, however, the
perception of causality virtually always arises. Other researchers replicating his experiments have similarly found that launching is not perceived by
all subjects on first presentation. For example, Boyle (1960) found that
50% of potential subjects did not see the relation as causal on first presentation. Thus, replication of the two types of events does seem to play a
role. It is not clear, however, that the role of replications is to increase the
reliability of the estimates; Michotte also reported that the subjects who
did not perceive causality did not see a noncausal sequence either, but
were generally confused. Regardless of the interpretation, only a few
replications, if any, seem to be required.

A further complication to the issue of the role of replications is that
specific replications may not be the sole contributor to reliability. Reliability could be based, not only on the specific events in question, but also
more generally on events involving causal relations of the same general
type. For example, based on the small variability directly or indirectly
observed in events involving mechanical phenomena, people might judge
even a single occurrence of an effect to be highly reliable (cf. Thagard &
Nisbett, 1982). Analogously, results from well-controlled physics experiments are often accepted without replication. In contrast, domains that
impose less stringent spatiotemporal constraints, or that are less well
controlled, and hence more subject to noisy data, would require more
observations to achieve the same level of reliability. In sum, replications
yield evidence for reliability, but the reliability indicated depends on the
variability of the type of phenomenon.

3. Innateness and Contrast

The small number of replications required, together with other evidence,
suggest that the perception of the causes of motion reflects the workings
of an innate modular system (Leslie, 1988). This type of causality seems

impervious to our conscious knowledge—subjects in Michotte's experiments knew perfectly well that no collisions of real objects were involved. That is, although no causality at the conceptual level is involved,
subjects nonetheless visually perceived causality. Moreover, such perception develops relatively early, by 27 weeks of age (Leslie & Keeble,
1987).

What does the innateness or modularity of a specific relevance criterion imply for the issue of whether there is a general criterion that involves some form of relevance? Innateness and the generality of a
process are separable issues. A distinction should be made here between
the innateness of the process incorporating a criterion and that of the
output of such a process. It is clear that the output of the process—
knowledge that A causes B to move—is not innate, because without
perceptual input showing object A colliding into object B in a way that
satisfies the specific contrast criterion, there certainly cannot be any perception that A causes B to move. Therefore, it is the innateness of the
process that is in question. An innate and modular information process
that tests relevance is nonetheless a process. One might think that psychologists should start with whatever evolution handed us. However, for
the goal of understanding human information processing, there is no reason to stop modeling once we encounter innateness. Many processes in
vision are innate, yet cognitive scientists have made progress in modeling them (see Marr, 1982). In fact, the general relevance criterion (whatever it may turn out to be) is typically assumed to be a fundamental
process that is innate. Thus, being innate does not distinguish the specific criterion for the perception of visible mechanical causality from the
general criterion. In particular, the existence of an innate specific criterion for perceptual causality that incorporates relevance certainly does
not preclude the existence of an innate general-relevance criterion—
rather, it supports it.

4. Can Perceptual Causality Provide a General Criterion?

Michotte thought that his findings suggest that Hume's criterion of constant conjunction should be replaced by the "causal impression" as the
"origin" of the idea of causality. But, the criteria proposed by Michotte
and Hume address very different issues. Michotte's causal impression
concerns the output of a causal inference process that occurs early in life
and early in the flow of information from the sensory input. Hume's
criterion, wrong as it may be, concerns the nature of the input that, given
the human causal inference process, gives rise to an output of causality.
Hume attempted to trace this output back to the sensory input, which he

proposed may be acquired directly through one's own sensory experience or indirectly through another person's. For Michotte the question concerning origin meant, across pieces of causal knowledge, which come early in information processing or in development? In contrast, for Hume the question concerning origin meant, across time and people, how does any particular piece of knowledge come to be causal?

The specific criterion indicated by Michotte's findings could not possibly be a general criterion by which we come to learn that a relation is causal. It is not applicable to types of causality other than motion due to collision. But people are able to discover causal relations that have very little to do with motion and collision. For example, this criterion would not be able to yield the inference that touching a flame causes one's finger to burn. Nor would it be able to tell us what caused malaria in the poor fellow who was both stung by a bee and bitten by a mosquito; or why we would predict the next piece of butter to melt when heated to 150 °F, but would not predict the next coin to go in Goodman's pocket to be silver. A criterion for perceptual causality leaves the problem of causal inference for other domains unsolved.

D. Criticism 2: Causal Inferences Are Based on Knowledge of Power

Whereas Michotte held that causal inferences are rooted in our perception of causal powers, other psychologists have espoused the position that causal inferences are based on our knowledge of causal powers (e.g., Bullock et al. 1982; Koslowski et al., 1989; Shultz, 1982; White, 1992). White (1989, p. 431) summarizes his "causal powers" theory of causal processing as follows, "In essence, the theory states that people understand the causal relation as a generative relation involving a causal power of some thing, the operation of which actually produces an effect." The following example illustrates an application of his theory. In discussing how people, in judging the cause of a train derailing, would entertain as a candidate a faulty rail but not the train driver eating cornflakes for breakfast, White writes (1989, p. 433), "The solution for which I would argue is that people discriminate between the faulty rail and cornflakes as causal candidates by means of their knowledge of the causal powers of those things." A faulty rail has the power to produce derailment, whereas eating cornflakes does not.

According to the power view, power is a more fundamental criterion than relevance, which is a consequence of power rather than its source. For example, Shultz and Kesterbaum (1985) note that it is possible that a criterion of statistical relevance is derived from, and develops subsequent to, the criterion of generative transmission. Bullock et al. (1982) showed that even when statistical relevance is equated, people (including children) still systematically differentiated between causal and noncausal relations, and that they appeared to do so on the basis of power. Finally, if power and relevance are pitted against each other, power apparently prevails, as several studies are often cited to show (Shultz, 1982, Experiments 2 and 5; Shultz, Fisher, Pratt, & Rulf, 1986, Experiment 1).

These researchers are clearly addressing an issue different from that concerning the discovery of causal relations—knowledge of power already *assumes* knowledge of causality. Whatever has power to produce an effect is by definition a cause of the effect. To think that power theorists are addressing the issue of how causal relations are discovered would imply assuming their answer to be, "If a particular relation belongs to a causal category, then it is causal," an answer that begs the question, "How did that category come to be causal?" Notice an important difference between the kind of prior causal knowledge assumed here and that required by the assessment of conditional contrasts: Power theorists assume prior causal knowledge of the relation in question, whereas conditional contrasts require prior knowledge of causes alternative to it. For power theories prior causal knowledge is used for supplying candidate causes from an established repertoire; for conditional contrast it is used for control, for getting established causes out of the way so the causal status of a candidate factor can be evaluated. Thus whereas induction by the assessment of conditional contrasts allows the possibility of a novel type of relation becoming a member of the causal repertoire, induction by knowledge of power involves the recognition that a novel token of a relation is of a type that has already been established as a member of the repertoire.[9]

The two views need not contradict each other. Knowledge concerning potential sources of power is the output of an inference process that might well be based, at least in part, on a relevance criterion. No internal contradiction is involved for a relevance theorist to agree, for example, that a typical adult understands that eating cornflakes for breakfast per se cannot cause (i.e., does not have the power to produce) derailment, whereas a faulty rail does, as long as these understandings are the outputs of a process involving statistical relevance. The role of relevance lies, not in describing our explicit understanding of a cause, but in pro-

---

[9] There are borderline cases—reasoning by analogy with a known cause, for example—for which the distinction between discovery and instance recognition is tricky to apply. The existence of borderline cases, however, does not prevent applying this distinction to clear cases, such as the instances of power discussed in the psychological literature.

viding a component of the criterion for how one comes to know—when the input and the inference are traced to their source—that one relation is causal and another not. Thus, whereas studies supporting power address the nature of the output of a process of inference (e.g., our conclusion that a faulty rail can cause derailment) and the subsequent influences of such output, studies of relevance address the nature of the input and the criterion by which causal knowledge emerges from not-yet-causal input.

Because power theorists pose relevance and power as conflicting alternatives, it is easy to be misled into thinking that these theorists are attempting to address the issue of how causal relations are discovered. This is particularly so because some of the criticisms they raise are legitimate concerns with respect to that issue. Moreover, power theorists sometimes explicitly claim what appears to be a compatible goal. For example, Shultz (1982, p. 1) states his goal as the identification of "the principles or rules by which the child comes to attribute causation." What has been left ambiguous are the "givens" from which the answers are assumed to begin: Relevance theories do not assume that the category of relations to which a target relation belongs is known to be causal, whereas power theories do.

If power theories begin their explanation by assuming knowledge of causality, do the types of evidence purported to favor the power view over the statistical-relevance view have any implications for the viability of the relevance view? Even though the answer given by power theorists does not address the question of what first led to the inference of the power assumed, if we take a further step and examine the nature of the assumed causal knowledge, it is possible in principle to show that statistical relevance is an insufficient criterion for discovering causes: This would be the case if subjects prefer to make causal inferences based on knowledge of power over an alternative that does not involve power but that has equal or greater relevance. A major source of difficulty for the relevance view is the differentiation between causal and noncausal relations that appear to have equal relevance.

However, none of the studies to my knowledge control for relevance at the level of abstraction of the power in question. In the following sections, I will examine the implications of these studies by considering their operational definitions of power and relevance. Power entails statistical relevance; whatever has power to produce an effect increases the probability of the effect. I will argue that the variant of the relevance view that is rejected is operationally defined over a narrow set of events, excluding related events in the subject's knowledge base. In contrast, the variant of the power view that is supported implies relevance that is more reliable and predictive than relevance as defined by the power theorists. If the relevance view had been instead defined so as to specify that when subjects are given a choice between a reliable and predictive relevance relation and a less predictive and reliable relation, they are more likely to choose the former as the cause, then the findings reported are in fact perfectly consistent with this view.

1. Pitting Power against Relevance

Shultz pursued the strategy of pitting power against relevance in three experiments (1982, Experiments 2 & 5; Shultz et al., 1986). He notes (1982, p. 4):

> Diagnosing the operation of such rules [generative transmission as opposed to "Humean" rules] is not ordinarily very easy to do, however, because of the fact that in many causal situations these rules are invariably confounded. . . . Consequently, it would be necessary to design rather contrived situations in order to unequivocally diagnose which rule is being used, situations in which some rules are rendered neutral or useless while others lead to contrasting attributions.

This approach often involves isolating what probably are components of a complex cause involving a conjunction of factors (e.g., covariation, spatial contiguity, and temporal contiguity) and pitting them against one another. Using this approach, one might analogously ask a question such as, What causes fire—oxygen, high heat, or combustible material? For components that interact to produce the effect, a question that forces a choice would be incorrectly framed. Shultz's attempt to "unconfound" the rules of covariation and generative transmission, however, is problematic for a different reason. He invariably created situations in which there was conflict between what the researcher defined as covariation and the subjects' prior knowledge about covariation regarding the type of events in question. Moreover, he invariably defined generative transmission to involve that prior covariational knowledge.

Let us first consider the definitions of covariation and generative transmission in Experiment 2 of Shultz (1982). In the relevant part of this experiment (the covariation condition), the target effect was a spot of light on a wall, and the critical task was to judge which of two lamps pointing at that spot caused it. The subjects, aged 3 to 13 years, were divided into two groups. For one group, two lamps (A and B) were first presented separately, providing what Shultz defines to be covariational information: The spot appeared when A was present but not when it was absent; in contrast, the spot did not appear when B was present. Note that the subjects could not see whether the lamps were on. The lamps were then hidden behind a screen. When the screen was removed, both lamps were present, as was the spot of light. The subjects still could not tell whether either of the lamps was on. At this point they were asked to judge, for the first time, which lamp was making the spot on the wall. Then, without the intervention of a screen, the lamps were turned to face the subjects so that they could see that only B was on. They were then asked again to judge which lamp made the spot on the wall "when the lamps were both facing the wall" (Shultz, 1982, p. 23). The perception and knowledge of a lamp being on or off was defined as information on generative transmission. Shultz reported that most subjects answered the first question according to covariation, saying that A was the lamp that made the spot. However, when they came to the second question, most subjects switched their answer to one based on generative transmission, saying instead that B made the spot.

Shultz showed that the switching was not due to subjects basing their answer on the most recently presented information. He ruled out this explanation by reversing the order of presentation of the covariational and generative-transmission information for a second group of subjects. He drew the following conclusion (Shultz, 1982):

"The results . . . indicated that children 3 years old and older favored the generative transmission rule over the covariation rule in a situation where it was contrived for these two rules to conflict. Children were observed to continue to utilize generative transmission information even when it appeared to conflict with subsequent covariation information; and they switched from initially using covariation information to using subsequent, conflicting information on generative transmission" (p. 28).

Notice that subjects were asked to choose between (1) the lamp that they could see was off but the mere presence of which covaried with the spot of light (covariation) and (2) the lamp that they could see was on but the mere presence of which did not covary with the spot (generative transmission). This narrow definition of covariation does not seem well justified.[10] It seems plausible to assume that children of the ages studied do have some form of knowledge about the covariation of lights and shadows, for example, knowledge about a lamp being turned on, and the surface closest to it in any particular direction becoming brighter, while surfaces beyond these blocked points in the same direction are cast in shadow. It also seems plausible to assume that children would tend to know at least implicitly that this covariational relation is more statisti-

[10] With the exception of Experiment 5, which I will discuss, other conditions in this experiment and other experiments in Shultz (1982) define covariation in similarly restricted ways.

cally predictive and reliable than that between the mere presence of a particular lamp in the experiment and a spot of light. After all, prior to the experiment, the children have experienced covariation of the first type but not of the second. Even if the potential cause is defined more generally as the presence of any lamp, its contrast with respect to light appearing would still be lower than if it is defined as a lamp that is not merely present but also turned on. Shultz's results, therefore, can be interpreted to mean that when highly predictive prior covariational knowledge based on relatively substantial evidence (lamps being on and light appearing) is pitted against current covariational knowledge that is either less predictive or based on small amounts of evidence (the presence of a particular lamp, or of lamps in general, and light appearing), the more reliable and predictive covariational knowledge wins.

In sum, as in White's application of power in his derailment example, knowledge of generative transmission in Shultz's experiment is simply assumed. Because knowledge of transmission (knowing that light is transmitted to the wall from the lamp that is on) implies knowledge of causality (knowing that light from the lamp causes the spot on the wall), and because subjects enter the experiment equipped with this knowledge, Shultz's findings are not relevant to the issue of how a causal relation is discovered. Moreover, because knowledge of power entails relevance with higher reliability and predictiveness than what is defined as covariation in these studies, the findings are consistent with the view that relevance is a component of the criterion for differentiating causal from accidental relations.

An analogous interpretation can be given to the results obtained by Shultz et al. (1986, Experiment 1). In the part of the experiment most relevant to the discussion here (the "obvious condition" in which information on generative transmission is obviously available), the subjects (children 3 to 7 years old) saw two flashlights pointing at a spot of light on the wall: They could see that both flashlights were on but that Flashlight A had its path to the spot blocked by a wooden disk, whereas Flashlight B did not. They were asked to indicate which of the two flashlights was making the spot on the wall. Generative transmission was defined in terms of whether or not the light coming from a shining flashlight was blocked. Prior to this critical situation, the children were shown that when A was on—and unblocked—the spot of light appeared, but when A was off, there was no spot. They were also shown that when B was on—but blocked—there was no light, and that when B was off, the spot appeared only when A was on and unblocked. Covariation was defined in terms of a flashlight's being seen as either on or off, regardless of whether it is blocked, with respect to the spot appearing. Accordingly,

A covaried with the spot, whereas B did not. The results showed that most children chose B as the cause, leading Shultz et al. to conclude that (when information on generative transmission is obviously available) people prefer to infer causality based on generative transmission over covariation.

Applying my argument, we see that knowledge of generative transmission as defined carries relevance (i.e., covariational) information that is more predictive than is knowledge of relevance as defined. In this case, knowledge that obstructing a shining flashlight blocks light beyond the point of obstruction implies knowledge of relevance: When a shining flashlight is obstructed by an opaque object, there is no light beyond that object; but when there is no obstruction, other things being equal, there is light beyond the same point. Assuming that children know the above relevance relation, it seems arbitrary to restrict the operational definition of relevance to the perception of the light being on or off, regardless of whether there is blocking. The relevance relation including information on blocking is clearly more predictive of the target effect than that excluding it. Because prior knowledge of power is inherently confounded with higher predictiveness of the relevance relation, the findings are consistent with relevance being a component of the process of induction.

Rather than being just an artifact created by a researcher, Shultz's definition of covariation raises a key issue: What is the appropriate level of abstraction for defining the cause in a relation? There are indefinitely many possible levels. The potential cause of a spot of light, for example, might be represented as the presence of a particular lamp during the experiment, as Shultz (1982) did. In this case, covariation is computed over a small set of events during the experiment. Another possible representation is the conjunction of a source of light with a certain intensity, the lack of obstruction between the source of light and the spot, and a maximum distance between the source and the wall that is a function of the intensity of the light. In this case, covariation is defined over many events of this type (whether the source be a lamp, a flashlight, or the sun) encoded by subjects in their lives. A yet more general representation might replace a source of light in the last representation with a source of energy. The defining level clearly could not be left arbitrary in a relevance theory: The value of contrast depends on it. I have argued that it seems more plausible to assume that children do have the knowledge of relevance corresponding to what Shultz calls knowledge of transmission. However, a deeper issue is, what determines the level of abstraction at which we encode a causal relation? As we will see, this issue of the level of abstraction at which a cause is defined recurs in many applications of contrast.

2. *Equating Statistical Relevance*

A study that is often cited to show the role of power when relevance is equated is described in Bullock et al. (1982). In this experiment (Bullock, 1979), children judged what caused a jack-in-the-box to pop up from its box. Before it popped, two identically timed events simultaneously occurred: A ball rolled down a slope toward the box, and a series of lights "rolled" down a parallel slope toward the box (the lights produce the phi phenomenon). Both the ball and the "light" were occluded from sight for a second before "Jack" was seen to pop. The above sequence was repeated multiple times, thus defining identical covariational relations for the rolling of (1) the ball, and (2) the light, with respect to Jack's popping. To manipulate the plausible underlying causal power or mechanism, there were two conditions. In the standard condition, the entire apparatus appeared to be in a single box. The popping of Jack was thus consistent with a plausible mechanism involving impact by the ball ("rolling and hitting [by an object with mass] can produce movement in another object through impact," [Bullock et al., 1982, p. 225]). The traveling series of lights, in contrast, is presumably less consistent with prior knowledge about mechanisms that can produce the movement in another object. A consideration of plausible mechanisms should therefore lead a subject to attribute the popping to the ball, despite identical covariational relations for the ball and the light. In the unconnected condition, a 6-in. gap was seen between the box containing Jack and the boxes containing the ball and the light. The popping of Jack was thus clearly inconsistent with being hit by the ball. Bullock et al. (1982) reasoned that for older children who were familiar with electrical phenomena, the light then may seem to provide the more plausible mechanism. These children might assume that the light is produced by electricity, which also causes Jack to jump. The results show that 3- to 5-year-old children were more likely to attribute the popping to the ball than to the light in the standard condition. In contrast, the children (with the exception of the 3-year-olds) were more likely to attribute it to the light in the unconnected condition. Bullock et al. concluded that children's causal inferences reflect a use of the "principle of mechanism."

Although the rolling of the ball and the light each covaried perfectly with Jack's popping, subjects might not have restricted their assessments of covariation to the sequences of events presented in the experiment. The rolling of the ball and the series of lights are likely to be represented not only at the specific level used by the researchers in equating covariational information but also at more abstract levels. The ball is not only a specific ball but also an object with mass; the series of lights is not only a specific series of lights but also an electrical device. Knowledge about causal mechanisms clearly implies knowledge about covariational relations at an abstract level: The "mechanistic" knowledge about motion in an object produced by the impact of a moving object includes the fact that when there is impact by a moving object with mass on another object with mass, motion in the latter object is likely, but when there is no such impact, other things being equal, motion in the latter object is less likely. Notice that according to this knowledge, although the cause is general enough to include all moving objects with mass, it is not so general as to include all moving entities. Therefore, consistency between a target relevance relation and a relevance relation defined at a more abstract level can explain the observed difference between the two conditions.

3. Comparing Contrasts Conditional on More versus Fewer Alternative Potential Causes

In all the experiments discussed so far, knowledge of power was defined in terms of familiar types of causal relations. Experiment 5 in Shultz's (1982) research is distinctive in that it involves a novel causal relation. This experiment used an unusual instrument, a Crookes radiometer. The radiometer has a little windmill whose vanes, black on one side, white on the other, are enclosed in a glass bowl. When light shines on the vanes, the vanes spin. The unusualness of the instrument served to ensure that prior covariational knowledge did not intrude. In fact, none of the subjects was familiar with the radiometer, nor was anyone able to explain its rotary motion, even if they believed the light was somehow relevant.

Because the power in question is novel, this experiment asked subjects how they would test a particular causal hypothesis, rather than how they would judge whether a relation is causal. After watching the apparatus— a flashlight shining on the radiometer and the vanes spinning—the subjects were asked to test whether light is a cause of the "propeller" spinning. The experimenter offered five methods of testing. Each suggested method was intended to answer a question corresponding to one of five rules of causal inference: generative transmission, covariation, temporal contiguity, spatial contiguity, and similarity. For the purpose of this discussion, I will focus only on the generative transmission and covariation methods. Corresponding to covariation, the suggestion was put as follows: "Whenever the light is on is the propeller spinning? Over here we have a light and propeller exactly the same as this one, except the light is off. You can remove this screen to see whether or not the propeller behind it is spinning" (Shultz, 1982, p. 42). For generative transmission, the suggestion was the following: "Is there some invisible thing that goes from the light to the propeller? You can put this black square into the slot [located between the flashlight and the radiometer in the stand holding the apparatus] to see if you can block that invisible thing before it gets to the propeller" (Shultz, 1982, p. 42). After choosing their preferred method, subjects were allowed to execute it. They were invited to try the remaining methods until they indicated that they did not need to try anything else.

Shultz reported that the generative transmission method was most frequently chosen as the most preferred method by subjects at all age levels, and that the older groups were more certain of their answer after testing the generative transmission rule than after using any of the other methods. Fewer subjects continued to test with other methods after using generative transmission than after using another method. Shultz concluded that subjects from 4 years to adulthood showed a clear preference for an inquiry based on the generative transmission rule as opposed to the other rules of causal attribution.

Although this experiment cleverly overcame the confounding with prior covariational knowledge that occurred in the other experiments, it nonetheless allows an alternative interpretation consistent with the relevance view. First, both methods generate relevance information, including the method operationally defined to be using "generativity." Although the subjects were not familiar with the causal relation between light and the rotation of the vanes, they were likely to be familiar with light and shadows, as noted earlier. Thus, if the blocking of a light source, which covaries with the absence of light on the vanes, leads to the stopping of their rotation, the light source would covary with the rotation. Second, note that the method defined to be using covariation is an indirect one involving more ambiguity in its interpretation than does the generativity method. It is dependent on a different apparatus that has not been demonstrated to work. The subject would have to take the experimenter's word that the apparatus is truly identical to the first one. Because there are potential differences between the two radiometers other than the light being on or off, blocking the light in the radiometer that was shown to be operating is the more clear-cut method—it ensures that the only difference is the factor that was manipulated. Thus, the results may be interpreted to show that when the choice was one between two covariational methods, one clear-cut and the other ambiguous, subjects preferred the clear-cut one; moreover, once they have tested using a clear-cut method and have obtained an answer, they are less likely to continue with ambiguous methods than if they had started with an ambiguous method.[11]

In sum, the inherent problem with the methodology of manipulating knowledge of power is that, whatever extra information a power relation may include, all power sources are understood to systematically produce statistical relevance. Thus, the introduction of power is inevitably accompanied by the corresponding relevance relation. Although it is in principle possible to "unconfound" relevance and power, none of the studies adopting this approach have succeeded in doing so. Moreover, because knowledge of causality (i.e., power) did not emerge because of an experimental manipulation, findings in these studies cannot inform us on how a causal relation is discovered.

E. Criticism 3: People Do Not Compute Contrasts

Once we peel apart the misplaced overlays in the debate, we see that the power view does not offer any solution at all to the issue of how a causal relation is discovered. However, one might ask, why should one even bother to consider statistical relevance as an alternative when the literatures in multiple fields apparently converge with overwhelming evidence to show that people do not systematically use the criterion of statistical relevance? Deviations from statistical relevance have been discussed in social psychology (e.g., Jaspars, Hewstone, & Fincham, 1983; Nisbett & Ross, 1980), philosophy (e.g., Hart & Honoré, 1959/1985; Mackie, 1974), and cognitive psychology (e.g., Jenkins & Ward, 1965; Schustack & Sternberg, 1981; Shaklee & Tucker, 1980).

In a series of articles (Cheng and Novick, 1990a, b, 1991, 1992; Novick, Fratianne, & Cheng, 1992), we argue that people have appeared to be unable to compute contrasts because they do not compute contrasts over the same set of events assumed by the researcher. We term the set of events over which the reasoner computes contrasts a *focal set*. The discrepancy between the focal set adopted by the subject and that assumed by the researcher explains many of the apparent deviations from the normative criterion of contrast. Extending Cheng and Novick's

---

[11] Recall that in Experiment 1 of Shultz *et al.* (1986), covariation was defined in terms of a flashlight being on or off. If Shultz had defined covariation in Experiment 5 as the flashlight shining on the operating radiometer being turned on and off, conditional contrasts would predict no difference between this and the generative-transmission options, both of which involve the contrast of light conditional on the same constant status (either presence or absence) of all alternative causes.

argument, Cheng and Holyoak (in press) propose that many "cue inter-action" effects (findings showing the influence of the strengths of other factors on the causal strength of a potential factor) which have been interpreted as evidence against the criterion of contrast, can be explained by conditional contrasts.

Because we (Cheng & Novick, 1992) recently reviewed our work, I will only briefly summarize our findings and arguments here. Ruling spu-rious causes outside our scope for the sake of simplicity, we evaluated the criterion people use to make causal judgments. We (1990a, b, 1991, 1992) noted that the focal set adopted by the subject is the one over which the hypothesis of contrast should be evaluated. We called our model, which defines the computation of contrasts specifying simple and conjunctive causes over focal sets, the *probabilistic contrast model*. We were agnostic on the issue of what determines the adoption of a focal set. To avoid circularity in our argument, however, we invariably provided evidence for the focal set independent of subjects' causal judgments (Cheng & Novick, 1990a; 1991; Novick et al., 1992). In every paper, we manipulated subjects' focal sets, independently assessed them, or both. Contrasts computer over subjects' focal sets systematically predicted their causal judgments. I will return to the critical issue of what deter-mines the choice of a focal set.

According to the social psychology literature, people suffer from a variety of biases, including a bias toward attributing an effect to a person rather than a situation, a tendency for actors and observers to make different causal attributions for the same event, and a tendency to make attributions to conjunctions of factors that are unpredicted by any vari-ants of Kelley's covariation principle or of the ANOVA model. In philos-ophy, considerable attention has been given to the intuitive distinction that lawyers, historians, and ordinary people make between a cause and an enabling condition. They do so even though each causally relevant factor has the same logical relation to the effect in terms of necessity and sufficiency. For example, when a lightning strike in a forest is followed by a fire, people might consider the lightning as the cause of the forest fire, but they will view the presence of oxygen as merely an enabling condition, even though the lightning and the oxygen (along with other factors, such as the presence of combustible material) were individu-ally necessary and jointly sufficient to yield the fire. Finally, many cognitive psychologists reported that their subjects used a variety of nonnormative heuristics based on linear combinations of the four cells of a 2×2 contingency table formed by crossing the presence and absence of a potential cause with the presence and absence of a target effect.

1. Causes and Enabling Conditions

This distinction between causes and enabling conditions has often been explained in terms of normality (Hart & Honoré, 1959/1985; Mackie, 1974). An abnormal necessary factor (e.g., lightning in the forest) is a cause, whereas a normal necessary factor (e.g., oxygen in the forest) is an enabling condition. This criterion is a heuristic that often gives the right cause but has no normative justification. Instead, we explain the distinction in terms of contrast computed over the contextually determined focal set: A potential causal factor that covaries with the effect (i.e., has a noticeable contrast with respect to the effect) within that focal set (e.g., lightning with respect to forest fires in the context of a forest) would be viewed as a cause, whereas a factor that is constant within that focal set (e.g., oxygen in a forest), but that is known to covary with the effect in some other focal set (e.g., oxygen covaries with fire in special environments in which the occurrence of oxygen varies) would be viewed as an enabling condition. This analysis differs from previous psychological models of causal induction in at least one of two respects. First, rather than being based on the universal set of events, causal judgments are based on subsets of events over which the reasoner computes covariation. Such subsets often have certain factors kept constant. Second, the analysis is probabilistic. For lightning to covary with forest fire, our analysis does not require that fire always occurs in the presence of lightning or never occurs in its absence.

To distinguish between enabling conditions and alternative causes that are constant in the focal set, Cheng and Novick (1992) refined their definition of an enabling condition as follows. Let i be a factor that is constantly present in the current focal set. Factor i is an enabling condition for a cause j in that focal set if i covaries with the effect in another focal set, and j no longer covaries with the effect in a focal set in which i is constantly absent. In contrast, i is an alternative to cause j if i covaries with the effect in another focal set, and if there exists a focal set in which i is constantly absent, but j continues to covary with the effect in that set. I will return to this distinction in my discussion of the level of abstraction of the representation of a potential cause.

We (Cheng & Novick, 1991) tested our model against four alternative views: normality in the sense of prevalence, normality in the sense of the ideal, and two variants of the conversational pragmatics view. Here I will summarize only our test against the prevalence variant of the normality view. We separated two concepts that are conflated in that view—the constant presence of a potential cause factor and the preva-

lence of such factors. We independently manipulated (1) which of two
factors in a scenario covaried with a target effect rather than being constantly present (as were several other factors), and (2) the prevalence of
the covarying factor and of the effect. We thereby changed the events in
the focal set implied by the causal question, as confirmed by our mea-
surements of subjects' perceived focal set. We found that the prevalence
of the covarying factor and of the effect in the perceived focal set had
absolutely no impact on causal judgments, but that the covarying factor
in that focal set (regardless of its prevalence) was judged to be causal.
Constant factors that covaried with the effect in a focal set in subjects'
prior knowledge were judged to be enabling conditions. Therefore, the
distinction between causes and enabling conditions—rather than being a
capricious bias—is consistent with the computation of contrasts. We explained the statistical normality criterion as a special case of our model,
the case in which contrast is computed for an effect that is rare in the
context in question; in such cases, the cause is also rare, unless the
case involves a factor whose contrast value is small but nonetheless
noticeable (e.g., prevalent sunlight as the cause of skin cancer, a rare
effect).

2. Deviations from Normative Inference in Social Psychology

We similarly explained the inductive biases reported in the social psychology literature by a discrepancy between the focal sets assumed by
the researchers and the subjects. Unlike philosophers who consider the
universal set as the focal set, psychologists often limit the focal set to the
set of events presented in an experiment. Rather than being too broad,
the psychologist's focal set is often too narrow, for the reason that subjects often recruit relevant events from their prior experience for inclusion. For example, in research on Kelley's ANOVA model (1967), subjects are often presented with information about one row, column, and
beam of a cube defined by the dimensions of persons, stimuli, and time.
Based on that information, they are asked to explain what caused the
person to react in a certain way to the stimulus on the occasion (i.e., to
explain the event represented by the intersection of the row, column,
and beam). Subjects' answers were typically evaluated against covariation computed over the presented information. Such an evaluation
carries the plausible but probably erroneous assumption that information
on how other people react to other stimuli on other occasions lies outside
the focal set relevant to an explanation of what caused a particular person to react in a certain way to a particular stimulus on a particular
occasion. To test our hypothesis that the inclusion of events in these

parts of the cube in the subjects' focal set explains the reported biases, my collaborators and I manipulated these events in two ways. We specified variations in these previously unspecified parts (Cheng & Novick, 1990a), and we left these parts unspecified, but manipulated and measured assumptions about these events (Novick et al., 1992). We found that our manipulations produced variations in causal attribution— variations that have been regarded as biases, but that are systematically predicted by the computation of covariation over the focal set consisting of the entire cube.

3. Criticisms of Kelley's ANOVA Model

Many criticisms from power and other top-down theorists against covariation have been directed at the ANOVA model. For example, White (1992) writes that the ANOVA and other regularity models can work only by a "coarse-grained" analysis, permitting discrimination between different causal "loci." For example, according to White, such models can conclude that someone's success is due to something about that person, but not to the person's high ability. Lalljee and Abelson (1983, pp. 67 & 71) raise a similar objection. Read (1987) notes that Kelley's model suggests that the reasoner "should give quite abstract explanations of social behavior in terms of something about the person or something about the situation" (pp. 298–299). It seems to me that these criticisms apply to the ANOVA model but not to statistical relevance in general. There is no reason why relevance cannot be applied to more fine-grained variables such as high ability. If the contrast for high ability versus low ability (across people) with respect to success is larger and more reliable than that for this particular person versus all other people, then covariation would predict that high ability is a more satisfactory attribution. White objects to applying relevance theories to variables such as high ability, grief, and sense of humor, on the grounds that they are not observable. However, the study of such variables by formal methods of statistical relevance are no longer taboo in psychology, as long as satisfactory operational definitions are provided for such variables. A person's intuitive definition might differ from a psychologist's explicit operational definition, but if one does not object to the study of such variables in science by formal statistical-relevance methods, why should one object to the use of such variables in everyday reasoning by intuitive versions of these methods? High ability, for example, might be intuitively indicated in everyday reasoning by the lucidity of a person's answer to a complex question, the construction of a solution that satisfies many constraints, and so on. As long as there are objective indicators to which a variable can be traced, it seems unwarranted to limit the computation of contrast to directly observable variables such as those in Kelley's theory.

4. Linear Heuristics

Cheng and Novick (1992) ruled out linear heuristics as candidate explanations of causal induction because these methods make predictions that are clearly false. For example, heuristics that have a positive weight for the frequency of the joint occurrence of the cause and the effect and a negative weight for the frequency of the cause occurring without the effect, regardless of their weights on the other two types of events (e.g., Arkes & Harkness, 1983; Schustack & Sternberg, 1981; Shaklee & Tucker, 1980), predict that factors that are constantly present in one's experience (e.g., gravity) should be facilitatory causes when the effect (e.g., rain) is prevalent, but inhibitory causes when the effect is rare. Accordingly, these models predict that inhabitants of Edinburgh (where rain is prevalent) should believe that gravity causes rain, whereas inhabitants of Los Angeles (where rain is rare) should believe that gravity inhibits rain. They make the same predictions for constant factors that do not normatively covary with the effect (e.g., houses with respect to rain) as for those that do (e.g., gravity with respect to rain). For example, they predict that inhabitants of Edinburgh would believe that houses cause rain, whereas inhabitants of Los Angeles would believe that they inhibit rain.

5. Cue Competition

Experiments in human causality judgments have shown that even when unconditional contrast is held constant for two potential causal factors, their causal strengths differ as a function of the strengths of other factors (Chapman, 1991; Chapman & Robbins, 1990; Shanks, 1991, Experiments 2 & 3). Such effects are often referred to as cue competition, reflecting the root of interests in such phenomena in classical conditioning, in which a potential conditioning factor is often called a cue. These findings have been interpreted as refuting statistical relevance. The refutation, however, applies only to unconditional contrasts, because these effects can be explained by conditional contrasts. Let me illustrate this with a phenomenon called "blocking" in the classical conditioning literature. The within-subject design schematized in Table I, adapted from Shanks (1991, Experiment 2), is one of many blocking designs. Results showing blocking using other designs (e.g., Kamin, 1969; Rescorla, 1981) can like-

TABLE I

Trial Types in a Design That Equates Unconditional Contrast Across Conditions[a]

Condition	Cue[b]						Effect	
	A	B	C	D	E	F	1	2
Unblocked	+	+	0	0	0	0	Yes	No
	0	+	0	0	0	0	No	No
	0	0	+	0	0	0	Yes	No
Blocked	0	0	0	+	+	0	No	Yes
	0	0	0	0	+	0	No	Yes
	0	0	0	0	0	+	No	No

[a] From "Categorization by a connectionist network," by D. R. Shanks, 1991, *Journal of Experimental Psychology: Learning, Memory, and Cognition, 17*, 433–443. Copyright 1991 by the American Psychological Association. Reprinted by permission.

[b] Rows indicate trial types: + under a cue in a row indicates that the cue is present on that trial type; 0 indicates that the cue is absent on that trial type. Large letters indicate the critical cues.

wise be explained by conditional contrasts. Effect 1 occurs in the presence of compound-cue *AB*, but it does so also in the presence of cue *C* alone. However, the effect does not occur in the presence of cue *B* alone, neither does it in the absence of *A, B,* and *C*. Effect 2 occurs in the presence of compound-cue *DE*, as in the presence of cue *E* alone. However, this effect does not occur in the presence of cue *F* alone, neither does it in the absence of *D, E,* and *F*. The critical comparison is between the strength of cue *A* in the unblocked condition (with respect to effect 1) and of cue *D* in the blocked condition (with respect to effect 2). As can be seen by an inspection of the table, assuming an equal number of trials of each type, the contrasts reflecting these strengths computed over the entire set of events presented is equal. Contradicting predictions based on these unconditional contrasts, subjects in Shanks's (1991) experiment rated *D* as less associated with effect 2 than *A* with effect 1.

A statistical-relevance analysis of this experiment is provided by Melz, Cheng, Holyoak, and Waldmann (in press). Their analysis was presented in terms of an iterative model proposed by Cheng and Holyoak (in press) to illustrate the computation of conditional contrasts at an algorithmic level. According to this model, contrast for a potential facilitatory factor is computed conditional on the simultaneous absence of all plausible causes (except the factor itself). If this is not possible, then contrast will be computed conditionalized on the absence of as many plausible causes as possible. The rest of the conditionalizing cues are preferably constantly present. Without going into the specifics of how our algorithm arrives at the set of conditionalizing causes at any point (see Cheng &

Holyoak, in press), one can nonetheless see that with respect to effect 1, when conditionalized on the absence of C, cue A has a contrast of 1.0 (see Table I). This is the most informative contrast for A, because C is a plausible cause whereas B is not: C has a contrast of 1 conditional on the absence of A and B, whereas B has a contrast of 0 conditional on the absence of A and C. In contrast, with respect to effect 2, cue D has a contrast of 0 conditional on the presence of E. (Because D never occurs in the absence of E, its contrast can only be calculated conditional on the presence of E.) This is an informative contrast for D, because cue E is a plausible cause: It has a contrast of 1.0 conditional on the absence of D, the only other plausible cause. F is not a plausible cause because it has a contrast of 0 conditional on the absence of D and E. The difference between the computed contrast for cue A with respect to effect 1 (1.0) and that for cue D with respect to effect 2 (0) provides an explanation for cue competition—lower ratings are given to D than to A. As will be seen later, cue competition is a case of Simpson's (1951) paradox. Cheng and Holyoak (in press) explained a number of findings about cue interactions in the classical conditioning and causal judgment literatures in terms of statistical relevance.

In sum, rather than being characterized as a collection of diverse heuristics and biases, as often suggested in the previous literature, the bottom-up component of the causal induction process can be characterized more simply—as the systematic computation of contrasts over focal sets.

F. CRITICISM 4: A FACILITATORY CAUSE CAN BE NEGATIVELY RELEVANT

1. Spurious Causes and Simpson's Paradox

A criticism of statistical relevance is that a facilitatory cause can be negatively relevant to its effect. This is a critical problem because it cuts against a fundamental intuition on which probabilistic theories of causality are built. Hesslow's (1976) hypothetical example illustrates this case. There is some evidence that consumption of oral contraceptives causes thrombosis. Suppose that pregnancy also causes thrombosis, and moreover is a more potent cause of it. However, taking birth-control pills reduces the probability of pregnancy. Then it is possible that the probability of thrombosis is lower in the class of women of child-bearing age who use oral contraceptives than in the class of women of this age range who do not, because oral contraceptives prevent a more potent cause (pregnancy) from being present. That is, taking oral contraceptives is negatively relevant to thrombosis despite being a cause of it.

The concept of conditional contrasts provides a solution to Hesslow's criticism (Cartwright, 1989; Salmon, 1984). If we take the class of women of child-bearing age and partition it according to whether a woman takes birth-control pills and whether she is pregnant, we get four classes: (1) women who do not take birth-control pills and are not pregnant, (2) women who do not take birth-control pills and are pregnant, (3) women who take birth-control pills and are not pregnant, and (4) women who take birth-control pills and are pregnant (but probably do not know it). If we compare the incidence of thrombosis across women who do not take birth-control pills but who are either pregnant or not (Classes 2 and 1, respectively), we may find that it is significantly higher among women who are pregnant, providing evidence that pregnancy causes thrombosis. If one is willing to assume that Class 4 is realistic, a similar comparison between Classes 3 and 4 may support the same conclusion. Similarly, comparing across women who are not pregnant but who either take or do not take birth-control pills (Classes 3 and 1, respectively), we may find the incidence of thrombosis to be significantly higher in women who take the pills, indicating that taking birth-control pills causes thrombosis. A comparison between 2 and 4 may support the same conclusion. That is, holding the alternative cause constant, each cause is positively relevant to the effect. The negative relevance of oral contraceptives in the unpartitioned class is therefore spurious.

The change in relevance relations upon partitioning involves a fact about probabilities sometimes known as Simpson's paradox (1951). Cartwright (1983) illustrates this paradox with the following real-life case. The graduate school at Berkeley was accused of discriminating against women in their admission policies, thus raising the question of whether being a woman was an inhibitory cause of admission to Berkeley. The accusation appeared to be born out in the relative frequencies: The relative frequency of acceptance was much lower for women than for men across the university as a whole (i.e., there was a negative relevance for women). Upon more careful examination of the data, however, it was discovered that this was no longer true if the analysis was applied to each department separately. In a majority of the departments, the relatively frequency of admission for women was just about the same as for men, and in some even higher for women than for men. The paradoxical reversal of relative frequencies was due to the fact that women tended to apply to departments with high rejection rates so that department by department women were admitted at about the same rate as men, but across the whole university a considerably lower proportion of women were admitted. This analysis exonerated Berkeley from the charge of discrimination. Thus, a negative contrast can disappear or even reverse when it is computed conditional on a causal variable. It involves the same rule for screening off spurious positive causes discussed earlier. More generally, the moral is that any relevance relation—positive, zero, negative—between two variables that holds in a given population can be changed in the subpopulations by finding a third variable that is correlated with the two.

Cartwright (1983) pointed out that Berkeley is exonerated from the charge of discrimination only because it is reasonable to partition by department. By contrast, if the unconditional relevance relation reversed when the applicants were partitioned according to their roller-skating ability, the reversal would count as no defense. The difference between the two situations lies in our belief that applying to a popular department causes rejection, whereas being a poor roller skater does not. This example illustrates an important point: Only partitions by causally relevant variables count in evaluating the causality of a candidate variable.

2. Negative Relevance of a Link in a Causal Path

There is another type of situation involving the negative relevance of a facilitatory cause that is harder to deal with. Suppes (1970, p. 41) discusses an example due to Deborah Rosen that illustrates this problem. Following is a slightly modified version of Rosen's problem taken from Salmon (1984, p. 193). Suppose a golfer tees off on a hole at a golf course. The shot is badly sliced, but by the sheerest accident the ball hits a branch of a tree near the green and drops into the hole for a spectacular hole in one. What is disturbing is that the probability of a hole in one given the ball hitting a branch along the way seems lower than that probability given the ball does not hit a branch. Yet when we see the event happen, our intuitions tell us that hitting the branch exactly the way it did was essential to the ball's going into the hole. It might be argued that if one only knows the specific details of the angle, speed, and spin with which the ball hit the branch, the contrast would be positive. This argument is not persuasive, however, because knowing those details might be impossible.

Instead, Salmon (1980) proposed the solution of successive "reconditionalization." The basic idea behind this solution is that once a particular event in a causal chain has occurred, it does not matter what other events might have happened, but did not. Contrasts for subsequent events are conditionalized on events in the chain that in fact occurred. In Rosen's example, let A stand for teeing off, B for a swing that produces a slice, C for the sliced ball traveling toward the tree, D for the ball hitting the branch, and E for the ball dropping into the hole. The causal chain can be symbolized by $A \rightarrow B \rightarrow C \rightarrow D \rightarrow E$. The following relevance relations hold:

$$P(C \mid B \cdot A) > P(C \mid \overline{B} \cdot A)$$
$$P(D \mid C \cdot B) > P(D \mid \overline{C} \cdot B)$$
$$P(E \mid D \cdot C) > P(E \mid \overline{D} \cdot C)$$

These inequalities, respectively, say that (1) given teeing off, the ball is more likely to be traveling in the direction toward the tree if the tee shot is a slice than it is if the swing is a good shot, (2) given the slice, the ball is more likely to collide with the branch if it is headed in the direction of the tree than it is if it is going in another direction, and (3) given the ball traveling toward the tree, it is more likely to go into the hole if it hits the branch than it is if it does not hit the branch. Each of these assertions seems plausible. By this analysis, each relevant relation in the causal chain is positive. Whether this analysis describes intuitive causal reasoning remains to be tested.

G. SUMMARY

Power theorists have often argued that statistical relevance is not important for inferring causality. In its place they propose innate specific criteria or knowledge of specific powers. I have noted that there is no contradiction between understanding a cause as a source of power and evaluating evidence using statistical relevance. As long as relevance is a criterion for acquiring knowledge of specific powers, the use of such knowledge to recognize new instances as causal can peacefully coexist with the discovery of causal laws using relevance as a necessary criterion. Neither is there any conflict between the specific criteria so far observed and statistical relevance as a component of a general criterion. Criticisms of the necessity of relevance based on the perception of causality are valid only if an arbitrarily defined experimental trial is considered a single event. Without this assumption, converging evidence shows that the criterion observed in perceptual causality incorporates relevance rather than refutes it.

Criticisms of relevance based on knowledge of power refute neither its necessity nor its sufficiency for the discovery of causes. The methodology based on manipulating knowledge of power confronts the problem of the confounding of such knowledge with relevance: The introduction of power is inevitably accompanied by the introduction of the relevance relation regarding the power in question. None of the studies adopting this approach have succeeded in controlling for relevance. With a more reasonable definition of the scope of the causes, the lines of evidence supporting the role of knowledge of power in fact support relevance.

Explanations in terms of knowledge of power might have obscured the issue of the genesis of that knowledge. Likewise, explanations in terms of specific innate criteria might have obscured the issue of how we reach the unifying notion of causality from the seemingly disparate criteria. Relevance as defined by conditional contrasts provides a potential resolution of both issues: It is a candidate for a necessary component of a general criterion for discovering causes. Indeed, relevance so defined not only explains the lines of evidence based on the perception and knowledge of power, it also explains a number of other kinds of evidence that have been regarded as refuting relevance. These include the intuitive distinction between causes and enabling conditions discussed in law and philosophy, apparent deviations from normative inference reported in social psychology, cue-interaction effects reported in classical conditioning, and spurious positive and negative relevance discussed in the philosophy of science. In all these cases, apparent deviations from relevance arise as the result of a mischaracterization of the focal sets on which causal judgments are based. Thus, rather than being characterized as a collection of diverse heuristics and biases, as suggested in the previous literature, the statistical component of the causal induction process can be characterized more simply—as the systematic computation of contrasts over focal sets (i.e., conditional contrasts).

III. Some Problems and Limits of Statistical Relevance

Although statistical relevance can accommodate many of the criticisms directed at it, it does have its problems and limits. I will first discuss two problems that look perilous but perhaps not necessarily fatal: (1) how conditionalization gets started and is constrained, and (2) the level of abstraction at which a cause is defined (for further discussions of problems with conditional contrasts, see Cartwright, 1983, Essay 1; 1989; Salmon, 1984, Ch. 7; 1989). Then I will illustrate the limits of statistical relevance with two examples that I find particularly striking. Each example points to a different aspect of coherence.

A. Constraints on Conditionalization

Conditionalization is a two-edged sword. As Cartwright (1983) notes, Simpson's paradox implies that without constraints on a conditionalizing variable, almost any true causal law could be defeated by finding, somewhere, some third variable that covaries in the right ways to reverse the required positive relevance between cause and effect. It is therefore crucial to have prior knowledge about other causes and to limit conditionalization to these causes. Because contrast for a factor depends on prior knowledge concerning alternative causes, one might wonder how the conditionalizing process ever gets started. Two compatible possibilities are innate specific constraints and the independent manipulation of potential causal factors. First, innate specific constraints allow the induction of specific causes (e.g., Baillargeon, 1986, 1987; Garcia, McGowan, Ervin, & Koelling, 1968; Gelman, 1990; Leslie & Keeble, 1987; LoLordo, 1979), and these "bootstrap" the assessments of other causes. Conditionalization is only one of the ways in which innate constraints can bootstrap the induction process. Such constraints are almost certain to play a role, but the specifics of the bootstrapping explanation, as well as its scope, are yet to be worked out. Could such constraints, for example, explain how our ancestors milleniums ago inferred that organic fertilization enhances plant growth, or how we inferred that exposure to the sun causes skin to tan? And if so, what role do such constraints play? A second possibility, one that seems more generally applicable, is that by the manipulation of a target factor independent of other factors, we can isolate the influence of that factor. The beauty of independent manipulation is, of course, that other factors can be kept constant without their being identified. The drawback, however, is that well-controlled experiments hardly ever occur outside the laboratory. Do people loosely assume and interpret everyday manipulations as controlled experiments? If the reasoner throws a baseball on one or more occasions at a glass window, for example, and the window breaks, does she assume that other (known and unknown) causes of the window breaking are kept constant before and during the crash? If so, causal conclusions can be reached, and they in turn can aid the induction of other causes in observational and other "experimental" situations.

There are purely observational situations in which people are nonetheless able to make causal inferences. Cheng and Holyoak (in press) hypothesized that in such situations, in the absence of prior causal knowledge, people start with a tentative conditionalizing set consisting of factors that are associated with the effect (i.e., the effect occurs when one or more of these factors are present), then iteratively update the causal status of every factor (including ones that are not in the initial conditionalizing set), and hence the composition of a subsequent conditionalizing set, by computing conditional contrasts. We have applied our model to explain cue-competition effects in only a few studies; clearly, work on how conditionalization gets started and is constrained has hardly begun.

B.   LEVEL OF ABSTRACTION AT WHICH A CAUSE IS DEFINED

This issue emerged in several contexts discussed earlier. Michotte's findings either support or refute contrast depending on the temporal scope of the "cause." Similarly, results in Shultz's (1982) Experiment 2, Shultz et al.'s Experiment 1 (1986), and Bullock et al.'s (1982) experiments testing covariation against power are consistent with contrast if the causes are defined in terms of certain types of events, rather than being restricted to the particular events presented in the experiments.

Let me illustrate the role of the level of abstraction of the definition of the cause in two other contexts. First, it is important in differentiating between an enabling condition and an alternative cause. Consider a typical focal set for a forest fire in which lightning is the cause of the fire. By our intuition, oxygen is an enabling condition rather than an alternative cause that happens to be constantly present in the target focal set. To differentiate between the two, Cheng and Novick's (1992) model specifies that if the cause (lightning in this example) no longer covaries with the effect (forest fires) when a constant factor in question (oxygen) is absent, then that factor is an enabling condition. Otherwise, it is an alternative cause. Now, if lightning is represented as lightning, our model does not have the required information for deciding whether oxygen is an enabling condition or an alternative cause. Whenever lightning strikes a forest, there is always oxygen. However, if lightning is represented more abstractly as high heat, then presumably we do know that in the absence of oxygen, heat does not covary with fire. Our model then correctly classifies oxygen as an enabling condition.[12] Notice that lightning is not represented yet more abstractly as high energy. We do not perceive a stone with high mechanical potential energy, for example, as a cause of fire.

Second, there are situations in which people are able to form systematic causal judgments but in which conditional contrasts cannot be computed, either because one does not know a plausible cause to conditionalize on or because the genuine cause covaries perfectly with a spurious one. For example, someone who does not know that a true cause of storms is a drop in atmospheric pressure might nonetheless judge that

---

[12] It seems equally justifiable to differentiate between an enabling condition and an alternative cause by varying the factor in question (e.g., oxygen) in the absence of the cause (lightning): If that factor, which does covary with the effect in some focal set, no longer covaries with the effect when the cause is absent, then it is an enabling condition. Otherwise, it is an alternative cause. A similar conclusion about the level of abstraction follows from this definition: If lightning is represented as lightning, oxygen will be an alternative cause (in the absence of lightning, oxygen still covaries with forest fires; e.g., when someone carelessly leaves a campfire). However, if lightning is represented more abstractly as high heat, oxygen is correctly classed as an enabling condition (in the absence of sufficient heat, oxygen does not covary with fire).

the drop in the barometric reading does not cause the storm. Similarly, someone who has never encountered a defective barometer (and has not been instructed about it) would still be likely to reach a similar conclusion. In that case there is insufficient information for computing the relevant conditional contrast—the probability of a storm given a drop in atmospheric pressure and no drop in the barometric reading is undefined. One possible solution involving contrast is that in such cases one would resort to knowledge about more abstract relevance relations. For the storm example, one might make use of knowledge about laws of mechanical motion, according to which the small movement of a small object (the mercury in the barometer) predicts no movement of masses of air and rain. In such cases, the inference has a top-down influence.

The topic of the level of abstraction of causal relations has seldom been discussed. The only discussion I am aware of in the psychological literature is by Anderson (1990). He reports an experiment showing that people do base inferences on abstract causal relations, but he does not explain the particular level of abstraction of the inferred cause. Anderson's model allows this level to vary depending on the value of a parameter (the "coupling probability"), and no explanation is offered for the particular parameter values that are assumed.

What defines the scope of a cause? It may seem that relevance as defined by contrast is hopelessly circular. The definition of contrast—the indicator for a causal relation—is dependent on the definition of a potential cause, but how can a cause be defined independently of the causal relation under question? The definition need not be circular, however, because for any type of effect, there is a level of generality of its cause at which contrast is at a maximum. I am assuming that the descriptions of the cause at various levels of generality are of equivalent complexity. The maximum-contrast level then could provide a criterion for the definitions of both the cause and its contrast with respect to the effect. (Factors that are causally irrelevant to the effect will have relatively low contrasts regardless of their level of abstraction.) To see why there is a level at which contrast for a causal factor is at a maximum, consider the simple case in which the causal relation is deterministic. The Euler circles in Fig. 1 illustrate the situations for this case in which the set of events in which cause C occurs is, respectively, larger and smaller than the set of events in which effect E occurs. When set C is larger than set E, $P(E \mid \overline{C})$ is reduced from its optimal value of 1. When set C is smaller than set E, $P(E \mid \overline{C})$ is increased from its optimal value of 0. In both cases $P(E \mid C) - P(E \mid \overline{C}) < 1$. But when set C coincides with set E, $P(E \mid C) = 1$ and $P(E \mid \overline{C}) = 0$, giving the maximum contrast. An analogous argument applies to the probabilistic case, in which the sets cannot

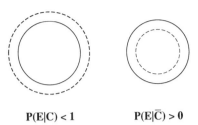

$$P(E|C) < 1 \qquad\qquad P(E|\bar{C}) > 0$$

Fig. 1. Conditional probabilities of the effect as a function of the level of generality of the cause. Solid lines denote effect E; dashed lines denote potential cause C.

completely coincide. There is a subset of events in E that never overlaps with C, and conversely there is a subset of events in C that never overlaps with E. Since these subsets are constant, they do not affect the solution. We see that for the rest of the events, including events in E that potentially overlap with C, the argument above applies. Therefore, as in the deterministic case, there is a level of abstraction that yields a maximum contrast. The maximum contrast solution for defining the level of abstraction of a cause and its contrast does require, however, that there be a predefined effect at a certain level of abstraction.

For each of the phenomena I explained by consistency with contrast at a certain level, there is an intermediate level of abstraction of the representation of the cause at which contrast seems to be at a maximum. For example, lightning is likely to have a lower contrast with respect to fire than does high heat; in the absence of lightning, fire still occurs often if there are other sources of high heat. High energy also seems to have a lower contrast with respect to fire than does high heat; in the presence of other kinds of energy (e.g., high mechanical or electric potential energy) but in the absence of high heat, fire seldom occurs.

C. COHERENCE AND THE LIMITS OF STATISTICAL RELEVANCE

So far in this article I have tried to see, perhaps with some squinting through a telescope, how far statistical relevance can take us, because it seems to constitute the more tractable part of the discovery of causes. There are clear cases of acquired causal judgments, however, in which relevance is not what makes the difference. In the context of illustrating the limits of a deductive theory of scientific explanation, Salmon (1989) gives this example of the correlation between the moon and the tides. This example also illustrates the limits of relevance as a criterion for causal inference. Long before the time of Newton, mariners were fully aware of the correlation between the position and phase of the moon and the rising and falling of the tides. They did not infer a causal connection between the moon and the tides, and they had no explanation for the ebb and flow of the tides. It was not until Newton furnished his law of universal gravitation that the tides were explained by a causal connection. How did Newton's law make the connection between the moon and the tides causal? This law is a functional relation that in itself involves no notion of cause or power; it may be regarded as a specific counterpart of contrast for continuous variables. Moreover, it does not increase the value or reliability of the relevance relation between the moon and the tides, which presumably was already at a maximum. What it does add is the subsumption of diverse phenomena under a single general principle—in this case celestial and terrestrial motion under universal gravitation.

Deductive consistency also plays a role in causal inference.[13] Consider Galileo's (1638/1933, pp. 62–64) conclusive refutation of Aristotle's proposal that bodies of different weights travel in the same medium with speeds proportional to their weights. If we regard this as an argument concerning whether weights "cause" bodies to travel at different speeds, we have a clear example of a refutation of a plausible causal relation by a deductive argument (a *reductio ad absurdum*):

> There can be no doubt but that one and the same body moving in a single medium has a fixed velocity which is determined by nature and which cannot be increased except by the addition of momentum or diminished except by some resistance which retards it. . . . If then we take two bodies whose natural speeds are different, it is clear that on uniting the two, the more rapid one will be partly retarded by the slower, and the slower will be somewhat hastened by the swifter. . . . if a large stone moves with a speed of, say, eight while a smaller moves with a speed of four, then when they are united, the system will move with a speed less than eight; but the two stones when tied together make a stone larger than that which before moved with a speed of eight. Hence the heavier body moves with less speed than the lighter. . . . Thus you see how, from [Aristotle's] assumption that the heavier body moves more rapidly than the lighter one, I infer that the heavier body moves more slowly. . . . a conclusion that is contrary to [his] hypothesis. We infer therefore that large and small bodies move with the same speed provided they are of the same specific gravity.

Notice that conditional contrasts contribute to coherence in that spurious relations will be screened off, thus reducing the number of factors considered causes. Coherence matters, however, even when contrasts are irrelevant, as the above examples show.

---

[13] I am grateful to Robert and Denise Cummins for making this point to me.

The idea that explanatory and deductive coherence are critical in explaining how a causal relation comes to be established is not new. The importance of the subsumption of various phenomena under a single principle can be traced to Kant (1781/1950; see Kitcher, 1986). However, to my knowledge, the role of coherence in forming causal relations has never been given any attention in psychology. Attempts in psychology and cognitive science to test the role of coherence in evaluating explanations *begin* with causal relations as primitives (Read & Marcus-Newhall, in press; Schank & Ranney, 1992; Thagard, 1989, 1992). A more basic question concerns how coherence might guide the initial formulation of causal relations.

IV. Conclusion

Superimposing the debates involving different questions might have created the illusion that a solution offered for one question fits a different question. I hope that separating the various issues reveals that we cannot comfortably think that the problem of how we discover causes has been solved. It seems that we are not entirely clueless, however. Although its formulation needs refinement and extension, the much criticized statistical-relevance view appears more viable than has often been supposed.

Beyond statistical relevance in its general and specific forms lies a gap of knowledge about the role of coherence in the discovery of causes. Although relevance and coherence are independent concepts, they need not be viewed as competing alternatives. Hume called causation a "cement of the universe." If I had to make a guess, I would say that statistical relevance sorts out potentially adjacent bricks, paring them to appropriate sizes, and coherence is the still mysterious cement that works only on the right bricks.

ACKNOWLEDGMENTS

The preparation of this article was supported by NSF Grant DBS 9121298. I thank Keith Holyoak, Yunn-wen Lien, Douglas Medin, and Barbara Spellman for their valuable comments on an earlier draft. I thank Anthony Dickinson, Randy Gallistel, Alan Leslie, and Michael Morris for discussions of Michotte's findings. Remaining unclarities and misconceptions are of course mine.

REFERENCES

Anderson, J. R. (1990). *The adaptive character of thought.* Hillsdale, New Jersey: Lawrence Erlbaum.

Arkes, H. R., & Harkness, A. R. (1983). Estimates of contingency between two dichotomous variables. *Journal of Experimental Psychology: General, 112,* 117–135.

Baillargeon, R. (1986). Representing the existence and the location of hidden objects: Object permanence in 6- and 8-month-old infants. *Cognition, 23,* 21–41.

Baillargeon, R. (1987). Young infant's reasoning about the physical and spatial properties of a hidden object. *Cognitive Development, 2,* 179–200.

Boyle, D. G. (1960). A contribution to the study of phenomenal causality. *Quarterly Journal of Experimental Psychology, 12,* 171–179.

Bullock, M. (1979). *Aspects of the young child's theory of causation.* Unpublished doctoral dissertation, University of Pennsylvania.

Bullock, M. (1985). Causal reasoning and developmental change over the preschool years. *Human Development, 28,* 169–91.

Bullock, M., Gelman, R., & Baillargeon, R. (1982). The development of causal reasoning. In W. J. Friedman (Ed.), *The developmental psychology of time* (pp. 209–254). New York: Academic Press.

Cartwright, N. (1983). *How the laws of physics lie.* Oxford: Clarendon Press.

Cartwright, N. (1989). *Nature's capacities and their measurement.* Oxford: Clarendon Press.

Chapman, G. B. (1991). Trial order affects cue interaction in contingency judgment. *Journal of Experimental Psychology: Learning, Memory, and Cognition, 17,* 837–854.

Chapman, G. B., & Robbins, S. I. (1990). Cue interaction in human contingency judgment. *Memory & Cognition, 18,* 537–545.

Cheng, P. W., & Holyoak, K. J. (in press). Complex adaptive systems as intuitive statisticians: Causality, contingency, and prediction. In J.-A. Meyer & H. Roitblat (Eds.), *Comparative approaches to cognition.* Cambridge, MA: MIT Press.

Cheng, P. W., & Novick, L. R. (1990a). A probabilistic contrast model of causal induction. *Journal of Personality and Social Psychology, 58,* 545–567.

Cheng, P. W., & Novick, L. R. (1990b). Where is the bias in causal attribution? In K. J. Gilhooly, M. T. G. Keane, R. H. Logie, & G. Erdos (Eds.), *Lines of thinking: Reflections on the psychology of thought* (Vol. 1, pp. 181–197). Chichester, England: Wiley.

Cheng, P. W., & Novick, L. R. (1991). Causes versus enabling conditions. *Cognition, 40,* 83–120.

Cheng, P. W., & Novick, L. R. (1992). Covariation in natural causal induction. *Psychological Review, 99,* 365–382.

Einhorn, H. J., & Hogarth, R. M. (1986). Judging probable cause. *Psychological Bulletin, 99,* 3–19.

Galileo, G. (1933). *Dialogues concerning two new sciences.* Macmillan: New York. (Original work published in 1638)

Garcia, J., McGowan, B., Ervin, F., & Koelling, R. (1968). Cues: Their relative effectiveness as reinforcers. *Science, 160,* 794–795.

Garcia, J., McGowen, B., & Green, K. F. (1972). Sensory quality and integration: Constraints on conditioning. In A. H. Black, & W. F. Prokasy (Eds.), *Classical conditioning II: Current research and theory* (pp. 3–27). New York: Appleton-Century-Crofts.

Gelman, R. (1990). First principles organize attention to and learning about relevant data: Number and the animate-inanimate distinction as examples. *Cognitive Science, 14,* 79–106.

Goodman, N. (1983). *Fact, fiction, and forecast* (4th ed.). Cambridge, MA: Harvard University Press. (Original work published in 1954)

Hart, H. L., & Honoré, A. M. (1985). *Causation in the law* (2nd ed.). Oxford, England: Clarendon Press. (Original work published in 1959)

Hesslow, G. (1976). Two notes on the probabilistic approach to causality. *Philosophy of Science, 43,* 290–292.

Hume, D. (1975). *Enquiries concerning human understanding and concerning the principles of morals* (3rd ed.). Oxford, England: Clarendon Press. (Original work published 1748)

Hume, D. (1987). *A treatise of human nature.* (2nd ed.). Oxford, England: Clarendon Press. (Original work published 1739). Also contains "An abstract of *A treatise of human nature*")

Jaspars, J. M. F., Hewstone, M. R. C., & Fincham, F. D. (1983). Attribution theory and research: The state of the art. In J. M. F. Jaspars F. D. Fincham, & M. R. C. Hewstone (Eds.), *Attribution theory: Essays and experiments* (pp. 3–36). London: Academic Press.

Jenkins, H., & Ward, W. (1965). Judgment of contingency between responses and outcomes. *Psychological Monographs, 7,* 1–17.

Kamin, L. J. (1969). Predictability, surprise, attention, and conditioning. In B. A. Campbell & R. M. Church (Eds.), *Punishment and aversive behavior* (pp. 276–296). New York: Appleton-Century-Crofts.

Kant, I. (1950). *Critique of pure reason.* (N. K. Smith, Trans.). London: Macmillan. (Original work published in 1781)

Kelley, H. H. (1967). Attribution theory in social psychology. In D. Levine (Ed.), *Nebraska symposium on motivation, 15,* (pp. 192–238). Lincoln: University of Nebraska Press.

Kelley, H. H. (1973). The processes of causal attribution. *American Psychologist, 28,* 107–128.

Kitcher, P. (1986). Projecting the order of nature. In R. Butts (Ed.), *Kant's philosophy of physical science* (pp. 201–235). Dordrecht: D. Reidel.

Koslowski, B., Okagaki, L., Lorenz, C., & Umbach, D. (1989). When covariation is not enough: The role of causal mechanism, sampling method, and sample size in causal reasoning. *Child Development, 60,* 1316–1327.

Lalljee, M., & Abelson, R. P. (1983). The organization of explanations. In M. Hewstone (Ed.), *Attribution theory: Social and functional extensions* (pp. 65–80). Oxford, England: Blackwell.

Leslie, A. M. (1982). The perception of causality in infants. *Perception, 11,* 173–186.

Leslie, A. M. (1984). Spatiotemporal continuity and the perception of causality in infants. *Perception, 13,* 287–305.

Leslie, A. M. (1988). The necessity of illusion: Perception and thought in infancy. In L. Weiskrantz (Ed.), *Thought without language* (pp. 185–210). Oxford, England: Oxford University Press.

Leslie, A. M. & Keeble, S. (1987). Do six-month-old infants perceive causality? *Cognition, 25,* 265–88.

LoLordo, V. M. (1979). Selective associations. In A. Dickinson, & R. A. Boakes (Eds.), *Mechanisms of learning and motivation: A memorial volume to Jerzy Konorski.* Hillsdale, NJ: Lawrence Erlbaum.

Mackie, J. L. (1974). *The cement of the universe: A study of causation.* Oxford, England: Clarendon Press.

Marr, D. (1982). *Vision.* San Francisco: W. H. Freeman and Co.

Melz, E. R., Cheng, P. W., Holyoak, K. J., & Waldmann, M. R. (in press). Cue competition in human categorization: Contingency or the Rescorla-Wagner learning rule? Comments on Shanks (1991). *Journal of Experimental Psychology: Learning, Memory, and Cognition.*

Michotte, A. E. (1963): *The perception of causality.* New York: Basic Books. (Original work published in 1946)

Mill, J. S. (1973). A system of logic: Ratiocinative and inductive. In J. M. Robson (Ed.), *Collected works of John Stuart Mill* (Vols. 7 & 8, 8th ed.) Toronto, Canada: University of Toronto Press. (Original work published in 1843)

Nisbett, R. E., & Ross, L. (1980). *Human inference: Strategies and shortcomings of social judgment.* Englewood Cliffs, NJ: Prentice-Hall.

Novick, L. R., Fratianne, A., & Cheng, P. W. (1992). Knowledge-based assumptions in causal attribution. *Social Cognition, 10,* 299–333.

Read, S. J. (1987). Constructing causal scenarios: A knowledge structure approach to causal reasoning. *Journal of Personality and Social Psychology, 52,* 288–302.

Read, S. J., & Marcus-Newhall, A. (in press). The role of explanatory coherence in social explanations. *Journal of Personality and Social Psychology.*

Reichenbach, H. (1956). *The direction of time.* Berkeley: University of California Press.

Rescorla, R. A. (1968). Probability of shock in the presence and absence of CS in fear conditioning. *Journal of Comparative and Physiological Psychology, 66,* 1–5.

Rescorla, R. A. (1981). Within-signal learning in autoshaping. *Animal Learning and Behavior, 9,* 245–252.

Rescorla, R. A. (1988). Pavlovian conditioning: It's not what you think it is. *American Psychologist, 43,* 151–160.

Salmon, W. C. (1965). The status of prior probabilities in statistical explanation. *Philosophy of Science, 32,* 137–146.

Salmon, W. C. (1971). Statistical explanation. In W. C. Salmon, R. C. Jeffrey, & J. G. Greeno, *Statistical explanation and statistical relevance* (pp. 29–87). Pittsburgh, PA: University of Pittsburgh Press.

Salmon, W. C. (1980). Probabilistic causality. *Pacific Philosophical Quarterly, 61,* 50–74.

Salmon, W. C. (1984). *Scientific explanation and the causal structure of the world.* Princeton, NJ: Princeton University Press.

Salmon, W. C. (1989). Four decades of scientific explanation. In P. Kitcher & W. C. Salmon (Eds.), *Scientific explanation: Minnesota studies in the philosophy of science* (Vol. 13). Minneapolis: University of Minnesota Press.

Schank, P., & Ranney, M. (1992). Assessing explanatory coherence: A new method for integrating verbal data with models of on-line belief revision. In *Proceedings of the 14th Annual Conference of the Cognitive Science Society* (pp. 599–604). Hillsdale, NJ: Lawrence Erlbaum.

Schlottmann, A., & Shanks, D. R. (1992). Evidence for a distinction between judged and perceived causality. *Quarterly Journal of Experimental Psychology, 44A,* 321–342.

Schustack, M. W., & Sternberg, R. J. (1981). Evaluation of evidence in causal inference. *Journal of Experimental Psychology: General, 110,* 101–120.

Shaklee, H., & Tucker, D. (1980). A rule analysis of judgments of covariation between events. *Memory & Cognition, 8,* 459–467.

Shanks, D. R. (1991). Categorization by a connectionist network. *Journal of Experimental Psychology: Learning, Memory, and Cognition, 17,* 433–443.

Shanks, D. & Dickinson, A. (1987). Associative accounts of causality judgment. In G. Bower (Ed.), *The psychology of learning and motivation, 21,* 229–261.

Shultz, T. R. (1982). Rules of causal attribution. *Monographs of the Society for Research in Child Development, 47* (No. 1).

Shultz, T. R., Fisher, G. W., Pratt, C. C., & Rulf, S. (1986). Selection of causal rules. *Child Development, 57,* 143–152.

Shultz, T. R., & Kesterbaum, N. R. (1985). Causal reasoning in children. *Annals of Child Development, 2,* 195–249.

Simpson, E. H. (1951). The interpretation of interaction in contingency tables. *Journal of the Royal Statistical Society* [Series B (Methodological)], *13,* 238–241.

Suppes, P. (1970). *A probabilistic theory of causality.* Amsterdam: North-Holland.

Thagard, P. (1989). Explanatory coherence. *Behavioral and Brain Sciences, 12,* 435–467.

Thagard, P. (1992). *Conceptual revolutions.* Princeton: Princeton University Press.

Thagard, P., & Nisbett, R. E. (1982). Variability and confirmation. *Philosophical Studies, 42,* 379–394.

Turner, M. (1987). *Death is the mother of beauty: Mind, metaphor, criticism.* Chicago, IL: University of Chicago Press.

White, P. A. (1989). A theory of causal processing. *British Journal of Psychology, 80,* 431–454.

White, P. A. (1992). Causal powers, causal questions, and the place of regularity information in causal attribution. *British Journal of Psychology, 83,* 161–188.

CATEGORIES, HIERARCHIES, AND INDUCTION

Elizabeth F. Shipley

I. Introduction

This article presents an account of psychological categories of physical objects based upon Nelson Goodman's (1955/1983) work on induction. It concerns categories of physical objects such as *dog* or *toy* or *rocking chair* and hierarchical relations among such categories.[1] It will attempt to answer four interrelated questions: What determines which classes of objects are categories? What determines the goodness of a category as a category? How do hierarchies influence category goodness? What is the role of hierarchies in induction?

The belief that induction is basic to both the formation and the use of categories has led to answers to these four questions that borrow heavily from Goodman's (1955/1983) work on inductive inference.

After consideration of three pre-theoretical psychological characteristics of categories (Section II), Goodman's work on induction is summarized briefly (Section III). Then, modifications of Goodman's position are suggested to make his approach more relevant to category formation and use (Section IV). In Section V prior studies of categories and induction are examined from the perspective presented here, and an integration is proposed of the theoretical work of Rips (1975), Carey (1985), and Osherson, Smith, Wilkie, Lopez, and Shafir (1990) with this approach.

[1] As a notational convention the names of categories and other classes are italicized, as are hypotheses.

THE PSYCHOLOGY OF LEARNING
AND MOTIVATION, VOL. 30

II. The Nature of Categories

In this article the term *class* will be used to refer to any specifiable set of objects: all red things, everything whose name begins with the letter *r*, all roses, everything smaller than a breadbox, and so on. Of the infinite number of possible classes of objects that a human can recognize, only some, such as *robin, robot,* and *rose,* are commonly considered categories. The term *category* will be used to refer to classes of physical objects that, for some person, have the characteristics described below.

A. CATEGORIES COMPARED TO OTHER CLASSES OF OBJECTS

Three psychological properties appear to characterize categories: (1) they have labels that are used to identify objects, (2) they serve as the range of inductive inferences, and (3) their members are believed to share a "deep" resemblance.

Mention of a category name is usually the most appropriate answer to the question, "What's that?" (Anglin, 1977; Brown, 1958; Ninion, 1980; Shipley, Kuhn, & Madden, 1983). When asking about an unknown object, "rose" or "flower" are satisfactory answers, "a red thing" or "something whose name begins with *r*" are less so. Similarly, "penny" is a better answer than "a round thing." Although each of these answers names a class of objects, those that merely describe the class, "red things" or "round things," seem inadequate. Requests for identification usually seek something more than a description. Category names appear to supply the needed "something more."[2]

A second characteristic of categories that distinguishes them from other classes is that they are the natural range of inductive inferences. Newly learned properties of an object are more likely to be attributed to other members of the same category than to members of different categories (e.g., Carey, 1985; Gelman, S. A., 1988; Gelman, S. A., & Markman, 1986, 1987; Holland, Holyoak, Nisbett, & Thagard, 1986).

Third, the members of a category belong together; they seem to have a "deep" resemblance beyond the surface properties that people use to assign them to the category (Murphy & Medin, 1985). To be sure, some categories have members with a strong physical resemblance. Indeed some categories, such as *robin,* have members that are physically indis-

---

[2] Undoubtedly, the most appropriate answer to "What's that?" varies with the context and the interrogator's presumed knowledge. One can even imagine a situation in which "a red thing" is a sufficient answer, perhaps when the question is asked of an interior decorator who is seeking to unify separate sections of a room with common color accents. The concern here is the default answer to "What's that?" Category labels are supplied unless the context demands otherwise.

tinguishable for most nonmembers. However, many other categories have members with less surface resemblance. Great Danes and Pekingese are hardly similar, yet *dog* is as compelling a category as *robin*. Thus, strong surface resemblance among the members of a category is not necessary.[3]

What is the source of a person's belief in a deep resemblance among members of a category? A little introspection suggests that the source can be based upon beliefs about at least three types of resemblance.[4] The first type is resemblance with respect to known properties that are not immediately evident, for example, the belief that all robins sing a specific, known melody. The second type is resemblance on a specific dimension without specification of the value on the dimension, for example, the belief that all robins have a similar, unknown body temperature. The third type is resemblance in unknown, as yet to be discovered, ways, for example, the belief that further study of a sample of robins will yield additional properties of all robins. (Also see Medin & Ortony, 1989, on psychological essentialism.) The approach to categories presented here will account for these three types of beliefs.

In brief, any specifiable set of objects is a class. For a given person, some classes of objects are categories. Categories are special classes in that their labels are used to inform others of the identity of an object, and they are more likely than other classes to support inductive inferences. Finally, category members are believed to resemble one another in ways that are not immediately evident, nor even necessarily known.[5] The position to be developed here will explain why categories have these three characteristics.

---

[3] Members of artifactual categories also may be said to have a ''deep resemblance'' based upon subtleties in their use, a resemblance that is not apparent in surface appearance. Think of *money* and the differences between preschoolers and adults regarding the knowledge of its use. The term *deep* is not intended to suggest physical depth but rather depth of knowledge.

[4] This is not meant to be an exhaustive list of the sources of a belief in a deep resemblance. For instance, it has been suggested (Medin & Ortony, 1989) that a belief in a causal relationship between surface properties and nonapparent properties may heighten the psychological coherence of a category.

[5] Note that this definition of a category is not consistent with some uses of the term in psychology literature. For instance, Barsalou (1983) defines an ''ad hoc category'' as a class of dissimilar entities ''created spontaneously for use in specialized contexts'' (p. 211) such as *things to take on a picnic*. Such classes are not categories by the criteria suggested here because (1) their characterizations (labels) would never be used for the identification of an isolated object, (2) they would not serve as the range of inductive inferences, and (3) their members are not thought to share a deep resemblance. In his theoretical work on categories, Anderson (e.g., 1991) specifies that a category need not have a label. If it does have a label, the label is treated like any other attribute.

B. CATEGORY GOODNESS

Not only do categories differ from other classes, they apparently differ among themselves in their "categoricalness," that is, in their goodness or coherence as a category.

Decades ago Brown (1958) pointed out that, for an unknown object in isolation, some category names are preferred to others as an answer to the question "What's that?" For an object that exemplifies several categories related by inclusion, one category name seems best for identification. For instance, "dog" is better than "animal" or "collie" in most situations (Anglin, 1977; Rosch, Mervis, Gray, Johnson, & Boyes-Braem, 1976).

For an object that exemplifies several categories not related by inclusion, again one category name may seem best for identification. For a pet peccary, "peccary" is usually a better identification than "pet." Of course, there is variation in the category label applied to a specific object in various contexts, depending upon the listener's presumed knowledge (Anglin, 1977; Mervis & Mervis, 1982), the speaker's knowledge (Shipley et al., 1983), the context of other objects (Olson, 1970), and the purpose of the communication (White, 1982). The "best" category label is the label used when the context does not dictate otherwise. (See also Cruse, 1977, for characterization of so-called "unmarked" or default labels.)

Similarly, some categories are more likely than others to determine the range of an induction. S. A. Gelman (1988) and S. A. Gelman & O'Reilly (1988) found that children are more likely to attribute a newly learned novel property of an object such as a rabbit to another rabbit than to a member of a more general category. Such results are not necessarily a matter of similarity facilitating generalization. Induction has been shown to occur more readily with dissimilar-appearing members of the same category than with similar-appearing objects from different categories (Gelman, S. A., & Markman, 1986; 1987).

Obviously, the relative goodness of categories is not the only constraint on induction. As work such as that of Carey (1985) and S. A. Gelman (1988) demonstrates, there are complicated relations between the nature of the category, the type of property, the knowledge of the inducer, and the range of induction. (Some of these relationships are considered in Section V.) Further, resemblance plays a role in determining the force of an inductive inference (Osherson et al., 1990; Rips, 1975). However, other things being equal, it appears that the category with the preferred label is the preferred range of induction. Shipley (1992) reports evidence for this relationship in preschool children. The children used so-called "basic-level" category labels (e.g., "dog") rather than "subordinate-level" category labels (*e.g.,* "collie dog") for individual animals, and they made inductive inferences more readily over basic-level categories than over subordinate categories.[6]

What of a deep resemblance among category members? Is deep resemblance also greatest for the category that is best for identification and induction? If the deep resemblance of a category is equated with the total number of properties that are actually shared by all members of a category (assuming that such a number could be determined), then the answer is clearly negative. Deep resemblance will always be greatest for the most specific category. For instance, robins have the same properties in common as do all birds, but in addition robins share properties such as diet, egg color, and song, properties that differ among different kinds of birds. However, if for a given person the relative degree of deep resemblance of several categories depends upon the organization of that person's knowledge about the categories, then the category with the greatest deep resemblance among its members will not necessarily be the most specific. For someone whose knowledge is organized with a number of properties attributed to birds (e.g., wings, beaks, hollow bones, fly, lay eggs, etc.), and with only a few properties attributed to robins (eat worms and lay blue eggs), then the more general class, *bird,* could well be the category with the greatest deep resemblance. (Also see Lakoff, 1987, & Murphy, 1982 for the argument that an individual's maximum knowledge is not necessarily stored at the most specific level). Hence, it is not implausible to suggest that for categories in an inclusion relation, the greatest deep resemblance among category members may occur with the preferred label and the preferred range of induction, rather than with the most specific category.

In brief, just as categories differ from other classes with respect to the use of their names in identification, in serving as the range of inductive inferences, and in possessing deep resemblance among members, so also categories apparently differ from one another in these same ways. Hence, I propose that the factors that determine whether or not a class is a category also determine the relative goodness of a class as a category. The term *coherence* will be used to refer to the psychological property of the goodness of a class as a category.

[6] The phrases "basic-level category," "subordinate category," and "superordinate category" will be used to refer to categories that have been found to be basic, subordinate to basic, or superordinate to basic by one or more of the Rosch et al. (1976) criteria. The use of these terms is for communicative purposes and is not intended as support for the theoretical positions expressed in Rosch's writings, nor is it intended to suggest that basic level is an inherent property of any specific category.

C. Where Do Categories Come From?

It is clear that we are born with the disposition to perceive bounded objects as discrete entities (Spelke, 1984), and with a sensitivity to surface resemblance among objects (e.g., Roberts, 1988; Tomikawa & Dodd, 1980). These dispositions could account, in part, for universals in categories from culture to culture (e.g., Berlin, 1978; Hunn, 1977). In addition, the approach presented here will assume that we are born with processes that can be used to build systems of categories. These systems initially honor, but later transcend, the original perceptually based classes. Variation in the use of the processes, in interaction with the environment, could account for individual differences in categories, both within and between cultures (e.g., Bulmer, 1967; Lancy, 1983; Tanaka & Taylor; 1991).

A single process is proposed as the basis for the transformation of a perceptually based class into a category. It is the attribution or projection of properties onto a set of entities. Projection acts upon two kinds of entities, individual objects, such as individual dogs, Fido and Rover, and classes of objects, such as the class of all dogs and the class of all cats.

When a person projects a property onto individual members of a class, both previously observed and never-observed members of the class, then the class becomes a category. For the person who hypothesizes of the class of things called "dogs" that *Dogs bark, Dogs eat meat,* and *Dogs wag their tails when happy,* the class of dogs is hypothesized to become a category.

The second way in which a class becomes a category is via the attribution or projection of properties to members of a class of classes that has the class at issue as a single member. Consider the class of different kinds of animals, which has the class of dogs as one member. Hypotheses can be projected over the class *kind of animal.* If a person hypothesizes *Every kind of animal makes a characteristic sound* and *Every kind of animal has a characteristic diet,* then every kind of animal, even a completely novel kind, is hypothesized to become a category.

In brief, the major presupposition of this paper is that categories are formed by the organism by means of induction. Initially, an innate quality space (Quine, 1969) provides the class that is the basis for a category. That is, inductive inferences are first made over classes of similar-appearing entities.

A complete account of categories must explain how people determine whether or not an object is an instance of a category, that is, it must specify identification routines (Miller & Johnson-Laird, 1976). This article has virtually nothing to say about identification, except to assume that humans can classify unfamiliar objects on the basis of similarity. Rather, I am concerned with what it means for a class to be a category, and with the acquisition and use of categories.

III. Entrenchment and Induction: The Goodman Position

Given that making inductive inferences about a class enhances the status of the class as a category and that categories serve as the range of inductive inferences, then these two assumptions, taken together, lead to the rather banal conclusion that the more a class has served as the range of inductive inferences in the past, the more likely that it will be the range of future inductive inferences. Hence, changes in the relative goodness of categories should be unlikely and the acquisition of category status by a novel class should be slow and rare. The relationship proposed here between category goodness and induction becomes more useful when it is combined with Goodman's (1955/1983) insights on induction.

In *Fact, Fiction and Forecast* (1955/1983) Goodman analysed what people do in making inductive inferences. He was concerned with characterizing the relative legitimacy of competing inductive inferences about unobserved instances. On the basis of this analysis Goodman proposed several factors that enhance the tendency of a class to be the range of an inductive inference. The central thesis of this article is that most of these factors also enhance the status of a class as a category. Hence, Goodman's analysis provides a way of explaining how classes become categories and of predicting the relative goodness of classes as categories. (See Rips, 1975, for a prior application of Goodman's position to experimental studies of induction and Sternberg, 1982, for use of Goodman's position to account for learning performance.)

This section will characterize briefly those aspects of Goodman's position that are most relevant to this account of categories. In Section IV Goodman's approach will be modified slightly to make it even more relevant to category goodness.

A. Emerubies and Grue: Predicates without Entrenchment

Goodman (1955/1983) argued that, logically, the objects in any finite set are members of an infinity of classes. For instance, the objects in the finite set consisting of my two dogs are members of the class of dogs, of the class of pets, of the class of brown mammals, and so forth. Goodman used "emerubies" to illustrate his argument. All emeralds examined to date are members of the class containing all emeralds as well as the class containing all emerubies, where emerubies are the set of emeralds examined prior to some future time t plus all rubies unexamined prior to time t. Thus observing that all examined emeralds are green provides equal support for the two hypotheses, *All emeralds are green* and *All emerubies are green*. Although the evidence supports both hypotheses, only *All emeralds are green* is induced from the evidence. Why?

Goodman's answer is based in part upon the history of use of the two predicates, *emerald* and *emeruby*, in prior inductive inferences. Hypotheses have been projected more often about emeralds than about emerubies, for example, *Emeralds are hard, Emeralds are expensive*, and so forth. The greater prior use of *emerald* than of *emeruby* is assumed to give greater inductive validity to hypotheses about emeralds than to hypotheses about emerubies. It is irrelevant that all emerubies examined to date have been found to be both hard and expensive. It is the projection of a regularity that is important, not its existence.[7]

In universal conditional hypotheses such as *All emeralds are green*, which is the only type of hypothesis that Goodman considers in detail, he distinguishes antecedent predicates, such as *emerald*, from consequent predicates, such as *green*, but treats the two types of predicates in the same way for purposes of induction. Thus, he presents an argument for consequent predicates that is analogous to his argument for antecedent predicates. Observing emeralds and finding that each one is green supports the inductive inference *All emeralds are green*. However, such observations also support the inductive inference *All emeralds are grue*, where *grue* applies to all green things examined before a future time t, as well as to all blue things not examined before time t. Again the induction of *All emeralds are green* and the failure to induce *All emeralds are grue* is attributed to the different histories of use of *green* and *grue* in prior inductive inferences.

The difference between *emerald* and *emeruby*, as well as the difference between *green* and *grue*, is characterized by Goodman (1955/1983) as a difference in a property he calls "entrenchment." The more frequent projection of hypotheses about emeralds than of hypotheses about emerubies results in greater entrenchment of *emerald* than of *emeruby*. The greater entrenchment of *emerald* than of *emeruby* means that a per-

---

[7] Goodman (1955/1983) proves that hypotheses with predicates such as *emeruby* cannot be dismissed because they contain mention of a specific time. If *emeruby* is considered a primitive, to be used in defining *ruby* and *emerald*, then *ruby* and *emerald* will contain mention of a specific time in their definition.

son is more willing to induce *Emeralds are green* than *Emerubies are green* from observation of green emeralds. In general, the greater the entrenchment of the predicates of a hypothesis, the greater the inductive force—the "projectability"—of that hypothesis with respect to unobserved instances.

Goodman claims that predicates gain entrenchment from their use in inductive inferences and that inductive inferences are more readily made with more entrenched predicates. However, use in an inductive inference is not the only way that predicates gain entrenchment. Goodman also proposes that predicates inherit entrenchment. The inheritance of entrenchment is mediated by parent predicates and over-hypotheses. These concepts are examined in the next two sections.

B. Inherited Entrenchment: The Contribution of Parent Predicates

A parent predicate of a given predicate is a predicate that applies to classes: Among the classes to which it applies is the extension of the given predicate (Goodman, 1955/1983). For instance, *kind of gemstone* is a parent predicate of *emerald*. *Kind of gemstone* applies to classes of gemstones; one of the classes is the extension of *emerald*. The same is true for consequent predicates. *Uniform in color* is a parent predicate of *red* and *green*. *Uniform in color* applies to classes of things of the same color; one of these classes is the class of all green emeralds.

Predicates that have the same parent predicate will be called offspring predicates of that parent predicate. Offspring predicates inherit entrenchment from their parent predicates. *Emerald* and *ruby* inherit entrenchment from the parent predicate *kind of gemstone*. *Green* and *red* inherit entrenchment from the parent predicate *uniform in color*.[8] The in-

---

[8] It must be noted that a predicate has separate entrenchment as an antecedent predicate and as a consequent predicate. A predicate gains entrenchment as an antecedent predicate from the projection of hypotheses in which it is the antecedent predicate. The same is true for consequent predicates. A predicate gains entrenchment as a consequent predicate from the projection of a hypothesis in which it is the consequent predicate. In addition, antecedent predicates and consequent predicates must be distinguished in inheritance. A predicate inherits entrenchment as an antecedent predicate from the entrenchment of its parent predicates as antecedent predicates. It inherits entrenchment as a consequent predicate from the entrenchment of its parent predicates as consequent predicates. For instance, *emerald* inherits entrenchment as an antecedent predicate but not as a consequent predicate, and *red* inherits entrenchment as a consequent predicate but not as an antecedent predicate, from the predicates in *Kinds of gemstones are uniform in color*. Psychologists usually conceptualize antecedent predicates and consequent predicates as referring to things and properties respectively (as in Gupta, 1980). Because Goodman (1955/1983) does not distinguish predicates in this way, he makes explicit the distinction between the entrenchment of a predicate as an antecedent predicate and as a consequent predicate.

heritance of entrenchment means that a novel predicate will be well entrenched provided it has a well-entrenched parent predicate. Thus, an unfamiliar predicate such as *peridot*, corresponding to a previously unknown kind of gemstone, will be well entrenched, and hypotheses about this unfamiliar kind of genstome will be projectable because *peridot* inherits entrenchment from *kind of gemstone*. (Changes in feature salience in Billman's focused sampling model play a role similar to the inheritance of entrenchment by properties [Billman & Heit, 1988].)

Although the concept of a parent predicate may seem unfamiliar, in fact it is not. Parent predicates are often "lexicalized" in English with the phrase *kind of*, as in *kind of tool*, which is a parent predicate of *hammer* and *saw*. One kind of tool is the class of hammers. Further, collective terms such as *family, tribe,* and *army division* are parent predicates.[9]

Parent predicates, such as *kind of tool*, which apply to classes, must be distinguished from predicates that apply to individuals, such as *tool*. This distinction may be unclear because many so-called "superordinate category terms" (Rosch et al., 1976) such as "tools" and "animals" are ambiguous; they can refer either to classes or to individuals (Carlson, 1977; Lyons, 1977). The question "Tell me what animals are at the zoo?" is likely to be answered by listing kinds of animals such as lions and elephants, rather than individual animals such as Leo and Jumbo. However, the question "How many animals are at the zoo?" is likely to be answered by counting individual animals; among them will be Leo and Jumbo.

 In sum, according to Goodman, predicates gain entrenchment in two ways. They earn entrenchment by appearing in projected hypotheses, and they inherit entrenchment from their entrenched parents.

C. OVER-HYPOTHESES: A SOURCE OF ENTRENCHMENT AND OF SUPPORT FOR INDUCTION

How do parent predicates such as *kind of animal* gain entrenchment? Goodman (1955/1983) proposed that parent predicates gain entrenchment as do other predicates, namely from the projection of hypotheses in which they appear. The parent predicates *kind of gemstone* and *uniform in color* gain entrenchment from the projection of a hypothesis such as *Kinds of gemstones are uniform in color*. Such hypotheses, in which both the antecedent and consequent predicates are parent predicates, are

---

[9] For example, *family* is a parent of predicates such as *member of the Jones family;* one family is the Jones family. *Tribe* is a parent of the predicate *member of Tribe X;* one tribe is Tribe X. *Army division* is a parent of the predicate *soldier in the 26th division;* one army division is the 26th (Goodman, 1955/1983).

called over-hypotheses. An over-hypothesis is an induction over hypoth-eses containing offspring predicates such as *Emeralds are green* and *Rubies are red.*

Over-hypotheses not only supply entrenchment, they also support in-ductive inferences. To see how this works let us start with hypotheses about the sounds made by different kinds of animals—*Dogs ' bark, Horses neigh,* and *Sheep baa.* To project this type of property, the mak-ing of a particular sound, onto each kind of animal, one uses an over-hypothesis, *Kinds of animals are uniform in sound.* The over-hypothesis specifies a type of property that is invariant within classes at the same level in a class-inclusion hierarchy.

By specification of the properties that are invariant within kinds, an over-hypothesis contributes to the projectability of specific hypotheses about individual kinds. For instance, the projection of an over-hypothesis about all animals of the same kind making the same sound supports a hypothesis about a specific kind of animal such as *armadillo,* namely *All armadillos make the same sound.* If one armadillo is ob-served making a specific sound, perhaps squealing, then one can use the over-hypothesis to induce from this limited sample *Armadillos squeal.*

Thus, over-hypotheses support inductive inferences about types of properties for both known and novel categories, and permit inferences about specific properties to be drawn from limited samples. Holland et al. (1986) present a similar position in their analysis of the role of vari-ability in generalizations.

Experimental evidence for over-hypotheses is found in the work of Nisbett, Krantz, Jepson, and Kunda (1983). Subjects who believed that tribes of people are uniform in skin color, but not obesity, were willing to predict skin color, but not obesity, in an unfamiliar tribe from a small sample. A belief in the homogeneity of skin color within tribes is, of course, an over-hypothesis.

D. SUMMARY: THE GOODMAN POSITION

Goodman was concerned with the relative projectability of competing inductive inferences or hypotheses. He proposed that the entrenchment of the predicates in a hypothesis gives the hypothesis projectability. In turn, a predicate gains entrenchment from the actual projection of hy-potheses with the given predicate and by inheritance from the entrench-ment of its parent predicates. Parent predicates, in turn, gain entrench-ment from the projection of over-hypotheses in which they appear. Finally, over-hypotheses support hypotheses about types of uniformities within classes of individuals. In addition, over-hypotheses support in-ductive inferences about specific properties from limited information.

IV.   Categories, Entrenchment, and Induction:
A Psychological Perspective

To make use of Goodman's (1955/1983) insights in an account of categories it is proposed that:

> The entrenchment of a predicate as an antecedent predicate determines the goodness of the corresponding class as a category.

In the remainder of this article both predicates and their corresponding classes will be referred to as having entrenchment.

Goodman (1955/1983) saw his theoretical efforts concerning valid inductive inferences as "describing or defining the distinctions it [the human mind] makes between valid and invalid projections" (p. 87). He used the concept of entrenchment as a means to this goal. In contrast, I wish to use the concept of entrenchment to account for category goodness. This change of focus suggests modification of Goodman's position to permit a better integration of the concepts of entrenchment and projectability with current knowledge of categories.

Those aspects of Goodman's analysis of induction that are considered essential to an explanation of category goodness are (1) the projection of hypotheses and (2) the role of parent predicates and overhypotheses. Three specific changes from Goodman's analysis seem necessary. These are examined next. Then kind hierarchies, a type of structure that derives from Goodman's analysis, are compared to the more familiar class-inclusion hierarchies with respect to their support of inferences.

Goodman is concerned with inductive inferences within a category, with going from a sample to an entire class exemplified by the sample. However, many inductive inferences are made from one category to another. An expansion of Goodman's work on entrenchment and induction to between-category inductive inferences was proposed by Rips (1975) and is considered in Section V.

A.   Modifications

Three specific changes are suggested. These concern the effect upon entrenchment of (1) the parameters of the projections of hypotheses, (2) the nature of the projected hypotheses, and (3) the sources of hypotheses. Although the details of these modifications require empirical evaluation, the need for such changes seems obvious.

1. *Quantifying Entrenchment*

Goodman proposed that the relative entrenchment of a predicate depends upon the number of "actual projections" of hypotheses with that predicate (1955/1983, p. 94). However, an actual projection is difficult to characterize. Does an actual projection occur each time a person says, "Dogs bite"? Does one have to "really mean" the hypothesis—whatever that might mean? Is some sort of a commitment necessary, such as a prediction in a specific situation, for an actual projection to occur? Clearly such questions can be answered only empirically.

Further, the variety of hypotheses would seem to be important. Imagine person A who believes that redheaded people have a number of traits in common—for instance, that they are good at arithmetic, poor at spelling, absent-minded, nearsighted, have a good sense of direction, and enjoy arguments. Suppose further that person A has projected hypotheses about each property several times for a total of n projections about redheaded people. Now consider person B who has projected the same hypothesis, *Red-headed people are absentminded,* n times, but who has no beliefs about other properties of redheaded people. Does it not seem reasonable that A more than B would consider redheads to be a special kind of people with other, as yet unknown, traits in common?

In brief, I am suggesting that the entrenchment of a category is a function of the number of types of projected hypotheses, as well as the number of tokens of projected hypotheses. The relative contributions of these two sources of entrenchment awaits empirical investigation.[10]

2. *Generic Hypotheses with Bare Plural Subjects*

According to the account of categories proposed here the entrenchment of a predicate (and the goodness of the corresponding class as a category) is enhanced by the use of the predicate in projected hypotheses. Hence, it is necessary to consider which projected hypotheses are relevant to the entrenchment of categories.

The hypotheses that Goodman (1955/1983) used in his analysis of induction are universal conditional hypotheses. Such hypotheses, for instance *All dogs bark,* are violated by observation of a single exception, a dog who cannot bark. For Goodman, both the making of past projections,

---

[10] It is also an empirical question whether or not the frequency and the recency of projections of a specific hypothesis influence the entrenchment of the predicates in the hypothesis. My intuition is that recency is irrelevant; as time passes one does not lose the sense that some class of objects forms a category, although one may forget the label of the category. A more specific determination of the role of the frequency of projections awaits clarification of what constitutes an actual projection.

that is, the making of predictions, and the outcomes of these predictions are relevant to the entrenchment of predicates. Using knowledge of the outcome of predictions means that violated hypotheses will cease to be projected, and classes will become less entrenched when predictions about the classes are violated. Thus, inductive inferences about future instances will be guided by the success of past inferences. Although evidence is a natural component of a theory of induction, its status as a central component of a theory of categories is more problematic.

Many of the hypotheses we project in everyday life are in the form of generic statements with bare (unmodified) plural subjects, such as *Birds lay eggs* or *Birds fly*. The first hypothesis cannot be paraphrased as *All birds lay eggs* because only mature female birds lay eggs. The second hypothesis cannot be paraphrased *All birds fly* because some kinds of birds, such as ostriches and penguins, as well as very young birds, do not fly. Yet few people who know anything about birds would consider *Birds lay eggs* or *Birds fly* false statements. Thus our projected knowledge includes generalizations with well-known exceptions.

Carlson (1977) and other linguists have argued that acceptable paraphrases of generic statements refer to kinds. The two sentences above could be paraphrased *Birds are a kind of animal such that the mature female lays eggs* and *Birds are a kind of animal such that most species fly*. If generic statements are actually statements about a single entity, a kind, then it seems plausible that a commitment on the part of an individual person to a statement such as *Birds lay eggs,* which presupposes the conceptualization of the class of birds as a single entity, should enhance the psychological coherence of the class of birds for that person.

The acceptance of generic hypotheses as relevant to entrenchment means that a more natural formulation of over-hypotheses is possible. Instead of an over-hypothesis specifying that various classes of the same kind are completely homogeneous with respect to a specific type of property, characteristic types of properties can be mentioned. For example, we project the over-hypothesis *Each kind of animal makes a characteristic sound* even if we know of exceptions within the classes of kinds, such as barkless dogs.[11]

---

[11] It may be that our propensity to express our knowledge in generic hypotheses is responsible in part for the psychologically compelling belief that categories have necessary and sufficient properties, the so-called "classical position" (Smith & Medin, 1981). See Mahmood and Armstrong (1992) for conflicts arising from the expression of beliefs about ethnic groups in generic statements and knowledge of individuals who violate the generalizations.

3. *Source Credibility: Another Determiner of Projectability*

Adults, and perhaps to a greater degree children, often accept information provided by another as a projectable hypothesis without evaluation or even knowledge of relevant evidence. Of course, we do not treat all people as equally good sources of hypotheses. Indeed, the projectability of different kinds of hypotheses provided by the same person may vary. Thus, the credibility in a relevant domain of the person who supplies a hypothesis should contribute to the projectability of the hypothesis and to the entrenchment of the predicates in the hypothesis.

B. KIND HIERARCHIES, CLASS-INCLUSION HIERARCHIES, AND INFERENCES

The hierarchical structure formed by a parent predicate, such as *kind of animal,* and its offspring predicates, such as *dog* and *cat,* I have called a "kind hierarchy" (Shipley, 1989). The upper level of a kind hierarchy consists of a class of kinds, *kind of animal* in the case of the kind hierarchy of animals. One member of *kind of animal* is a class of individuals of a single kind, for example, the class of dogs is one member of the class *kind of animal.* The lower level consists of classes of individuals, such as the class of dogs with Rover as one member and the class of cats with Garfield as one member (Fig. 1A).[12]

Corresponding to each kind hierarchy is a class-inclusion hierarchy with individuals at each level. For instance, corresponding to the kind hierarchy of animals is a class-inclusion hierarchy with individual animals as members of the classes at every level. In the class-inclusion hierarchy of animals Rover is a member of the superordinate category *animal* as well as the included category *dog* (Fig. 1B).

---

[12] Consideration is limited here to two-level kind hierarchies because three-level hierarchies seem conceptually odd, for instance *poodle, kind of dog,* and *kind of kind of animal.* Goodman (1955/1983, p. 112) gives an example of an over-hypothesis of an over-hypothesis (whose predicates are parent predicates of parent predicates), but has to use geometric properties to specify the antecedent predicate and to explicitly define the consequent predicate to make it at all comprehensible: "*Every stack [of bags] of marbles in Utah is homogeneous in color variegation.*" My intuition is that people often have overlapping two-level kind hierarchies that correspond to a single three-level class-inclusion hierarchy. For example, one kind hierarchy might have the parent class *kind of animal* at the upper level and classes of different kinds of animals, including the class of individual dogs, at the lower level. A second kind hierarchy could have the parent class, *kind of dog* at the upper level and classes of different kinds of dogs, such as the class of individual poodles, at the lower level. The effects of such structures is beyond the scope of this paper.

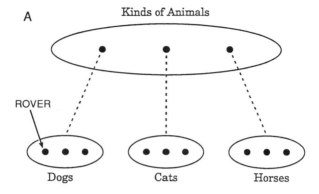

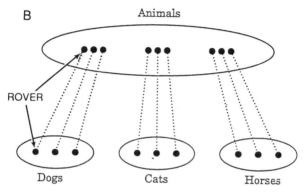

Fig. 1.   (A) illustrates the kind hierarchy of animals. The hypotheses *Dogs eat meat* and *Horses eat hay* are projected over the classes of individual dogs and individual horses respectively. The over-hypothesis *Each kind of animal has a characteristic diet* is projected over the parent class of kinds of animals. (B) illustrates the class-inclusion hierarchy of animals. The hypotheses *Dogs eat meat* and *Horses eat hay* are projected over the classes of individual dogs and horses respectively. The general hypothesis *All animals eat* is projected over the superordinate class of individual animals.

Analogous to the differences between superordinate-category terms and parent predicates is the distinction between general hypotheses that refer to properties of individuals (e.g., *Animals move*) and over-hypotheses that refer to properties of classes, (e.g., *Each kind of animal has a characteristic movement*). The projections of these two types of hypotheses have different effects. The projection of a general hypothesis enhances the entrenchment of a superordinate category of individuals, such as *animal*, but has no effect upon the entrenchment of the corresponding class of classes, *kind of animal*. The projection of an over-hypothesis enhances the entrenchment of a parent class, such as *kind of animal*, but has no effect upon the entrenchment of the corresponding superordinate category of individuals *animal*. (Of course, the increase in entrenchment of *kind of animal* does increase the entrenchment, by inheritance, of specific kinds of animals such as *dog* and *cat*.) In Section V it will be argued on the basis of recent experimental work that young children may have the parent class *kind of animal* as an entrenched class, but not the superordinate class *animal* (Carey, 1985; Davidson & Gelman, S. A., 1990). In brief, the entrenchment of a superordinate class of individuals is different from the entrenchment of the corresponding parent class.

Because the entrenchment of a parent class and the entrenchment of the corresponding class of individuals are logically independent, a person could have projected beliefs about kinds of animals, for example, *Each kind of animal has a characteristic movement,* and projected beliefs about individual animals of different kinds, for example, *Monkeys climb* and *Seals swim,* but no beliefs about properties common to all animals, that is, no beliefs such as *Animals move.* Although it might seem reasonable that a person who projects an over-hypothesis, such as *Each kind of animal has a characteristic movement,* would also project a corresponding hypothesis about individual animals, such as *Animals move,* it is an empirical question whether or not humans make inferences from an over-hypothesis about classes to the individual members of the corresponding superordinate class.

As was noted in Section III,C, projected over-hypotheses about parent classes support inductive inferences about offspring classes. If, for example, the over-hypothesis *Each kind of animal has a characteristic diet* is projected, and if a novel class such as *aardvark* is placed in the animal kind hierarchy, then one will believe *Aardvarks have a characteristic diet* even though one knows nothing of the specific diet of any individual aardvark. Given this belief in the uniformity of aardvarks' diet, one can induce the characteristic diet of aardvarks, namely termites, from observation of a few aardvarks eating termites. Note that one can make deductive inferences about the classes in a kind hierarchy, such as *Aardvarks have a characteristic diet.* However, one cannot use a kind hierarchy to make deductive inferences about individuals.

In contrast to kind hierarchies, class-inclusion hierarchies support deductive inferences about individuals. If, for instance, one knows that every member of the superordinate category *animal* eats, then one can deduce for any kind of animal (such as *aardvark*) that all animals of that kind eat and one can also deduce that every individual animal eats.

It should be emphasized that a kind hierarchy supports inductive inferences only if it includes an entrenched class of kinds resulting from the projection of over-hypotheses over the class of kinds. A class of kinds without entrenchment does not support inductive inferences. Consider the goal-derived classes that Barsalou (1983) has called "ad hoc" categories. The class of kinds *kind of thing to carry out of one's home in a fire* contains such classes as family members, pets, family pictures, manuscripts, paintings, and so forth. This class of classes will not become entrenched because there are no hypotheses that project the same types of properties onto the individual kinds and hence no projectable over-hypotheses. Even though each class, *family member, pet, manuscript,* and so forth is a well-entrenched category, there is no common thread among the projected properties of each category to unite these categories and their properties by a projected over-hypothesis.

In brief, kind hierarchies, which consist of a parent class and classes of individuals, support inductive inferences about individuals providing the parent class is well entrenched. In contrast, class-inclusion hierarchies, which consist of classes of individuals in inclusion relations, can support deductive inferences about individual.

V. Prior Experimental Work on Induction

Four sets of studies of induction are particularly relevant to the account of categories presented here (Carey, 1985; Gelman, S. A., 1988; Gelman, S. A., & Coley, 1990; Gelman, S. A., Collman, & Maccoby, 1986; Gelman, S. A., & Markman, 1986, 1987; Gelman, S. A., & O'Reilly, 1988; Osherson, Smith, Wilkie, Lopez, & Shafir, 1990; Rips, 1975). The concepts discussed above, entrenchment of predicates, projectability of hypotheses, parent predicates, kind hierarchies, and over-hypotheses, are used below in an attempt to provide a more unified account of the findings of these studies and to expand the account of categories proposed here.

A. CHILDREN'S INDUCTION OF DIFFERENT TYPES OF PROPERTIES OVER DIFFERENT KINDS OF CATEGORIES

S. A. Gelman and her colleagues have examined the inductive inferences of preschool and young school-age children. Two of their results have already been mentioned and can be interpreted as support for the use of entrenchment in an account of categories. The first result is the primacy of membership in the category over perceptual resemblance in the determination of induction (Gelman, S. A., & Markman, 1986; 1987). In these studies a common label was used to signify membership in the same category. The second result is the greater effectiveness of basic-level categories compared to superordinate categories in constraining inductive inferences (Gelman, S. A., 1988; Gelman, S. A., & O'Reilly, 1988).

Other studies by S. A. Gelman and her colleagues also can be interpreted as providing evidence for the role of the entrenchment of categories in supporting inductive inferences. For instance, 4-year-olds made more inductive inferences when stimuli were labeled "boys" than when the same stimuli were labeled "children who play with trains." The first label refers to a well-entrenched category, *boy*, the second to a class lacking in entrenchment, *child who plays with trains* (Gelman, S. A., et al., 1986). Two-year-olds who were told that a familiar depicted bird lives in a nest were more likely to attribute the property of living in a nest to a dodo bird if both birds were given the label of a well-entrenched category, *bird*, than if both birds were given the label of a class with little if any entrenchment, *wide awake* (Gelman, S. A., & Coley, 1990).

Other findings by S. A. Gelman (1988) can be interpreted as showing that well-entrenched properties are more likely to be projected than are poorly entrenched properties. She examined a variety of properties including properties characterized as "generalizable for natural kinds" (former states, parts, or substance), "generalizable for artifacts" (functions), and "nongeneralizable properties" (temporary states, historical accidents, or temporal aspects). Children were told that one member of a familiar category (e.g., a white rabbit) possessed a property and were asked if other individuals possessed the property. All properties except the nongeneralizable properties were readily attributed by the children to other members of categories exemplified by the taught-on individual (the white rabbit).

Although S. A. Gelman (1988) characterized the experimental properties as novel, all except the nongeneralizable properties were familiar types of properties, such as function (*is used for putting in brackets*) and diet (*likes to eat alfalfa*), types of properties that young children apparently project (Shipley, 1989). These familiar types of properties could have parent predicates with entrenchment (e.g., *has a characteristic function, has a characteristic diet*), entrenchment that would be inherited by the experimental properties. In contrast, for nongeneralizable properties both the type of property and the specific property undoubtedly had little if any history of past projections. For example, it is hard to imagine a context in which anyone would project *has a little scratch on it* over some class of objects. Further, the nongeneralizable properties lack entrenched parent predicates. Hence, all properties except the nongeneralizable properties should have been readily projected, as they were.[13]

In brief, the concepts of entrenchment and over-hypotheses are consistent with the intuitions that motivated S. A. Gelman's studies and with the findings of these studies.

B. ASYMMETRIES IN INDUCTION BY ADULTS

Rips (1975) examined the inferences of adult subjects who were told to imagine an isolated island on which all members of a certain species had a contagious disease. For instance, one group of subjects was told that all members of *robin*, the given category (GC), had an unknown disease. The subjects were asked to estimate the proportion of individuals with the disease in various target categories (TCs), such as *duck* and *sparrow*. Other subjects had different GCs.

Rips found that two factors influenced induction: (1) the similarity of the GC and TC: Induction was greater the more similar the two categories; and (2) the "centrality" of the GC: Induction was greater the more central the GC. Centrality was defined operationally as the distance in a scaling space between a category and its superordinate category; for example, *robin* is considered a central category because it is close to *bird*.

Rips interpreted the increase in induction with an increase in the similarity of the GC and the TC as an instance of generalization by similarity. He made two interrelated interpretations of the finding that centrality facilitated induction. The first interpretation was that members of central categories, such as *robin*, share more properties with members of other bird categories than do members of less central categories, such as *hawk*. Thus, a robin shares more properties with birds of other kinds than does a hawk. Lacking other information, the subject assumes that the distribution of a novel property mirrors the distribution of better-known properties. Hence, *have disease X* is more readily projected onto other species of birds from *robin*, a central category, than from *hawk*, a peripheral category. That is, an inductive inference from *robin* to *hawk* will be stronger than an inductive inference from *hawk* to *robin*.

Rips also suggested that the facilitation of induction by central categories is equivalent to the greater inductive force of well-entrenched predi-

---

[13] Interestingly, Gelman (1988) found that younger children were equally willing to attribute properties to categories of artifacts and to categories of natural kinds. However, older children more readily attributed properties to categories of natural kinds than to artifacts. Hence, relative entrenchment of categories as a determiner of inductive inferences must change with age, presumably, in this case, as a result of acquiring greater knowledge about categories of natural kinds.

typical?

cates posited by Goodman. Rips assumed that predicates corresponding to central categories have greater entrenchment. Indeed, if subjects know more about central categories, that is, have projected more properties over them, it follows from Goodman's (1955/1983) analysis that central categories will be better entrenched than more peripheral categories. Thus, *robin,* a central category, will be better entrenched than *hawk,* a more peripheral category.

Rips's (1975) discussion of entrenchment presupposes facilitation of an inductive inference from one category to another by the entrenchment of the given category. However, Goodman (1955/1983) did not deal with intercategory induction. His analysis is of induction from a sample to classes exemplified by the sample. Hence, Rips's use of the concept of entrenchment is an expansion of Goodman's position. This expansion of Goodman's position seems natural and useful. However, the specific use of entrenchment by Rips to account for the effects of centrality may be unnecessary. See the similarity-coverage model of Osherson et al. (1990) (also Section V,D) for an alternative explanation of Rips's findings of asymmetry of induction with central categories.

In sum, Rips's (1975) findings on induction, as well as the spirit of his interpretation of the findings, are consistent with the approach suggested here. However, according to this approach it is the greater entrenchment of central categories, not the centrality of the categories per se, that makes them a more potent source of induced properties. Hence, induction should be greatest from the most entrenched category, even when it is not the most central category.

Let us look next at Carey's (1985) work, which suggests that the category *person* is a best-entrenched but not central category for young children.

C. ASYMMETRIES IN INDUCTION BY CHILDREN

Carey (1985) studied the projection of novel properties within the animal kingdom by children of different ages and by adults. In one procedure subjects were told a novel property of a depicted individual (such as a dog) and then asked about possession of the property by depicted members of various test categories (such as another dog, a person, an aardvark, and a bee). The measure of induction was the percentage of subjects who attributed the property to the test-category member.

Carey, like Rips (1975), found that the similarity between the given category and the target category facilitated induction for all subjects. In addition, she found that induction varied with the GC for the 4- and 6-year-olds, but not for the adults. For the younger subjects, a novel property was more readily projected when it was taught as a property of a person than when it was taught as a property of a dog. For instance, young children more readily projected the unknown property of having a spleen (something inside the body) from a person to a dog, than from a dog to a person. In addition, they more readily projected having a spleen from a person to an aardvark than from a dog to an aardvark.

According to Carey, the projections of the younger and older subjects differed because the conceptual status of *person* differs for the two groups. *Person* is the prototypic category of animals for young children, and their biological knowledge is based on their knowledge of *person*. (It should be noted that Carey is using the term *prototypic* in the sense of original rather than central or average.) When young children were taught a novel property of a person, they extended the property to other kinds of animals on the basis of the similarity between those animals and people. However, when young children were taught a novel property of a dog, Carey proposed that the children observed Gricean conventions (Grice, 1975) when asked to consider other categories. The children inferred from the experimenter's failure to mention a person as a possessor of the novel property that people lack the property, and, consequently, that other kinds of animals also lack the property. That is, a property that people lacked was not a general property for the young child.

In terms of entrenchment, the fact that young children have more knowledge about *person* than about other animal categories means that *person* is the most highly entrenched category in the animal kingdom for them. Hence, according to the assumption that inductive inferences are facilitated by the entrenchment of the GC, a property initially attributed to a person should be more readily extended to other categories than a property initially attributed to a dog, as Carey found.

Carey (1985) also taught 6-year-old children and adults a novel property of two individual animals of different kinds. For instance, subjects were told that both a dog and a bee had the same internal organ, a spleen. They were then shown pictures of other animals, such as the aardvark, and asked whether the depicted animal had a spleen. The adults projected the property from the dog and bee to all other kinds of animals. This pattern of projection is different from that of adults told that one kind of animal, either dogs or bees, had a spleen. When told that one kind of animal possessed the property, the projection of the property to other kinds of animals depended upon the similarity of the animal possessing the property and the test animal. Carey concluded that when adults learned that two very different kinds of animals possessed the same property, they inferred that the property was possessed by all kinds of animals. They made an inductive inference over a category of individuals, *animal*.

In contrast, the children's projections from the two animals, dog and bee, to other kinds of animals depended upon the similarity of the test animals to dogs and bees. For instance, attribution of a spleen to the aardvark was no more likely for children told that both dogs and bees possessed a spleen than for children told only that dogs possessed a spleen. Carey argued that the children, unlike the adults, did not infer that all animals possessed spleens when told that dogs and bees possessed spleens. The children did not use the category of individuals, *animal,* to make inductive inferences. In terms of entrenchment, *animal* was not an entrenched category for children, although it was for adults.

Of course, young children have some knowledge of the term "animal." We have asked preschoolers to explain to a pretend alien the word "animal." They listed and gave similar types of properties for different kinds of animals, but supplied few, if any, properties of all individual animals. Apparently, children initially interpret "animal" as referring to the parent class *kind of animal* and may even formulate over-hypotheses.

In sum, I basically agree with Carey's interpretation of her findings. However, more explicit consideration of developmental changes in entrenchment might contribute to a more unified explanation of the various studies of induction. Specifically, I suggest the following: (1) The special status of the category *person,* compared to other categories, is one of greater entrenchment; (2) differences in children's readiness to project properties from different categories can be attributed to differences in the entrenchment of these categories; and (3) the development of biological knowledge can be characterized in part as an increase in the entrenchment of more general categories of individuals, such as *animal* and *living thing*.

D.   INFERENCE STRENGTH AS A FUNCTION OF SIMILARITY AND CATEGORY RELATIONS IN ADULTS

Osherson et al. (1990) presented an elegant model of the relative strengths of inductive arguments for various relations among the categories in the arguments. They also reported a number of experiments that provide support for their model. To anticipate, their model will be shown to be relevant in several ways to the position developed here:

1. A failure of the model when applied to children's inductive inferences (Carey, 1985) will suggest that the power of the model could be enhanced by incorporation of a concept such as entrenchment.

2. A specific modification to incorporate entrenchment will be proposed, namely to drop the assumption that similarity is a symmetrical relation and to use the relative entrenchment of two categories in determining the similarity of one to the other.
3. Certain successful predictions of the model, which are contrary to the predictions based on the concept of entrenchment presented here, will indicate a needed elaboration of the entrenchment approach. These points are considered after a brief characterization of the model.

The Osherson et al. (1990) model is concerned only with the effects of category relations on argument strength. It compares arguments in which the same property is attributed to different categories and tacitly assumes no interaction between the categories and properties. The model, called the similarity-coverage model, makes the strength of an inductive argument an increasing function of two factors. The first is the similarity between the category (or categories) in the premise and the category in the conclusion. The second is the similarity between the category (or categories) in the premise and the lowest-level category that includes all the categories in the premise and the conclusion. This latter category "covers" the premise and conclusion categories. The concept of coverage accounts for the facilitation of induction by centrality.

One aspect of the Osherson et al. (1990) definition of similarity is especially relevant here: The similarity between two categories in an inclusion relation, such as *dog* and *animal,* is a function of the similarity between *dog* and each kind of animal. Thus, the Osherson et al. definition of similarity may be applicable for young children who do not have an entrenched category of individual animals but who do have knowledge of various kinds of animals, that is, who have a kind hierarchy of animals.

Although the Osherson et al. (1990) model makes predictions about multiple premise arguments as well as single premise arguments, the nature of the model can be illustrated with single premise arguments. Arguments (1) and (2) illustrate the effect of the similarity between the premise and conclusion categories. In each argument the sentence above the line is the premise and the sentence below the line is the conclusion.

(1) $\underline{\text{Robins have property Q.}}$ (P)
        Sparrows have property Q.   (C)

(2) $\underline{\text{Robins have property Q.}}$ (P)
        Geese have property Q.   (C)

According to the model the strength of argument (1) is the weighted sum of two terms. One term represents the similarity between *robin* and *sparrow*, the other term represents the similarity between *robin* and *bird*. *Bird* enters into the determination of argument strength because it is the most specific category that includes (covers) both *robin* and *sparrow*. The same is true for argument (2). One term represents the similarity between *robin* and *goose*, the other term represents the similarity between *robin* and *bird*. The parameter r weights the two factors. Thus, (3) and (4) give the relative strengths of arguments (1) and (2) respectively.

(3)   Strength of (1) = rSIM(robin; sparrow)
$\qquad\qquad\qquad\quad$ + $(1 - r)$SIM(robin; bird)

(4)   Strength of (2) = rSIM(robin; goose)
$\qquad\qquad\qquad\quad$ + $(1 - r)$SIM(robin; bird)

Because the similarity of *robin* and *bird* is the same for both arguments, the relative strengths of arguments (1) and (2) depends upon the similarity of *robin* and *sparrow* compared to the similarity of *robin* and *goose*. Because robins are more similar to sparrows than to geese, argument (1) is predicted to be stronger than argument (2). This prediction is supported by the experimental results of Osherson et al. (1990) and Rips (1975).

Now consider arguments (5) and (6) in which the categories in the premise and the conclusion are interchanged. Again, the lowest-level category that includes both the category in the premise and the category in the conclusion is *bird* for both arguments.

(5) $\underline{\text{Cardinals have property Q.}}$ (P)
$\quad\;\;$ Penguins have property Q.   (C)

(6) $\underline{\text{Penguins have property Q.}}$ (P)
$\quad\;\;$ Cardinals have property Q.   (C)

(7)   Strength of (5) = rSIM(cardinal; penguin)   ~~bird~~
$\qquad\qquad\qquad\quad$ + $(1 - r)$SIM(cardinal; penguin)

(8)   Strength of (6) = rSIM(penguin; cardinal)
$\qquad\qquad\qquad\quad$ + $(1 - r)$SIM(penguin; bird)

Osherson et al. (1990) assume that similarity is symmetrical in comparisons of argument strength; hence the similarity of *cardinal* to *penguin* equals the similarity of *penguin* to *cardinal*. Thus, the relative strength of arguments (5) and (6) depends upon the similarity between *cardinal* and *bird* compared to the similarity between *penguin* and *bird*. Because cardinals are a relatively typical bird, they are more similar to many kinds of birds than are penguins. Hence, argument (5) is stronger than argument (6). Again this prediction is supported by the experimental results of Osherson et al. (1990) and Rips (1975). Note that this prediction of asymmetries in induction depends upon relative centrality. Rips (1975) used entrenchment to account for such asymmetries.

Recall that Carey (1985) also gave her subjects arguments in which the categories in the premise and in the conclusion were interchanged. She found that 4- and 6-year-old children more readily make inferences from *person* to *dog* than from *dog* to *person*. That is, argument (9) is stronger than argument (10) for young children.

(9) <u>People have property Q.</u>   (P)
     Dogs have property Q.   (C)

(10) <u>Dogs have property Q.</u>   (P)
     People have property Q.   (C)

The application of the similarity-coverage model to children has been tested by Lopez, Gelman, Gutheil, and Smith (1992). For kindergarten children (ages 5;2–6;4) they found no evidence that coverage influences judgments of argument strength. For second-graders (ages 8;5–9;8) coverage played no role when the covering category was not mentioned in the arguments. From the results of Lopez et al. it follows that only the similarity component of the similarity-coverage model is relevant to Carey's (1985) finding of asymmetries in induction between *dog* and *person* for 4- and 6-year-olds. Consequently, the relative strengths of arguments (9) and (10) are given by (11) and (12).

(11) Strength of (9) = rSIM(person; dog).

(12) Strength of (10) = rSIM(dog; person).

If similarity is symmetrical, as Osherson et al. (1990) assume, then the similarity of people to dogs is the same as the similarity of dogs to people. Hence, arguments (9) and (10) should be equal in strength, contrary to Carey's (1985) findings for young children.

One way to use the similarity-coverage model to account for Carey's results is to drop the assumption that similarity is symmetrical.[14]

---

[14] Another possible way to reconcile Carey's (1985) findings of asymmetries in induction with the Osherson et al. (1990) similarity-coverage model, including the assumption of symmetry of similarity, is to assume two things. One assumption is that for young children *person* is a more central category than is *dog* in relation to the animal kingdom. (Although I think this is unlikely, it should be checked empirically.) The second assumption is that, contrary to the findings of Lopez et al. (1992), the coverage component of the similarity-coverage model does apply to young children.

Tversky's (1977) work on the asymmetry of similarity suggests a way to predict the asymmetry found by Carey (1985) for young children. Tversky proposed that the similarity of a less salient entity to a more salient entity is greater than the similarity of a more salient entity to a less salient entity (e.g., North Korea is more similar to China than China is to North Korea). Equating entrenchment with salience, it follows that the similarity of dogs (the less entrenched category) to people (the more entrenched category) is greater than the similarity of people to dogs. Hence, argument (9) should be stronger than argument (10), as Carey found. Entrenchment has been incorporated into the similarity-coverage model by use of the asymmetry of similarity (Tversky, 1977).[15] See Carey (1985) for a discussion of the relevance of Tversky's model to her findings.

Some tests of the Osherson et al. (1990) model produced results contrary to what would be predicted by the analysis of entrenchment presented so far. For instance, Osherson et al. found, as they predicted, that argument (13) is stronger than (14).

(13)   Crows secrete uric acid crystals.   (P)
       Peacocks secrete uric acid crystals.
       _____
       All birds secrete uric acid crystals.   (C)

(14)   Crows secrete uric acid crystals.   (P)
       Peacocks secrete uric acid crystals.
       Rabbits secrete uric acid crystals.
       _____
       All birds secrete uric acid crystals.

The reason that argument (13) is stronger than (14) according to the Osherson et al. analysis is that the similarity of the premise categories in (13), *crow* and *peacock,* to *bird* is greater than the similarity of the premise categories in (14), *crow, peacock,* and *rabbit,* to *animal.* (*Bird* and *animal* are the categories that cover the premise and conclusion categories in (13) and (14), respectively.)

In contrast, consider the relative entrenchment of the property *secrete uric acid crystals* in the conclusion of the two arguments. Projecting three hypotheses with the same property, instead of two hypotheses, should make the property better entrenched in (14) than in (13). A better-entrenched property would be projected more readily than a less well entrenched property over the conclusion category. Hence, (14) should be

_____

[15] It remains to be seen whether asymmetry of similarity also enters into calculation of the coverage component. This possibility could be tested by examining adult performance with arguments using categories from a domain in which maximum typicality and maximum entrenchment differ—providing that they exist.

stronger than (13), contrary to experimental findings (Osherson et al., 1990).

This, among other findings reported by Osherson et al., indicates that an explanation of intercategory induction based upon entrenchment must include a concept such as coverage. We have already argued that Carey's (1985) findings indicate that the similarity-coverage model must include a concept such as entrenchment. Hence, it is proposed that the coverage model and a model based upon entrenchment be combined to account for between-category induction with neutral properties. The coverage model of Osherson et al. (1990) will account for the effects of the relations among categories; asymmetry of similarity (Carey, 1985; Tversky, 1977) will account for the effects of entrenchment.

It is important to note the extent of the similarity-coverage model. It was formulated to compare the relative strength of inductive inferences or arguments when (1) the same property appears in both arguments and (2) all categories appear in a single hierarchical-inclusion structure. Further, a lack of interaction between the categories and the property in the argument is assumed. A role for the entrenchment of the categories has been proposed. It remains to be seen how other aspects of the entrenchment position, such as over-hypotheses and the inherited entrenchment of properties, can be combined with the similarity-coverage model.

VI. Discussion

Finally, I would like to relate the position proposed here to two more general issues: (1) the role of theories in conceptual coherence and (2) kind hierarchies and over-hypotheses as adaptive specializations.

A. THEORIES AND OVER-HYPOTHESES

Recently, theories and models have been given an important role in determining the coherence of categories (Carey, 1985; Keil, 1989; Lakoff, 1987; Medin & Wattenmaker, 1987; Murphy & Medin, 1985). Theories are evidently formulated at a very early age. Three- and 4-year-olds give evidence of organized knowledge and causal explanations in their answers to questions about biological matters, self-initiated movement, and origins. See Carey (1985) for relevant evidence and summaries of earlier work (also Gelman, S. A., & Kremer (1991); Keil, 1989; Massey & Gelman, R., 1988).

In this paper I am proposing that inductive inferences contribute to the coherence of categories. These inferences, although insufficiently interconnected to be characterized as a theory, might be considered predecessors to theories and to share with theories the ability to enhance category coherence. Thus, a continuum is proposed from the projection of isolated hypotheses (*Dogs eat meat*) to over-hypotheses (*Each kind of animal has a characteristic diet*) to simple causal explanations (*Animals need food for energy*) to more elaborate general theories, such as a theory of metabolic activity. With each elaboration of belief, the categories involved become more coherent.

Notice the changing status of a specific category such as *dog* as a person's knowledge becomes more theory-like. The initial projections are about members of the category. Next come over-hypotheses that relate the given category, and one of its properties, to other categories of the same kind, and to their properties of the same type. Next comes a generalization that refers to a more inclusive category that includes members of the category at issue. Finally come theories that interrelate properties of members of the category at issue but that do not necessarily predicate properties of category members themselves.

This order appears to capture the child's changing knowledge of biological categories (Carey, 1985; Davidson & Gelman, S. A., 1990; Shipley, 1989). It also puts similarity-based accounts of categories and theory-based accounts of categories, as analysed by Murphy and Medin (1985), at the extremes of a continuum, with over-hypotheses and generalizations between the two extremes. Although Murphy and Medin discuss the inadequacies of similarity-based accounts, an argument can be made that novices' initial projections apply to similarity-based classes, which are their initial classes. (Also see Medin and Ortony, 1989.) For instance, recent experimental work with children and adults makes clear that overall shape plays an essential role when classifying unfamiliar objects for the purpose of naming them (Landau, Smith, & Jones, 1988).

B. OVER-HYPOTHESES AND KIND HIERARCHIES AS ADAPTIVE SPECIALIZATIONS

Medin and Wattenmaker (1987) have suggested that "organisms reflect the (evolutionary) history of their interaction with their environment in terms of adaptive specializations" (p. 53). Could the ability to formulate and use over-hypotheses be an adaptive specialization that facilitates survival?

The benefits of dividing the world into categories of equivalent objects, rather than treating each object as a unique entity, are self-evident. Such a strategy is essential in order to cope with new instances of familiar kinds of things. The ability to form and honor categories is obviously an adaptive specialization for humans.

But what of over-hypotheses? Our remote ancestors not only encountered new instances of familiar kinds, they also, as a result of habitat changes and migration, encountered novel objects that could not be assigned to existing categories. To the extent that they accurately attributed properties relevant to their own survival to these new objects, they would thrive. The inference that vegetation that looks alike is uniform in edibility provides a way to deal with novel classes of objects on the basis of very limited samples. For instance, getting sick after ingesting the leaves of a previously unknown plant should prevent a person from eating leaves of that kind of plant in the future.

This argument might seem an argument for "prepared learning" in which an organism is pre-wired to avoid food associated with a single episode of sickness. Indeed, rats exhibit such prepared learning (Garcia & Koelling, 1966; Seligman, 1970). However, there are two vital benefits for an organism whose ability to learn from a single instance is based on the ability to project over-hypothesis rather than on built-in biases specific to food. First, single-instance induction will not be limited to food consumption, but can also occur in such important domains as food location and the selection of material for tools and shelter. In addition, when over-hypotheses are explicitly formulated, one person can teach another how to make useful inductive inferences about novel classes from limited information.

Of course, it is the structure of the plant and animal kingdoms, the homogeneity of the same types of properties within different species, that ensures that over-hypotheses are useful. If humans are sensitive to such structure, they will be able to form useful over-hypotheses.

These considerations suggest that people should be biased to form sets of classes that support the projection of over-hypotheses. In such a set of classes contrasting classes will be homogeneous in the same types of properties. Apparently people are biased in just this way.

Quinn (1987) demonstrated with infants that exposure to a contrasting class of geometric figures similar in shape (e.g., a set of deformed triangles) facilitates the recognition by infants of the set of deformations of another shape (e.g., circles) as an equivalence class.

Imai and Garner (1968) asked adults to sort sets of objects without any restrictions on the number or nature of the resulting classes. For instance, subjects were given blocks that differed in shape (square and circular) and color (red and blue). Individual subjects formed classes that were either all uniform in shape, or all uniform in color, or all uniform in both shape and color. Subjects did not sort red squares into one class and the remaining objects, blue squares, blue circles, and red circles, into a second class. Shipley and Kuhn (1983) found the same bias when children were asked to form classes for purposes of comparison. They called this a bias to form equally detailed alternatives, that is, to form contrasting classes with the characteristic features of each class specified in the same detail.

Young children can use the information in contrasting classes to make inferences about the properties of a single class from a single instance. Macario, Shipley, and Billman (1990) found that four-year-olds are guided by perceptual uniformities in contrasting classes in inferring from a single instance the characteristic features of a class exemplified by the single instance. Such properties as shape, color, texture, and substance, as well the appendages of toy animals, were used by the children. Counterbalancing ensured that it was the homogeneity of the property in the contrasting classes, rather than the specific property, that guided inductive inferences. Further, providing a label for the classes, including the class exemplified by a single instance, facilitated induction. As mentioned previously, induction from a single instance by adults has been demonstrated by Nisbett et al. (1983).

In brief, the natural environment is structured in ways that can be described by over-hypothesis. Over-hypotheses about various biological kinds would have great value as an aid toward survival in a changing world. Humans of all ages have an ability to organize objects in their environment into contrasting classes with characteristic properties of the same type. That is, humans exhibit an equally detailed alternative bias in the formation of classes; they are biased to form sets of classes that have the potential to support over-hypotheses.[16] Four-year-olds and older humans apparently use over-hypotheses. Hence, an ability to form kind hierarchies in accord with the equally detailed alternative bias and to formulate and use over-hypotheses is a worthy candidate for adaptive specialization.

The intriguing question remains: How do over-hypotheses get started? Let us consider again the inference that vegetation that looks alike is uniform in edibility. This is an over-hypothesis of such hypotheses as *X-plants taste good, Y-plants don't ease my hunger, Z-plants make me sick,* and so forth. To project such an over-hypothesis it is necessary that X-plants, Y-plants, and Z-plants are considered different kinds of the same type of entity, different kinds of plants in this case. Further, it is

---

[16] The fact that much of the work cited in this argument deals with perceptual properties is not contrary to the position that over-hypotheses are nascent theories. Medin and Wattenmaker (1987) argue that constraints on theories may also be found in more basic processes such as perception, learning, or memory. They cite as an example the parallels between causal attribution and animal conditioning.

necessary that tasting good, easing hunger, inducing sickness, and so forth, are considered properties of the same type; in this example all these properties concern the effects of ingestion. Once a person has knowledge in which there is a mapping from different categories of objects of the same kind to different properties of the same type, that person has the knowledge base to project an over-hypothesis. What accounts for the projection of the over-hypothesis? Is it an inevitable consequence of such an organization of knowledge? Alternatively, does the ability to project an over-hypothesis grow out of the apparently innate tendency to form classes of objects that are uniform in the same types of perceptual properties? I do not have an answer to these questions.

VII. Summary

This article began with a pre-theoretical characterization of categories of physical objects as (1) having labels that are used to inform others of the identity of an object, (2) being the natural range of induction, and (3) having members whose similarity does not reside in surface resemblance. It was suggested that whether or not a class of objects is a category, and the relative goodness or coherence of the class as a category, depend upon the same factors.

Next, a theoretical account of categories was presented, (based upon Goodman's [1955/1983] analysis of induction) that attributes the coherence of a category to beliefs (hypotheses or inductive inferences) about the category and to beliefs about parent classes of the category, where a parent class, such as *kind of animal,* has the class at issue as a single member.

In addition, a role was specified for kind hierarchies, such as the hierarchy of different kinds of animals, in the establishment of novel classes as coherent categories and in the support of specific inductive inferences. A novel class becomes a good category when given an entrenched parent. Once one learns that aardvarks are a kind of animal, *aardvark* becomes a well-entrenched category. Further, inductive inferences, such as *Cats meow,* gain inductive force (projectability) from the projection of an over-hypothesis about the parent class, *kind of animal,* such as *Kinds of animals have characteristic sounds.*

To make Goodman's analysis of induction more applicable to category coherence, three modifications were proposed.

1. The entrenchment of a predicate is a function of the number of different projected hypotheses (types), as well as or instead of the fre-

quency of actual projections of hypotheses (tokens) containing the predicate.

2. The projection of a generic hypothesis, even if there are known exceptions, enhances the entrenchment of the predicates in the hypothesis. The projection of such hypotheses presupposes the unity of the category mentioned in the hypothesis, even when the specific property is possessed by only a minority of category members, as in *Birds lay eggs*.

3. The credibility of the source of a hypothesis contributes to the projectability of the hypothesis. In this way a category honored by a community can become entrenched for an individual who has little if any direct experience with members of the category.

Four important sets of studies of induction were examined: S. A. Gelman (1988), Rips (1975), Carey (1985), and Osherson et al. (1990). Using the approach developed here, the results of these studies were interrelated. In accord with Rips's (1975) suggestion, the entrenchment of the given or premise category was assumed to facilitate inductive inferences. It was proposed that the Osherson et al. (1990) model be elaborated to include an asymmetrical similarity measure; this would provide a role for entrenchment in the model and would allow it to predict asymmetries in children's inductive inferences (Carey, 1985). However, the Osherson et al. results indicate a need for elaboration of the entrenchment position with respect to intercategory induction, a need that can be satisfied by use of the Osherson et al. (1990) concept of coverage.

According to the account of categories presented here, the preferred category label for an object is the label for the best-entrenched category exemplified by the object. That is, the preferred label carries with it the richest set of inductive beliefs. Further, this account makes a category the natural range of induction as a consequence of previous inductions over the category, and as a consequence of the induction of hypotheses over its parent classes. This explanation attributes psychological belief in the deep resemblance of category members to entrenchment—both direct entrenchment from the projection of hypotheses over the category and inherited entrenchment from parent categories—and to projected hypotheses, both those projected over the category and those projected over a parent category. Three suggested components of deep resemblance, (1) resemblance in nonperceptible ways, (2) resemblance in specific kinds of ways with the specific values unknown, and (3) resemblance in as yet to be discovered ways come from (1) projected hypotheses, (2) over-hypotheses, and (3) total entrenchment, respectively.

Finally, two issues were considered briefly. The first was a comparison of the entrenchment-based concepts presented here with more elaborate theories in accounting for category coherence (Murphy & Medin, 1985). The second was the possibility that over-hypotheses and kind-hierarchies can be considered adaptive specializations (Medin & Wattenmaker, 1987).

Implicit in the position presented here is the conviction that what it means to "have" a category of objects is to have a set of projected beliefs about members of the category. This position has nothing to say about how a person decides whether or not a specific entity is in a category.[17] Nor does the position have anything to say about the "meaning" of category terms. This is not to imply that such issues are trivial or uninteresting. (See Armstrong, Gleitman, L. R., & Gleitman, H. [1983] for a discussion of these issues and the shortcomings of other positions in these respects.) Rather, the intention is to argue that the questions that motivated this inquiry are best answered by examination of people's beliefs about properties of category members, properties of categories, and relations among categories.

ACKNOWLEDGMENTS

This work was supported in part by Grant BNS-8310009 from the National Science Foundation and Grant HD-12821 from the National Institutes of Health. I am especially grateful to Dorrit Billman, Pamela Blewitt, Maureen Callanan, Barbara Malt, and Sandra Waxman for helpful discussions.

REFERENCES

Anderson, J. R. (1991). Is human cognition adaptive? *Behavioral and Brain Sciences, 14,* 471–517.

Anglin, J. M. (1977). *Word, object, and conceptual development.* New York: Norton.

Armstrong, S., Gleitman, L. R., & Gleitman, H. (1983). What some concepts might not be. *Cognition, 13,* 263–308.

Barsalou, L. W. (1983). Ad hoc categories. *Memory and Cognition, 11,* 211–227.

Berlin, B. (1978). Ethnobiological classification. In E. Rosch & B. B. Lloyd (Eds.), *Cognition and categorization.* Hillsdale, NJ: Lawrence Erlbaum.

Billman, D. & Heit, E. (1988). Observational learning from internal feedback: A simulation of an adaptive learning method. *Cognitive Science, 12,* 587–625.

Brown, R. (1958). How shall a thing be called? *Psychological Review, 65,* 14–21.

Bulmer, R. (1967). Why is the Cassowary not a bird? A problem of zoological taxonomy among the Karam of the New Guinea Highlands. *Man, 2,* 5–25.

---

[17] Indeed, recent work by Malt (e.g., in press) suggests that there may be a rather loose connection between a person's beliefs about members of a category and a person's judgments about the membership of specific objects.

Carey, S. (1985). *Conceptual change in childhood*. Cambridge: MIT Press.

Carlson, G. N. (1977). *Reference to kinds in English*. Bloomington, IN: Indiana University Linguistics Club.

Cruse, D. A. (1977). The pragmatics of lexical specificity. *Journal of Linguistics, 13,* 153–164.

Davidson, N. S., & Gelman, S. A. (1990). Inductions from novel categories: The role of language and conceptual structure. *Cognitive Development, 5,* 121–152.

Garcia, J., & Koelling, R. (1966). Relation of cue to consequence in avoidance learning. *Psychonomic Science, 4,* 123–124.

Gelman, S. A. (1988). The development of induction within natural kind and artifact categories. *Cognitive Psychology, 20,* 65–95.

Gelman, S. A., & Coley, J. D. (1990). The importance of knowing a dodo is a bird: Categories and inferences in 2-year-old children. *Developmental Psychology, 26,* 796–804.

Gelman, S. A., Collman, P., & Maccoby, E. E. (1986). Inferring properties from categories versus inferring categories from properties: The case of gender. *Child Development, 57,* 396–404.

Gelman, S. A., & Kremer, K. E. (1991). Understanding natural causes: Children's explanations of how objects and their properties originate. *Child Development, 62,* 396–414.

Gelman, S. A., & Markman, E. M. (1986). Categories and induction in young children. *Cognition, 23,* 183–209.

Gelman, S. A., & Markman, E. M. (1987). Young children's inductions from natural kinds: The role of categories and appearance. *Child Development, 58,* 1532–1541.

Gelman, S. A., & O'Reilly, A. W. (1988). Children's inductive inferences with superordinate categories: The role of language and category structure. *Child Development, 59,* 876–887.

Goodman, N. (1983). *Fact, fiction, and forecast*. New York: Bobbs-Merrill. (Original work published 1955)

Grice, H. P. (1975). Logic and conversation. In D. Davidson & G. Harman (Eds.), *The logic of grammar*. Encino, CA: Dickenson.

Gupta, A. (1980). *The logic of common nouns*. New Haven: Yale University Press.

Holland, J. H., Holyoak, K. J., Nisbett, R. E., & Thagard, P. R. (1986). *Induction: Processes of inference, learning, and discovery*. Cambridge: MIT Press.

Hunn, E. S. (1977). *Tzeltal folk zoology*. New York: Academic Press.

Imai, S., & Garner, W. R. (1968). Structure in perceptual classification. *Psychonomic Monograph Supplements, 2*(9, Whole No. 25).

Keil, F. C. (1989). *Concepts, kinds, and cognitive development*. Cambridge: MIT Press.

Lakoff, G. (1987). *Women, fire, and dangerous things*. Chicago: University of Chicago Press.

Lancy, D. F. (1983). *Cross-Cultural studies in cognition and mathematics*. New York: Academic Press.

Landau, B., Smith, L. B., & Jones, S. S. (1988). The importance of shape in early lexical learning. *Cognitive Development, 3,* 299–321.

Lopez, A., Gelman, S. A., Gutheil, G., & Smith, E. E. (1992). The development of category-based induction. *Child Development, 63,* 1070–1090.

Lyons, J. (1977). *Semantics*. Cambridge: Cambridge University Press.

Macario, J. F., Shipley, E. F., & Billman, D. O. (1990). Inducing a category from a single instance: The role of contrasting categories. *Journal of Experimental Child Psychology, 50,* 179–199.

Mahmood, C. K., & Armstrong, S. L. (1992). Do ethnic groups exist? A cognitive perspective on the concept of cultures. *Ethnology, 31,* 1–14.

Malt, B. C. (in press). Concept structure and category boundaries. In G. Nakamura, R.

Taraban, & D. L. Medin (Eds.), *The psychology of learning and motivation* (Vol. 29). New York: Academic Press.

Massey, C., & Gelman, R. (1988). Preschooler's ability to decide whether a photographed unfamiliar object can move by itself. *Developmental Psychology, 24,* 307–317.

Medin, D. L., & Ortony, A. (1989). Psychological essentialism. In S. Vosniadou & A. Ortony (Eds.), *Similarity and analogical reasoning.* New York: Cambridge University Press.

Medin, D. L., & Wattenmaker, W. D. (1987). Category cohesiveness, theories, and cognitive archaeology. In U. Neisser (Ed.), *Concepts and conceptual development: Ecological and intellectual factors in categorization.* Cambridge: Cambridge University Press.

Mervis, C. B., & Mervis, C. A. (1982). Leopards are kitty-cats: Object labeling by mothers for their thirteen-month-olds. *Child Development, 53,* 267–273.

Miller, G. A., & Johnson-Laird, P. N. (1976). *Language and perception.* Cambridge, MA: Belknap Press.

Murphy, G. L. (1982). Cue validity and levels of categorization. *Psychological Bulletin, 91,* 174–177.

Murphy, G. L., & Medin, D. L. (1985). The role of theories in conceptual coherence. *Psychological Review, 92,* 289–316.

Ninio, A. (1980). Ostensive definition in vocabulary teaching. *Journal of Child Language, 7,* 565–73.

Nisbett, R. E., Krantz, D. H., Jepson, C., & Kunda, Z. (1983). The use of statistical heuristics in everyday inductive reasoning. *Psychological Review, 90,* 339–363.

Olson, D. R. (1970). Language and thought: Aspects of a cognitive theory of development. *Psychological Review, 77,* 257–273.

Osherson, D. N., Smith, E. E., Wilkie, O., Lopez, A., & Shafir, E. (1990). Category-based induction. *Psychological Review, 97,* 185–200.

Quine, W. V. (1969). Natural kinds. In *Ontological relativity and other essays.* New York: Columbia University Press.

Quinn, P. C. (1987). The categorical representation of visual pattern information by young infants. *Cognition, 27,* 145–179.

Rips, L. J. (1975). Inductive judgments about natural categories. *Journal of Verbal Learning and Verbal Behavior, 14,* 665–681.

Roberts, K. (1988). Retrieval of a basic-level category in prelinguistic infants. *Developmental Psychology, 24,* 21–27.

Rosch, E., Mervis, C. B., Gray, W. D., Johnson, D. M., & Boyes-Braem, P. (1976). Basic objects in natural categories. *Cognitive Psychology, 8,* 382–439.

Seligman, M. E. P. (1970). On the generality of the laws of learning. *Psychological Review, 77,* 406–418.

Shipley, E. F. (1989). Two kinds of hierarchies: Class inclusion hierarchies and kind hierarchies. *The Genetic Epistemologist, 17,* 31–39.

Shipley, E. F. (1992). *Inductive inferences by preschoolers and level of category label.* Paper presented at the 33rd annual meeting of the Psychonomic Society, St. Louis, MO.

Shipley, E. F., & Kuhn, I. F. (1983). A constraint on comparisons: Equally detailed alternatives. *Journal of Experimental Child Psychology, 35,* 195–222.

Shipley, E. F., Kuhn, I. F., & Madden, E. C. (1983). Mothers' use of superordinate category terms. *Journal of Child Language, 10,* 571–588.

Smith, E. E., & Medin, D. L. (1981). *Categories and concepts.* Cambridge, MA: Harvard University Press.

Spelke, E. S. (1984). Perceptual knowledge of objects in infancy. In J. Mehler, M. Garrett, & E. Walker (Eds.), *Perspectives on mental representations.* Cambridge, MA: Harvard University Press.

Sternberg, R. J. (1982). Natural, unnatural and supernatural concepts. *Cognitive Psychology, 14,* 451–488.

Tanaka, J. W., & Taylor, M. (1991). Object categories and expertise: Is the basic level in the eye of the beholder? *Cognitive Psychology, 23,* 457–482.

Tomikawa, S. A., & Dodd, D. H. (1980). Early word meaning: Perceptually based or functionally based. *Child Development, 51,* 1103–1109.

Tversky, A. (1977). Features of similarity. *Psychological Review, 84,* 327–352.

White, T. G. (1982). Naming practices, typicality and underextension in child language. *Journal of Experimental Child Psychology, 33,* 327–346.

INDEX

CONTENTS OF RECENT VOLUMES

ISBN 0-12-543330-1

90040